T0374945

Beyond Orientalism

Beyond Orientalism

AHMAD IBN QĀSIM AL-HAJARĪ BETWEEN
EUROPE AND NORTH AFRICA

Oumelbanine Zhiri

UNIVERSITY OF CALIFORNIA PRESS

University of California Press
Oakland, California

© 2023 by Oumelbanine Zhiri

Library of Congress Cataloging-in-Publication Data

Names: Zhiri, Oumelbanine, author.
Title: Beyond Orientalism : Ahmad ibn Qāsim al-Hajarī between Europe and
    North Africa / Oumelbanine Zhiri.
Description: Oakland, California : University of California Press, [2023] |
    Includes bibliographical references and index.
Identifiers: LCCN 2023002576 (print) | LCCN 2023002577 (ebook) |
    ISBN 9780520390454 (hardback) | ISBN 9780520390461 (ebook)
Subjects: LCSH: al-Ḥajarī, Aḥmad ibn Qāsim, active 17th century. |
    al-Ḥajarī, Aḥmad ibn Qāsim, active 17th century—Travel—Europe. |
    al-Ḥajarī, Aḥmad ibn Qāsim, active 17th century—Travel—Africa, North. |
    Orientalism. | Africa, North—Intellectual life—17th century.
Classification: LCC DP103.7.I26 Z45 2023 (print) | LCC DP103.7.I26 (ebook) |
    DDC 946/.051—dc23/eng/20230222
LC record available at https://lccn.loc.gov/2023002576
LC ebook record available at https://lccn.loc.gov/2023002577

32 31 30 29 28 27 26 25 24 23
10 9 8 7 6 5 4 3 2 1

To Gary

CONTENTS

ILLUSTRATIONS

ACKNOWLEDGMENTS

My thinking about the early modern world and its scholarly networks has taken shape through conversations with many people, and it is my pleasure to acknowledge them here. I offer my gratitude to my colleagues of the Mediterranean Seminar who have created an incomparable forum to exchange knowledge and ideas, and to discuss from different perspectives how regions and cultures connect. I have presented bits and pieces of the work that eventually became this book during several quarterly workshops, and I owe a debt of gratitude to the codirectors Brian Catlos and Sharon Kinoshita. Discussions with and interventions by fellow seminarists have always been helpful, including those of Fred Astren, Mohammad Ballan, Christine Chism, John Dagenais, Andrew Devereux, Daniel Gullo, Sergio LaPorta, Toby Liang, Karla Mallette, Ignacio Naverette, Karen Pinto, Nuria Silleras-Fernandez, David Wacks, Joshua White, and Fariba Zarinebaf. I am also grateful to colleagues of the University of California Maghreb Studies group helmed by Camilo Gomez-Rivas, which allowed me to discuss parts of this book with Carla Freccero, Emily Gottfried, and Susan Gilson Miller.

The scholarly community at the University of California San Diego has always been supportive and engaging, sometimes through our dynamic GEMS (Group of Early Modern Studies), and sometimes in less structured formats. In both these ways, many fruitful conversations have occurred over the years with Jody Blanco, Lisa Cartwright, Page duBois, Fatima El-Tayeb, Stephanie Jed, Sara Johnson, Todd Kontje, Lisa Lampert-Weissig, Jin-Kyung Lee, Lisa Lowe, Sal Nicolazzo, Jim Rauch, Roddey Reid, Daniel Vitkus, and with many of our great students.

I have presented portions of this book in numerous conferences and colloquia. I am very grateful to Edwige Tamalet Talbayev and to Toby

Wikström, who welcomed me at Tulane University, and to Jonathan Haddad and Elizabeth Wright, who invited me to present my work in the series of events called "The Southern Strategies of Early Modern Empires" and to meet with their wonderful students in the University of Georgia at Athens. I have also benefited from listening to and discussing with many colleagues at the conventions of the Renaissance Society of America, the MLA, the Sixteenth-Century Society and Conference, and other gatherings, including: Jocelyne Dakhlia, Eric Dursteler, Daniel Hershenzon, Mercedes García-Arenal, Claire Gilbert, Seth Kimmel, Nabil Matar, David Nirenberg, Dwight Reynolds, Fernando Rodríguez Mediano, Gerard Wiegers.

Many travel grants awarded by the UCSD Academic Senate financed research trips to libraries in Europe and Morocco. Librarians in many countries have helped me access documents and obtain images. I thank the archivists and librarians of the Biblioteca Nacional de España; the Bibliothèque Nationale de France; the library of the University of Bologna; the John Rylands Library at the University of Manchester. I also thank Ahmad Shawqī Binebine and Sidi Mohammed al-Idrissi of the Hasaniyya Library in Rabat; Mohammed Sghir Janjar of the Foundation of King ʿAbd al-ʿAzīz in Casablanca; Barnaby Bryan of Middle Temple in London; Ulrike Polnitzky of the Österreichische Nationalbibliothek in Vienna; René Janssen of the Nationaal Archief of the Netherlands in The Hague. I also thank Eric Schmidt and Lisa Moore, the fantastic editors of the University of California Press, for their help and support, and the reviewers for their incisive remarks and their generosity.

My many conversations with friends have deepened my thinking and widened my intellectual horizons more than they know. Thanks to Ahmed Alami, Elisabeth Arnould-Bloomfield, Ali Benmakhlouf, Doris Bittar, Lisa Bloom, and Françoise Canter.

Finally, I would like to express to Gary Fields my deepest gratitude for his unwavering support, his enthusiasm for this project, his kindness and willingness to support me, and for everything he has brought to my life.

INTRODUCTION

In 1665, Thomas Le Gendre, a wealthy trader from Rouen, wrote a memoir of the years 1618–25, which he had spent in Morocco. His text was published anonymously in 1670, probably at the behest of merchants interested in founding a trading society in Morocco who needed information about the region. Among other events, the memoir recorded a remarkable occurrence: the time the Saʿdī Sultan Mūlay Zaydān (d. 1627) received emissaries sent to his court by the government of the Dutch Republic:

> In the year 1622, an ambassador of the Gentlemen of the States,[1] a squire of the Prince of Orange, and a disciple of Erpenius, professor of oriental and foreign languages in Leiden, came to Marrakesh, both with presents that were very pleasing to King Zaydān, but mostly the one from Erpenius, which was an atlas and a New Testament in Arabic; and the eunuchs told us that the king would not stop reading the New Testament. As the ambassador was annoyed not to have been authorized to leave, he was advised to present the king with a petition or request, which was written by this disciple of Erpenius, whose name is Golius, in the Arabic language, and in a Christian style. The king was very much stunned by the beauty of the request, by the writing and the language as well as by the style that was extraordinary in that land. He called immediately for his *talips* or secretaries, and showed them the request, which they admired. He asked for the ambassador and asked him who wrote it. He answered that it was Golius, a student sent by Erpenius. The king asked to meet him and spoke with him in Arabic. The student answered in Spanish that he understood very well all that His Majesty was telling him, but that he could not answer him in the same language, because his throat would not help him, since one speaks with the throat as well as with the tongue; and the king, who understood Spanish well, liked his answer. He responded favorably to the request and gave the ambassador the authorization to return. And today, this Golius is in Leiden, professor of oriental and foreign languages in the stead of Erpenius, who is now dead.[2]

As recounted by Le Gendre, this anecdote stages an encounter between Islam and Christendom, and between East and West, that doubles as a meeting between knowledge and power and that features three protagonists. The first is Thomas Erpenius (1584–1624), professor of oriental languages at Leiden University since 1613; the second is his student Jacob Golius (1596–1667), who accompanied the Dutch embassy in Morocco from 1622 to 1624, and who would succeed his mentor as the chair of oriental languages;[3] the third and final protagonist is the Sultan Mūlay Zaydān (d. 1627), portrayed as an admiring spectator of Golius's accomplishments as a translator and as a wit. Curiously absent from the account of Le Gendre, however, is a fourth character, intimately connected to the other three, who played an instrumental role during the early modern period in the circulation of knowledge between Arab countries and Europe, the transnational Muslim polyglot Ahmad ibn Qāsim al-Hajarī.[4] Born in Spain, Hajarī was a prolific mediator between Europe and North Africa, translating diplomatic, religious, and scientific texts between Arabic and Spanish, and a remarkable writer in his own right, authoring lengthy autobiographical texts. In Morocco, Tunisia, Egypt, and Europe, he maintained contact with famed and influential scholars, like Erpenius, whom he met in Paris in 1611 and to whom he taught Arabic, and his student Golius, who, on Erpenius's advice, contacted Hajarī. Hajarī's biography testifies to a dense system of networks in which knowledge and information were circulating between regions in both directions. He was an important figure in this nuanced and multidirectional phenomenon that included the European study of Islamic and West Asian culture and languages known as Orientalism. Authors such as Thomas Le Gendre too often kept silent about the networks of scholars outside Europe that made this study possible. *Beyond Orientalism* corrects the record by exploring these webs without limiting itself to the European Orientalists, and focuses on the life and career of Hajarī.

EUROPEAN ORIENTALISM: PERCEPTIONS AND PRACTICES

Le Gendre likely encountered Hajarī during the years he spent in Marrakesh, and he might even have counted him among the secretaries to whom the sultan showed Golius's Arabic letter. The trader from Rouen, however, when he was writing about his time in Morocco, did not feel that his readers would be interested in knowing about Hajarī and other local scholars. Instead, he painted Orientalism as a purely European enterprise, severed from the practices and networks that made it possible. Le Gendre knew that, in the years following his Moroccan mission, Golius had become a distinguished scholar, famous among learned Europeans as a specialist in oriental languages. The prestige of Orientalism as a field of knowledge was sufficiently high, even among trading communities, for Le Gendre to include in his memoir the story recounted at the beginning of this introduction. Traveling beyond these circles, this anecdote would be recorded in the annals of European scholarship. Through a citation by an erudite librarian in 1675,[5] it was incorporated in new editions of widely read encyclopedias, such as the *Grand dictionnaire* by Louis Moréri and the *Dictionnaire historique et critique* by Pierre Bayle, in entries devoted to Golius. This widespread circulation suggests that the story, and its representation of an encounter between a European scholar and a Moroccan sultan, resonated with contemporary readers.

This rich account provides interesting information about the perception of Orientalist knowledge by Europeans in the second half of the seventeenth century, including how it is inflected by the erasure of Hajarī. Remarkably, of all the members of the Dutch mission, Le Gendre named only Golius. Even the ambassador Albert Ruyl remained anonymous, as well as Pieter van Neste (1567–1625), the squire of Maurits of Nassau, prince of Orange, and stathouder of the Dutch Provinces. In contrast, Erpenius, who was not part of the delegation, is mentioned by name. For Le Gendre, clearly, two encounters occurred at the same time: the anonymous Ruyl and van Neste represented the Dutch state, but their exchange with the sultan paled in comparison to the other meeting. The audience of Golius in the court of Mūlay Zaydān is at the center of the account, and Golius was presented not as a mere adjunct to the ambassador, but as an envoy himself, sent by his mentor Erpenius. On behalf of the latter, he offered the sultan two books, including the Arabic New Testament that Erpenius had published in Leiden in 1616. Le Gendre paints Erpenius as the holder of a kind of authority that enabled him to address a monarch as an equal, like the Gentlemen of the States. The main encounter was not the one occurring between two political entities (the Sa'dī kingdom and the Netherlands), but the one happening between the sultan and a very different type of power, not political but intellectual: the European Republic of Letters, as the early modern networks of European writers and thinkers were called, whose correspondence advanced scholarship and transcended national and even religious boundaries. In this encounter, Europe, through the learned Golius, was able to demonstrate that it had acquired a command of a foreign culture. His Arabic epistle provoked the surprise and the admiration of the sultan and his entourage of professional scribes and secretaries, and, when Golius was received in court, he even turned his lack of speaking proficiency to his advantage when he found a clever way to excuse this shortcoming. No wonder other citizens of the Republic of Letters were taken by that story. It promoted a flattering image of their own eminence as intellectuals, and as Europeans who could master other cultures. In such a picture, the role of Hajarī or of any local scholar in the construction of Orientalist knowledge was better left unmentioned.

In broad outline, Thomas Le Gendre's account is an affirmation of Edward Said's celebrated notion of Orientalism.[6] It reveals how Europeans sought mastery of the oriental "other," while the political work of the Orientalist is concealed behind the dream, or ideological fantasy, of a Republic of Letters that transcended politics. The portrayal of the Moroccans as passive admirers of Golius's achievement is a striking feature of Le Gendre's account, situating it in a genealogy that has not yet ended, a "trap that still besets many historians of early modern encounters: attributing all the initiative in matters of bridge-building to European agents alone."[7] *Beyond Orientalism* argues that this trap has hindered our understanding of early modern European Orientalism. It proposes a broader view, and considers that Europeans were not the sole agents in the construction of this field of knowledge. Many subjects of Muslim polities played a crucial part in its development, and taking their contribution into account opens the door to a deeper understanding of the field, and, more broadly, of the history of the cultural, scholarly, and technological interactions between Europe and its Islamic neighbors. The story of Hajarī, in terms of his writings, his work at court, and his political and intellectual contacts, illustrates precisely how the flow of knowledge, power, and diplomacy, which included Orientalism, circulated at cross-currents.

His undermining of the relevance of the location in which the anecdote took place significantly frames the meaning of European Orientalism in Le Gendre's account. For him, Morocco is merely the stage on which the European scholar deploys his learning and displays his knowledge of Arabic, rather than the site where he acquires the tools and information needed to perfect his understanding of a foreign culture. This view ignores the fact that during his time in Morocco, Golius was busy expanding his knowledge of Arab culture and language, and seeking out manuscripts to complete his collection, which would become very well known among European scholars.

It also dissimulates that in practice the Dutch scholar needed the active contribution of local scholars, including Hajarī. Most importantly, their collaboration was fruitful not only for Golius, but also for Hajarī's own intellectual pursuits. Documents reveal complex exchanges between them, in which Hajarī was the collaborator and informant of Golius, and Golius could in turn be the collaborator and informant of Hajarī.

Another of Thomas Le Gendre's silences is just as noteworthy. Officially, Golius participated in the Dutch embassy not as an interpreter, but as an engineer; his work as an Arabist (as when he translated Ruyl's request addressed to Mūlay Zaydān) was secondary. Although he undoubtedly sought this appointment as a member of the Dutch embassy at least partly in order to further his Arabic studies, the official reason for his participation was unconnected to this academic pursuit. The mission in Morocco was about the sultan's ill-fated plan to build a port on the Atlantic coast of his country, for which he enlisted the help and expertise of his Dutch allies. Golius was such an important character in this project that in the Hague on July 24, 1624, he authored the final report detailing why Mūlay Zaydān's venture was unfeasible.[8] The reader of Thomas Le Gendre's account would not know any of this. Philology and science were closely connected in the career of Golius, who would become professor of mathematics at Leiden University in 1629 (after taking the chair of oriental languages in 1625). His interest in Arabic stemmed originally from his mathematical research, as he wanted to read some Greek texts that survived only in Arabic translation, and to study the contributions of scholars writing in Arabic. His case exemplifies that the strict distinction between science and philology that the nineteenth century has made familiar was much more porous in the early modern period.[9] In sum, Le Gendre's account is silent about Golius's connection with local scholars, and about the intermingling of the humanities and the sciences in Golius's career. The two erasures intersect. Hajarī was himself much involved in science and technology, not only out of personal interest, but also as translator for Mūlay Zaydān. His engagement in this field outlasted his career in Morocco, and, in his later years, he produced an important work, an Arabic translation of a Spanish-language treatise on gunnery written by another exile from Spain, Ibrāhīm Ghānim, who was in charge of the defense of the port of Tunis.

The study and understanding of Orientalism in the centuries that followed have prolonged to a great extent the silences of Le Gendre's account. This field is still understood mostly as a humanistic discipline, mainly comprised of literary representations and of philological studies, and deprived of its scientific and technological dimensions. As to the many subjects of North African and Middle Eastern countries who contributed to the field, they are reduced to the role of shadowy informants. Approaching Orientalism this way precludes a full retracing of the practices through which it developed. Mapping these practices is necessary for a full understanding of this subject.

A MEDITERRANEAN INTERCESSOR, IN ORIENTALISM AND BEYOND

By uncovering what is erased in an account such as Le Gendre's, *Beyond Orientalism* seeks to modify our understanding of the early modern cultural connections between Europe and its Islamic neighbors. Its analyses engage with scholars who reexamine the relations between Islam and Christendom in the early modern period, and reimagine those interactions in a context of sustained connections, despite the political and confessional antagonisms that often fueled hostility or violence. The study of the Mediterranean has changed considerably in recent decades.[10] The contest between, on the one hand, a bifurcated model based on the binaries of East versus West, and Islam versus Christendom, and, on the other hand, a more unitary representation highlighting commonalities and interactions, has been going on for a long time. Recently, a more nuanced approach has privileged the study of networks, and of patterns of connection, promoting an integrated reading of the Mediterranean through close attention to the practices and modalities of the contacts between the different regions, and seeking, without denying diversity, to explore forms of commonality. This paradigm has been particularly advanced by the greater awareness of the large presence in early modern Europe of "Muslim slaves, mercenaries, merchants, diplomats, travellers and scholars."[11]

The present study belongs in this trend, taking at its starting point the cultural formation called Orientalism. Before going further, some clarification is warranted about the terms *Orientalism* and *Orientalist*. This book will use them in a precise sense, what Edward Said described as "the most readily accepted designation for Orientalism," an "academic one .... Anyone who teaches, writes about, or researches the Orient . . . is an orientalist."[12] Although "readily accepted" when Said first published his book in 1978, this designation has now been mostly superseded by his own newer definitions.[13] In the present book, Orientalism will be understood in the sense that the word had before Said's analyses changed its import. One caveat, however, is in order, since the words *Orientalism* and *Orientalist,* in these meanings, were not in use in the English nor the French language before the very end of the eighteenth century or the beginning of the nineteenth (although the phrase "oriental languages" did exist). Since this book will concern itself mostly with cultural history up to the mid- to late-seventeenth century, the practices or people to which it will refer to as Orientalism or Orientalists would not have been thought of in those terms by contemporaries. These words will nevertheless be used for the sake of convenience. Furthermore, this premodern Orientalism, or oriental studies, can also be thought of as "predisciplinary," marked by "the independent and idiosyncratic efforts of individual scholars in particular lines of inquiry."[14] Arabic and other oriental languages were beginning to be taught in a few European universities, and publication programs were undertaken, often as an aid to biblical studies or to missionary efforts. Much of the work in the field, however, was still taking place in a less structured way. It largely developed through encounters, fortuitous or willed, between Europeans and people from Arab and Ottoman lands. The exchange between Golius and Hajarī is but one example of such encounters. Far from being unique, it takes place in a wider horizon of the dynamics and mediations that made possible the production of Orientalist learning.

As for the many people hailing from Eastern cultures, long deleted for the most part from the history of the European Orientalism, beginning with accounts such as Le Gendre's, some are now better known. More work is still needed, however, to understand and analyze their contribution, and to map out how their role should alter the way the field itself should be understood. The central protagonist in this book, Ahmad al-Hajarī, is an ideal actor and guide for examining the networks of cultural and scholarly exchange in the early modern Mediterranean world. Through a close examination of his life, career and works, this study will retrace the ways in which he, like many other scholars from North Africa and the Middle East, influenced his Europeans counterparts and helped shape the development of early modern Orientalism. Even more importantly, the book examines this collaborative experience not only inside, but also beyond the confines of the European Republic of Letters. His substantial body of work was produced mostly in North Africa (or the Maghrib) and was thus situated in the Maghribi culture of his time, following some of its forms and modalities. Hajarī's work was also inflected by multiple personal and intellectual experiences with Europe, in Spain where he was born, as a traveler and envoy of the sultan in France and Holland, and as an interlocutor to European Orientalists. By looking at both these contexts, the European and the Maghribi, this study will show that, when it comes to Hajarī's connections with Erpenius, Golius, and other Orientalists, these networks do not arbitrarily stop at the frontiers of Europe. The intellectual interactions between Europeans and subjects of Muslim countries, which helped shape Orientalism, also affected the societies and cultures of Arab countries, in ways that have not yet been considered in all their dimensions.

Focusing on matters of intellectual history, *Beyond Orientalism* analyzes Hajarī's career and his cultural production, and portrays him as much more than a mere intermediary between two supposedly stable and discrete ensembles (whether they are called the West and the East, or Christendom and Islam), but as an actor and a contributor in a global intellectual history. Using the experience of Hajarī as a kind of case study, this book reveals that early modern Orientalism was not simply an intellectual discipline derived from knowledge constructed by Europeans about their Islamic neighbors. Orientalism was instead a cultural formation born of the circulation and exchange between two interrelated civilizational ensembles. Thanks to a series of networks and knowledge practices situated in Europe, and in Arab and Ottoman lands, it connected the forms of learning that prevailed in Europe and in the Islamic countries, and their respective webs of scholarship or "Republics of Letters."

PLAN FOR THE BOOK

Beyond Orientalism tells the story of Ahmad al-Hajarī in three parts. Part 1, "A Connected Republic of Letters," looks at ways in which early modern Europe related with its Islamic neighbors, and how their spheres of learning, or Republics of Letters, interacted. Chapter 1, "Ahmad al-Hajarī: Trajectories of Exile," takes the figure of Hajarī as an exemplar of these connections, and sketches what we know of his eventful life story, focusing on his intellectual and political activities from Spain to Morocco, from France to the Netherlands, from Egypt to Tunisia. It highlights his many journeys, as well as his successful career as a translator and as a mediator between cultural, political, and legal systems. Working with Orientalists, including Erpenius, Golius and others, was only one aspect of his manifold experience as cultural broker. To underscore that Hajarī's work in Orientalism was not unique in his time, but was inscribed in a larger pattern of intellectual exchange, chapter 2, "Networks of Orientalism: Out of the Shadows," offers an overview of the many people from Islamic countries who played important roles in the field in its first formative period, from the sixteenth through the mid- to late seventeenth centuries. It proposes ways of categorizing these contributors who taught European scholars the languages and cultures of their neighbors, helped them build the first oriental libraries in Europe, and provided them with some understanding of the institutions and practices of knowledge of the Muslim lands. These people brought about an encounter between European and Arabic Republics of Letters, albeit often overdetermined by the prevalence of religious controversy. The chapter explores how the connection between European and the Arabic (or more largely Islamic) Republics of Letters in the early modern period helped European scholars to begin producing a body of Orientalist knowledge about the different Islamic cultures. This sketch of a larger context of sustained contributions of men hailing from Islamic cultures, and this reflection on the modalities and import of this continuous exchange, sets the stage for a closer engagement with Hajarī's work, in Part 2, "Ahmad al-Hajarī: Becoming an Arab Writer." Chapter 3, "Hajarī: A Morisco Writer in the Arabic Republic of Letters," examines the literary and social approaches that he adopted in order to carve a place for himself in the knowledge webs of the Arabic-speaking and writing world. He was born and raised as a secret Muslim in the peripheral site of the vanishing Islamic Spain, and was a member of a vulnerable minority, now dispersed across Mediterranean lands, and to the defense of which he remained dedicated his whole life. He thus needed specific modes to be included in these elaborate scholarly networks. His strategies, which include translation, connections with established scholars, and autobiographical writing, will be shown to be that of a minor author, albeit in the complex sense of "a marginalized, minority people re-appropriating a major language" outlined by French philosophers Gilles Deleuze and Félix Guattari.[15] Chapter 4, "Hajarī in the World," then turns to the ways in which he combined, connected, and considered his eclectic experiences, as a traveling polemicist, a student of European cosmography, a skilled translator of scientific texts, an official in charge of the Saʿdī relations with Christian powers, and a thinker reflecting on the place of Islam and Arabic in the world.

Part 3, "Technology in the Contact Zone," focuses on an early seventeenth-century shared technological culture between the Maghrib and Europe, a culture in which Hajarī was both a witness and an actor. Participating in the trend of reconsidering the history of science and technology in Islamic countries, it challenges the notion, still largely accepted despite the many revisionist studies that have shown its inadequacy, according to which the West became modern by developing science, while Islam remained premodern, having abandoned the cultivation of secular and rational learning. The present study will contribute to this project by focusing on the role of cultural mediators between Europe and North Africa, and by uncovering overlooked developments of the study and practice of technology in the Maghrib. Chapter 5, "A Harbor on the Atlantic Coast," analyzes the episode which brought Golius to Morocco as an engineer, Mūlay Zaydān's harbor project. Through a study of Golius's and others' roles, it examines how Orientalism intersected with diplomatic and technical exchanges, and explores the transnational figure of the technical expert that was playing an increasingly important part in the early modern European state.[16] Hajarī, a witness and a secondary player in this episode, was in the position to make observations that suggest a similar development in North Africa, albeit smaller in scale. He again takes center stage in chapter 6, "Artillery and Practical Knowledge in North Africa," which will analyze his Arabic translation in Tunis of a fascinating technological document, an artillery manual authored in Spanish by a fellow exile from Spain, and will situate it in the context of a written middle culture, between the high academic forms of the learned and the popular culture of the illiterate.

Drawing on the insights of Mediterranean studies, global history, and science and technology studies, this book proposes a relational inquiry that challenges the tendency to situate Golius and Hajarī in discrete cultures, with only barely meaningful connections: Golius as a representative of the European Republic of Letters, as a founding father of the discipline of oriental studies, as an early representative of Enlightenment, whose years spent in Morocco and the Levant, and whose copious connections with scholars of these regions, were simply the inert means through which he acquired mastery over oriental culture; and Hajarī as a mere intermediary who happened to collaborate with influential Orientalists like Erpenius and Golius, but whose work and career are subsumed within Arabic civilization, or even more narrowly, within the subculture of the Muslim exiles from Spain. It will paint the fluid zone in which oriental studies flourished, thanks to the networks that connected Europeans and non-Europeans. These webs of relations trace an intellectual landscape to which both Golius and Hajarī, among many others, belonged, and that included but also extended beyond Orientalism.

PART ONE

A Connected Republic of Letters

THE MEETING BETWEEN GOLIUS AND HAJARĪ was not due to mere chance. When Jacob Golius, an Arabic and other Eastern languages student from the University of Leiden, came to Morocco, he was not only carrying an offering of books for Mūlay Zaydān on behalf of his mentor, the famed European Orientalist Thomas Erpenius, he was also bringing a letter of introduction addressed to Erpenius's friend and Arabic teacher Ahmad al-Hajarī. Despite arriving in a foreign land, Golius was still in a familiar, albeit metaphorical, territory, which contemporaries described with a special moniker—the Republic of Letters. Golius even helped connect between different Republics of Letters.

Since the beginning of the Renaissance, Europeans had enlisted this notion of the Republic of Letters to designate the international and interreligious networks of scholars. The phrase *Respublica litteraria* itself was coined in 1417 by an Italian humanist, Francesco Barbaro, seeking to revive the spirit of letters in antiquity. Members of this community of peers kept in touch through travel and correspondence, even in times of religious and political conflict. In *Worlds Made by Words*, Anthony Grafton describes the Republic of Letters as an "interdisciplinary, international community of scholars" from the early modern period that created "rules for the conduct of scholarly life and debate."[1] More recently, scholars of early modern Orientalism have begun to analyze how exchanges between the European students of oriental cultures and their Islamic neighbors integrated awareness of Eastern forms of knowledge in the increasingly institutionalized disciplines devised by the citizens of this Republic of Letters.[2]

In parallel, some critics argue that the Republic of Letters concept could be profitably used for the premodern Islamic world, in which networks, sustained by intellectual exchange and extensive travel, crisscrossed over a vast expanse of land and undeniably connected scholars and writers over the centuries.[3] This argument is situated within recent research that aims at reevaluating the history of Orientalism. Examining Ottoman manuscripts owned by early modern Orientalists, philologist Paul Babinski noted that in Europe they propagated not only Eastern texts but also foreign practices of reading, collating, glossing. He strikingly proposed that these manuscripts "form a kind of philological contact zone . . . between distinct 'republics of letters,'" and, taking an even larger perspective, that "the emergence of oriental studies as a field of Western European knowledge belongs within a longer process of Islamic philology's globalization."[4]

The present study, rather than focusing on manuscripts, will examine a more embodied form of the circulation of learning, and analyze the role played by the bearers of Eastern knowledge in inflecting the course of early modern Orientalism. Historian E. Natalie Rothman analyzes the significance of late seventeenth-century Venetian dragomans, interpreters, and translators operating in Istanbul in the development of Orientalism as a field of study.[5] This book will consider earlier connections, when cultural brokers, including translators, teachers, and authors—like Golius and Hajarī—created crucial exchanges between the spheres of learning in European and Islamic countries. It focuses especially on transactions in the western part of the Arab world, the Maghrib, which is still too often overlooked in the study of the early modern Mediterranean circulation.[6]

Jacob Golius and Ahmad al-Hajarī's relationship is an instance of the two Republics of Letters interacting by taking advantage, and extending, the still limited but nevertheless significant shared intellectual landscape that resulted from sustained exchange. As a quintessential mediator, Ahmad al-Hajarī—whether he was teaching European students Arabic and helping them obtain manuscripts, or assisting them in reading grammar books and accessing the cultures of Islam—was, as we shall see, a representative of the Arabic Republic of Letters, albeit a rather modestly ranked member of that scholarly network. His work and career are situated at the intersection of the European and the Islamic spheres of knowledge and contributed to connecting them, despite, or maybe because of, his marginal position in both. He also deployed his talents in a number of other professional paths that allowed him to contribute to the development of shared practices in the fields of diplomacy, translation, and even law—as did a number of his European interlocutors. His career, inside and beyond Orientalism, helps map the landscape of intellectual encounters that produced mutually influential processes in different domains, honing in on the path toward a connected Republic of Letters.

Chapter 1 will follow Hajarī's remarkable life between Spain and North Africa. Hajarī was born and raised in Spain and then made a successful career in North Africa as a courtier, translator, and writer that largely built on his knowledge of the cultures of Europe. He belonged to many networks—connecting him to merchants and scholars, diplomats and warriors, rulers and doctors—and through these various networks he had many intellectual and practical interactions with Orientalists. By carefully retracing how these multiple experiences inflected his life and taught him precious skills, this biographical sketch will propose that his contribution to Orientalism is not to be separated from his other qualifications and professional involvements. These also led him to cross boundaries and mediate between communities and cultures and enabled him to emerge as a significant intercessor.

Chapter 2 widens the lens beyond Hajarī. This larger focus argues that Orientalism was not merely a body of knowledge built by European scholars about the East but also the product of interactions among modalities of learning in Europe, North Africa, and the Middle East. Intermediaries hailing from Muslim countries helped Europeans build languages skills and furthered their knowledge of Islamic cultures. Some were accomplished enough to expose them to a different learning system, organized through schools and libraries and through teaching, reading, and writing practices. These brokers collaborated with scholars from Rome, Paris, London, or Leiden. These collaborators, in various capacities depending on the level of their education, created critical connections between European and Arab cultures. In sum, since the sixteenth century, the sustained encounter between polities, regions, and spheres of knowledge brought to life a connected Republic of Letters, of which Orientalism was an early manifestation.

ONE

Ahmad al-Hajarī

TRAJECTORIES OF EXILE

WHEN GOLIUS MET HIM IN MARRAKESH, Ahmad al-Hajarī had been a trusted servant of the Sultan Mūlay Zaydān for many years. Like other members of his court, he was an exile from Spain, where he was born around 1569 to Moriscos, as Muslim converts and their descendants were called. In 1499, forced conversion was the only legal option for Muslims, other than death or exile, and those who stayed in Spain were known as *nuevos cristianos,* "New Christians." This distinguished this ostracized group from "Old Christians," who were said to be of *sangre limpia* (pure Christian blood), and marked them as suspect and inferior. Hajarī, outwardly a Christian, spent his formative years as a crypto-Muslim under the surveillance of the Spanish Inquisition. Though mistreated and marginalized, the Moriscos were forbidden to leave Spain during this period lest they foment aggression among Spain's Muslim enemies. But Hajarī managed to escape in 1599, ten years before the expulsion of the Moriscos from Spain in 1609. This chapter focuses on his extraordinarily compelling life story.

The main features of the life of Ahmad ibn Qāsim al-Hajarī are known well enough, thanks to his copious autobiographical writings and to other documents, including diplomatic and personal correspondence, even though mystery still surrounds some crucial elements. Any biographical account of Hajarī has to rely on a few texts. His main extant work, titled the *Supporter of Religion against the Infidels,*[1] itself an abridgement of a lost text, focuses on his travels to Europe, without ignoring other times in his life. Another important source consists of documents included in a manuscript held in the University of Bologna library. It first belonged to a wealthy Morisco expelled from Spain and settled in Tunis, Muhammad Rubio of Villafeliche in Aragon, who sponsored some of the translations it contains.[2] Written almost entirely in Spanish, it collects texts composed or translated by several Moriscos in the first third of the seventeenth century, including a few by Hajarī. Among these, one piece stands out: the Spanish translation of a long Arabic letter he signed in Paris in May 12, 1612, and addressed to Morisco friends living in Istanbul. Many years after writing it, Hajarī, then settled in Tunis, himself translated this essential missive that contains invaluable information about his life.[3] Another important text, one of the last translations he made, also in Tunis, was of an artillery manual authored in Spanish by the Morisco Ibrāhīm Ghānim.[4] Hajarī translated it into Arabic and added a postscript that recounts episodes of his life and events he witnessed.[5] Finally, a number of documents and letters found in archives, some of which have been published, provide more information.

Early on, readers could have been confused by the fact that the author known to modern scholarship as Ahmad ibn Qāsim al-Hajarī also bore other patronyms. Hajarī himself used different names depending on the time of his life and on the audience he was addressing. Born in Spain, he had a Spanish patronym: Diego Bejarano. However, he preferred his full Arabic name: Ahmad ibn Qāsim ibn Ahmad al-faqīh Qāsim ibn al-Shaykh al-Hajarī al-Andalusī.[6] Al-Hajarī and al-Andalusī are his *nisba*s, or names of relation, the first referring to his hometown of al-Hajar al-Ahmar, and the second indicating his country of origin, al-Andalus, as Muslims of the time called Spain. He also had a *laqab,* or honorific nickname, Shihāb al-Dīn, that he used in the title of one lost text he authored. His *kunya,* or tektonym or name derived from the name of the oldest child, was Abū al-ʿAbbās. Another name, Afuqāy, was used for him, and by him, although its meaning and origin remain obscure. He also sometimes used hybrid forms of his names such as "Ehmed ben Caçim Bejarano."

During his remarkable life, Hajarī faced discrimination and danger but was also honored by heads of state and theologians—and never wavered in his commitment to serve the Morisco community during their years of persecution and exile. The biographical sketch in this chapter traces his encounters with traders, scholars, and public officials, to reveal a multifaceted career largely built on his understanding of the cultures of Europe, that allowed him to emerge as a significant intercessor between communities and cultures. However, he was not unique in his time. He could, to some extent, be seen as but one example whose case illuminates the trajectories of many people coming from Arabic and other Eastern cultures, and who, like him, played a part in the field of Orientalism.

Hajarī came from al-Hajar al-Ahmar, also called Hornachos, a small town in Extremadura populated by Moriscos. Like the other Hornacheros, his family, consisting of his parents and a sister, were secret Muslims who spoke Arabic despite the decree promulgated in 1567 that forbade the use of the language in Spanish territory. He was born during the bitter Morisco revolt of 1568–71, known as the Second War of the Alpujarras, when the Moriscos of Granada opposed the Spanish Crown. Not long before the rebellion, Morisco leader Francisco Núñez Muley (ca. 1492–1570) explained the reasons that would lead to this explosion: "With each day that passes we are in worse shape and more mistreated in all respects and by all manners, as much by the secular as by the ecclesiastical arms of justice."[7]

After mercilessly crushing the rebellion, the Crown deployed massive efforts to forcibly assimilate the vanquished, during a dark period for the minority when many found themselves the victims of institutional and popular violence. The policy toward them, now considered an "utterly alien element within the body politic," was to coercively bring about their "outright, total, and final Christianization."[8] In this threatening context, Hornachos remained a special case, and acquired an importance disproportionate to its size, "because it afforded a relatively inaccessible place of refuge where Muslims might live away from the constant surveillance of Christian neighbors."[9] It was considered the very symbol of the Morisco danger, and its population fiercely resisted acculturation attempts.[10] Hajarī was raised in this atmosphere of defiance. Not only did he speak colloquial Arabic from childhood, but a family member taught him the rudiments of reading and writing the classical form. During his time in Spain, he also learned Spanish so well that he could pass as an Old Christian, as few Moriscos could. This mastery of the two languages would mark his whole life and career.

Hajarī did not stay in Hornachos, however, and spent time in several cities, including Madrid, Granada, and Seville, although the reasons for these moves remain unclear. Documents show that he came from a privileged background and that he knew wealthy and influential characters belonging to or connected to the Morisco community in Spain. Many of Hajarī's acquaintances had been able to secure for themselves a reputation as trustworthy translators and enjoyed the advantages this position yielded. Cultural historian Claire Gilbert has shown that such recognition could earn interpreters "employment, reward, legitimacy and—in some cases—protection," as well as "agency and benefits for themselves, for their families, and sometimes for their communities."[11] While in Granada, Hajarī was awarded a license to translate, which gave him a salary and placed him among the Arabic-speakers who could proudly display their mastery of Arabic in a country where the knowledge of this language was effectively criminalized and could have devastating consequences. He obtained this license as a result of his involvement in one of the most influential events in his life: the Lead Books or *libros plúmbeos/plomos* affair. Most accounts of the culture of the Moriscos in Spain in the late sixteenth century focus on this extraordinary religious and political incident.

On March 19, 1588, in Granada, during the demolition of a tower known as the Torre Turpiana, workers found a lead chest which contained several relics, including bones attributed to Saint Stephen and others, a piece of cloth identified as the handkerchief of Mary, and a parchment written in Arabic, Latin, and Spanish, containing a prophecy about the end of the world by Saint John. During the years 1595–99, treasure hunters also discovered lead books in caves located in the hillside of Granada, soon to be called the Sacromonte, or the holy mountain (see fig. 1). These tablets bore engraved texts in Arabic and other languages that were ostensibly ancient Christian writings. Seekers also found more bones and ashes. Objects and texts were first identified as dating from the beginning of Christianity in Spain, written in Arabic by Saint Ctesiphon, and by Saint Caecilius, a missionary who was, according to legend, ordained by Peter and Paul to evangelize southern Spain and who became the first bishop of Granada. The archbishop of Granada Pedro de Castro Vaca y Quiñones (1534–1623) embraced the holy relics, and they became the focus of intense popular devotion. Nevertheless, from the very beginning, there was controversy over their authenticity. Some defended the finds as authentic Christian documents and objects. Others were convinced that these were contemporary forgeries rather than ancient and venerable relics, and pointed not only to the obvious anachronisms contained in the texts but also to several indisputably Islamic statements that they conveyed. While the Crown and the Vatican monitored developments, many scholars were asked to examine, translate, and interpret the parchment and the Lead Books. Hajarī was among them. The relics were transferred to Rome in 1643, where they were again examined by experts, and eventually condemned in 1682 by Pope Innocent XI who sided with the opponents of the *plomos,* as the finds were generically called, and declared them to be heretical artifacts created by Muslims in order to undermine the Christian faith. Only in the year 2000 were they returned to Granada.

FIGURE 1. The discovery of the Lead Books near Granada. Engraving made by Francisco Heylan (ca. 1584–ca. 1635), published in Diego Nicolás Heredia Barnuevo, *Mystico ramillete historico . . .*, Granada, Imprenta real, 1741. Creative Commons. Digitized by the University of Granada, http://digibug.ugr.es/handle/10481/32212.

Hajarī probably got involved through his acquaintance with Muhammad ibn Abī al-ʿĀsī, also known as Muhamed Vulhac, and as Pérez Bolhaç.[12] Muhammad was a translator, a physician, and the grandson of the man Hajarī calls "the pious shaykh al-Jabbis."[13] "Al Jabbis" has been identified as the wealthy merchant Lorenzo Hernandez El Chapiz, who belonged to a network of Moriscos attempting to obtain the official status of Old Christians in order to avoid expulsion from Spain. Muhammad's grandfather Lorenzo was, like Muhammad, a translator of Arabic. He was also a member of a committee tasked with interpreting the parchment found in the Torre Turpiana.[14] Through Muhammad, Hajarī met Maldonado, an abbot who, discovering that he knew Arabic, introduced him to Archbishop Pedro de Castro. Asked to translate the parchment, Hajarī testified to his delight at this appointment, since he was for the first time able to reveal his knowledge of Arabic without fear of the Inquisition. His most important contribution to this effort was his 1598 translation of the parchment, still extant in the archives.[15] According to him, this version was sent to Rome, although this has not been corroborated. Hajarī was a secondary figure in this affair, but he attached to it an immense importance, and he kept reflecting on it until his later years.[16] Its impact on his own religious and intellectual thinking was considerable.

Critics have proposed different approaches to assess how these falsifications negotiated the connection between Islam and Christianity in Granada, analyzing the parts played by the many constituents involved in the examination of the evidence, including the Morisco community, the ecclesiastical and political authorities of Granada, the Crown, and the papacy. Hajarī's involvement offers a rare look at this episode from the point of view of a Morisco. By counterfeiting documents that celebrated Arabic as a Christian language and emphasized the points of agreement between Islam and Christianity, the forgers pursued the goal of creating "a heritage that would have guaranteed Morisco cultural survival by merging the separate pasts of the two communities."[17] From the perspective of the *plomos* forgers, this was an attempt to integrate Arabic and Arabic-speaking people into the polity of Spain while efforts to eradicate all remnants of the culture of Islamic Iberia were underway. This experience in mediating officially between linguistic, cultural, and religious systems foreshadows many later episodes when Hajarī would do the same, in both North Africa and Europe. His involvement in the *plomos* episode places him among the Morisco scholars and translators whose work is being increasingly recognized as belonging in the history of Orientalism.

After his participation in the *plomos* episode, he left Granada for Seville. In this thriving city, where the learning necessary for the colonial enterprise was supported by state institutions such as the Casa de Contratación, the central trading house and procurement agency for Spain's New World empire, he developed a curiosity for cosmography, which might have led to his acquaintance with the prominent astronomer Rodrigo Zamorano (1542–1620). Hajarī's continuing interest in this field would serve him well in his Moroccan career, when he found the Sultan Mūlay Zaydān to be similarly inclined. Hajarī probably spent a few months in Seville, perfecting his Spanish in order to be able to move to a seaport by passing as an Old Christian, since Moriscos were not allowed in the coastal towns. He met with other influential members of the Morisco community, including some who would end up in Istanbul, such as Muhammad ibn Abī al-'Āsī, who became a recipient of the letter Hajarī sent from Paris that related his views on assimilation and expulsion. Muhammad and Hajarī would indeed enjoy a long friendship. In the mid-1630s, Hajarī was still involved in business with Muhammad, who at that time owned a shop in Cairo.[18] Hajarī also cultivated the friendship of 'Abd al-Karīm ibn Tūda, governor of Arzila in northern Morocco, who spent years in exile in Spain.[19] Ibn Tūda might have helped Hajarī when the latter escaped from Spain, as Inquisition documents show he had done for others.[20] Less happily, Hajarī entered into some kind of business with two Morisco brothers named Villegas, which ended in a quarrel and the cessation of their relations. This mishap cannot distract from the fact that, during his first decades in Spain, Hajarī had already created networks of friends and associates that he would be able to rely on for the rest of his life, for his own advantage, and also in order to help less lucky members of his community. He would still be in touch with acquaintances from Spain in Morocco, France, Egypt, and Tunis, and he would keep creating and maintaining new international connections that have left traces in many domains. These early decades in Spain deeply influenced his outlook on life, and taught him skills that he would rely on for his later career in North Africa.

ESCAPE TO MOROCCO

What is probably the major event in his life occurred in 1599, at about age thirty, when he escaped from Spain. He writes, "Allah inspired me with leaving that country for the land of the Muslims," and describes how his fluency in Spanish aided him in this very risky adventure, since the Moriscos were strictly forbidden from leaving Spain:

> Now when I found out that the unbelievers [Christians] at the frontiers made a practice of investigating everyone that passed to see if they could find a Spanish Muslim in disguise, so as to be able to send him for trial (for they had forbidden Muslims to approach the frontiers so as to prevent them from fleeing to Muslim territory), I studied for many years to learn their speech and to pick up their writing, so that, when I came to their country on my way to Muslim lands to escape, they would think me one of them.[21]

His escape route, one often taken by Moriscos, took him from Seville to Puerto Santa Maria in the northeast of Cádiz, where he joined a fellow Morisco, whom Hajarī described as a "Cordobese boy" and an "excellent, religious person."[22] A ship brought them to the heavily fortified Portuguese stronghold of Mazagan (al-Burayja in Arabic, now the city of al-Jadīda) on the Atlantic coast of Morocco. He spent two months in Mazagan where, in order to better disguise his intentions, he fought against the Muslims when

FIGURE 2. View of Marrakesh in 1641, after the print by Adriaan Matham (1599?–1660). Bibliothèque Nationale de France. ID/Cote:GE D-21463. Public domain.

called upon. Finally the opportunity to flee arose, and he escaped with his companion to Azammūr, under the jurisdiction of the Saʿdī dynasty which ruled over most Moroccan territory. He then went to Marrakesh, the capital, where he would reside for decades. He encountered in the city previous acquaintances, such as the Villegas brothers with whom his relations were no better than they had been in Seville. When Hajarī arrived in Marrakesh in 1599, his old friend Ibn Tūda had regained an eminent status in Morocco, and proposed to help him obtain a position in the court of the powerful Saʿdī Sultan Ahmad al-Mansūr (r. 1578–1603). Hajarī declined this opportunity but was nevertheless introduced to the sultan on July 4, 1599, and was impressed by the magnificence of his army. He settled in Marrakesh and, in another proof of his connections with the Morisco elite, married the daughter of El Partal, "one of the most famous Alpujarras rebels exiled in Morocco."[23] He fathered two sons and two daughters. He also studied and frequented learned circles, entertaining friendships with famed and sometimes influential scholars (see fig. 2).

The death of Ahmad al-Mansūr in 1603 was the beginning of a bitter civil war among his sons. During this troubled time, Hajarī attached his career and fate to Mūlay Zaydān, who would end up winning the war, although he would reign on a diminished territory. Hajarī was only one among many Morisco members of the sultan's court. His knowledge of Spanish served him well, and he worked for Mūlay Zaydān and then his two sons and successors,

as a secretary and translator of official documents. In the bilingual chancellery of Mūlay Zaydān, he held a position he calls *kātib sirrihi fī al-lisān al-ʿajamī*,[24] which means literally "the secretary for his secret in the foreign [Spanish] language." Positions similarly named, using the word *sirr* or secret, are attested in the history of Arab states, including the Moroccan *makhzan*—as the Moroccan government and court was called—where they were held by high-ranking officials of the chancellery who could use the sultan's seal (though these officials were not on the level of ministers or chamberlains).[25] The title highlights that Hajarī enjoyed not only great success in his career, but also, at least during the reign of Mūlay Zaydān, a relationship with the sultan based on trust and closeness. Beyond diplomatic correspondence, he also put in Arabic for the learned Mūlay Zaydān European scholarly texts, mostly of astronomy and geography. Many of his translations have unfortunately been lost.

Even before Zaydān secured his power, Hajarī was involved in the affairs of the court, and able to exert some influence. He met the Dutch ambassador Pieter Maestersz. Coy. Coy had been sent to deliver Moroccan captives that the Dutch navy had released from seized Spanish galleys as a sign of good will on the part of the government of the Netherlands and in order to smooth the way for a potential alliance.[26] Coy's mission was supposed to last two years, but he stayed longer in Morocco, when turmoil was engulfing the region. He arrived on June 18, 1605, in the port of Safi, when Abū Fāris, brother of

Zaydān, was reigning, and only left in 1609. A few months after his arrival, the civil war broke out again. In February 1607, Mūlay Zaydān entered Marrakesh and soon stabilized his power. Coy was arrested after an altercation between a Dutch warship and a vessel belonging to an English pirate, and he was released on July 19, 1607, fifty-five days after his arrest. Hajarī claims that he was instrumental in Coy's liberation, and that, grateful to him for having released Muslim captives, he asked his influential friend the judge Muhammad ibn 'Abd Allāh al-Ragraguī (d. 1614) to intercede on behalf of the diplomat. Although no document corroborates this version of events, Hajarī would again meet Coy a few years later in his native Holland. The Dutch official introduced him to high-ranking members of the government, including the Stathouder Maurits of Nassau, as a testimonial to their cordial relationship.

TRAVELS IN EUROPE

Hajarī's travels in Europe, where he met Coy again, comprised another crucial period in his life. The reason for this long trip to France and the Netherlands stemmed from the tragic final episode in the history of Muslim Spain, when the Spanish Crown decided in September 1609 to expel the Morisco population. This event had wide-ranging repercussions in North Africa, where many of the Moriscos took refuge. Hajarī translated for the sultan a letter about this decree addressed by Felipe III to the grandees of Valencia, and would later include his version in the *Supporter*.[27] That was only part of his involvement in the events surrounding the expulsion. Some Moriscos from Cordoba, Hornachos, Ecija, and Sanlucar rented their passage on four French ships as France, already hostile to Spain, counted the expulsion as "barbarous" and helped the refugees reach Islamic lands.[28] However, as happened to many Moriscos during such journeys from Spain, the captains stole their belongings and abandoned the passengers on an island. An English ship rescued them and transported them to Morocco, where the sultan and the population showed them compassion, and gave them money and food. Learning that the king of France was suing the robbers, the Moriscos decided to send members of their own community so they might also seek retribution. Indeed, the archives bear traces of affairs involving thieving French ship captains and expelled Moriscos who sued their robbers and obtained at least partial restitution.[29] French justice even punished some culprits, including by death in some notorious cases.[30] Hajarī, as a respected and prominent member of the Morisco community of Marrakesh, was authorized by Mūlay Zaydān and encouraged by his friend the judge Ragrāguī to accompany the delegation and to represent the wronged Moriscos. He was not the sole Morisco sent from North Africa to represent victims of theft in French courts.[31] Holding a letter of recommendation from the sultan, he traveled with five of the victims. The names of two are known: Jacques Fernandez of Seville and Harné Garsia of Luque.[32] The ship transporting them to France left Safi probably in early 1611, and arrived thirty days later in Le Havre. From there, the travelers went to Rouen, where Hajarī and presumably his companions dressed in French clothes that would be their attire for the rest of the trip.

His European travels show him able to rely on webs of acquaintances for his court case and other affairs and to extend them further. As soon as he arrived in Rouen, he encountered a French merchant he knew from Morocco. In Paris, which the travelers reached three days later, Hajarī met Étienne Hubert (1567–1614) and Arnoult de Lisle (1556–1613), other former residents of Marrakesh whom he had probably already met when both were physicians employed at the Moroccan court. They were also studying Arabic, which was an important language in medicine.[33] Hajarī's involvement with European students of Arabic is a crucial part of his story and legacy as a participant in the Republic of Letters networks that helped advance oriental scholarship in Europe.

He mentioned de Lisle's help in his court case in the letter he addressed in Paris to Morisco friends settled in Istanbul.[34] This diplomat and physician to the king of France is a considerable character in the history of early modern French Orientalism. Henri III had made him the first professor of Arabic at the prestigious Collège Royal in 1587, a position deemed necessary considering the usefulness of the language in medicine, philosophy, and biblical studies. However, de Lisle appears to have rarely, if ever, taught in the Collège, spending instead many years in Morocco as an agent to Henri III, and then Henri IV, and as a physician in the service of Ahmad al-Mansūr. He sojourned in Marrakesh from 1588 to 1599, and then again in 1606 and 1607. After his first stay, de Lisle was replaced by Étienne Hubert, a physician from Orléans, who arrived in 1598 in Marrakesh, where he spent a year in the service of Ahmad al-Mansūr, as his personal doctor, and also, according to Hajarī, as a spy for the French Crown.[35] In a private letter, Hubert simply stated that he was sent to Marrakesh to renew the peace between the French and Moroccan monarchies.[36] He learned Arabic well enough to gain the respect of many learned contemporaries, such as Isaac Casaubon (1559–1614) or Joseph Scaliger (1540–1609). When Hajarī arrived in Paris, the two men struck a deal: in exchange for Hubert's assistance in navigating the French government for his court case, Hajarī helped him in his Arabic studies. At that time, Hubert was professor of Arabic at the Collège Royal, a position he would hold until 1613.[37]

Beside Hajarī's own testimony, the traces of his work with Hubert are found in printed and manuscript texts. Hajarī might have related to his interest in medicine, being himself curious enough of this field to be able to quote established authorities of early modern medicine like the Greek physicians Galen and Hippocrates and the Persian polymath Ibn Sīnā (also known as Avicenna).[38] Hajarî was also proud of his ability to cure the sick, albeit mostly by using methods akin to magic.[39] Hubert's copy of the Arabic *Qānun al-tibb* (Canon of Medicine) by Ibn Sīnā published in 1593 in Rome by the Medici Press bears annotations in Spanish by Hajarī.[40] An Arabic-Latin lexicon, maybe authored by Hubert, is preceded by a transliterated Arabic alphabet which provides the "pronunciation d'Affricque par Ben Caçin," as his name was mangled, and contains Latin glosses referencing Hajarī.[41] The latter also made copies of Arabic manuscripts for Hubert, including a mnemonic poem on the verbal system by the Andalusian grammarian Ibn Mālik with its commentary, to which Hajarī added interlinear Spanish translations in a few pages, and, in the end, appended more personal contributions in prose and verse. He signed this work in April 1612. An Arabic alphabet within a volume comprised of printed and manuscript folios is attributed to "Ben Caçin de Maroque,"[42] meaning Ibn Qāsim from Marrakesh. In a note on the manuscript of a famous collection of prayers, Hajarī attested to its Maghribi provenance.[43]

As his main contact in Paris among the learned, Hubert opened to Hajarī the doors of libraries and abbeys, and introduced him to some luminaries of European cultural life. Hajarī certainly heard Hubert mention François Savary de Brèves (1560–1628), who was an important figure in the culture and politics of early seventeenth-century France. He served as ambassador of France, first in Istanbul then in Rome, and was an ardent promoter of oriental studies.[44] Through Hubert, Hajarī met a famed and respected connoisseur of poetry.[45] This unnamed scholar might have been Jacques Davy du Perron (1556–1618), "Grand Chaplain" (Grand Aumônier) of France from 1606 to 1618, and thus, *ex officio,* head of the Collège Royal in which Hubert taught.

He was a learned controversialist, a Hebrew scholar, a proponent of the study of Arabic, and a prolific writer, renowned for his poetry.[46] Hajarī was also aware that Hubert was teaching Arabic to a small cohort. He met Jean-Baptiste Duval (d. 1632), who first studied Arabic with Hubert in Paris in 1600, then traveled to Rome, and went on to become royal secretary and interpreter in oriental languages. In a preface to his Arabic-Latin dictionary, which he completed in 1613 and based on the work of two Maronite scholars, he attested that in April 1612, Hajarī had examined the Arabic books Duval brought back from his travels, and had told him that he would love to live in Asia where books were easy to find.[47]

Better known and much more significant in the history of Orientalism is Thomas Erpenius, quietly studying Arabic in the little town of Conflans near Paris at this time, avoiding the tumult of the city and on the lookout for Arab visitors who would help him in his studies. In September 1611, Hubert sent Hajarī to visit Erpenius, who mentioned their first encounter in a letter dated September 28 and addressed to the famous scholar Isaac Casaubon.[48] The Dutch student took an immediate liking to Hajarī, whom he described as "a cultured and highly intelligent man." The feeling was mutual, and the two men delighted at having met each other: "For his part, he found a man in this place who was studying Arabic; and for my part, I met an Arab who I hoped would be able to teach me something. I was not disappointed." Judging that Hajarī was a much better professor of Arabic than a previous instructor, the Egyptian Copt Yūsuf ibn Abī Dhaqn, Erpenius decided to move back to Paris so that he could meet his new teacher more often. Another letter he wrote in Arabic to Hajarī that same month detailed why this encounter made him so happy.[49] Erpenius deplored the difficulty of learning Arabic given the "lack of books and teachers in this country," and expressed his eagerness to pick up something from "every Arab who came here." Thanking Hajarī profusely for his help, he asked him to explain Quranic phrases in Spanish. This letter is notable for the respect and admiration Erpenius expressed for his new friend and teacher (see fig. 3).

Parallel to his work with Orientalists, Hajarī made progress in his lawsuit, thanks to the help of Hubert and de Lisle, who probably introduced him to the secretary of the king he calls "Monsiur Manjan," and who might have been Claude Mangot (1556–1624), secretary of state and later keeper of the seals (garde des sceaux). With their assistance, he was received by the royal chancellery. Pleading for the robbed Moriscos before Christian judges and officials, he might have been building on experience acquired in Spanish

THOMAS ERPENIVS ARABI.
CÆ LINGVÆ PROFESS

FIGURE 3. Portrait of Ahmad al-Hajarī's friend Thomas Erpenius (1584–1624), engraving by Jan van de Velde (1593–1641). Rijksmuseum, http://hdl.handle.net/10934/RM0001. COLLECT.334016. Public domain.

courts when he was licensed to translate between Arabic and Spanish. In France he met many jurists and lawyers, and obtained valuable practical knowledge about the workings of the law in Europe. His writings show that he was aware of and maybe familiar with some scholarly European legal texts.

News about Hajarī's efforts spread among the Morisco diaspora, and, after he had spent about a year in France, he was contacted by other victims of thefts asking for his help. Among those who reached out to Hajarī was Alonso de Campos, who had been robbed by Genoese sailors, and who said he could provide information about the French thieves. Another was Jeronimo de la Cueva of Baeza, whose goods had been stolen by a Frenchman. In parallel to these cases of robbery, Hajarī had also been entrusted by Moriscos from Marrakesh to represent some of the distraught mothers whose young children had been taken away from them in Seville: "The cries were so loud that the Sevillians said that it was like the Day of Judgement."[50] At one point during his time in Paris, he met with the Spanish ambassador Íñigo de Cárdenas, who had arrived in Paris in 1609, to discuss their situation, although there is no indication that any result came from this encounter.

To deal with the case of the robbed Moriscos, Hajarī traveled to other French cities. His movements and activities around France, as well as his correspondence, show that, in advancing the Morisco cases, he was activating the network of diplomats cum Orientalists whom he knew from Morocco and who were now helping him navigate the intricacies of the French government and legal system; and, at the same time, he was relying on another web of relations, the international network of Moriscos who were working toward facilitating the settlement of their compatriots after their forced exile, toward, in the words of Dutch historian Gerard Wiegers, "managing disaster."[51] Sometime during the winter of 1611–12 winter, he went to Bordeaux to meet the man he calls *qādī al-Andalus,* the judge of the Andalusians, meaning the magistrate appointed by the French government to deal with the Morisco issue. The French magistrate, Marc-Antoine de Gourgues (1575–1628), was a scion of a distinguished family of *noblesse de robe* (i.e., nobles awarded their aristocratic rank for their service in judicial or administrative posts). When Hajarī arrived in Bordeaux, he learned that Gourgues was in Saint-Jean-de-Luz. This city on the Basque coast near the Spanish border had been a frequent destination for Moriscos fleeing Spain since decades before the expulsion, and during the years when it occurred.[52] Hajarī traveled to Saint-Jean-de-Luz, where he spent a few months, and met with some influential Moriscos he had known in Spain. His efforts not leading to the desired result, he went back to Paris, probably with Gourgues, to focus on obtaining a letter from the king endorsing his attempt to obtain retribution on behalf of the robbed Moriscos, and giving him procuration to sue in their name. To secure this important document, he mobilized the assistance of many: besides de Lisle, Hubert, and "Manjan," Hajarī also met with a Morisco named Tapia, himself an acquaintance of two of the aforementioned Frenchmen. Tapia had been sent from Istanbul by Sultan Ahmad I to urge the king of France to help the exiled in their endeavors. Indeed, the king's missive mentioned that the orders it conveyed were given "in honour of the great lord," meaning the Ottoman ruler.[53]

The importance of Hajarī's networks extending over Europe and the Mediterranean is underscored by the aforementioned letter. Directed to Moriscos living in Istanbul, he signed it with a hybrid version of his name, "Ehmed Bencaçim Bejarano Andaluz." Among the named adressees were his good friend from Spain Dr. Pérez Bolhaç (Muhammad ibn Abī al-'Āsī), another acquaintance named Luis de Baldivia, who had passed through Saint-Jean-de-Luz on his way to Istanbul,[54] and Tapia, whom Hajarī had recently met in Paris. This important missive narrates his escape from Spain and his settlement in Morocco, and details his observations about the difficulties that most of the refugees encountered in North Africa, although, "wherever they are, they will be at a better place, as they will not be subjected to the Inquisition."[55] Hajarī then focuses on his efforts on behalf of the robbed Moriscos and described his time in Saint-Jean-de-Luz. He also urged the recipients to lobby and seek an attestation from the Ottoman sultan to help him in his affairs, or at least a letter penned by the French ambassador in Istanbul Achille Harlay de Sancy (1581–1646), whom the Moriscos considered an ally. He asked to have this document sent to Hubert. This letter shows Hajarī strategizing with other community leaders in order to better the situation of the Morisco diaspora around the Mediterranean, and places him within a "milieu of wealthy and influential Granadan and Castilian Moriscos."[56] These men had the ear of European diplomats, and archives show that Tapia was in contact with Achille Harlay de Sancy.[57] As for Muhammad ibn Abī al-'Āsī, he had a short correspondence with Cornelius Haga (1578–1654), the first Dutch ambassador in Istanbul, and played a part in facilitating the signature of a treaty between the Ottoman Porte and the Dutch government.[58] In fact, historians Mercedes García-Arenal and Fernando Rodríguez Mediano suggest that the Hajarī-Bolhaç link was instrumental in successfully bringing about this alliance.[59]

In the French capital, Hajarī continued working with Hubert and other European students of Arabic. Hajarī sometimes felt lonely and nostalgic for the warmth of his household, and even wrote a poem that poignantly expresses his longing for his wife and children: "I separated from my loved ones for a purpose, / And the separation caused my torment."[60] Despite these moments of despondency, he also enjoyed some lively social occasions. He attended in the Place Royale the grandiose celebrations upon the engagements of Louis XIII with the Spanish princess Anne of Austria, and Elisabeth of France with the Prince of the Asturias, future King Felipe IV. On May 13, 1612, at a dinner at the house of Marc-Antoine de Gourgues, he met several notables, including the judge's mother-in-law, Marie Tudert, widow of the powerful high official Jean Séguier, lord of Autry, and had a spirited discussion with them concerning religious difference.

Armed with the document signed by the king of France, Hajarī went to Olonne, where twenty-two of the robber captains resided. He sojourned in the house belonging to a man he calls the "commander of the Seal," maybe Nicolas Brûlart de Sillery who was chancellor of France in the years 1607–24, as well as *garde des sceaux,* or keeper of the seals, during part of that time. There he met some ladies with whom he discussed religion and, in a trial for his faith, engaged in a chaste romance with a brunette. Without having obtained the sought-for restitution, he went again to Bordeaux, where he had an incident with the police. Hajarī and his companions were denounced for openly practicing Islam and eating meat on Friday and Saturday.[61] On a more pleasant note, he met with members of the parliament of Bordeaux, including one named Fayard, from a family of local notables.[62] With him and some of his associates, he engaged in debates about religion, as he had done throughout his travels. From Bordeaux, he took a boat on the Garonne River, that led him to Toulouse. Although he does not state the reason for this trip, one can surmise that it is related to the funds that the international network of Moriscos had deposited in that city.[63] Indeed, a "member of the Chapiz family . . . acted as a depositor of Morisco capital in Toulouse."[64] As seen earlier, Hajarī had been acquainted with members of this wealthy family while in Spain and maintained a connection after his exile. This trip away from Paris was successful. He settled the case and obtained restitution of some stolen merchandise, as well as monetary compensation: "As for the goods deposited in Bordeaux, which had been stolen by the captain from the people of al-Hajar al-Ahmar, I got hold of them after one and a half years had gone by. Praise be to God that every Andalusian who appointed me as his legal representative, received some money."[65]

Hajarī went back to Paris, where he met two Turkish ladies who had been captured in the eastern Mediterranean and brought to Paris, and were now part of the household of Queen Marie de Medici, though they longed to return to their homeland. When he went to the Netherlands, Hajarī again activated his networks to arrange for their successful escape. After more than two years in France, and after winning his lawsuit and obtaining restitution for the robbed Moriscos, Hajarī left the country, taking the same route through Rouen and Le Havre. A Dutch ship led him from France to Holland, where he stayed between June 13 and September 13, 1613. The reasons for this trip are not entirely clear. Some speculate that he was sent on a secret mission by Mūlay Zaydān. Maybe he was also working on behalf of the Moriscos and in association with exiled community leaders to ameliorate the fate of the refugees. His visit might be also related to his acquaintance with the Moriscos settled in Istanbul who were facilitating the alliance between the Dutch Republic and the Porte. Whatever the case, just like in France, Hajarī could count on his network of friends. In Amsterdam and the Hague, he encountered traders from Marrakesh. Through Pieter Coy, he met four times with Maurits of Nassau in the Hague, and they discussed the Morisco situation.

Another earlier acquaintance that he met in Holland was Thomas Erpenius. When Hajarī came back to Paris from a trip to Bordeaux, Erpenius had left the city. Soon after he arrived in Holland, Hajarī heard that his student had been appointed professor of Arabic in Leiden, and wrote to him on June 16, 1613, from Amsterdam.[66] In the *Supporter,* he described him as a man "who was studying Arabic and teaching it to others, receiving a salary for this."[67] That was the year in which the Dutch scholar published his widely influential *Grammatica arabica,* the main textbook used by European students of Arabic until the nineteenth century. The two men met again, and Hajarī was invited to Erpenius's house. He considered his encounters with the Dutch scholar important enough to mention them in some detail in the excerpts from the *Supporter* included in the Bologna manuscript and translated into Spanish.[68]

The two men worked together again in Holland. In a note, added on September 1613, to a manuscript of a grammatical text, Erpenius mentioned that his "Spanish Muslim friend" who was then in Amsterdam inspected the book.[69] During that time, the Dutch scholar, in his preparatory manuscript for his edition of Arabic proverbs, attested in many pages to the help provided by Hajarī.[70] It may have been at this time that the latter copied for Erpenius the well-known thirteenth-century grammar book known as *al-Ajurrūmiya*, written by Muhammad al-Sanhājī ibn Ajurrūm, with complete interlineal Spanish translation.[71] Like Hubert did in Paris, Erpenius introduced Hajarī to learned men in Leiden, which, with its "several schools . . . for the study of science,"[72] was a capital of European culture. In his home, Hajarī met a famous physician, identified in the edition as Petrus Pauw (1564–1617), and other unnamed scholars. He also met through Erpenius the young Pieter Nuyts (1598–1655). Hajarî signed an entry in his *Album amicorum* on September 11, 1613.

A Dutch ship brought him back to Morocco in December 1613. This long European sojourn was very fruitful. He had done well by his fellow Moriscos, helping them obtain justice and restitution, and had experienced the cultures of France and Holland, in ways that would inform his own reflection on the world. He also met many scholars, and worked with a number of them. Back in Marrakesh, he told learned friends about his religious debates with Christians and Jews in Europe, and some urged him to write about these encounters. He did not yet follow their advice, and simply resumed his functions in court.

FROM MARRAKESH TO TUNIS

Back in Marrakesh, one of his assignments also concerned questions of law. As secretary and translator for Mūlay Zaydān, Hajarī became involved in the legal and political case of the inheritance of the sultan's brother al-Shaykh al-Ma'mūn, ally of the Spaniards, assassinated on August 21, 1613. Zaydān contested the claims of his nephew ʿAbd Allāh to be the sole inheritor of his father's estate, most of which was located in the northern city of Tangiers, under Spanish control. This dispute was thus occurring "across religious, linguistic, and legal systems."[73] Both Mūlay Zaydān and his nephew petitioned the king of Spain, claiming to defend the rightful heirs of the deceased. Beyond the issue of the inheritance, the two adversaries were engaging in a political and strategic struggle over the Saʿdī throne and over their alliances with competing powers, Spain for ʿAbd Allāh and the Dutch Republic for Zaydān. These political and strategic issues were couched in legal and religious terms. Mūlay Zaydān addressed his letters in Arabic to the Spanish authorities, but also had them translated into Spanish. Dated February 24,

1614, and November 11, 1614, they explained that according to Islamic law, all of his brother's male and female children and his widows should have a share in the inheritance. If accepted, this argument had the advantage of limiting 'Abd Allāh's access to his father's wealth, which he was trying to acquire in its entirety by using the European and Christian practice of primogeniture. To support his claims, Zaydān joined to his correspondence a *fatwa* (legal opinion), issued by the chief judge and other scholars and jurisconsults of Marrakesh. Hajarī was charged with putting all these documents into Spanish.[74] His versions were signed "Ehmed Bencaçim Andaluz," and "Ehmed Bencaçim Focay, secretario de Su Magestad." Analyzing this episode in fascinating detail,[75] Claire Gilbert highlights Hajarī's awareness of the "protocol for 'converting' Islamic legal knowledge into evidence or arguments that could be used in Christian courts,"[76] and illustrates his navigation between the two systems. He might have learned, as a licensed translator in Spain, how to address Christian judges, and he certainly acquired more valuable experience when he represented the robbed Moriscos in France. Despite the skills of his secretary and translator, Mūlay Zaydān did not obtain satisfaction, since the case was adjudicated on political grounds and his nephew was Spain's ally.

Hajarī intervened in other matters. He advocated for the release of a captive monk, in all likelihood the Irish Dominican Antoine de Sainte-Marie, released in 1622 after eight years of captivity.[77] He was also involved in the relations of the Sa'dī government with the Dutch Republic. In November 21, 1619, he translated into Spanish a letter addressed by Mūlay Zaydān to the States General, protesting against the arrest in Amsterdam of the French merchant Jacques Fabre, who represented the *makhzan*.[78] More importantly, in 1622, the Dutch state, in response to the sultan's queries, sent a mission to Morocco whose goal was to investigate the possibility of building a harbor on the Atlantic coast. Hajarī was an active participant in the negotiations between the Dutch diplomats and the Sa'dī court, and appears several times in the diary of Albert Ruyl, head of the mission. He enjoyed a very good relation with the envoys, including Jacob Golius, whom Erpenius had counseled to get in touch with his friend Hajarī. This was the latter's last episode of sustained involvement with a European scholar of oriental studies. Letters he wrote from Marrakesh to Golius during his sojourn in Safi, which acknowledged the reception of missives from the Dutch scholar, have been published.[79] They testify to the many difficulties that Orientalists encountered in obtaining manuscripts, including robberies. As noted by

Robert Jones, "Golius, no doubt acting on Erpenius's instructions, sought manuscript copies of specific texts cited in Leo Africanus's *Description of Africa*,"[80] including texts by al-Masʿūdī, al-Harīrī, Ibn Khallikān, and Ibn Khaldūn. His Moroccan contacts helped him obtain copies. Among them was Hajarī, who also procured and completed for Golius a copy of a famous book on plant remedies, Ibn Baklārish's *Mustaʿīnī,* still held in Leiden, which demonstrates his ability to perform complex editorial work.[81]

In a letter to Golius written on February 2, 1624, Hajarī stated: "On another day I will write for you the answer to your Sheikh, the learned professor Erpenius."[82] His response to Erpenius is probably an unpublished Arabic missive held in the John Rylands Library at the University of Manchester.[83] It provides invaluable information on the scholarly and personal relations between the two men. The address to "Monsuor Arpenios Flamenco" is the only Spanish part. The letter responds to points made by Erpenius, some of which seemingly echo the praise of the Arabic language that the Dutchman had pronounced in Leiden University, and which had been recently published.[84]

Hajarī liked Erpenius's respect for knowledge, and quotes four hadith, or sayings attributed to the Prophet Muhammad, commending learning. Hajarī obviously shared his friend's admiration for Arabic, stressing that the elegance and concision of the language come from its exceptional system of declination and its rules of syntax and quoting a version of an often-cited anonymous verse: "If the birds knew the delight of grammar / They would bow to the earth and beat it with their beaks." Then, in response to a remark about the explanation of Quranic terms, Hajarī reminds Erpenius that to understand the Quran and its meaning, one needs to be very learned in grammar, logic, and language. He indicates some books: *Kitāb al-zabīd wa al-jawhar* (The Book of the Substance and the Essence) might refer to a brief and very popular treatise on rhetoric by the sixteenth-century Algerian author al-Akhdarī, titled *al-Jawhar al maknūn* (The Hidden Essence). Hajarī also mentions Ibn ʿAtiya, the twelfth-century Andalusian author of a famous book of *tafsīr* or exegesis. As for "al-imām Fakr," Hajarī probably has in mind the Persian Fakhr al-Dīn al-Rāzī (d. 1210), who wrote another important work of exegesis. Hajarī then humbly explains that he knows very little of *tafsīr,* and nothing at all of rhetoric (*bayān*), and apologizes for his shortcomings. At the end of the letter, obviously answering a question concerning the headings of diplomatic letters, he compares the simplicity that prevailed during the time of the Prophet with the flowery displays of modern missives and their overwrought compliments, which, in his view, only amounted to lies and hypocrisy. One might surmise that he is answering complaints from Erpenius, who was sometimes asked to translate epistles sent by the Moroccan court to the Dutch Republic and might have found it difficult to produce Dutch versions of the florid introductions.[85] Finally, the letter is signed "your friend (*habībukum*) Ahmad ibn Qāsim al-Andalusī."

This substantial missive demonstrates that years after the sustained periods of collaboration between Erpenius and Hajarī in France and Holland, the Dutchman was still eager to obtain his opinion and advice on his studies, even though Hajarī did not disguise his lack of mastery of the most prestigious fields of learning. It also gives a glimpse of the tenor of the oral exchanges between the two men, with Hajarī answering questions and counseling him to seek books, as well as introducing him to reference works considered important in the Arabic Republic of Letters (see fig. 4).

Hajarī was also busy translating cultural and scientific texts for the service of Mūlay Zaydān. He put into Arabic the Spanish translation of an astronomical treatise, influential in ocean navigation, that had been written in Hebrew by Abraham Zacuto and then translated by his disciple José Vizinho into Latin as *Almanach perpetuum,* or the *Perpetual Almanac,* and into Spanish as well. Hajarī might have worked on his Arabic version during the time that Golius was in Morocco, if we consider as a clue a passage in a letter in which he asks the Dutchman about astronomical vocabulary.[86] After the death of the sultan in 1627, Hajarī kept working for his sons 'Abd al-Mālik (r. 1627–31) and then al-Walīd (r. 1631–36), at a time when their power was declining until it barely extended beyond Marrakesh. The last extant documents about his work for the dynasty were recorded toward the end of his career in the Sa'dī court. The French trader Antoine Cabiron wrote a memoir of his diplomatic mission in Marrakesh at the court of Mūlay al-Walīd, which ended in April 1634. The memoir often mentions Hajarī, who is called "Talbe Hemed Becassem," and who conveyed messages from the sultan, translated letters, and received payment from the Frenchman in return for his help, his translations, and his advice.[87]

That same year, 1634, Hajarī left Marrakesh on his *hajj* (pilgrimage) to Mecca and Medina. He never returned to the Sa'dī capital. On his way, he sojourned in the kasbah of the Ūdāya, the castle of Rabat-Salé. This port on the Atlantic coast of Morocco was an independent corsair republic, mostly populated by Moriscos, many of them hailing from Hajarī's hometown of

Hornachos. His many years in Marrakesh had not lessened his feeling of belonging to the Morisco "nation." He was welcomed by "Habdu Rrehhmen Bencaçim Ximenez Andaluz," 'Abd al-Rahmān ibn Qāsim Ximenez al-Andalusī, a citizen of Rabat of Granadine stock. Ximenez presented him with a poem in Spanish, a panegyric that testified to the prestigious reputation that Hajarī enjoyed in the Morisco community, as a learned man, a respected official, and a faithful defender of the exiled minority:

> You are unique in art, the repository of science,
> A courtier in the presence of Kings, steeped in the Qur'an . . .
> The whole nation [of Moriscos] loves you dearly, you are a friend of all.[88]

Thanks to Ximenez's sponsorship, Hajarī began to translate Arabic religious texts into Spanish to help Moriscos access sources of the Islamic faith in their native language. After his time in Rabat, Hajarī went on to accomplish the *hajj*. During this trip, he spent time in Cairo. There he struck one of the most important friendships in his life, with 'Alī al-Ujhurī (1559–1656), a famous professor in the college of al-Azhar in Cairo, the most prestigious institution of learning in Sunni Islam. Thanks to him, Hajarī took the leap to compose extensive texts. Hearing of Hajarī's travels and of his polemical discussions about religion with Christians (and some Jews), he forcefully encouraged him to write them down. Hajarī followed his advice, and, still in Egypt, wrote a travelogue, now lost, titled *Rihla al-Shihāb ilā liqā' al-ahbāb* (The Voyage of Shihāb Toward the Meeting of His Loved Ones). After reading this book, Ujhurī asked him to write an abbreviated version that would focus more closely on the religious controversies. Hajarī produced this compendium, *Supporter of Religion against the Infidels,* which has already been referred to many times under the shortened title of the *Supporter.* Its earliest, and shortest, version was completed on September 11, 1637, and a copy is now held in the library of al-Azhar.

After his travel to Arabia and Egypt, rather than going back to Marrakesh, Hajarī settled in Tunisia, where at least one of his children lived. This Ottoman province was at that time, according to Hajarī, the best place for the Morisco diaspora, who had been welcomed by the local power and by the population while Morocco was going through a long period of political troubles.[89] In Tunis, Hajarī became friends, or maybe reacquainted, with an eminent intellectual, Ahmad al-Hanafi (d. 1650), himself a Morisco who had left Spain for Bosnia, then under Ottoman rule, and later relocated to Tunis, where he attained a position of great influence as a religious scholar. In these later years, Hajarī kept revising the *Supporter,* producing at least two longer versions. One extant copy was completed on October 25, 1641, and is now held in the Dār al-Kutub Library in Cairo.

He continued to translate Arabic works, mostly devotional texts, into Spanish, aimed at helping the Morisco exiles to learn about Islam in their native language. The Bologna manuscript contains some of these, and includes also the Paris letter addressed to Moriscos of Istanbul. The missive is preceded by an introduction telling about the circumstances of its writing "from the court of Paris to the Andalusians who were then in Constantinople or lived there," and how it was taken to Tunis by the noted Morisco writer Muhammad ibn 'Abd al-Rafi' (d. 1643). Hajarī translated it into Spanish on the order of Muhammad Rubio, who sponsored some of his translations. He was thus prominent enough among the Morisco diaspora that his letter circulated beyond its addressees, and was considered worthy of translation and of wider dissemination. The collection also contains the poem written by Ximenez in 1634 and Hajarī's response, as well as a Spanish-language paraphrase of some parts of the *Supporter.*[90]

While in Tunis, according to Gerard Wiegers, Hajarī might have also written two Spanish-language religious texts, the only copies of which, held in the Biblioteca Nacional de España, do not mention their author. One is an incomplete theological commentary on a poem by Ibrāhīm Bolfad, a blind Morisco writer from Algiers. The other focuses on religious rituals according to the Hanafi school of Islamic jurisprudence. There is, however, no doubt that Hajarī made a translation into Arabic of a manual of artillery, completed in 1638, soon after his relocation in Tunis. This work, the shortened title of which is *Kitāb al-ʿizz* (Book of Glory), holds an important and still understudied role in the history of the circulation of technological knowledge in the premodern Mediterranean. To produce this version, Hajarī collaborated with the author, the Morisco Ibrāhīm Ghānim, who was in charge of the defense of Halq al-Wādī, the harbor of Tunis. Hajarī added a long appendix in which he reflected on his eventful life, and on his successful career, during which, he said, "were opened to me . . . the doors of princes that were shut to many people."[91] This essential translation, extant in a number of illustrated manuscripts, many produced by his son Muhammad Khūja, is the focus of the last chapter of this book.

Hajarī died in Tunisia sometime in 1641 or later, after a long and productive life, during which he pursued fruitful and durable relationships with many people of different backgrounds. Several of these associations were with persons belonging to circles of power, members of the scholarly, social, and political elites of many countries. He was willing, however, to help the less fortunate and less well connected, especially the Morisco exiles. He made many efforts in Spain, Morocco, France, the Netherlands, and Tunisia in order to help them survive and ameliorate their perilous circumstances, and his work is a vital contribution to the memorialization of the history and culture of the Moriscos in Spain and North Africa. This biographical sketch has demonstrated a trait that deeply impacted Hajarī's life as well as his intellectual production: he was a man of many overlapping networks. This essential feature has also left its trace on the way his reputation developed over the centuries.

AFTERLIVES

Tellingly, the oldest mention of Hajarī in scholarship after his death might well have been in a European text. This book is one of the most famous in the history of early modern Orientalism, the *Bibliothèque orientale,* composed by Barthélemy d'Herbelot, who adapted Arabic, Persian, and Turkish scholarship to produce a French reference book on Islamic history and literature.[92] In this early encyclopedia of Islam, d'Herbelot does not present Hajarī as a collaborator of famed Orientalists. Rather, he mentions him in relation to the Lead Books, foreshadowing the recent reevaluation of this forgery as being not merely an episode of the religious history of the Moriscos but also a chapter in the history of Orientalism, as the notoriety of the affair advanced the knowledge and study of the Arabic language in Spain. Not only does Hajarī appear in the entry "Gharnatah" (Granada), but he has a special entry devoted to him, as "Ahmed Ben Cassem al-Andaloussi." Both articles mention the discovery near Granada of the *plomos,* and tell of the "fabulous" stories about Jesus Christ and the Virgin Mary that they contain. D'Herbelot found the necessary information in a text that Hajarī added to the copy of Ibn Mālik's mnemonic poem on verbal structure that he wrote in April 1612 for Étienne Hubert. He knew about the recent papal condemnation of the documents but did not include in these entries particulars about the discovery itself other than what he read in that manuscript.[93]

The other early scholars who mention Hajarī while focusing on different aspects of his work and experience are Moroccan writers who quoted from the lost *rihla* or travelogue. Muhammad ibn al-'Ayyāshī al-Miknāsī (d. 1727), a trusted servant of Sultan Mūlay Ismāʿīl (r. 1672–1727), of the ʿAlawī dynasty which succeeded the Saʿdī, wrote a book commissioned by Hālima al-Sufyānyya, wife of the sultan, to teach her son Zaydān his genealogy on his maternal side from the Sufyān lineage. Referencing the lost travelogue, he cites a long passage about Hajarī's escape with a companion from al-Burayja to Azammūr, where the governor was a Sufyānī. This governor then led Hajarī, whom the author calls "Shihāb al-Dīn al-Hajarī al-Andalusī, known as Afūqāy," to the court of the Sultan Ahmad al-Mansūr, who was accompanied with more than a thousand horsemen.[94] The *rihla* is also quoted by a more eminent contemporary of Ibn al-ʿAyyāshī. Muhammad al-Ifrānī (ca. 1670–1745), author of an influential history of the Saʿdī dynasty, cites a very short passage by "Ahmad Afuqāy al-Andalusī" about Ahmad al-Mansūr's army.[95] He cites Hajarī more abundantly in his bibliographical dictionary, a work that belonged to the vast literature that memorialized members of the scholarly class.[96] The author did not devote an entry to Hajarī, whom he called "Abū al-ʿAbbās Ahmad Afuqāy al-Andalusī," or "Abū al-ʿAbbās Ahmad al-Andalusī," but he mined the travelogue for anecdotes about scholars, none of which was kept in the *Supporter*. He relied on Hajarī for stories about Ahmad al-Manjūr (d. 1587), an eminent scholar from Fez, and a professor of many notable Moroccans, including the Sultan Ahmad al-Mansūr.[97] In his entry on the renowned religious scholar and Sufi Ridwān al-Jinwī (d. 1581), who was the son of a native of Genoa who converted to Islam, Ifrānī quotes Hajarī to tell the conversion story of the father.[98] Obviously, Hajarī did not know these two men, dead before he arrived in Marrakesh. Both Manjūr and Jinwī had been professors of Hajarī's friend Ragrāguī, his probable source for the anecdotes. Ifrānī relied again on Hajarī's travelogue in the entry devoted to ʿAlī al-Ujhurī, to underscore the fame he enjoyed in Marrakesh.[99]

After these authors, no one that we know of has ever quoted from the original travelogue. In fact, only much later would scholars begin to cite its abridgment, the *Supporter*. One of the readers of the copy which is now preserved in the library of al-Azhar university in Cairo is noteworthy.[100] The first and last pages bear notes written by one Hasan al-ʿAttār (1766–1835). Well known for having entered into relations with French scholars after Napoléon Bonaparte's 1798 invasion of Egypt, ʿAttār was a prolific and prominent author, who eventually became rector of al-Azhar, extensively reforming its curriculum.[101] He added a comment on the first page of the manuscript about its polemical content, and, on the last page, he highlighted the pleasure he took in reading this travel account and the curious details (*gharā'ib*) it contains. He also added a few notes on the manuscript.[102]

These early references to Hajarī already show how different he could appear to scholars, depending on their interests. This trend was not destined to abate in the following decades and centuries, especially when the Bologna manuscript, written in a different language from the lost travelogue and its abridgment, was to attract a new set of scholars interested in Morisco history who were at first unaware of the existence of the travel account. This collection was first described by the Spanish Arabist Eduardo Saavedra in 1889,[103] and analyzed by another Spanish scholar, Jaime Oliver Asín.[104] When L. P. Harvey published and translated the appendix to the *Kitāb al-'izz*, he identified its translator as the author of some of the texts of the Bologna manuscript.[105] At about the same time, the Moroccan historian Muhammad al-Fāsī had access to a manuscript fragment of the *Supporter* that belonged to the French Orientalist Georges Colin,[106] and described its contents.[107] In his important article about translation under the Sa'dī dynasty, the Moroccan erudite Muhammad al-Manūnī identified the translator of the *Kitāb al-'izz* as the translator of Abraham Zacuto's astronomical treatise, and as the author of the travelogue quoted by Ibn al-'Ayyāshī and Ifranī, as well as of the text mentioned by Fāsī.[108]

A new step in the scholarship about Hajarī was taken when the Egyptian scholar Fu'ād Sayyid described a complete manuscript of the *Supporter* held in the library Dār al-Kutub in Cairo,[109] to which the Italian Arabist Clelia Sarnelli Cerqua soon began to devote a number of studies.[110] The manuscript was published by the Moroccan historian Muhammad Razzūq in 1987, finally making this important text widely available and opening a new period in studies on Hajarī.[111] The following year, Robert Jones defended his thesis on the study of the Arabic language in Renaissance Europe, which included documents recording the connection between Hajarī and the many Orientalists with whom he collaborated.[112] That same year, Gerard Wiegers published a book that began the crucial task of bringing together the different threads of Hajarī's career.[113] The interest in Hajarī has since grown considerably, especially thanks to the increasing number of studies on the Lead Books affair and to the discovery of more documents of his connection with French and Dutch Orientalists. An important juncture is the publication in 1997 of an edition of the *Supporter* by P. S. van Koningsveld, Q. al-Samarrai, and G. A. Wiegers. This edition collated both the Dār al-Kutub manuscript from Cairo and the fragment from the Bibliothèque Nationale de France, alongside an English translation. Both of these texts were revisions made by Hajarī in Tunis, and present differences. Revised and republished in 2015 after the discovery of the 1637 manuscript, this edition allows to follow the different stages of the text, and is particularly notable for its erudite introduction, footnotes, and bibliography.

. . .

Hajarī's work provides historians with a treasure of information on the early modern Mediterranean world. It has attracted the attention of scholars interested in the religious outlook of the Moriscos, especially in connection with the Lead Books affair, and the indispensable work of Gerard Wiegers (sometimes in collaboration with Pieter S. van Koningsveld) will be frequently referenced throughout this book. Critics have shown interest in his work, especially the *Supporter,* and in his career as a diplomat, traveler, intellectual, and translator.[114] Historians of the Moriscos have found in his texts a precious source, especially concerning the life of exiles in North Africa.[115]

Beyond the scholars focused on the Moriscos, Hajarī has attracted the attention of the students of early modern Orientalism. Indeed, the network of Orientalists is one of the intellectual communities to which Hajarī belonged, and only one of the many fields in which he was called to exercise his skills as a mediator. We have seen that, as a translator since early on, he learned to negotiate between communities and between legal and cultural systems. He even played an important part in bringing about a shared diplomatic culture and in ushering practices of legal pluralism into North Africa and Europe. This experience was parallel to his role as cultural broker when he was working with Orientalists. He acquired the necessary skills in negotiating, at different stages in his life, the relationship between the Morisco community and the Spanish state, between the Islamic and Christian legal systems, between the Moroccan *makhzan* and the European governments, and at the same time between the European and the Arabic Republics of Letters. He was only one of many translators whose competence went beyond the mere linguistic but involved social and cultural proficiency. He belonged to a considerable group of people who were put in position to negotiate with more or less ability between spheres of learning. These transactions are crucial to understand the early formation of European Orientalism. This discipline could not have developed without the contribution of numerous people who hailed from Arabic-speaking lands and communities, and who taught

Europeans the necessary linguistic skills, while providing cultural background. The coming chapter will situate Hajarī's contribution to Orientalism within a wider network frequently overlooked in the history of Orientalism and offer a succinct sketch of the role played by mediators from North Africa and the Middle East. It will also reveal Orientalism to be in large part the result of close interaction between neighboring, often antagonistic, regions, and the spheres of knowledge that they produced.

TWO

Networks of Orientalism

OUT OF THE SHADOWS

WRITING IN 1612 TO HIS FRIENDS in Istanbul, Hajarī summed up his observations about scholarly life in Paris and elsewhere in Europe: "In this city all sorts of sciences are studied, and various languages, like Latin, Hebrew, Greek, and Arabic. Everyday books on Arabic science are printed. In Rome, as well as Flanders, Germany, and Paris they translate them as well, and not badly."[1] This description reveals the scale of Orientalism in Europe, which Hajarī understood because of his own contributions to the field, and because of his friendships with a network of European scholars, which gave him the opportunity to make informed observations about this early modern intellectual development in Europe. In addition to Hajarī, other individuals from Islamic countries played crucial roles in building the field of oriental studies as it gradually became institutionalized in the centers of European learning. Though the mainstream history of Orientalism has mostly long erased these individuals, recent studies have rescued them from the shadows of footnotes or cursory mentions.[2] The sheer number of contributors from the East who provided Europeans with critical knowledge about the literature and culture of their neighbors belies a definition of Orientalism as a solely European field. Their large presence is an integral element of the early modern movement that created a "geography of knowledge that linked Europe, western Asia, and northern Africa,"[3] of which Orientalism was a visible manifestation.

The previous chapter helped situate Hajarī in this geography. This chapter highlights the role played by other Easterners, mostly from Arab and Ottoman lands, in these critical exchanges. Some of these intellectuals from the East occupied coveted positions in European institutions of learning as professors, librarians, or authors of influential books and treatises and are thus well known.

Less prominent collaborators with Orientalists left only the faintest of traces in the record. Whether established or obscure, however, these Eastern intellectuals helped shape the contact between Europe and the neighboring Islamic countries. These encounters between the Republics of Letters were by no means easy and straightforward, but were instead often difficult, fitful, and precarious. Moriscos, for example, contributed knowledge of the languages and the culture of the East but belonged to a threatened minority. Other Eastern intellectuals were captured and brought to Europe as part of war and piracy. Luckier ones were sent by rulers as diplomats. And some who visited Europe were simply motivated by wanderlust. European Orientalists themselves traveled to Islamic countries, where they encountered local scholars who assisted them in advancing their knowledge of Oriental languages and cultures. These encounters delineate a landscape of cultural interactions, in and out of Europe.

This chapter's reflection on this context of cultural exchange will be framed by several issues of central importance in the development of Orientalism. One is religious polemic, which is an essential feature of early modern Orientalism—one that considerably inflected the involvement of native speakers of Eastern languages, dictating how they were allowed in the field and how their contribution was understood and disseminated. Another is the different situations of those contributors, whether they were Moriscos trying to establish themselves within a dominant culture, captive collaborators, Eastern Christians whom papal institutions wanted to bring closer to Catholicism, or learned Easterners freely collaborating with Orientalists. In addition, the sites themselves are a crucial element to consider as the possibilities of exchange were different within and outside Europe, and this affected the type and depth of Eastern influence. Providing a picture of many overlooked contributors to Orientalism, particularly those from the Islamic world, this chapter argues that, with all kinds of variations, significant intellectual exchange between the European and Eastern spheres of learning did indeed occur, and that, in the words of Sonja Brentjes, this "communication . . . was a dialogue, not a monologue."[4]

ORIENTALISM IN SPAIN: CONVERTING THE MUSLIMS

Let us begin by examining the country in which Hajarī was born. Spain was the European country with the longest, closest, and most intimate connection—albeit conflicted—with the Islamic world, given that most of the Iberian Peninsula had been under Muslim rule from the eighth to the eleventh century. Spain was a prominent site of intellectual exchange, and multilingual Toledo, after its capture by Christians, became "the principal center for the translation of Arabic scientific and philosophical texts into Latin."[5] Small Muslim states still flourished later, and Granada, the last Iberian Muslim kingdom, was conquered in 1492. Spain hosted the largest Arabic-speaking population in Europe, and this population had direct access to Islamic texts. However, the contribution of Spain in early oriental studies has long been masked by Spanish ambivalence about its Islamic history. The Spanish Crown displayed great hostility toward the Islamic religion and the Arabic language, requiring conversion in 1502 and outlawing Arabic in 1567. Thus, it was thought, Spain stayed on the margins when oriental studies entered the learning landscape in Europe. Recent research has amended this view to show that Spain played a part in the development of oriental studies, albeit one that is strongly colored by the specific circumstances of the Muslim or formerly Muslim minority in Spanish society.[6] Indeed, the enduring vitality of Arabic in early modern Spain influenced the development of the scholarly discipline in the peninsula and even in the rest of Europe.[7]

In all of Europe, until the end of the early modern period, missionary projects and religious polemic were essential in the development of oriental studies, which only slowly and fitfully became more secular. Early philological interest in Arabic was mostly spurred by an awareness of its closeness to Hebrew and a desire to advance the study of the Bible. Religious concerns were particularly evident in Spain, where the conversion of Muslims was a pressing political issue when the capture of Granada opened the question of what should happen to the Muslim minority living in Catholic Spain. The Crown first chose toleration, in agreement with the articles of the capitulation of the last Islamic kingdom of the peninsula, letting the vanquished live as Mudéjars, a term used for those who stayed in Spain as "subject Muslims who accepted Christian rule,"[8] as opposed to Moriscos or converted Muslims. Between toleration and coercion, there was a time when conversion by persuasion was the preferred official policy, and at this point knowledge of Arabic and Islamic texts and doctrine was considered an asset for missionary purposes.

The serious study of Islam and Arabic for the aim of conversion was building on Iberian medieval antecedents, such as the Dominican Ramon Martí (d. 1285), and the Franciscan Ramon Llull (1232–1316), who studied oriental languages, the Torah, the Talmud, and the Quran.[9] The influential collaboration between Christian missionaries and learned Muslims is foreshadowed by Juan de Segovia (1393–1458), who advocated an interreligious dialogue based on the knowledge of the other's religion, a dialogue aimed at persuading Muslims to become Christians. As early as 1454, Juan was discussing the use of Muslim "rites, observances, and customs as ways by which Muslims might be converted to Christianity."[10] He initiated a translation of the Quran into Spanish with the help of ʿĪsā ibn Jābir (Yça Gedelli), *alfaquí* of the Mudéjar community of Segovia (the word *alfaquí* is the Spanish transcription of the Arabic word *faqīh* [pl. *fuqahāʾ*] which designates a scholar trained in Islamic law).[11] Juan then rendered this version in Latin. Thus, collaboration between a Christian and a Muslim produced the first attested Spanish translation of the Quran. Although the translations are lost,[12] their precedent could be inscribed in another narrative, the history of European Orientalists who benefited from the help of learned native speakers.

At the time of the conquest, the Spanish Crown was suspicious of its religious minorities and sought permission from the pope to select two or three priests as inquisitors under the Spanish Crown to root out heresy. Granted in 1478, this helped to solidify royal power, as it shifted inquisitorial authority from the pope to the state. In 1492, Isabella and Ferdinand issued the decree of expulsion for Jews who refused to convert. However, the terms of the capitulation of the kingdom of Granada forbade coercion to obtain conversion concerning Muslims. Hernando de Talavera (1428–1507), confessor of Isabella and first archbishop of Granada, was even willing to allow New Christians to make confession in Arabic.[13] Early on, he expressed his opposition to forced conversion and his belief that "heresies need to be corrected not only with punishment and lashes, but even more with Catholic reasoning."[14] His opposition to coerced conversion would lead to his own victimization by the Inquisition, including a trial for heresy in 1505–6. Though acquitted, the privations of prison and persecution made him ill, and he died in poverty.

To aid in the effort of learning Arabic in order to convert Muslims, Talavera encouraged the publication of a Spanish-Arabic dictionary and a grammar book by Pedro de Alcalà, who consulted with informants he called "learned *alfaquís*" without more detail.[15] Some Muslim converts also became missionaries and produced more visible work, which provided readers with a glimpse of texts of the Islamic tradition. This information traveled beyond the limits of conversion, and, in an unintended twist, would help those who were beginning to gesture toward a philological and scholarly approach to the study of Islam. These converts acquired a new prominence not only as "informants and mediators, but also authorities."[16] Their work can be sketched out thanks to the new authorial dignity afforded to them as evangelists to the Muslim community. The most important of these is undoubtedly Juan Andrés, a Mudéjar and *alfaquí* of Xátiva in the kingdom of Valencia. Juan Andrés recorded his conversion in his 1515 polemical work titled *Confusión o confutación de la secta mahomética y del Alcorán* (Confusion or Confutation of the Muhammadan Sect and of the Quran).[17] In the *Confusion,* Juan Andrés describes his conversion on April 15, 1487, in the cathedral of Valencia: "Suddenly, the shining rays of divine light . . . removed and cleared the shadows of my understanding, and then opened the eyes of my soul. Because of the understanding I had of the sect of Muhammad, I clearly recognized that the goal of salvation for which men were created was not by that perverse and evil [law] but through the holy law of Christ."[18] This narrative "directly evokes the New Testament model of the conversion of Saul of Tarsus,"[19] and similar to Paul (formerly Saul), he received the new name Juan Andrés when he became a Christian. He was then ordained a priest and devoted himself to proselytizing. His zealous activity took an important turn when he became the collaborator of Martín García (ca. 1441–1521), who was named a general inquisitor in 1484 and bishop of Barcelona in 1515. He enlisted a number of collaborators, like Juan Andrés, with knowledge of Arabic and Islam, who could cite Arabic passages from the Quran to dispute the Islamic faith in order to convert Muslims.

In the absence of corroborating documents, scholars have raised doubts as to the reality of a historical Juan Andrés. They point to errors in the *Confusion* that seem inconsistent with Juan's claim that he was trained in Islamic law.[20] Other scholars counter that the text displays indubitable, if flawed, knowledge of Quranic exegesis.[21] Some speculate that he might have belonged to a team of authors,[22] or that his text had simply gone "through the significant filters of its sponsors and printers."[23] Whatever the case, there is little doubt that a Muslim convert baptized Juan Andrés had constructed his authority by insisting on his knowledge as a former *faqīh* (though he might have exaggerated his level of learning) and on his deeply sincere conversion to Christianity. Some chapters of the *Confusion* read as a manual for evangelizers, suggesting arguments on how to use Islamic texts to convince a Muslim audience of their falsity. Other passages in the *Confusion* illustrate this method, directly addressing Muslims and pointing to what Juan Andrés presented as contradictions or unbelievable stories. Juan Andrés's influential polemic was published in French, Dutch, Latin, and English translations based on the 1537 Italian version. These editions often stressed the political and ideological battle against the Muslims, and readers used it accordingly, including influential Christian polemicist Filippo Guadagnoli (d. 1656), notable for his study of languages, who incorporated it into his virulent 1631 *Apologia pro christiana religione*.[24]

Religious debates did not, however, exhaust the uses of the *Confusion* in Europe. Indeed, in the early modern period, "religious polemics were neither exclusively read as polemical or religious."[25] This point is crucial when analyzing sixteenth- and seventeenth-century Orientalism, in which missionary concerns could coexist with often less robust philological interest. The role of the *Confusion* in the slow development of the scholarly study of Islam and Arabic in Europe should not be downplayed, and it was widely read by Orientalists.[26] Thanks to Juan's descriptions and quotations, scholars have gained some access to a bibliography of original sources that comprise what he calls the "complete faith of the Muslims,"[27] including the Quran (with many passages transliterated and translated), the Sira (the biography of Muhammad), the Sunna (traditions about the Prophet), and some *tafsir* or exegesis, with a few authors and titles directly mentioned. Juan Andrés gave readers a sense, however skewed and narrow, of the textual web of the Islamic scriptural and theological tradition.

CHRISTIAN KABBALIST READERS OF SPANISH MUSLIM CONVERTS

Among those who mined Juan's text for this sort of information are early modern Christian kabbalists, who adapted to Christianity the Jewish esoteric tradition known as the kabbalah. This trend spurred the interest in the study of Hebrew and connected languages, such as Arabic, and strongly influenced Orientalism.[28] Crucially, it encouraged scholars to view non-Christian cultures as coherent philosophical traditions deserving of study, and not merely as heretical distortions of the religious truth. This does not negate polemical concerns. The celebrated, prolific, and controversial Orientalist—and committed kabbalist—Guillaume Postel (1510–81) was an attentive reader of Juan Andrés's book. In one of his works, he referred to "Johannes Andreas Maurus," Latinizing Juan's name. He mentioned some Arabic theological treatises that he only knew through Juan, and, citing the

Confusion, noted that there were seven hundred such texts.[29] The poet Guy Le Fèvre de la Boderie (1541–98) was likely encouraged by his mentor Postel to translate the *Confusion.*[30] In the preface and annotations to his 1574 French translation, he describes his reasons for undertaking this task as polemical concerns and scholarly interest. Le Fèvre also offers a remarkably inclusive view of the contemporary culture of Europe: "I think that today we have the legacy not only of the Latins and the Greeks ... but also of the Persians, the Arabs, the Chaldeans, the Egyptians, and the Hebrews."[31] Le Fèvre thus accepts this Eastern heritage as part of a renewed European civilization and considers that its study is not essentially different from that of the philologists who were resurrecting the Greek and Latin "good letters." He saw it as a needed complement to this "Renaissance," which may be surprising in light of later efforts to conceptually cut off a secularized Europe from a reified Orient, and even from the Semitic roots of its religion.[32]

The kabbalah provided its Christian adherents with a synthetic system that made sense of the diversity of the world, metaphysically by allowing mediations between God and the world, as well as religiously and politically by looking for points of agreement between religions.[33] Their ultimate goal was a universal conversion to Christianity, which Postel colored with his apocalyptic beliefs. These views nevertheless promoted the collection of an archive of the world cultures, languages, and religions, as was shown when a student of Le Fèvre, the barely remembered Claude Duret, wrote an enormous tome on the history of the languages of the universe, filtered through kabbalistic concepts, which doubled as a global encyclopedia of civilizations. Duret, like Postel, relied on Juan Andrés's authority to underscore that Islam had a coherent written doctrinal corpus, and offered a succinct bibliography of these theological texts, which comprised eight hundred books, he said, inflating Juan's count.[34]

Juan was not the only converted Muslim who influenced early modern Orientalists. Another convert, who also belonged to the general inquisitor Martín García's circle of collaborators, did not leave any writing of his own but his influence was nevertheless significant. The former *alfaquí* Juan Gabriel of Teruel, named Ali Alayza before his conversion, provided the preacher Martín de Figuerola with quotations from the Quran and from works of exegesis in his still unpublished 1521 manuscript *Lumbre de fe contra el Alcorán (The Fire of Faith against the Quran).* His work circulated beyond Iberia. When the erudite cardinal Egidio da Viterbo (1469–1532), an important Orientalist and student of the kabbalah, visited Spain, he obtained an

Arabic copy of the Quran, with a transcription in the Latin alphabet and a Latin translation made by Juan Gabriel. The original manuscript with the Latin translation is now lost, but Egidio later sponsored a revision in Italy by a much more famous convert, a protégé of Egidio's, Hasan al-Wazzān, known as Leo Africanus, who is discussed later in this chapter. In the absence of the lost original, the two remaining copies of Leo's translation allow scholars to assess it as a groundbreaking annotated bilingual Quran.[35] This edition, without eliminating polemical concerns, "was set up in such a way as to over-whelmingly favor philological reading,"[36] and is thus a paramount example of scholarship advancing in the shadow of religious polemic.

BEFORE THE EXPULSION: FICTIONS OF CONVERSION

There is no record of how much Hajarī knew about the vast contribution of former Muslims to the evangelization effort in the early-sixteenth century, or their less important but not inconsequential role in disseminating knowl-edge of oriental languages and cultures. Unlike them, Moriscos who contrib-uted to Orientalism in the last decades of the century often did so in circui-tous ways, as they were constrained by hostility toward their religious identity. Besieged by suspicion, they produced works that attempted to shore up their place in Spanish society as true Christians, and chapter 1 describes how Hajarī would become involved in this work.

The culmination of the effort to eliminate the Arabic and Islamic "taint" in Spain included the official ban on Arabic in Spain in 1567. The possession of Arabic texts was outlawed, and Arabic books were ritually burned, even though Arabic translation kept playing an important role in Spanish politics and culture. Coercive measures were adopted against the use of Arabic names, and any characteristic of Morisco culture was attacked, including Morisco dress (such as distinctive turbans or head sashes, pantaloons for women, and belted tunics for men). In this environment, Arabic speakers hid their knowledge of Arabic. Like Hajarī, some Moriscos however pursued careers as interpreters, working for the Crown or for the Inquisition or the Church. Most important are Alonso del Castillo and Miguel de Luna, who were licensed translators and belonged to elite learned Morisco circles well integrated within the dominant political culture. Alonso del Castillo was born in the late 1520s in Granada.[37] His father's name was very likely Hernando del Castillo Alcahal—this last word comes from the Arabic *al-kahhāl,* which means apothecary.[38] He appears in Hajarī's *Supporter of Religion Against the Infidels* as al-Ukayhil, a diminutive of *al-kahhāl.* He worked as an interpreter of Arabic for the Inquisition and for the king.[39] He was also a physician, and, in Spain, as in the rest of Europe, Arabic medical texts were studied and collected. As an Orientalist, Castillo performed classic philological work, translating the Arabic inscriptions of the Alhambra in 1564, and cataloging the Arabic books held at the Escorial Library in 1574. These tasks are another illustration of early modern Spain's ambiguous rapport with its Islamic past. Although trying to eradicate the language and culture of the vanquished, the Crown also wanted to preserve the memory of the victory. Examining this ambivalence, scholar Barbara Fuchs wonders: "Does the Alhambra stand for the Christian triumph, or for centuries of Andalusi cultural achievement?"[40] For the elite Moriscos, ideally it could do both, ensuring the descendants of Andalusians a place in Spanish history, culture, and society. Castillo translated the Arabic inscriptions of the palace that testified to the glory of the Islamic Nasrid dynasty who built the Alhambra, but he did so in the service of the Spanish Habsburgs who ruled Spain in the sixteenth and seventeenth centuries.

Cataloging the Arabic manuscripts of the Escorial in a country that had burned so many Arabic books presented its own ambiguities. But by founding a royal library, Felipe II was also affirming his own stature as king by emulating other European monarchs who were creating libraries and collecting books in different languages, including Arabic. Some of the manuscripts of the Escorial had been seized from Moriscos by the Inquisition.[41] Their inclusion in the library was the result of coercive policies enacted by the king, and at the same time allowed him to paint himself as an enlightened patron of learning. As a fitting symbol of how the library expressed the political power of its owner, among the items described by Castillo was an Ottoman flag captured by Juan of Austria at the Battle of Lepanto, where allied Christian forces defeated the Ottoman Turks in 1571.[42] These ambiguities might have escaped the later scholars who used Castillo's catalog to get a sense of the larger landscape of Arabic knowledge and literary history and included it in their own texts, thus incorporating his work in European Orientalism.[43]

Miguel de Luna (c. 1550–1615), also a physician, learned Arabic in his youth, and succeeded Castillo as interpreter to the Crown.[44] Vastly erudite, he not only composed medical treatises but also published the bestselling *Historia verdadera del Rey Don Rodrigo* (The True History of King Don

Roderigo).[45] This was ostensibly a mere translation of a historical account, presenting a favorable view of the Muslim conquest of Spain, allegedly found in the Escorial Library and attributed to the fictitious "Abulcacim Tarif Abentarique." Luna was not the only Golden Age Spanish writer to invent an Arab author for his text—the most famous being, of course, Miguel de Cervantes, who made Cide Hamete Benegeli the fictional author of *Don Quixote*. Miguel de Luna's novel introduced readers to Arabic modes of writing. The chronicle included, between its two parts, a biography of the magnanimous and righteous Arab king Jacob Almançor. The biography was attributed by the fictional Abulcacim to the no less imaginary Ali Abençufian and belongs to the mirror-for-princes literary genre that flourished in Islamic and other countries, instructing rulers on good governance.[46] The Englishman Robert Ashley liked this portrait so much that he translated only this biography.[47] Taking stock of the progress of oriental collections in European institutions, Ashley's preface includes an admiring description of the Oxford University library where he found this "Arabian Historie," and which held books and manuscripts in "Arabian" and other Eastern languages. The 1680 French translation of the chronicle by Le Roux also situated the text in the lineage of Orientalism in an appendix that examined its reliability, citing Erpenius among others. He emphasized how Luna's work, alongside the "science of Oriental Languages," should put firmly in the past the times when the discipline of history seemed to be made only "for the Greeks or the Romans."[48] At a time when the Inquisition was busy "recoding ever more Morisco customs and traditions as evidence of dissimulation and heresy,"[49] Luna introduced readers to Arab discourses and literary forms, and extended the domain of the interest for Arabic beyond the utilitarian political usages to which it was confined in Spain, whether for the needs of diplomacy or the law. His revisionist history of the Muslim conquest of Spain included a philological apparatus, learned notes, and the invention of supporting documents. It was denounced by later critics as an egregious hoax, but in recent decades, it has been read more sympathetically as an effort to bestow on the Moriscos a recognition of their specific history, while at the same time integrating them into Catholic Spain, by "writing themselves into a culture that increasingly attempted to define them as an irreducible Other."[50]

The *plomos* affair, much better known thanks to important studies over the past three decades, developed in this context. For several centuries, the consensus has been that the relics were indeed fabrications perpetrated by Moriscos. Alonso del Castillo and Miguel de Luna were the most important

Morisco protagonists in the *plomos* affair in two different capacities: immediately called to decipher the finds, they are also the prime suspects for the forgery. If they were indeed the culprits, by producing the fakes which are "beyond doubt the last works written in the Iberian Peninsula in the Arabic language,"[51] the forgers also attempted to anchor Arabic, still outlawed, deep in the history of Spain, and in Spanish society, while reinforcing their own position as specialists of the language, as Arabic speakers and philologists. Theologically complex, the *plomos* addressed two audiences. For Old Christians, they appealed to local patriotism as the finds made Granada one of the most important Catholic cities in Spain. In addition, a passage translated from the Lead Books indicated that the apostles had found *a Maria no le tocó el pecado original*' ("Mary was untouched by original sin"), ostensibly offering proof to proponents of the Immaculate Conception of the Virgin Mary, a controversial doctrine at the time that was nevertheless widely popular in Spain.[52] To former and maybe crypto-Muslims, the *plomos* toned down problematic aspects of Christianity, especially the Trinity and the divinity of Jesus, while painting Arabic as an ancient Christian language, and thus attempting to dissociate it from Islam in the Spanish imagination.

Despite the Church's early embrace and the enthusiasm of a population eager for a local Christian history and for relics of its own, the Lead Books affair ended in failure. Not only did the papacy condemn the documents as heretical, but long before that determination, the Crown decided that Spain could no longer accommodate this minority—whose Christianity was deemed an insincere cloak for potentially rebellious subjects—and expelled the Moriscos in 1609. However, a faint victory should be recognized for the forgers. The *plomos* episode gave a boost to the philological study of Arabic in Spain, even though use of the language had been outlawed for decades.

While efforts to eradicate all remnants of the culture of Islamic Iberia were underway, Moriscos produced fictions that made European scholars more aware of the scale of the written Arabic and Islamic tradition and of the different modes it comprised: scripture and theology, historical and philosophical styles, not to mention the hybrid discourses of the Lead Books themselves. Regardless of the fact that they were pursuing other goals, Moriscos introduced a better (if not entirely accurate) knowledge of the religious texts of Islam. These discourses—including polemical texts and translations—traveled beyond the boundaries of Spain and were influential in Orientalism and sometimes cited in the nascent oriental studies. Therefore, although the *plomos* forgers failed at integrating Arabic and Arabic-speaking people into the polity of Spain, by deploying specific scholarly strategies, they succeeded at making them more firmly a part of learned culture. They thus contributed to making Arabic an acceptable language in Spain, at least in scholarly circles, and included Spain and its Islamic heritage in the broader formation of early modern oriental studies. These fictions of conversion were heavily marked by the attempt to assimilate a vulnerable minority in Spanish society. There and elsewhere, religious polemic helped to slowly advance knowledge of Islam in Christian milieus, but also hindered the communication between the spheres of knowledge.

CAPTIVE KNOWLEDGE IN EUROPE

The prevalence of war and captivity created circumstances of exchange and circulation that included the contribution of prisoners and slaves from the East to Orientalism. Captivity and ransoming were part of the unwritten rules of war, if the captives were able to reach out to those with the means to pay for their freedom. Ransom was determined by the status of the captive. Conversion was a necessary step toward greater freedom for those who could not be ransomed, and the few captives who led visible and successful careers as authors or teachers were baptized. Lamenting the fate of those captured by Christians, an Algerian chronicler wondered: "How many scholars have they taken captive?"[53] Indeed, captive scholars played essential roles in introducing the learned of Europe to Arabic language and culture. A well-known medieval precedent occurred when Ramon Llull bought a Muslim slave in Majorca to help him study Arabic.[54] In the following centuries, many more captive collaborators entered the field, as the confrontation on the frontier between Islam and Christendom intensified. Paradoxically, captivity "effectively connected communities across the Mediterranean. It facilitated the traffic of goods and ideas as well as people," and "revolutionized the production and transmission of information."[55] This includes the circulation of the knowledge that advanced Orientalism.

As seen earlier, in 1518 Egidio da Viterbo brought to Italy the translation of the Quran made by Juan Gabriel of Teruel, and revised it with the help of another convert, Hasan al-Wazzān or Leo Africanus, undoubtedly the most famous of these captive scholars. In recent decades he has stepped most decidedly from the shadows with several studies devoted to his life, career, and influence.[56] Born in a family of notables from Granada, who relocated to

Fez when he was a toddler, he studied theology and jurisprudence, and appreciated history and poetry. He served the Waṭṭāsī sultan Muhammad, called al-Burtuqālī or "the Portuguese" (r. 1504–26), who had himself been a captive in Lisbon for several years. The journey that disrupted Wazzān's life began in 1515 when he was sent to Istanbul. The ship bringing him back to Morocco in 1518 was seized by Sicilian pirates who delivered him to Pope Leo X of the Medici family. After a year of captivity, Wazzān was baptized by the pope himself on January 6, 1520. At his baptism, he took the Latin name Johannes Leo de Medicis (Giovanni Leone in Italian). Soon released, he spent several productive years in Italy. It is presumed that he went back to the Maghrib around 1529, and the date of his death is unknown. His complex identity as an emblematic figure of the early modern Mediterranean frontier between Islam and Christendom is often the focus of analysis. Of equal importance, however, is his vast influence on European culture, which extended through the centuries. In Italy, he first exerted it on the Italian humanists who had developed an early interest in oriental studies. Leo belonged to circles curious about Islamic culture for religious, political, and sometimes scholarly reasons.[57] In 1514, his godfather, Pope Leo X, sponsored the first book to be printed with Arabic types, the *Septem horae canonicae,* a prayer book addressed to Eastern Christians. Agostino Giustiniani (1479–1536) dedicated his very influential 1516 polyglot psalter, in which the psalms were edited in several languages, including Hebrew, Greek, and Arabic, to Leo X. Another patron was the learned prince Alberto Pio de Carpi (1475–1531), for whom Leo copied an Arabic version of the Pauline epistles in January 1521.[58] Leo's multifarious influence on Orientalism also included a grammar that facilitated the study of Arabic. Although it was soon lost, it was known to Guillaume Postel, who authored the earliest Arabic grammar published in Europe outside of Spain (1539),[59] and to the rabbi and physician Jacob Mantino (d. 1549), the dedicatee of Leo's 1524 incomplete trilingual vocabulary (Arabic-Hebrew-Latin), now held in the Escorial Library. Egidio da Viterbo, to whom Leo taught Arabic, might have encouraged him to write works about the history, geography, religion, languages, and cultures of North Africa, only some of which have survived. His extant works include his most widely read book, the groundbreaking geography and history of North and West Africa, the *Libro della cosmographia dell'Affrica.*[60] Written in Italian and completed in Rome in 1526, this treatise "long remained a principal source for European knowledge of the Islamic world."[61] During the first century following publication, it was translated into French, Latin, and

English, and widely quoted by cosmographers, cartographers, and philosophers. Some of his narratives even made their way into fiction.[62] It also contained many accounts of his author's adventurous life. Reflecting on his extensive and often perilous travels, Leo stated that if he "were to tell in detail the particularities of even one journey such a work would count more than a hundred folios."[63]

Leo's geographical description exerted a deep influence on Orientalism, providing vital inside information that helped scholars map out Arabic literary history and chart paths to pursue its exploration. The chapters on Fez in particular contain a comprehensive representation of North African culture that borrows liberally from the *Muqaddima* by the celebrated Ibn Khaldūn (1332–1406).[64] There, and elsewhere, the text features authors as influential as the theologian and philosopher Abū Hāmid al-Ghazāli (1058–1111), or the geographer Abū 'Ubayd Allāh al-Bakrī (ca. 1040–94). If Juan Andrés gave European scholars a glimpse of the theological texts that underpin Islamic doctrine, Leo introduced them to a much wider range of literature, including the secular fields of poetry, philosophy, science, history, and geography. Almost a century later, Erpenius heavily relied on Leo in a November 5, 1620, speech on the value of Arabic for the pursuit of knowledge, where, to prove his point, he stressed the number of universities and of trustworthy historians, mathematicians, excellent poets, and astronomers in Arab countries.[65] Leo provided European scholars with a sense of the Arabic sphere of knowledge, not only of disparate books, but also of a scholarly culture connected by networks and organized by institutions of schooling and patronage.

Another of Leo's texts played an important role in helping Europeans sketch this Arabic Republic of Letters, a Latin-language bio-bibliographical dictionary of Muslim, Christian, and Jewish authors, first published in 1664 by one of Jacob Golius's students, the Zurich-based Orientalist Johann Heinrich Hottinger (1620–67).[66] At that time, when scholars were tentatively mapping out oriental literary history, Leo's rather sketchy attempt was still considered relevant, although a much more formidable effort of assessing the scholarly heritage of the Islamic world had already been produced: *Kashf al-zunūn* (The Clearing of Doubts) by the great Ottoman scholar Kātip Çelebi (1609–57). This monumental and still authoritative bibliography of Arabic, Persian, and Turkish texts "had a significant impact on European oriental scholarship."[67] It would become a main source for the late seventeenth-century *Bibliothèque orientale,* Barthélemy d'Herbelot's grand attempt at a literary history of the Islamic world.[68]

Earlier, Leo had provided European scholars with an invaluable sketch of the Arab tradition of learning. The connection between Republics of Letters remained nevertheless tenuous. It might have been both helped and hobbled by the author's precarious situation in the Arab sphere of knowledge. As a well-read convert, he was allowed to pursue a career in Italy, adapting genres of Arab culture, informing readers about writing modes and styles, and producing work that bears the influence of the Italian intellectual circles that he frequented for several years. There is, however, no evidence that, in North Africa, he belonged to the higher echelon of the Arabic Republic of Letters, the prestigious circle of the ulama (lit. the learned). This term (the singular of which is *'ālim*) designates in Islamic countries scholars of any discipline, but came to mean almost exclusively the practitioners of the religious sciences, the "guardians, transmitters, and interpreters of religious knowledge, of Islamic doctrine and law,"[69] although a sizable number of these ulama also studied the natural sciences and wrote poetry and belletristic prose. Leo did present himself as a *faqīh,* which denotes a more narrowly conceived training in law, even when he was borrowing books from the Vatican Library.[70] However, in the Maghrib, he admits that he was only asked to adjudicate cases when he was traveling in remote regions with little access to trained scholars.[71] Thus, according to his own testimony, he was recognized as a specialist of law when no other more knowledgeable scholar was available. He did not teach in any madrasa, he was not a *muftī* qualified to issue legal opinions, nor a *qādī* or judge. The absence of such credentials makes him similar to Hajarī. Neither of them was memorialized in the bio-bibliographical dictionaries that record the life and work of Muslim scholars.

Most disappointingly, Leo did not leave any external trace about his life in North Africa before or after his captivity. His own work portrays him as a public servant rather than a scholar. His literary achievements before his capture, when he dedicated a poem to a local lord, and when he collected quotes engraved on tombs for a booklet he offered to a prince, were minimal, and connected to his position as a courtier. Concerning the impact of his work in North Africa, only a few tantalizing bits and pieces suggest possible avenues of study. His description of Africa could be found in the Maghrib in the hands of a few Europeans.[72] There is however no indication that local scholars knew about it. The closest might be Hajarī, who mentions Luis del Mármol Carvajal (1524–1600) and his *Descripción general de África,*[73] in his letter from Paris, although it is impossible to ascertain if he was aware that Mármol had borrowed a great deal of his information from Leo Africanus.

It took a few more centuries for Arab culture to reappropriate his work, by Butrus al-Bustānī in his 1876 encyclopedia, and in 1935 thanks to Muhammad al-Hajwī's brief book.

UNEASY ENCOUNTERS BETWEEN
REPUBLICS OF LETTERS

A generation after Leo Africanus, another captive, Muhammad Kharrūf al-Ansārī al-Tūnisī (d. 1558), worked with a European Orientalist, mirroring Leo's involvement with Egidio da Viterbo and others. In stark contrast with the experience of Leo, his story left many traces in Arab texts, since Kharrūf was a bona fide member of the scholarly class.[74] This rare opportunity to examine the collaboration between a European Orientalist and a Muslim captive scholar from both sides offers many insights on the entanglement of slavery and early modern Orientalism. European Orientalists celebrated the pioneering work of Kharrūf's European pupil and owner, the Flemish cleric Nicolas Cleynaerts (1495–1542), also known as Nicolas Clénard. His posthumously published, copious, and lively correspondence in Latin memorialized his heroic efforts to learn Arabic.[75] He was so eager to learn the language that he described himself as being an "Arabicomaniac."[76] He studied the influential 1516 Giustiniani psalter, and moved to Spain. In Seville, he bought a slave captured during the Spanish assault on Tunis in 1535, who would teach him Arabic, and was disappointed when his professor got ransomed only eight days later.[77] Cleynaerts bought another learned captive, also from Tunis, whom he described as an expensive "Arab merchandise," and began in 1539 to study with his help. He only named him once as "my Charuf."[78]

Kharrūf taught his new master Arabic grammar, helped him read the Quran, and copied manuscripts for him. Now aware of how little Europeans knew about Islam, Cleynaerts, whose main goal was the conversion of Muslims, decided to study Islamic religious texts and train missionaries who could debate Muslims in Arabic. Frustrated by the burning of Arabic books by the Spanish Inquisition, he left Kharrūf behind and went to Fez, where he stayed from May 1540 to August 1541. There, he discovered that his slave had been sending letters detailing his ordeal and seeking help in getting ransomed. Summoned by the Sultan Ahmad al-Wattāsī (r. 1526–45), Cleynaerts was forced to negotiate Kharrūf's freedom.[79] He was dismayed to lose another highly competent instructor of Arabic, although he boasted of making a handsome profit. He bought his slave for 180 ducats and obtained 500 for his ransom.[80] In Fez, he was already planning to buy a new teacher, and heard of educated slaves in Malaga, Cordoba, and Seville, all from Tunis, all presumably captured like Kharrūf during the 1535 assault.[81] Cleynaerts was dependent on slaves for his studies, because he was well aware that the religious polemic that spurred his interest in Arabic studies would also hinder his interaction with Muslim scholars. In Morocco, he denied any interest in religious debate, and tried to hide his polemical goals behind scholarly concerns, claiming only a desire to read in Arabic medical and philosophical works. This dissimulation was in vain, and the Flemish scholar blamed the learned community of Fez for discouraging any potential helpers since he was a "Christian dignitary" who might stir up trouble. He heard that some respected ulama met to discuss his case.[82] The deep distrust of Muslim scholars that Cleynaerts displayed in his correspondence is matched by their suspicion of his motives.

Kharrūf's account is not extant, but Moroccan sources recalled his experience, including the autobiography of his student Ahmad al-Manjūr, the renowned scholar later mentioned by Hajarī in the lost travelogue which was a source for a few Morrocan writers, as discussed in chapter 1.[83] Manjūr's information about Kharrūf, whom he described as "a rationalist and a versatile man of letters," mostly corroborates Cleynaerts's. Thanks to Manjūr, we learn that Kharrūf taught his master, who remained unnamed in his account, a grammar book by Abū al-Qāsim al-Zamakhsharī (1075–1144). Cleynaerts did own the treatise authored by the grammarian he called "Albucasim."[84] Manjūr revealed that Kharrūf sent letters describing his predicament to Muhammad al-Yasītnī (d. 1552), a prominent scholar and *muftī* (jurisconsult) of Fez, who urged the sultan to ransom the captive. The Tunisian scholar's liberation was thus due to his status as a respected academic, belonging to international networks of intellectual exchange and scholarly solidarity. Yasītnī also delivered the *fatwa*, or legal opinion, that the latter should not teach Cleynaerts, given his polemical aims.

Kharrūf spent the rest of his life in Fez, writing poetry, and teaching rhetoric and logic. His mentoring of local students would have far-reaching consequences in Islamic culture, as he is credited for having revived the study of logic in Morocco, and for ushering a new efflorescence of the rational sciences in the Maghrib, which would later influence many thinkers in the Ottoman Empire.[85] Thanks to his scholarly eminence, he would be, like his distinguished friends Manjūr and Yasītnī, memorialized by biographers who provided details about his ordeal, such as the fact that he lost all his books "due to the calamity of captivity, as they were sunk at sea."[86] This is in marked contrast with the silence surrounding Hasan al-Wazzān or Leo Africanus.

Furthermore, another influential scholar echoed and appropriated Kharrūf's experience. Ahmad ibn al-Qādī (1552–1616)—a mathematician, a prolific historian, and a captive in Malta in 1586 and 1587—did not devote to his story a stand-alone narrative, but embedded information about it in several texts. His friend 'Abd al-'Azīz al-Fishtālī (d. 1621), the minister and historiographer of the Sultan Ahmad al-Mansūr, described in detail the negotiations involving diplomats and merchants that led to his ransoming by the sultan and his release.[87] Significantly, Ibn al-Qādī in his own writings constantly connected his hardship to literature and scholarship, mourning the loss of many texts, including an autographed copy of his professor Manjūr's autobiography, "which I lost during my ordeal, and my copy is now in the hands of the infidels."[88] Indeed, not only people but also objects and texts were seized in the economy of captivity that supported early Orientalism, and the first constitution of oriental libraries in Europe largely depended on looting.[89] By invoking these stolen texts and by identifying with Kharrūf, Ibn al-Qādī inscribed his traumatic adventure in the Arabic Republic of Letters, recounting more than once the shortened story of the Tunisian scholar's captivity and ransoming by the sultan.[90] However, he never mentions Kharrūf's collaboration with Cleynaerts. In the cases of Kharrūf and of Ibn al-Qādī, the trauma of slavery mostly overshadowed the intellectual exchange. While captivity and religious polemic permitted and justified the communication between European and Arabic spheres of knowledge, they also hindered meaningful connections between their more prominent members. This is one of the limitations of this exchange during the early modern period.

Other less distinguished captives participated in oriental studies. None would make as big an impact in Europe as Leo did, and none has been remembered in their culture of origin as Kharrūf was. However, decades after Leo's time, Italy continued to be a major site of oriental studies, aided by the founding in 1543 of a school for neophytes (converts), two-thirds from Judaism and the rest from Islam. These Muslim neophytes were in all likelihood victims of piracy and war. Pope Gregory XIII revitalized the College of Neophytes in 1577. Some of its students contributed to one of the most important enterprises of early modern Orientalism, the Typographia Medicea, an oriental press founded by the grand duke of Tuscany, encouraged by Gregory XIII, and directed by the erudite Giovanni Battista Raimondi (ca. 1536–1614).[91] Religious concerns, as always, dominated this enterprise. The expressed goal of the press was to promote Catholicism among Eastern Christians by disseminating theologically orthodox material in their languages (Arabic and Syriac). Nevertheless, the few secular texts it published during its short existence exerted a profound influence on oriental studies,[92] including the anonymous abridgment of Idrisī's geography, which Hajarī read in Granada, and Ibn Sīnā's *Canon of Medicine*, which he studied in Paris in a copy belonging to Étienne Hubert. Students of the College of Neophytes also made contributions of varying importance and quality to the field.[93]

In other regions of Europe, captives, converted or not, assisted Orientalists, and more rarely produced their own work. The German scholar Bartholomeus Radtmann, produced his forgettable and brief Arabic grammar thanks to his collaboration with Paul Willich, a converted "Turk" (*Turk* at that time could mean Muslim in general rather than a Turkish national specifically).[94] The imperial librarian in Vienna, Sebastian Tengnagel (1573–1636), employed at least another "Turkish" captive, a poet and prisoner of war named Darwīsh Ibrāhīm, who was still imprisoned while working for Tengnagel and complained about the dreadful conditions of his detention.[95] In France in 1612, Hajarī's friend Étienne Hubert "retrieved from the king's guards" the converted "Turk" François de Boulogne and employed him as a scribe.[96] About two decades later, an account of the missions of the French envoy Isaac de Razilly (1585–1635) in Morocco was attributed to a converted "Turk," whose godfather was the powerful Cardinal de Richelieu, and who went by the hybrid name Jean Armand Mustapha.[97] His dedication informs the readers that he came from North Africa, and "changed his early slavery for a sweet freedom," probably an allusion to his captivity that ended after his conversion. In Paris, he taught "foreign" languages, presumably oriental ones.

One of the most distinguished members of the European Republic of Letters was the antiquarian and polymath Nicolas Fabri de Peiresc (1580–1637), who, to obtain information and documents, maintained vast Mediterranean networks, recently described in fascinating detail in *Peiresc's Mediterranean World* by historian Peter N. Miller.[98] Like others, his studies benefited from the presence of captives. In Marseille, he "saw the population of North Africans, most of them slaves, as potential sources."[99] In the late 1620s, when he was studying Arabic coins in Marseille, he enlisted the help of "Sayet son of Hamat from the country of Sussy of the city of Tarudan in the kingdom of Morocco."[100] This should be understood as Saʿīd ibn Aḥmad from the city of Tārūdānt in Sūs, a Moroccan region south of Marrakesh. Peiresc described him as a "Turkish slave" who possessed many interesting books and was well-read in Maghribi history.[101] Peiresc also consulted another slave about the origin of some petrifications: "Mattouk Chiassan" from Aleppo, whom he referred to as "my Turk," "was in the possession of Nicolas Crouset."[102]

Another captive worked with many scholars. Aḥmad ibn ʿAlī, an "Arab slave," in the words of Hottinger, was a Moroccan who had been captured by Spaniards about 1630, converted to Christianity, spent time in France and the Netherlands, then went back to his country and his religion.[103] He stayed in touch with some Orientalists, carrying out scholarly missions for Jacob Golius and his students, including buying manuscripts and collecting information. A number of the Arabic letters he wrote to and received from Golius are still extant and attest to a rather tumultuous life.[104] Later examples are found in Italian archives. The anonymous translator of excerpts from the Quran, based on the 1647 French version by André du Ryer, was helped by an unnamed coggia or hoça, a title used in Livorno to designate the slaves who were exempted from the galleys, since they were imams (religious guides). This Muslim collaborator was so well read that he could correct the mistakes and misunderstandings of the translation. The scientist and poet Francesco Redi (1626–97) might have been alluding to that same captive, whom he named "Chogia Abulgaith Ben Farag Assaid," describing him as a very knowledgeable and intelligent Moroccan, who led a career in the Tunisian court before his capture. The accomplished Abū al-Ghayth also worked with Barthélemy d'Herbelot, author of the famed *Bibliothèque orientale,* who sojourned in Tuscany from 1666 to 1671, and letters attest to their collaboration.[105] A later case concerns an Egyptian imam, who was captured in 1706 and left autobiographical information in the colophons of manuscripts he copied for the Vatican Library after his conversion.[106]

These examples show that the collaboration of Orientalists with captives was far from an uncommon occurrence. Some European scholars, like Cleynaerts, even contemplated shopping for a learned slave. So did François Savary de Brèves, who intended to staff a projected school of oriental languages in Paris with some free collaborators, but also by recruiting "two or three more from the prisons of Malta or those of the grand-duke," or by "buying in Malta and in Livorno two Persians and two Turks."[107] In the same way, the renowned Italian mathematician Giovanni Alfonso Borelli (1608–

79), wanting to translate into Latin the *Conics* by the Hellenistic geometer Apollonius of Perga (third century B.C.E.), half of which were lost in the original Greek and only extant in Arabic, was looking in 1656 for "some monk or some slave knowing Arabic" in order to translate and explicate the "much desired four last books of Apollonius's conics."[108] These examples of European intellectuals shopping for knowledgeable slaves, as well as the number and quality of the captive scholars who contributed to the field, show that captivity was a not inconsiderable factor in the development of early modern Orientalism. As we will see later, on the other side Christian prisoners sometimes helped North African and Middle Eastern authors, including Hajarī, better understand the cultures of Europe.

EASTERN CHRISTIANS AS ORIENTALISTS

Another category of collaborators hailing from Islamic countries were originally Christians, and as such were allowed an easier entry into the institutions of learning. Their vital role in early modern oriental studies, however, also involved religious polemic. In the late sixteenth century, major crusading plans receded and were replaced by Catholic missionary activity. Counter-Reformation Rome made great efforts to bring Eastern Christians into the Catholic fold.[109] Roman Catholics wanted to reconcile Eastern Christian doctrines with those of the Roman Catholic Church, uniting Eastern and Western Churches in a common Christian faith. Eastern Christians were in fact brought to Europe explicitly to further the cause of the Roman Church, which considerably influenced their contribution to Orientalism. Syriac, the literary and liturgic language of many Eastern Christian Churches, began to be studied in Italy in the early sixteenth century, and the interest in Syriac grew thanks to the increasingly institutional relation between the papacy and the Eastern Churches. One crucial juncture was the Fifth Lateran Council (1512–17), in which a delegation of the Maronite Church participated. The long process of bringing the Maronites closer to the Catholic Church had begun at the time of the Crusades, with the aim of making them renounce beliefs that the papacy considered heretical.[110] During the time of the council, the learned humanist and linguist Teseo Ambrogio (1469–1540) studied with Elias, a young member of the Maronite delegation, who, like Leo Africanus, worked for Alberto Pio di Carpi, and who copied the first Syriac texts made in Rome.[111] Teseo also worked with an unnamed

Armenian.[112] These collaborations helped him produce his pioneering grammar of oriental languages.[113]

A few decades later, another great advance in Syriac studies also benefited from the help of a native speaker. Moses of Mardin, a Syrian Orthodox monk, was sent to Rome in about 1549 by the Patriarch of Antioch to inquire about printing Syriac Bibles to distribute in the East, and "systematically sought out the very few men in Europe who knew some Syriac."[114] He got in touch with Guillaume Postel and with the German humanist Johann Albrecht Widmanstetter (1506–57). The latter had already studied with visitors from the Levant, including Simon, the Maronite bishop of Tripoli who came to Rome in 1535.[115] During his time in Europe, Moses copied manuscripts and taught Arabic and Syriac.[116] Most important, he helped produce the first edition of the Syriac Gospel published in Vienna (1555), usually attributed to Widmanstetter, while the substantial contributions of Postel and Moses are overlooked.

During the following decades, the papacy made the concerted effort to sponsor the creation of several institutions to further its goals, including a number of schools that taught Arabic.[117] The important congregation of *Propaganda fide* was founded in 1622 to coordinate missionary activities. These efforts helped bring native speakers who would make collectively a major contribution to the field of oriental studies. One institution was particularly influential. In 1584, Pope Gregory XIII founded the College for Maronites,[118] which followed the model of other Catholic colleges created in Rome, usually directed by Jesuits, whose aim was to train priests and theologians from foreign lands in proper Catholic doctrine. Young Maronite boys were brought to Rome from the Levant to study. Many of them spent several years, and some of them most of their lives, in Europe, where they worked in various capacities and helped advance oriental studies. Some found employment in the oriental presses that were created in Italy and elsewhere, the most prestigious being the Medici Press.[119] Others staffed libraries.[120] A number of Maronites taught in schools, at the Maronite and Neophyte colleges, at the convent of San Pietro in Montorio, or the university La Sapienza.[121] Some published instructional tools, often rudimentary grammars of Arabic and Syriac.[122]

The more successful became eminent citizens of the European Republic of Letters, willing to address the larger educated public beyond the missionaries. Among those, some held prestigious positions in France, in great part thanks to the aforementioned François Savary de Brèves. Planning to found a school and a press for oriental languages in Paris, he convinced Jibrā'īl al-

Sahyūnī / Gabriel Sionita (1577?–1648), who had already cowritten a still unpublished Arabic-Latin dictionary,[123] to move to Paris, where he succeeded Étienne Hubert in 1615 in the prestigious position of professor of oriental languages in the Collège Royal. He was accompanied by another graduate of the Maronite college, Yūhannā al-Hasrūnī / Johannes Hesronita, who was named royal interpreter. Together, they authored *Grammatica Arabica Maronitarum* (1616).

Even after Savary's forced retirement in 1618, when he bore the consequences of his closeness to the now disgraced Queen Regent Marie de Medici, the two Maronites continued publishing, most notably, in 1619, under the title *Geographia Nubiensis* (The Nubian Geography), an influential Latin version of the abridgment of Idrisī's geography, earlier published anonymously by the Medici Press. In the same volume, they coauthored a modern description of the orient, notable, unsurprisingly, for its chapters on Lebanon, where the Maronites came from, and demonstrating their willingness to seek a general learned readership beyond a specialized audience. Sionita stayed in Paris until his death in 1648. A well-known scholar, his reputation was sullied, however, by accusations of laziness and dishonesty.[124] The most important project in which he participated was the Polyglot Bible published in Paris in 1645.[125] This publication of the Bible in several languages was only one of many such undertakings in Europe, that reflected the latest advances in philology.[126]

Another Maronite contributor to the Paris Polyglot Bible, Ibrāhīm al-Hāqilānī / Abraham Ecchellensis (1605–64), built a highly successful career in Europe, and joined the ranks of the Republic of Letters at a fairly prestigious level. Like many other graduates of the Maronite college, in Italy he was an editor, a teacher, a librarian in his later years, and an author of grammars of Arabic and Syriac.[127] His prolific authorial output extend beyond these standard productions, and he became the most important Orientalist of his time, at least in Catholic Europe.[128] Protected by powerful patrons and friend to many other intellectuals, including the famed Egyptologist Athanasius Kircher (1602–80),[129] he conducted part of his career in Paris, where he was invited to work on the Polyglot Bible, and taught at the Collège Royal. He published many editions or Latin versions of oriental texts, as well as original work. He translated medical and philosophical texts, and collaborated with Giovanni Alfonso Borelli in the first Latin translation of the books of the *Conics* by Apollonius of Perga that had been extant only in Arabic.[130] As usual for most Orientalists in his time, he was much involved in religious polemics. A fierce defender of the Catholic Church, he did not hesitate to enter into controversies against Protestant Orientalists.[131] A staunch apologist for the Maronites, he was also a declared enemy of Islam, and tended in his work to Christianize Arabic culture and language. In his later years, he worked at the Vatican Library, assisted by his three brothers-in-law of the Nimrūnī / Nairone family.[132] Mirhij al-Bānī / Fausto Nairone (1628–1711) became in his own right a member of the European Republic of Letters, albeit contested by some of its citizens.[133] Ecchellensis was succeeded in his chair of oriental languages at the Collège Royal around 1650 by another Maronite, Sarkis al-Jamrī / Sergius Gamerius (until 1658).[134]

The Maronites were the most visible of the Eastern Christians who led successful careers as members of the European Republic of Letters, but they were not the only ones. Marqus al-Du'ābili / Marcos Dobelo or Dobelio (c. 1575–?) was an Iraqi Kurd, probably a Christian from an Eastern Church considered heretical by Rome, who studied at the College of Neophytes.[135] He inventoried manuscripts at the Vatican Library, compiled an Arabic compendium of various treatises of medicine, and taught Arabic in Rome from 1605 to 1610. Invited to Spain to help assess the *plomos,* he deemed them a fabrication. He entertained unfulfilled hopes of pursuing his career in England, and spent the rest of his life in Spain, where he translated medical and historical works and composed an Arabic grammar that remained in manuscript.

Another alumnus of the College of Neophytes who led a remarkable career in Europe is Yūsuf ibn Abī Dhaqn / Joseph Abudacnus or Barbatus, who had the distinction of being a Copt at a time when very few of these Christians from Egypt traveled to Europe, and who is known thanks to the work of Alastair Hamilton.[136] Born in Cairo, probably in the late 1570s, he was sent in 1595 to Rome, and converted to Catholicism. In many European countries, he found powerful patrons and befriended distinguished scholars, including the famed astronomer Johannes Kepler. He taught Arabic in Paris in 1609, most notably to Erpenius, just before the latter met Hajarī, and became acquainted with Hajarī's friends Étienne Hubert and Arnoult de Lisle. Later, Joseph taught and worked in Oxford and Antwerp, and in the Bavarian court. He moved to Istanbul, where he found employment as an interpreter and as a manuscript buyer for Tengnagel, the imperial librarian. Beside a brief Hebrew grammar, and an Arabic grammar that is in manuscript, he authored a short history of the Copts, which exerted some influence on the field of Coptic studies.[137]

The effort to Catholicize the Eastern Churches changed considerably the religious and cultural life of the Christian communities in the Levant. It also greatly influenced the development of early modern Orientalism in Europe. A large number of Maronites and members of other Eastern Churches studied in Rome, and later staffed European institutions of learning and libraries, and some occupied positions of influence. Their contribution belonged to Counter-Reformation efforts, and was thus shaped by the hope that "the practices and beliefs of the Eastern churches could prove useful and instrumental in polemics between Protestants and Catholics."[138] Often virulently anti-Muslim, they were encouraged to create in Europe an archive of Eastern Christianity that to this day informs how the history of the Middle East is written in the West. The most important of these scholars, Ecchellensis, influenced the Republic of Letters' approach to the cultures of North Africa and the Middle East, in ways that downplayed Islam in favor of Christianity. As shown by Alastair Hamilton, Ecchellensis, in his Arabic-Latin dictionary, omitted Islamic terminology, and thus proposed a Christianized, de-Islamized version of Arabic.[139] This text remained in manuscript, but one wonders if such attempts might have explained why Le Gendre extolled the "Christian style" of Golius's epistle to Mūlay Zaydān. The work of these Eastern Christians, especially the ones who went through the College for Maronites, Christianized their representation of the Arabic Republic of Letters to bring it closer to European expectations in the struggle against Islam.

TRAVELERS FROM THE EAST: DIPLOMATS AND FREELANCERS

Captives, converts, and especially Eastern Christians continued to play an important part in oriental studies, but in the late sixteenth century, more sustained official and personal travel involved free men of different faiths, including Muslims. These learned visitors from Arab and Ottoman lands were welcomed and sometimes feted by Orientalists and their friends in Paris and Leiden, creating the conditions for more meaningful exchange between spheres of knowledge.

Many educated exiles like Hajarī found positions in Maghribi courts, especially in Morocco, where their mastery of Spanish ensured they were sent on diplomatic missions to Europe. Some envoys, whether Moriscos or not, worked with European scholars, as Hajarī did. In 1609, the secretary of a

Saʿdī embassy to The Hague, ʿAbd al-ʿAzīz ibn Muhammad al-Taghlibī, struck up a friendship with the student of Arabic Jan Theunisz (1569–between 1635 and 1640) and stayed with him after the mission ended, until April 1610.[140] ʿAbd al-ʿAzīz was introduced to Theunisz's friends, and made copies of Arabic texts for them, including the Gospels. He offered his own copy of the Quran to his host as a present. Two manuscripts bear traces of the religious, scholarly, and friendly exchanges between the two men. The first is an Arabic text with a Latin translation, and includes a recollection of their first meeting and their subsequent conversations on religion, giving a somewhat surprisingly fair representation of the Muslim's point of view on sensitive issues. The second is a large dictionary which reflects the strong influence of ʿAbd al-ʿAzīz as a native speaker.

Increasingly sustained diplomatic relations connected more visitors with European scholars, especially in Northern Europe. In 1639, for example, an embassy to the Duchy of Schkeswig-Holstein at Gottorf was sent by Shah Safi of Iran (r. 1629–42). Six members stayed in Europe, among them Haqq-vīrdī (d. 1650). The latter converted and began working for the Orientalist and cartographer Adam Öhlschläger, known as Olearius (1599–1671). The Eastern scholar taught him Persian, helped him translate the *Gulistān* by the illustrious poet Saʿdī (1210–92), and checked his information when he wrote his widely read travel account.[141] Olearius introduced Persian literature, history, and art to the German-speaking public, a cultural contribution that depended largely on Haqq-vīrdī's assistance. He also became secretary of the first German embassy sent to Isfahan in 1635–39.

Orientalists eagerly sought visitors learned enough to copy, explicate, or translate texts, and as was often the case with Easterners who worked with Orientalists, Haqq-vīrdī was employed by several scholars. In Holland, he copied manuscripts and translated texts for Golius from May 1642 to August 1643. They had a contract drawn before a notary that stipulated a twelve-hour work day for the copyist, including Sundays.[142] On his way back to Gottorf, he traveled with the aforementioned captive Ahmad ibn ʿAlī, and complained about his habits, which included constant smoking and drinking. A Jew from Marrakesh, named Saʿdīya ben Levi, who might have, at least for a while, converted to Islam[143] sojourned in the 1640s in Groningen, where he taught Hebrew to Hottinger, who described his fiery temper.[144] Besides procuring manuscripts, he translated from Arabic to Hebrew, and transcribed for Golius Maimonides' medieval masterpiece of Jewish thought, *Guide for the Perplexed,* in Arabic characters.[145] Another visitor to Golius was Mūsā b.

Mīkhā'īl ibn 'Atiyā / Moses Michaelis.[146] A priest of the Greek church of Damascus, he arrived in Leiden around 1645 and stayed until 1649, and assisted Golius in translating the official Dutch Protestant catechism into Arabic, to help in missionary efforts. International traders assisted the circulation of money to pay for services and procure manuscripts. Letters exchanged between the two men, or sent by Mūsā to his brother Yūhannā in Damascus, inform us about their arrangements concerning money exchanged through merchants, and about the many travails Mūsā endured before returning home.

Some free visitors led long careers in Europe, and some converted to Christianity. Isaac Pallache, connected to the Moroccan court, belonged to a Jewish family that served the Sa'dī *makhzan* for generations, and is probably the Moroccan Jew who was considered for the first chair of Arabic studies in Leiden University that Erpenius eventually obtained. Isaac stayed in the Netherlands and converted to Christianity around 1633.[147] Other migrants did not change religion. A gifted Turkish polyglot known as "Ossin," or Husayn, was Savary de Brèves's assistant,[148] and worked with Raimondi in Rome.[149] Savary introduced him to Étienne Hubert, who, in a letter to Joseph Scaliger attested that "Vafer Hussin" knew not only Turkish, Arabic, and Persian, but also Latin, "which is rare for a Turk."[150] De Brèves obtained in 1613 for this free Muslim, who refused to convert, the position of interpreter to the king.

In addition, European scholars who traveled to the East hired local assistants and then attracted them to Europe with the offer of jobs. These migrant freelancers played a decisive part in the history of Orientalism. Niqūlāwus ibn Butrus al-Halabī / Nicolaus Petri (c. 1611–c. 1661) is an especially important character in this milieu, whose many letters mostly to European scholars have been published.[151] This member of the Orthodox Church came from a family of silk weavers from Aleppo, owned property in Istanbul, and was well-educated in elite Arabic culture. He met the German Orientalist Christian Ravius during his stay in Istanbul (1639–41), when the latter collected about three hundred manuscripts, some apparently stolen from their rightful owners.[152] Traveling to Europe as Ravius's copyist and assistant, Niqūlāwus befriended Golius and the most important English Arabist of the seventeenth century, Edward Pococke (1604–91), professor at Oxford since 1636.[153] Niqūlāwus copied manuscripts for Golius, and stayed in touch with him after his return to Istanbul in 1647, buying books for him. He also worked with Golius's student Levinus Warner, helping him obtain manuscripts, and collaborating on his Turkish translation of the Bible.[154]

In 1657, like Niqūlāwus and Haqq-vīrdī, Shāhīn Kandī signed a contract with Golius, and with Leiden University as well.[155] This Armenian Christian, whose family Golius befriended in the Levant, was a cultivated man, knew Turkish and Persian, and wrote, in Arabic, a "lively literary prose of excellent style."[156] He copied manuscripts, was charged to review the Turkish translation of the Bible, and later helped catalog the manuscripts brought from the East by Warner. Another visitor to Europe was a Muslim who left fainter traces. The Jesuit of Irish origins Tomás de León (1613–90) spent most of his life in Spain, and had strong interest in oriental studies. In his letters, he mentions a certain "Rachman," described as a "Moorish Altaleb or student from here." Rachman was an unusual scholar: "as to [Arab] students, especially mature ones, very few reach here; the only one who is here, and who is my friend, told me today that he knows of no other anywhere in Spain who is *al-taleb* or student . . . he himself knows by heart the Grammar of Abibeker [Abū Bakr] . . . and the Zairagia or Kabbala of the Arabs." Elsewhere, León adds that that this student knew the Quran very well.[157]

It would be futile to try to disentangle religious concerns from scholarly pursuits. Religious polemic was still an essential element of oriental studies. We have already seen how the pursuit of oriental knowledge was supported for missionary purposes, and how Moriscos in Spain used their knowledge to defend Christianity against Islam. But polemic is a two-way street. In North Africa, Moriscos did the opposite, and produced polemical texts against Catholicism. Muhammad Alguazir or al-Wazīr from Pastrana in Spain, who might have been an acquaintance of Hajarī, wrote a text that exerted some influence on oriental studies.[158] Around 1611, Mūlay Zaydān commissioned him to compose an anti-Christian polemical work in Spanish, which contains new religious ideas, such as the notion of Muhammad as the Messiah. Orientalist circles ensured this book an interesting afterlife.[159] Most important, it was later used by another polemicist, Ahmad ibn ʿAbd Allāh al-Haytī al-Marūnī, a convert sent to the Netherlands by Mūlay Zaydān. Asked by Prince Maurits about the Muslim view of Jesus, he wrote a polemical treatise, of which only a Latin translation survives, and which was mainly an adaptation of part of Alguazir's treatise.[160] Protestant Orientalists spread its arguments in their own anti-Trinitarian and freethinking polemics.[161]

Beyond the time period to which this book confines itself, many more Eastern Christians traveled to and sojourned in Europe.[162] Some left testimonials about their interactions with Orientalists, in their country or in Europe. Solomon Negri (d. 1729), who taught Arabic in several European countries in the late seventeenth and early eighteenth centuries, wrote a memoir.[163] The Syrian Maronite Hannā Diyāb is especially noteworthy. Like Hajarī, he wrote his most significant work describing his experiences in Europe and his interactions with scholars in Arabic, and outside of Europe. As a young man, he was brought by the French envoy Paul Lucas from Aleppo to Paris, where he was presented to the aged Louis XIV in the royal palace of Versailles. He also met Antoine Galland, who translated into French one of the most famous texts of world literature, *One Thousand and One Nights*. Some of its better-known stories, such as "Aladdin and the Magic Lamp" and "Ali Baba and the Forty Thieves," were not part of the manuscripts Galland relied on but were "orphan tales" recited to him by Diyāb in Paris. The Frenchman kept silent about the young Syrian visitor in his published work. Years after his return to Aleppo, Diyāb wrote an account of his travels to Europe, preserved in only one manuscript, which reveals the true extent of his contribution: "Before the discovery of this manuscript, Diyāb had only a shadowy existence in literary history as the mysterious Maronite who related 'beautiful stories' to the more famous French translator."[164] Now published and translated into French and English, this long-ignored text not only highlights the heretofore barely acknowledged labor of the Eastern contributor but also changes our understanding of the production of the *One Thousand and One Nights* as a world text.[165] It is attracting attention in its own right as an inventive and artful memoir. This recently discovered text illustrates how fruitful it would be to look at the work of Eastern collaborators of Orientalists after they went back to their countries, and to examine the depth and extent of the intellectual continuum that encompassed Europe and its Islamic neighbors.

ORIENTALIST EXCHANGES OUTSIDE OF EUROPE: LOCAL SCHOLARS AND BOOKSELLERS

That Diyāb and others were hired in the East is a striking example of the connectedness of the early modern Mediterranean world. Some visitors to Europe continued to work with Orientalists after they returned home, extending the territory of the connected Republic of Letters, as Hajarī had done with Jacob Golius. Indeed, Europe was not the only site in which Orientalist knowledge was produced. Intellectual exchange happened in North Africa and the Middle East, often involving educated people who never traveled to Europe, such as the deacon Mīkhā'īl Krākū, from

Damascus, who assisted Golius,[166] or Thalja Karma, the brother of the patriarch of Antioch who worked with Pococke.[167]

Some of these Eastern interlocutors expected their interaction with European scholars would give them access to books and scientific instruments, and that the exchange of knowledge would go in both directions. Golius obtained manuscripts and information from the Syrian physician Yūhannā b. Mīkhā'īl b. 'Atiya / Johannes Michaelis and in return provided him with printed Greek books, and astronomical instruments.[168] Their travels and their connections with scholars in Eastern countries indeed allowed Europeans to enter into meaningful intellectual transactions with accomplished members of the Arabic and Islamic Republics of Letters. In Iran, the Italian traveler Pietro della Valle (1586–1652) entertained friendships with astronomers and mathematicians. In his travelogue, he expressed the high esteem in which he held them and recounted many of their conversations.[169] Orientalists also knew Muslim scholars who were distinguished enough to leave many traces in biographical dictionaries. A correspondant of Golius, Sheykhzāde Muhammad Efendi (d. 1658), was an eminent jurist who held prestigious positions in the judiciary and taught in a madrasa in Istanbul.[170] His acquaintance with Ravius was less happy, as the European scholar stole manuscripts from him.[171] Another eminent scholar and judge who helped Jacob Golius obtain manuscripts was the Egyptian polymath, judge, physician, and renowned poet Muhammad b. Ahmad al-Hutātī al-Misrī (d. 1641).[172] Golius and Warner were acquainted with several members of the learned 'Urdī family.[173]

In their quest for manuscripts, Orientalists also entered into relationships with librarians and booksellers, many of whom were themselves very accomplished. The Aleppo bookseller Ahmad al-Darwīsh acted as teacher, guide, copyist, and friend to many European Arabists. An adherent of the Gulshaniyya Sufi brotherhood, Ahmad taught Arabic to Jacob Golius and Pococke, among others, addressing them in his letters as pupils, and maintaining an interest in their progress long after they had left the Levant.[174] He also taught Pieter Golius (1597–1676), the brother of Jacob Golius. Pieter converted from Protestantism to Catholicism, and spent twenty years in Syria as a missionary. Writing to his friend Nicolas Peiresc, he described the bookseller as an "old and very learned Dervish."[175] Ahmad's letters show that he didn't only look for books his clients ordered but also counseled them on their purchases. Very well connected, he even had access to the library of the local lord Fakhr al-Dīn.[176] The Arabic literature scholar Hilary Kilpatrick noted the active role he played "behind the scenes": "He was much more than an informant: rather, he played an active part behind the scenes in the development of Arabic manuscript collections in England. The history of Orientalism needs to give due recognition to him and other scholars in the Arab world who guided Europeans in acquiring material."[177] Peiresc had heard from his Capuchin contacts of a rival of Ahmad in the Aleppo book market, "Mohammed Estacaoni, who is interested in mathematics, and who has a beautiful library of books in diverse oriental languages."[178] This letter badly mangles the name of the bookseller and writer Sayyīd al-Taqwā (d. 1650–51).[179] A fierce competitor, he often represented those fighting to possess the same manuscripts Ahmad was trying to procure for his European clients.[180] In another example of the two-way scholarly exchange between Europeans and Easterners, Ahmad asked Jacob Golius to help him acquire a globe and Pococke to provide him with a Medici Press print of the geographer Idrisī's treatise, two requests that attest to his interest in geography.[181] A sincere friendship connected Ahmad and Pococke, and the older man expressed his heartfelt condolences when he learned of the death of Pococke's father.

In the Maghrib, Jacob Golius also had a number of scholar or bookseller correspondents, in addition to Hajarī. He often was in touch with them through merchants and Dutch diplomats. An undated letter sent from Tunis mentioned manuscripts, named dealers and copyists, and reminded Golius that its author had been contacted by a Dutch envoy.[182] The latter bought eight books, for which he billed Leiden University. A local scholar sent a letter to Golius, dated July 14, 1634, in which he answered questions about ulama of the Hanafi school of Islamic jurisprudence, and about books of literature, history, or ethics written in the Maghrib and al-Andalus.[183] In the early 1660s, Golius exchanged letters with a Moroccan correspondent not only charged with finding books but also with collecting information such as names of cities and other sites, and inscriptions on tombs of kings, and with sending him objects, including carpets and an ostrich egg.[184]

. . .

As historian John-Paul Ghobrial has noted, a true social history of early modern Orientalism has yet to be written, and such a history would have to devote a much larger part to the subjects of Islamic countries who participated in it, not just as neutral conveyors of linguistic skills and as manuscript dealers but also as learned men who introduced scholarly practices and views:

"Any history of orientalism that ignores such figures remains incomplete, misshapen and disingenuous."[185] This chapter has explored their extensive and varied participation in the field, reflecting on the constraints placed on the work of native speakers who contributed to the development of oriental studies. European scholars depended to a large extent on these more or less learned men to teach them languages and copy manuscripts. The most accomplished also translated reference books and compiled dictionaries or grammars. The more creative authored historical or geographical treatises and literary compendiums, some of which exerted a profound influence on oriental studies and European culture in general.

The diversity of their circumstances considerably inflected their contribution. Born in Spain, converted Muslims and their descendants were members of a persecuted minority whose participation in Orientalism was determined by their search for acceptance in the dominant culture. Captives of war and piracy helped Europeans deepen their knowledge of the languages, the religion, and sometimes the high culture of Arabic and Ottoman countries, in the hopes of an amelioration of their circumstances. Eastern Christians led successful careers in European teaching institutions, publishing houses, and libraries. Diplomats and envoys entered into polemics and friendships with Europeans. Freelancers were employed as copyists and teachers and assisted with writing sometimes widely read books. In Islamic countries, local scholars and booksellers advised European scholars on which reference books or artifacts to acquire. This diversity of channels delineates a vast landscape of intellectual exchange, crisscrossed by networks that connected not only individual scholars from Europe and Islamic countries but also spheres of knowledge, contributing to the progressive emergence of a connected Republic of Letters. Scholarship needs to give its due to these numerous active contributors to the field of oriental studies in the sixteenth and seventeenth centuries who came from Islamic cultures.

While this brief survey is without doubt incomplete, it reveals an early modern world where numerous Arabs and Ottomans collaborated with Orientalists, though many did not stay in Europe in order to pursue successful careers. More cultural production by Eastern scholars probably awaits discovery in archives, letters, and memoirs that bear traces of their intellectual exchange with Europeans. Those that we know about, like the Maronite Hannā Diyāb writing in Syria, show great promise for the study of both early modern Arab and European cultures. Hajarī's particularity arises from the fact that he participated in the field through several channels: a Morisco called to help decipher the parchment found in Granada, an envoy sent to Paris and Holland by Sultan Mūlay Zaydān, and a local interlocutor who helped Jacob Golius collect manuscripts in Morocco. We know more about Hajarī because he is one of the few Arab and Muslim historiographers of early modern Orientalism who provided his own record of collaboration with European scholars. Most important, the study of Hajarī's output as an author and translator, in Arabic and Spanish, allows us to move beyond Orientalism and to pursue the study of the networks that sustained it past the frontiers of Europe. The following chapters will show how he extended his scholarly networks in the Maghrib and Egypt, and how he worked to be integrated into the Arabic Republic of Letters. His success made him one of the most important intercessors between spheres of knowledge in the early modern period, helping European Orientalists better understand Arab culture and introducing European cosmographical and technological advances to readers in North Africa.

—————

PART TWO

Ahmad al-Hajarī

BECOMING AN ARAB WRITER

DURING THE EARLY MODERN PERIOD, Eastern contributors to Orientalism participated in exchanges with European interlocutors that were at times precarious and uneasy but nevertheless connected Republics of Letters on both sides of the geographic divide. Some collaborators of Orientalists, mostly diplomats and freelance assistants, displayed an interest in European culture and in some cases asked their counterparts in Leiden or London to provide them with scientific instruments and with books.[1] Such requests suggest that certain individuals in Islamic countries, while participating in the practices of Orientalism, were at the same time constructing a knowledge of European culture during its early modern expansion, thus extending the discipline beyond the confines of Orientalism narrowly conceived as a European enterprise. Although documentation of such exchanges is limited, the career of Hajarī can help advance our understanding of this phenomenon. His role is all the more compelling given that that he had to find idiosyncratic ways to be a part of the sphere of learning in North Africa.

Leo Africanus is but one example that proved Eastern collaborators could be prolific and influential authors in their own right. Their work, however, was done in Europe where they could only prosper as converts to Christianity. Hajarī, by contrast, composed most of his texts in North Africa. As a Morisco, his quite unusual contribution to Arabic culture was largely predicated on his knowledge of European learning, institutions, and cultural productions. He could not count on years of schooling in a prestigious madrasa, nor on serious study with famed ulama, to open doors into the more prestigious circles that comprised the Arabic Republic of Letters. His intellectual output was strongly linked to his successful path as a high-ranking official, although he did enjoy friendships with respected scholars who devoted their studies to religious as well as secular disciplines. Both callings were dependent on his command of Spanish and his skills as a mediator between languages, polities, and legal systems.

His career at court inflected his intellectual production in specific ways, in good part thanks to his work as translator of cultural and scientific texts for Mūlay Zaydān. By relating his experiences of travel, by recounting his encounters with scholars in France and Holland, and by translating European texts, he not only secured his own specific place in the Arab intellectual landscape, he also helped situate Orientalism in a larger picture of exchange, which included polemical disputations, scientific work, and social interactions with Europeans. Chapter 3 will analyze the strategies that he deployed to carve out a place for himself in Arab culture, including autobiographical writing and friendships with established scholars, despite what he considered to be his shortcomings. Chapter 4 will turn to his representations of his contacts with Europeans, and with European culture, and the ways in which they framed and inflected his view of the world. These strategies and representations are anchored by his complex relations to both the Arabic and the Spanish languages.

———————

THREE

Hajarī

A MORISCO WRITER IN THE ARABIC
REPUBLIC OF LETTERS

AHMAD AL-HAJARĪ WAS NOT A MORISCO trying to find a place, like some did, in the political and intellectual landscape of an intolerant Catholic Spain, nor a captive forcibly converted, nor an Eastern Christian allowed to reside and thrive in Europe. Rather, Hajarī most clearly belonged to the category of visitors and travelers who freely befriended members of the European Republic of Letters. His work—whether he was assisting Arabists, writing about his experiences in foreign lands, or translating scientific and technological texts in North Africa—is entirely situated in a cultural continuum encompassing Europe and North Africa. In this continuum, Orientalism features as a cultural production, among others, that was created and sustained by political and intellectual networks. Like Leo Africanus and others, Hajarī produced substantial work that was deeply informed by his intimacy with Christian Europe. Unlike them, he wrote most of his texts in Arabic, and his influence was first and foremost felt in North Africa. The study of Hajarī's work shows that the practices of early modern Orientalism went beyond Europe, and beyond Orientalism itself. Arabs and Ottomans like Hajarī, when studied, are usually investigated in terms of their impact in Europe. Such insufficient study rarely considers how their experiences inflected their cultural output in the East. This neglect frames the way their contribution has been understood.

There is a larger stake in this debate. Admitting a few Easterners as participants in early modern Orientalism, though welcome, has not really transformed the way we envision the evolution of the discipline, nor its place in the cultural history of Arab and Islamic countries. It is still too often said that Eastern cultures remained hermetically closed to Europe. This view does not acknowledge that Europe was open to the world and able to become familiar with foreign civilizations due to their contacts with people from other countries. Writing global history in this way allows for some non-Westerners to be included in European cultural history without really inflecting it and without significantly changing the way the cultural history of their own countries is considered. Through the example of Hajarī, this study proposes to widen the perspective and situate Orientalists and this particular collaborator hailing from Arab culture in the same cultural landscape.

Thanks to the many traces he left in both the European and the Arabic Republics of Letters, Hajarī is a perfect object of study for advancing our understanding of the intellectual networks that connected North Africa to Europe. Looking at the texts and translations of Hajarī in a holistic way reveals in more detail the interplay of Arabic and Spanish in his work and the modalities of his emergence as an Arab writer. This chapter explores how he integrated himself into the Arabic Republic of Letters as a minor, though significant, writer. His original works and translations are due for a reevaluation as cultural productions that illustrate the shared ways of representing the world that connected different shores of the Mediterranean.

HAJARĪ, BETWEEN SPANISH AND ARABIC

In the spring of 1612, Hajarī was in Paris and copied a manuscript for Étienne Hubert about the Arabic verbal system authored by the well-known grammarian Ibn al-Mālik (d. 1274).[1] Not content with performing a task that Orientalists frequently requested from their Eastern collaborators, he also added his own marginal annotations in the text, often in Spanish. He included more comprehensive notes in the few last pages of the manuscript, all the more interesting for being among the earliest texts he authored. Some additions, such as a list of Arabic months, and a few proverbs, probably conveyed supplemental information to Hubert. Others were more personal, and more revealing.

Although he enjoyed a lively social life in the foreign capital, Hajarī also missed his family. Feeling lonely, he added to the manuscript a poem in Arabic written in a popular form and comprised of two stanzas. In this nostalgic piece, he touchingly expressed his longing for the day when "sadness would turn to happiness" and he would see again his loved ones, his children and their mother, his wife, whom he called the "white dove." He added to this poem its Spanish translation ending with the invocation of *la blanca paloma.* Finally, at the end of the manuscript, he appended a three-page text in Arabic telling a legend about Jesus, who, as a child, explained the mystical significance of letters of the Arabic alphabet. Answering potential objectors who would point to the historical impossibility of Jesus knowing Arabic, Hajarī then described the discovery of the parchment and the Lead Books of Granada to prove that the language was in use among early Christians.

Beside highlighting Hajarī's nostalgia for the warmth of his Marrakesh household, these pieces show him eager to extol the sanctity of the Arabic language, attested to by Jesus himself. He took great pride in his role as a sought-after professor to Orientalists, just over a decade after he escaped from Spain, where he often feared that his knowledge of the tongue would put him in deadly trouble with the Inquisition. However, apart from the convenience the language provided for communication during his travels in Europe, he still relied on Spanish to express feelings and ideas. Translating his own poem into Spanish signals that this devout Muslim retained an emotional connection to this language even though it might carry Christian connotations. This was the case for the words he used to describe his beloved wife: in southern Spain the words *la blanca paloma* had been included for centuries in the cult of the local *Virgen del Rocío* (Virgin of El Rocío).[2] The expression as it appears in Arabic was thus already a translation. Writing the Spanish phrase alongside the Arabic text, Hajarī invites readers to consider "La blanca paloma" as the Spanish title to an Arabic poem. These pieces demonstrate Hajarī's strong emotional attachment to the Spanish language, as well as his reverence for the Arabic tongue (see fig. 5).

Decades after his time in Paris, Hajarī left more traces interweaving Spain and North Africa, Spanish and Arabic, and braiding the threads of his life and experience. In 1534, on his way from Marrakesh to Mecca for the *hajj,* Hajarī began his journey with a stay at the kasbah of the Ūdāya, a walled castle complex in Rabat. His memories about his time in the kasbah are written in a short text included among a collection of seventeenth-century Morisco documents held in the library of the University of Bologna. This manuscript includes a number of mostly religious works and translations by Hajarī and other Moriscos. Introducing his own translation of excerpts from a famous book by the judge ʿIyād (1083–1149), Hajarī added some autobiographical information. He highlighted the usefulness of his version for the "Spanish Andalusians who understand better the Romance language than the grammatical Arabic" in which ʿIyād wrote.[3] He expressed his gratitude to the sponsor of this translation, ʿAbd al-Rahmān Ximenez, who had welcomed Hajarī

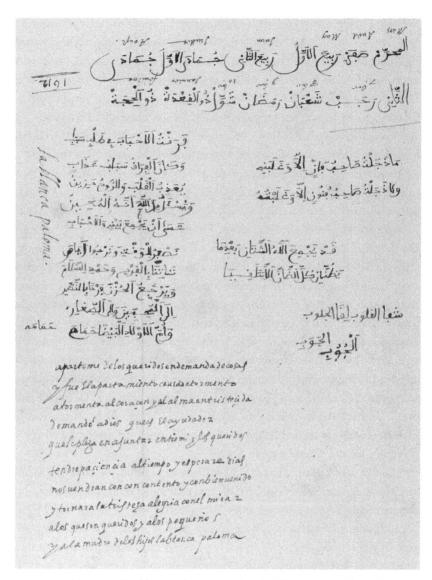

FIGURE 5. The poem "La blanca paloma," by Ahmad al-Hajarī, in Arabic and Spanish. Bibliothèque Nationale de France, MS Arabe 4119, folio 26r. By permission.

in the kasbah by presenting him with a panegyric he authored in Spanish. This poem, also included in the Bologna manuscript, sang the praises of Hajarī as a courtier, as a learned man, and as a steadfast friend to the Moriscos. It also informed readers that Ximenez had read "divine verses," presumably in Spanish, that Hajarī had written and "copied in his own hands."[4]

We do not know whether Hajarī composed those lost poems directly in Spanish, or, similar to "La blanca paloma," wrote Arabic poems that he translated. Indeed, in this case, the distinction between original and translation is blurry. The Bologna manuscript includes the poem that Hajarī wrote in response to Ximenez's panegyric. Like the latter, it is a classic romance in octosyllables, first eulogizing the Prophet Muhammad, while the last few strophes praised his host's literary style and nobility. What sets it apart is that Hajarī added some marginal notes in Arabic. The first describes Muhammad as the Seal of the Prophets, a classic phrase in Islamic theology that he rendered in his poem as *el ultimo embaxador,* while the others are sentences attributed by tradition to Muhammad, about souls and love, that helped him highlight the affective connection that united the Moriscos in their exile. Thus, like he did for the Paris poem, Hajarī put together Spanish and Arabic, going back and forth between them, and expressed his attachment to the Spanish language, and to the Moriscos, whom he was now serving by putting religious Islamic texts into their native tongue, as he did in Rabat and as he would continue doing in Tunis where he settled after completing the pilgrimage.

Hajarī was born a member of an endangered minority and decided at one point to move and join the community to which he aspired. As he put it in the title of his lost travelogue—*The Journey of al-Shihāb toward the Meeting with his Loved Ones*—he determined to journey toward his loved ones and a territory where what he held most dear, the Islamic religion and the Arabic language, were not under threat. On the other shore of the Mediterranean, he endeavored to rebuild his life and to make a career close to the Saʿdī court in Morocco and, later, to the Tunisian circles of power. He succeeded, thanks to his skills as an interpreter and translator.

Hajarī was a translator before he was a writer, given his fluency in Arabic and Spanish, and translation remained a constant in his life and work. (He also translated from French and Latin, sometimes with the help of a more proficient scholar.) But in North Africa, knowledge of Spanish marked him as an outsider, and he had to answer suspicious inquiries about how he could speak, read, and write fluently the language of the enemy. His answer was an autobiographical narrative, appended to his 1638 translation of a gunnery treatise, the *Kitāb al-ʿizz*, by the Morisco Ibrāhīm Ghānim: "If anyone should say, 'How do you know how to read Spanish . . .?' I studied for many years to learn their speech and to pick up their writing, so that, when I came to their country [the coastal cities] on my way to Muslim lands to escape, they would think me one of them . . . nothing they saw in me gave them any cause to doubt, either in my speech or in my manners, or my way of writing."[5] Any member of the Morisco minority caught attempting to pass as an Old Christian in the coastal towns would have to face the wrath of the Inquisition, given that Moriscos' freedom of movement was severely constrained. And it was not easy to pass as an Old Christian for the Moriscos, especially those who belonged to the lower classes. Their very distinctive dialect was often featured in Spanish comedies of the time.[6] But Hajarī was not the only Morisco who was able to do so. The author of the treatise on artillery could also pass as an Old Christian. In Seville, Ghānim attended workshops on gunnery that taught him cutting edge knowledge that found its way into his book: "I used to sit with them and memorize some of the discussion and try my hand at gunnery without any of them being aware that I was an Andalusian [Morisco]."[7] Both translator and author present their closeness to the enemy in speech and manners as the result of defiance, of courage, of heroism, even. This proficiency, as disquieting as it could be seen in North Africa, allowed for the acquisition of knowledge and skills that could become immensely useful for the Islamic societies in which they chose to live: the mastery of artillery for Ghānim, and the talent to translate difficult texts for Hajarī. Indeed, the latter's command of Spanish brought him many rewards: "I afterwards realised that by reason of the studies I had undertaken with the purpose of drawing near to Allah and to be able to approach the land of the Muslims, there were opened to me, because of this forbidden language, the doors of princes that were shut to many people."[8] These efforts not only helped both Hajarī and Ghānim escape Spain, they also won Hajarī a career in the *makhzan* of the Saʿdī sultans, and gave Ghānim an opportunity to contribute to the defense of North Africa.

When Hajarī worked hard at mastering the major language of Spanish, the Spanish of the Old Christians, and not the minor dialect that would immediately reveal him to be a Morisco, he did so, according to his defensive statement, merely in order to escape Spain, and not out of a personal desire to assimilate in Spanish society. This assertion might not reflect the entire truth, however. Although he never quotes in his extant texts from Spanish literary culture as other Moriscos did,[9] he did write or translate his own poems into Spanish. His work also demonstrates a good knowledge of Spanish cosmographical science, which certainly goes beyond what was needed for his escape and which betrays a desire to access forms of learning valued by the majority culture.

Reflecting on the difficulties of translating the *Kitāb al-ʿizz* led Hajarī to think more deeply about his trajectory and his task as a Morisco translator and about what bilingualism brought to him and, in the end, to the society in which he decided to live. In the appendix to the *Kitāb al-ʿizz,* he also insisted on the outstanding contributions made by many Moriscos to the defense of North Africa against Christian foes, helping their integration in Maghribi society by showing them as assets and not mere refugees and recipients of charity.

The complexities of his relationship to Spanish do not stop there though. He had also, since his stay in the kasbah of the Ūdāya, worked at facilitating this process of assimilation by translating Islamic devotional texts so that his fellow Moriscos, who could not read Arabic, would learn about their religious duties in their native Spanish. Doing so, he helped the refugees integrate more fully into the majority culture of North Africa, by learning about religious dogma and rituals in their native tongue, which was now, in this new context, the marginalized language of a vulnerable community. His use of Spanish at that time also reveals his active solidarity with the Morisco exiles.

When Hajarī was in Rabat, in his mid-sixties, most of his work to that point had consisted of translations from Spanish and other romance languages into Arabic, notwithstanding any lost poetry he might have written. He had not followed the counsel of scholarly friends to write about the religious controversies he engaged in during his travels in Europe. Only when he was in Egypt, where he sojourned during his time in the East, did he find the impetus to write in Arabic much longer autobiographical texts, one of which is extant. The catalyst to this momentous decision was his friendship with ʿAlī al-Ujhurī, who not only encouraged him, but, he said, ordered him to write down his experiences of controversial debates with learned men of other religions. The work Hajarī would write would also detail his involvement with the Lead Books affair, and would memorialize his deep commitment to serve the exiled Morisco community. It displayed however the ambition to address a larger audience than the diaspora. From belonging to a persecuted minority in Spain where Arabic was banned, Hajarī came to the point where he was urged by one of the prominent scholars of his time to join the Arabic Republic of Letters.

THE CONQUEST OF ARABIC

Crucial features of his project include his relationship to the Arabic language, but also to Spanish, as well as the literary strategies he deployed to situate himself in the learned tradition, through textual connections with scholars and through autobiographical writing. An analysis will help measure how willfully this exile from Spain and collaborator of European Orientalists anchored himself in the Arabic-Islamic tradition of learning and writing. It will make clear, when it will focus on his connection to and his reflection on the outside world, that the assessment of his work and of his import should not be limited to the help he brought to European scholars, nor to his polemical approach to other religions. Rather, these two aspects are contributing factors in the cultural horizon he envisioned for his work beyond the confines of Europe. Thus, Hajarī worked at interweaving what might at first glance look like separate threads holistically into his life, his work, and his thought.

Hajarī's *Supporter of Religion against the Infidels* was written in Arabic, and aimed at reaching a learned readership that was familiar with the conventions and forms of Arabic literature. The study of the idiosyncratic ways in which Hajarī adapted these literary traditions is all the more important since he clearly reflected a lot on his writing. He extensively revised the *Supporter,* his main extant text, demonstrating his care for his work and his high degree of self-awareness as a writer. A close reading will help delineate the expectations he had for his own work, who he imagined his readers to be, and how he situated himself in the literary and intellectual landscape of his time.

The linguistic situation of the Arab world is usually described as one of diglossia, that is with a high and low variant. *Fushā,* also called Classical Arabic (with a recent modified form called Modern Standard Arabic), is learned through formal education and is the language of most Arabic literature. Less grammatically complex, *'āmiyya* is reserved for colloquial oral communication. Strongly local, this dialect differs from region to region. Many scholars have, however, questioned the notion of a stark opposition between the two forms of Arabic and noted the constant and fluid interaction between the two varieties, as well as the widespread use of intermediate written forms, usually called Mixed or Middle Arabic, which manifest the interaction between the high written form and the low spoken mode. A number of texts have been composed in Middle Arabic since the medieval period, including what has undoubtedly become the most famous Arabic literary work, *One Thousand and One Nights.*[10] Linguists consider Middle Arabic to be a written form of Arabic that differs from *fushā* by being more attuned and permeable to the colloquial while still borrowing heavily from the classical form, and which underwent itself a measure of standardization.

This is the form in which Hajarī wrote his *Supporter*. In all likelihood, he would have found Classical Arabic beyond his reach. Erpenius recounted in a letter to a friend that Hajarī freely acknowledged his lack of mastery of the prestigious *fushā*. The Dutch scholar noted that "his speech is not very pure and, as he himself admits, he often fails to observe grammatical rules and mixes colloquial idioms with classical as he is not accustomed to the language of the learned."[11] The *Supporter* is in fact considered to be a paramount example of a text written in the mixed mode, combining classical, dialectal, and intermediate forms. Linguistic historian Jérôme Lentin has analyzed the hybrid nature of its language and shown that it contains, alongside grammatically standard passages, not only colloquialisms but also a number of characteristic traits of Middle Arabic.[12] These include, among others: a spelling that follows the dialectal pronunciation when some consonants had merged and when the distinction between short and long vowels had collapsed; the change of grammatical genders for some words; the use of propositions in ways that are different from Classical Arabic; and the indifferent use of negative prepositions. These traits are also pronounced in his extant letters to Erpenius and Golius. Critics have noted that in correspondence not intended for publication, premodern authors, even those who had perfect command of *fushā,* tended to relax strict grammatical rules. Hajarī's letters follow this tendency and can be compared with other letters from Maghribi correspondents of Golius, some of whom wrote in an Arabic barely different from the vernacular, and others in forms closer to Middle Arabic but still distinct from the formal *fushā*.[13]

Hajarī's use of Arabic demonstrates the complex movements that mark his practice of writing. The very existence of his work, and especially the *Supporter,* was a victory for him over his religiously, culturally, and linguistically threatened origins. It was also the culmination of processes of "reterritorialization" and "deterritorialization," to employ useful concepts made famous by Gilles Deleuze and Félix Guattari.[14] They can help propose a succinct mapping of Hajarī's different moves around languages and their uses, thanks to their concept of territory as a metaphorical (and not only physical) space that is not fixed but is constantly made and unmade. As scholar Simone Aurora notes in his examination of territory and identity, "Although the production of signs which mark a territory is not at all limited to linguistic formulations . . . it is however undeniable that language probably represents the most powerful semiotic system, and therefore one of the most efficient tools, to create a territory."[15] If Hajarī's move away from Spain was meant as a reterritorialization in Islam and Arabic, its holy language, he nevertheless had to use a deterritorialized form of it, meaning a minor form, that is, a form that differs from the standard.[16] He does not, however, offer a defense of the vernacular in writing as a few contemporary Egyptian authors did.[17] Indeed, the complexities of his relation to Arabic and language in general go well beyond his use of the middle or mixed form. Understanding them is both facilitated and complicated by the fact that Arabic is a frequent topic of discussion and reflection in his text. He demonstrates a high degree of self-consciousness in his use of both the Spanish and the Arabic tongues. However, there is more to Hajarī's relationship to language than his ability (or inability) to master Classical Arabic. Beyond his use of Middle Arabic, which blurs the neat distinction between colloquial and classical, Hajarī's practice of language and writing about language also exceed the high/low binary.

The paradox of learning perfect Spanish as a means to a literal as well as metaphorical reterritorialization in the "land of the Muslims," is compounded by the fact that Arabic had always been for Hajarī an essential part of this move. Arabic had accompanied him throughout his life but had also been for him since early on a conquest to dream of, for which he had to plan, and that he needed to defend against lethal enemies. His account of learning to read and write the classical form underscores that it was both a temporal achievement and a spiritual triumph for him: "One of the graces God bestowed upon me is that He created in me the love to learn to read in Arabic, after I had spent five years to learn in Spanish."[18] When he was ten, a relative taught him to read and write Arabic, despite his parents' fears that he would be found out and subjected to harsh punishment by the Inquisition. He was an extremely fast learner, for which he offered two explanations. One is secular, when he prosaically admits that his "knowledge of reading Spanish was of great help to me to learn reading Arabic as well." The other is spiritual: "Can it remain hidden from anyone that the fact that I learned to read in less than one day was due to a divine benefaction and to success granted by God—praised be He!—and by the blessings of the Andalusīs."[19] This juxtaposition of the practical and the otherworldly is a hallmark of Hajarī's representation of his life, and here, it offers a perfect encapsulation of his relationship to language, which also brings together the mundane and the heavenly.

Connected to the religious aspect, but nevertheless distinct from it, is the fact that Hajarī's work demonstrates that he could read and quote classic Arabic texts, and engage with another territory he aspired to, the Arabic

Republic of Letters. Whatever his incapacity to completely master Classical Arabic, which he acknowledged to Erpenius, he was still, in his work with European Orientalists, the representative of that Republic and the bearer of Arabic language and Arabic culture. He must have felt that his ability to fulfill this role was a sign of the success that he had achieved. However, taking the step of writing a book and submitting it to the judgment of the learned of North Africa was measurably different. In the absence of direct and unambiguous testimony from Hajarī, we can only venture to read the clues he left and cautiously surmise that it took time for him to feel confident enough about his skill as a writer to undertake this project. He might also have needed reassurance that, even if he did not entirely master the prestigious *fushā*, he was proficient enough in an acceptable form of Middle Arabic to fulfill this ambition. After his return from his European travels, Moroccan scholars suggested that he should write down his experiences, especially his encounters and polemical discussions with learned men from other religions. He seemed to have thought and talked about it enough that Ahmad Bābā, a famed scholar from Timbuktu, gave him stylistic advice.

Despite these possible early plans, he only composed his travelogue, and then its abridgement, when he was in Egypt. Maybe he could not resist the forceful wishes of a prestigious author such as Ujhurī. Besides, the place itself might not be fortuitous. Historian Nelly Hanna notes that seventeenth- and eighteenth-century Egypt witnessed a considerable expansion of prose texts written in Middle Arabic, or mixing classical with colloquial.[20] According to her analysis, this phenomenon developed in parallel with deep structural changes in Egyptian society. These transformations were brought about by the spread of a commercial culture that led to the increasing visibility and cultural power of a growing middle class of merchants and craftsmen, literate but not deeply learned in the higher forms. Most texts during that period were still written in Classical Arabic, especially when it came to theology, exegesis, and law. However, evidence points to a greater use and acceptance of the colloquial and the mixed forms in prose literature or chronicles. This, in turn, allowed for an increased inclusiveness of potential readers, and an expansion of topics, as shown when historical annals authors record public but also more mundane events concerning the lower classes.[21] Although some decried this phenomenon as a decline in standards, increasingly, even authors praised for their high degree of command of Classical Arabic would not disdain to mix it up to some extent with the lower forms. Middle Arabic, even among the learned, had become "an acceptable form of written communication."[22] Hajarī might have been influenced by the cultural atmosphere in Cairo, and encouraged by its acceptance of Middle Arabic.

ENGAGING THE ARABIC REPUBLIC OF LETTERS

These reflections are far from exhausting the complexities of Hajarī's relationship to Arabic and to language. It is important to stress again that writing in Middle Arabic does not mean that Hajarī was situating himself in opposition to the culture of the learned. The *Supporter* deploys diverse strategies to demonstrate that Hajarī could participate in scholarly exchange, though, not being one of the ulama, he could not directly join in their discussions as a member of this most prestigious circle. He clearly acknowledged that fact when, on May 13, 1612, he was having dinner in the Parisian house of Marc-Antoine de Gourgues, in the company of a few notables. The French guests were impressed by his witty responses when they were discussing religion. He gave them, however, a humble assessment of himself: "I told them: 'You should know that I am the interpreter of the Sultan of Marrakesh. He who occupies that post must study the sciences, as well as the books of the Muslims and Christians, in order to know what he is saying and translating in the court of the Sultan. But when I am in the presence of the scholars of our own religion, I am not able to talk about the [religious] sciences.'"[23] This conversation shows that Hajarī took pride in his proficiency as a political and cultural broker, and in the skills and learning that he had acquired. He nevertheless highlighted the limitations to this knowledge, and suggested that he was far from proficient in certain fields. This modest appraisal echoes the letter to Erpenius in which he admitted to his lack of mastery in the prestigious disciplines of Quranic exegesis and rhetoric.

A quick overview of the scholarly and educational landscape of Morocco at that time will help situate Hajarī's humble self-assessment.[24] The stabilization of the country during the first decades of the Saʿdī dynasty favored an "expansion of literacy and education."[25] In many regions, educational institutions flourished, and, after childhood instruction, young men, and a few women, could pursue further studies in madrasas in Fez, Marrakesh, and other cities, and in Sufi lodges in rural areas. As for the content, its foundational disciplines included: the Quran and exegesis; the hadith; theology; the law and its numerous ramifications; Sufism; the Arabic language and its many fields, such as grammar and rhetoric. Astronomy, mathematics, geometry, and logic could also be topics of learning. Instruction was based on texts, read and discussed under the guidance of a professor. The most successful students obtained employment or patronage. The ruler appointed judges (*qādīs*), or jurisconsults (*muftīs*). Endowments associated with mosques or madrasas, which often supported students and libraries, usually also paid for the less lofty positions of official witnesses, imams, and preachers.

Hajarī did not go through this curriculum in which "jurisprudence, theology and Sufism formed an inextricable backdrop for all intellectual activities."[26] He thus could not master the domains that were the purview of the ulama, and he is never described as belonging to this rarefied company. At best, he is said to be a *tālib,* a student, even later in life, as in 1634, by the Frenchman Cabiron, and by Ximenez in his poem. The evidence he has left as a member of the Saʿdī *makhzan* shows him to be an interpreter of legal, political, and cultural texts to and from (mostly) Spanish, and a representative of the sultan in his relations with Europeans. His expertise was of a different kind, based on a mastery of languages as a translator of diplomatic and scientific documents, and on a familiarity with more earthly texts than the religious treatises that only the ulama could compose.

However, as he suggested to his Parisian acquaintances, and as other passages of the text confirm, he was very proud of being allowed a more circuitous entry in learned circles, and of having friends and even mentors among the ulama. He must have attended assemblies in which those luminaries debated the finer points of grammar and poetry, and of religious doctrine and law. He was certainly eager to portray himself as a friend of prestigious members of the learned class. Four of these scholars stand out. Muhammad b. ʿAbd Allāh al-Ragrāguī (d. 1614), attained a degree of fame and power in Marrakesh, where he had been the most important judge since the days of Ahmad al-Mansūr.[27] Hajarī was close to this influential character, and enjoyed his respect. A passage of the Paris manuscript of the *Supporter* informs readers that Ragrāguī encouraged him to take the European trip and considered him a worthy representative of his adopted country in foreign lands. Earlier, Hajarī had approached the well-connected judge who successfully interceded in favor of Pieter Coy's release from incarceration. Other evidence of their closeness might be found in Ifrānī's prosopography, which quoted stories from Hajarī's lost travelogue about Manjūr and Jinwī. Ragrāguī was Hajarī's probable source, since both had been his teachers, as is mentioned in an authoritative biographical dictionary.[28] Another distinguished scholar on whose authority he relied is the judge he calls ʿĪsā al-Saktī, and who is usually known as al-Suktānī (d. 1652). This jurist was one of the most powerful judges in Marrakesh, and an important figure in the Moroccan culture of his time. He mentored many students who became prominent scholars and writers in their own right, and he is often cited and praised in collections of biographies, in autobiographies, and in historic chronicles. He told Hajarī "that refuting the falsehoods spoken by the Infidels concerning the religions is part of the *jihād*."[29] This opinion justifies a central feature of the *Supporter,* disputes with religious adversaries, and Suktānī was probably among the scholars who encouraged Hajarī to write them down. The latter attached such an importance to his advice that he mentioned it again in the appendix to the book of artillery.

A particularly noteworthy friend of Hajarī's appears in chapter 13 of the *Supporter.* Ahmad Bābā (1556–1627) was a scholar from Timbuktu in the Songhay kingdom when he was deported to Marrakesh in 1593 after Ahmad al-Mansūr's invasion. Fearing his influence, the sultan had him incarcerated for years until local scholars, admiring his knowledge and intellect, interceded on his behalf and succeeded in having him released, though he was not permitted to leave the city. He was then able to pursue his studies, figure prominently in the intellectual life of Marrakesh, and teach in the main mosque.[30] Ragrāguī was one of his numerous students.[31] Maybe through him, Hajarī established with Bābā a personal relationship. When Bābā was finally authorized in 1607 by Mūlay Zaydān to go back to his country, Hajarī was among a group of men who accompanied him outside the city to bid him farewell. He was still exchanging letters with him years later. During his travels in the East, Hajarī heard Bābā's work praised in Cairo and Tunis and thus learned that his fame extended far beyond Timbuktu and Marrakesh. He knew of some of his texts, including a commentary on a well-known book of theology and a book on tobacco that was part of a lively debate among Arab and Muslim scholars on the use of this substance in the early seventeenth century.

The most important of Hajarī's scholarly mentors also participated in this transnational discussion about the permissibility, and advisability, of the use of tobacco. ʿAlī al-Ujhurī was arguably the most important influence in his career as a writer. Beside teaching at al-Azhar, he was the head of the Mālikī school of jurisprudence, the author of numerous esteemed treatises, and, in the words of Hajarī, a "great scholar whose learning is widely praised in various countries."[32] The *Supporter* mentions him more often than any other contemporary writer. Hajarī's connection to the great Egyptian scholar was known in Morocco well enough that Ifrānī's biographical dictionary quoted his travelogue to attest to Ujhurī's influence on scholars from Marrakesh. By citing these four scholars, Hajarī situates his momentous decision to write about his life and travels in proximity with the higher culture, whose representatives encouraged him to compose his own work about his religious debates in Europe, which he framed as a peaceful jihad waged to defend Islam against its detractors.

These four scholars were not only his friends, they also had provided him with encouragements and advice for his literary project. They appear at several points in his writings to attest to the value of his contribution. Hajarī insists that he was spurred by the guidance of these esteemed scholars when he made the decision to write down his experiences. Without doubting this claim, one should note this was a familiar rhetorical move, "a common prefatory device found in many genres of writing in the Islamic Middle Ages."[33] This trope helped Hajarī build his authority, by borrowing the legitimacy of his accomplished friends. Ujhurī ordered him, he said, to write about his polemical discussions. Suktānī instilled in him the value of defending Islam against its enemies by refuting their distortions. A hopeful circumstance allowed for a connection with Ahmad Bābā. The very minute Hajarī completed in Tunis the revised version of the *Supporter,* "I heard the muezzin say: 'Allahu akbar' in the first prayer-call for the Friday prayer. So I regarded this as an auspicious sign that the book would be well-received."[34] This reminded him of Bābā, who wrote his treatise on tobacco in Tamagrūt just after he left Marrakesh and said "that when he concluded writing his work, he heard the prayer call for the salat [prayer], rejoiced and regarded this as an auspicious sign that the book will be well received. Likewise, I rejoiced when I heard the *takbir* after I had written the last letter of my book."[35] This symbolic connection with Bābā reminded Hajarī that the eminent scholar sent him encouragements and writing advice from Timbuktu: "After he had gone to his own country, I wrote to him and I informed him that I had gone to France and the Netherlands to arrange some affairs and that I had been detained in those countries. Then he wrote to me. . . . He also said 'When you write down everything you have seen, you should try to do so as concisely as possible!'"[36]

Hajarī also received oneiric blessings from Ragrāguī. Dreams played an important role in his spiritual journey, as they have for many Muslims throughout the ages.[37] They often feature in premodern autobiographies.[38] The *Supporter* contains many accounts of the dreams and visions that helped Hajarī navigate his life. In this case, he dreamed about telling his long-dead protector and friend of his plan of writing his book. In his vision, Ragrāguī predicted that it would be crowned with success. In the dream, his mentor was accompanied by Muhammad ibn Yūsuf al-Targhī, the most famous reciter of the Quran of his time in Marrakesh, whose presence reinforced the support that Ragrāguī was giving him.[39]

WRITING THE SELF

Going beyond the wishes of his friends among the scholars, Hajarī demonstrates that he was also following a more personal writerly impulse. In the introduction, he explained that Ujhurī advised him to write about his religious disputes with Europeans and that he exceeded the advice of his respected mentor by also writing a travelogue: "I complied with his order by writing more than he had asked and I compiled the book in the form of a travel account which I entitled 'The Journey of al-Shihāb towards the Meeting with His Loved Ones.'"[40] Hajarī then detailed the contents of the lost travelogue, which indeed go beyond what piqued Ujhurī's interest. The first part was devoted to a description and history of al-Andalus, as he almost always calls Spain, from the Muslim conquest to the time when the Christians took over the whole peninsula. This account relied on the work of the famous polymath from Granada Lisān al-Dīn ibn al-Khatīb (1313–74). Then, Hajarī moved on to his participation in the Lead Books affair, followed by his escape to Morocco. Finally, the text described the expulsion of the Moriscos, the author's own travels and the marvelous things he had seen, as well as the disputes he had with scholars from other religions. This summary indicates that Hajarī had his own agenda when writing. The Egyptian scholar, however, after hearing the text of the travelogue, still pushed Hajarī to edit his book into a shorter version by extracting his accounts of his debates with Christians and Jews. This was in line with his initial interest and with the advice of Hajarī's friends from Marrakesh, who first suggested that he write about his polemical discussions. He actually again went beyond the wishes of his respected friend, especially in the version he produced after leaving Egypt, when he enriched his account and added many illuminating passages.

His literary project exceeded the expectations of his mentors, which compounded his self-awareness as a minor author and made him more anxious about his decision to write about his own life. However, retracing Hajarī's life relies mainly on his many autobiographical writings. Despite the discovery of valuable documents, his own work is still the most important source to follow his trajectory. Even before he began producing extensive autobiographical texts, his May 12, 1612, letter to friends in Istanbul foreshadowed this concern and offers important information about his escape from Spain and his settlement, life, and position in Marrakesh, as well as his efforts on behalf of the robbed Moriscos in France and his acquaintance with scholarly and government circles in Paris. That might be one of the reasons why, much later, Hajarī translated it himself into Spanish, as a testimony to his service to the Morisco communities. In his later years, he also wrote his *rihla,* or travelogue, and its compendium, the *Supporter.* He produced the first version of the latter in Egypt and kept revising it in Tunisia. He also paraphrased and translated some passages of the *Supporter* into Spanish, which are included in the Bologna manuscript. Finally, in the appendix to his translation of Ghānim's treatise on artillery, the *Kitāb al-ʿizz,* he again recounted parts of his life story, including his time in Spain, his escape to Morocco, his service for the Moroccan sultans, especially Mūlay Zaydān, and his career in Tunisia. This commitment to autobiographical writing is a striking feature in Hajarī's career and is as important as his engagement with transcultural exchange and religious polemic. Two chapters of the *Supporter,* the introduction and chapter 13, the last chapter of the book, are especially revealing about his approach to this literary mode.

This personal autobiographical impulse is particularly noteworthy in the context of a renewed interest in the history of premodern Arabic autobiography, a genre of writing that had long been ignored if not denied. Ending a long and willful disregard of premodern Arabic (and all non-western) forms, critics have challenged the "assumption of western origin and exclusivity," and suggested ways to uncover and retrace the history of the genre in Arabic literature.[41] Hajarī clearly situated himself in this literary tradition. By demonstrating that he obeyed the wishes of respected scholars and ethical luminaries, who showed him, through encouragement, symbols, and visions that they approved of his work, he might have been alleviating feelings of anxiety generated by the very act of writing an autobiography.

Such apprehensions were detectable in many texts since the fourteenth century, as a mark of a growing self-consciousness on the part of Arab autobiographers.[42] Hajarī expressed his disquiet in the clearest way in chapter 13, extensively rewritten in Tunis. The additions greatly strengthened an aspect already present in the previous version, the recounting of events that, in his estimation, showed that God and His angels had been guiding him throughout his life. He was very hesitant to write about these occasions and to devote to them the best part of a chapter, feeling unworthy "because of the shortcomings, ignorance and sins I know of myself."[43] His anxiety worsened when he read a famous treatise in which the theologian Muhammad al-Sanūsī (1435/6–90) stated that one should be weary of pronouncing the Islamic profession of faith too often, giving the example of someone who did, and "used to find some money under his prayer rug, but when this became generally known, it stopped."[44] Hajarī feared that, if he were to publicize the graces God bestowed upon him, it would be seen as a boast, which would then put an end to these blessings.

His discomfort was alleviated by another vision, and by Ujhurī's assistance in interpreting it. He dreamed that he was reciting three Quranic verses (93:11, 41:53, 38:44) that supported autobiographical writing that extolled Islam:

> the first one of which was the saying of the Exalted God: "Speak about the blessing of your Lord!" The second verse was: "We shall show them our signs on the horizons and in themselves, so that it would be clear to them that it is the Truth. Is it not enough for your Lord that He is a witness of everything?" Finally, the third verse was: "Take in your hand a bundle of rushes, and strike herewith, and do not foreswear your oath." I understood that the first two verses contained the permission to write this chapter, nay the order to do so.[45]

Ujhurī certified that the third verse should be similarly understood, and other signs confirmed this reading to Hajarī. The latter was quite aware that the first verse, Quran 93:11 ("Speak about the blessing of your lord"), had at that time already become widely quoted in order to justify autobiographical writing and especially writing about the graces bestowed by God upon the writer.[46] Some even cited the verse in the titles of their life stories. These include two major Egyptian authors quoted by Hajarī, ʿAbd al-Wahhāb al-Shaʿrānī (ca. 1493–1565) and Jalāl al-Dīn al-Suyūṭī (1445–1505), whose work enjoyed wide readership during their lifetimes and long after their deaths.[47] Hajarī felt that he was the recipient of many special gifts and blessings, which included his ease in learning to write and read Arabic, the numerous times throughout his life when he miraculously recovered precious objects or writings he had lost, and his ability to cure sick people "merely by the sprinkling of water and by incantation by means of verses from the Noble Qur'an."[48] God also showed special attention to Hajarī by sending him a guardian angel who made sure he accomplished rituals such as prayer and the reading of the Quran in a timely and mindful fashion.[49] These signs of divine benevolence did not stop after Hajarī wrote about them, since he could add many such stories in his Tunis revision, alleviating his fear of bringing an end to the blessings by publicizing them.

His autobiographical anxiety might not have been a purely internal affair. He might have heard acquaintances express misgivings over his plans, and, in the Tunis revisions, he answers again potential doubters and defends more vigorously his project, in very telling ways.

> Should anyone say that it should have been [better][50] to have kept secret what I have mentioned in the last chapter, I would say to him: After I had composed the book to refute the Christians and the Jews on the basis of their own books, I mentioned in that chapter the experiences of a servant of God belonging to the Muhammadan community ... which will never happen ... to any Christian or Jew. ... The holy man ʿAbd al-Wahhāb al-Shaʿrānī, from Cairo, mentioned in his book entitled *Kitāb al-minan,* both miracles and marvels. ... A commentator of the Noble Qurʾan said about the meaning of the words of the Exalted God: "Speak about the grace of your Lord!": "Mentioning His blessings—He is Exalted!—is a form of gratitude to Him for them."[51]

Hajarī's defense of his writing against potential (or real) critics connects his blessings and the polemical part of his work, for which he was encouraged by famous scholars. Writing about divine benevolence is not to be read as boasting by an individual, but as illustrating that Muslim excellence is recognized by God. This argument tightens the connection between the body of the text and this last chapter, which is not a mere appendix, but a sort of apogee to the overall argument of the book, which extols the superiority of the last revealed religion over its two predecessors.

By mentioning Quran 93:11 again, Hajarī highlights how self-consciously he situates himself in a tradition of autobiographical writing, which is reinforced by the mention of Shaʿrānī who already felt compelled to write a defense of autobiography in the preface to his memoir.[52] Although Hajarī was far from alone in feeling autobiographical anxiety, his misgivings were clearly compounded by his self-consciousness as a minor writer. Nevertheless, thanks to his scholarly friends, especially Ujhurī, he overcame his fears and produced a text that he felt was well received by its learned readers and earned him a place in the Arabic Republic of Letters.

. . .

During his lifetime, Hajarī established himself as a courtier, secretary, envoy, translator, and writer. In all these roles, he drew on the many networks he established early on as member of a persecuted minority in Spain and kept extending throughout his life after his escape. His extant book records these associations and reinforces them. Narrating his life, he also connected with scholars who were among the most prestigious of their time. He thus situated his work in proximity to the more rarefied regions of Arabic learning, despite writing in Middle Arabic rather than the lofty classical form. Examining his career and his practice as a writer, chronicler, and autobiographer illuminates the complexities of his willful insertion into the Arabic literary field.

Although Hajarī is considered a minor writer in the Arabic Republic of Letters, this judgment, with which he probably would not have disagreed, should not be taken as disparaging. To return to Deleuze and Guattari, this word can imply an appreciation of the workings of a literary project rather than a harsh verdict on its import or quality. For example, the minor character of a work first reveals itself in the language it uses: "A minor literature doesn't come from a minor language; it is rather that which a minority constructs within a major language."[53] Exploring Hajarī's usage of a minor form of the Arabic language, his relation to Spanish and, most importantly, to Arabic, leads to a better understanding of his trajectory as a writer who fully accepts his status as minor but who nevertheless works at overcoming the limitations it might impose on him. Even his use of Spanish reveals his active solidarity with the Morisco exiles and thus exhibits a political dimension that Deleuze and Guattari consider to be an essential feature of the work of the minor writer.

Hajarī was well aware that his connections to the outside world, his travels, and his disputes with Christians and Jews were what most attracted the attention of those scholarly friends who encouraged him to write. If the book as an effort at reterritorialization in Arabic culture was successful overall, it also paints him as a man of the wider world, able to sustain networks and associations beyond his culture of choice, including with some of the most important European scholars of Arabic in his time. Throughout his work, he reflected on this position, relying not only on Arab-Islamic cultural references but also on his knowledge of others' scriptures, on his observations during his travels, and on a familiarity with European geography that he acquired out of personal interest and as a translator for Mūlay Zaydān.

If Orientalism as a field of knowledge is the product of a globalization of the culture of Europe in the early modern period, this development itself was made possible to an extent by an opening to the outside world that was happening at roughly the same time in the Arab and Ottoman lands—an opening that allowed for a more intense circulation of people and ideas. Exploring how Hajarī moved from the local to the global and participated in a transcultural phenomenon of a new imagination of the world, the next chapter analyzes how Hajarī integrated the Maghrib in a global intellectual history. It shows that the world Hajarī represents is itself multidimensional, and that his connection with European Orientalism played only a part in it.

FOUR

Hajarī in the World

IN CHAPTER 13 OF THE *SUPPORTER,* Hajarī describes a workday in the service of Mūlay Zaydān, probably sometime in the 1620s: "One day I was sitting, in the City of Marrakesh, to translate a treatise in Latin talking about the terrestrial and the celestial globe. Both of them were big globes, placed on a pedestal. On the celestial globe were drawn the stars, the fixed stars, the constellations, and the other figures known to the astronomers, provided with their names. Similarly, the terrestrial globe contained every known city of the world, the regions, countries and climates. Every country was provided with its name. So were the seas and the rivers."[1] This passage paints a striking portrait of Hajarī at work contemplating images of the earth and the heavens in the palace of the sultan. His interest in European cosmography not only helped his career in the court of Mūlay Zaydān but also nourished his own view of the world. Through his vast reading of texts and his exchanges with scholars and traders, clerics and diplomats, travelers and captives, he accumulated this new learning and assumed a critical position in transmitting knowledge across boundaries and between the different Republics of Letters.

This aspect of his work as a conveyor of knowledge and information is as important as the religious content that has been of primary interest to scholars. Religion is obviously essential, and his friends among the ulama were quite taken by his accounts of successful religious disputes. The *Supporter of Religion against the Infidels* makes an important contribution to that history of a storied tradition of Muslim-Christian polemics in the western Mediterranean, including the Lead Books controversy. The work is even considered as "one of the most important polemical treatises ever written in Arabic by a Morisco,"[2] while Hajarī himself is described as the "most famous of the polemicists of the Moriscos."[3]

Although a profoundly polemical work, the *Supporter* is far richer in scope. It broadens the meaning of the confrontation beyond its theological content as it belongs to the genre of travel literature and a long-standing tradition of Arabic autobiography from which it borrows tropes and references. The study of its literary form reveals a complex textual economy that includes the travel narrative, the autobiographical and the cosmographical, and a transcultural literature in the early modern period that proposed new ways to represent the world—a world much bigger than previously thought. The religious controversy, so important in the text, is tightly connected to these other meanings, and even the clearly polemical passages acquire supplemental significance beyond the dispute over dogma and rituals. From the local stage of southern Spain, Hajarī found himself presenting his arguments on a much larger scale, mostly during his travels in Europe, not only to defend his religion against detractors but also to bring back converts to Christianity to their former Islamic faith. Additional meanings emerge thanks to his relationships with captives in North Africa and Europe, intellectual interlocutors in the field of Orientalism, and even adversaries who could also be friends and allies and with whom he thus formed attachments. Religious controversy itself helped widen his vision of the world and of Islam's place in it.

Weaving together his performance as an apologist for Islam with his travel account and his knowledge of European cosmography, Hajarī reflected on the place of Islam and the Arabic language in a vast world. One of the most salient characteristics of his writing is the widening of vista in his description of the earth, which situated the author and his experience on an expansive worldly landscape. By connecting controversy to travel and cosmography, far from being confined to the local frame of early seventeenth-century Morisco polemical literature, Hajarī was able to situate his defense of Islam on a global stage.

HAJARĪ AS POLEMICIST: LEAD BOOKS BEGINNINGS

Hajarī's practice as a controversialist takes place in a long history in Islamic lands. In Spain in particular, "subject Muslims had a deep tradition of polemic,"[4] which helped defend a vulnerable population against forcible assimilation and produced numerous writings before and after the expulsion of the Moriscos.[5] After 1614, exiled Moriscos wrote to defend Islam and attack Christianity. Two main sites of this production were Marrakesh, especially the court of Mūlay Zaydān, and Tunis—two locales in which Hajarī became an eminent resident at different times. The Spanish-language polemical texts produced by Moriscos in Tunis include the two anonymous manuscripts tentatively ascribed to Hajarī by Gerard Wiegers,[6] and a text usually attributed to a friend of Hajarī's in Tunis, Ahmad al-Hanafī. Hajarī belonged in North Africa to intellectual milieus in which religious debate was part of the cultural landscape and was probably present in the upbringing and education of Moriscos.

His first experiences with polemical controversy were shaped by the Moriscos' dramatic confrontation with the Inquisition and their efforts to carve a place in Spanish society through the Lead Books forgeries of the Sacromonte and other fabrications.[7] By recounting the discovery of the relics of Granada in the first chapter of the *Supporter,* Hajarī assigned to it the function of a prologue to his polemical debates. His understanding of the *plomos* is unsurprisingly framed by his Islamic beliefs. The first critics to study the original documents since their anathematization described the parchment and analyzed the contributions of Hajarī, concluding that, contrary to many contemporaries, he was "convinced that the parchment was an ancient document, dating from the beginning of the Christian Era,"[8] to be read as a testimony to the truth of Islam. He considered the Lead Books to be proto-Islamic documents, an interpretation that contradicts many fellow exegetes, and, of course, the assessment of modern scholars.

In the *Supporter,* Hajarī first sketched a historical narrative, recounting the destruction of the Turpiana Tower and the discovery of the parchment and the handkerchief ascribed to Mary. Then, a few years later, the Lead Books were unearthed, and the search began for scholars able to decipher the documents. Historiography turned to autobiography, when Hajarī himself became a character in the plot and could thus obtain firsthand information about the momentous discovery. Later, he spread the knowledge of this episode beyond Spain, sometimes orally, mentioning it to Sultan Ahmad al-Mansūr and showing him a copy of the parchment,[9] and also in writing, in his 1612 appendix to his copy of Ibn Mālik's poem. The *Supporter* contains excerpts from the documents unearthed around Granada, including the text of the parchment and parts of some Lead Books. The Tunis version of the *Supporter* added texts in the first chapter, and in an appendix.[10] Hajarī thus took on the editorial task of the philologist, making available some *plomos,* adding commentary about the circumstances of their writing and of their discovery, and explaining why, in his estimation, the forms of the letters show

FIGURE 6. A Lead Book. Engraving made by Francisco Heylan (ca. 1584–ca. 1635), published in Diego Nicolás Heredia Barnuevo, *Mystico ramillete historico . . .*, Granada, Imprenta real, 1741. Creative Commons. Digitized by the University of Granada, http://digibug.ugr .es/handle/10481/32212.

that the documents had to be dated to the time of the Roman emperor Nero (see fig. 6).

In Granada, he held in his hands the parchment as well as some of the original Lead Books. In North Africa, he was able to consult and transcribe copies of these texts. The memory of the Lead Books circulated somewhat hazily among exiled Moriscos, as witnessed by John Harrison, an English agent in Morocco, who, in 1631, recalled that members of the diaspora in northern Morocco believed in prophecies of their return to Spain that were announced in a lead disc found near Granada.[11] Hajarī was a more reliable historiographer—and agent—of the dissemination of the *plomos*. He found transcripts of some documents in Marrakesh, including a copy of the *Book of the Maxims of Saint Mary*, which belonged to Fāris ibn al-ʻIlj, who, as a captive in Granada, had been asked to study the *plomos*.[12] Hajarī vouched for the similarity of this copy to the one he read in Granada, and cites verbatim the third maxim (out of 101). In Tunis, Hajarī discussed its meaning with the Morisco author Muhammad ibn ʻAbd al-Rafīʻ, and they agreed that this text announced Muhammad's mission. He also read a copy of the Lead Book called *Book of the Gifts of Reward,* brought to Tunis by Yūsuf al-Qalbu, and in 1637 added it as an appendix to the *Supporter.*

Hajarī did not doubt the weightiness and sanctity of the finds. He never questioned their authenticity and antiquity. He was aware that not all defenders of the Lead Books understood them to be proto-Islamic, many reading them as Christian. His editorial work tends to highlight what was easily understood as Islamic while ignoring passages about the Trinity that were more difficult to gloss away.[13] The translation he produced in Spain already promoted an Islamic reading of the texts, to the point that, he said, Archbishop Castro was displeased with his work.[14] Hajarī's religious beliefs filtered his understanding of the discoveries. His reading parallels the one offered by Spanish Christian defenders of the Sacromonte documents who, like him, took advantage of what cultural historian Seth Kimmel calls the "linguistic ambiguity and unstable theological grammar of the *libros plúm-beos*" to try to force them "through the process of canonization."[15] From the other shore, and a different religious perspective, Hajarī's aim was to establish the texts as quasi proto-scripture that announced the advent of Islam. According to him, the Sacromonte documents, buried for centuries and pro-tected from corruption, tell the truth about how original Christianity was aware of its own coming supersession by Islam and announced the mission of Muhammad. This is also how he read the scriptures of the Jews and the Christians, like all other Muslim polemicists. His historical and editorial approach to the Sacromonte documents in the first chapter accords with the hermeneutical method that he would deploy in his disputes.

The writing of the episode of the Lead Books on the *Supporter* also fore-shadows their literary form, where he would constantly anchor controversies in concrete detail and lived interaction, not restraining himself to abstract dogma and philological proof. His polemical accounts never let the reader forget that these are encounters between specifically situated people, whose exchanges include emotions and feelings. Telling of his involvement in the *plomos,* he intertwined it with anecdotes that highlight the plight of the Moriscos, and the tragic background against which the Sacromonte episode played out. When Archbishop Castro gave him the Medici printing of Idrisī's geography, he took it with him when he met visitors from his hometown, who were frightened by the sight of the book: "I told them: 'Do not be afraid. The Christians honour me and respect me for my ability to read Arabic. But all the people of my town thought that the Christian Inquisitors—who used to sentence and burn to death everyone who manifested his adherence to

Islam in any way or was reading the books of the Muslims—would condemn me as well.'"[16] Other passages show that despite his boast of being now respected by the Christians, he did not trust them, to the point that he was afraid of eating the food provided by Castro.[17]

The very end of the chapter recounts his last conversation with the archbishop before he left for Seville, and later for Morocco. They did not talk about the documents, their meaning, or their interpretation, but rather about the persecution of the Moriscos, their rejection by Spanish society, and the rarity of intermarriages between Old and New Christians. Connecting the reality of Morisco life in late sixteenth-century Spain with the deciphering of the Lead Books, Hajarī emphasized that the eventual failure of the Sacromonte episode to make a place for Moriscos in Catholic Spain was not rooted in mere philology and theology, but, more alarmingly, in society, politics, and emotions. This last exchange marked the abandonment of the hope that the *plomos* might have offered, "that religious discord and violence would end not when the truth of one religious tradition had dominated all the others, but rather when religion itself came to be defined by shared iconographies, histories and practices across traditional ecumenical lines."[18] This dream would stay unrealized, but it haunts Hajarī's recounting of his later disputes, which go beyond the strongly local face-to-face debates between Granadan Christians and Moriscos and are set on a much larger, even global, stage.

RELIGIOUS DEBATE AS PERFORMANCE

Hajarī's account of religious controversy doubles with a narrative of encounters with people. The religious debates are written as scenes, almost in a theatrical sense, very precisely situated in time and space, and for the most part incorporated within the story of his travels. The *Supporter* depicts Hajarī as a traveling debater who is moving from country to country and city to city, meeting Christians and a few Jews, and engaging in discussions about religion. The order of this narrative is more or less chronological and follows his peregrinations from Rouen to Paris, from Bordeaux to Toulouse, and from Amsterdam to Leiden, with only a few debates taking place in his adopted hometown of Marrakesh or in Cairo. The specific locations vary widely, with discussions set in the house of a French judge or the abode of a Dutch Orientalist, in the country castle of a high-ranking official or in a boat leading him from Bordeaux to Toulouse, in an apothecary shop or in a Parisian monastery.

To dismantle his adversaries' positions, he relied on a bibliography. He knew the Gospel presumably since his time in Spain. He read the Spanish version of the Old Testament in France, and later found again in Tunis the translation of the Bible by Cipriano de Valera.[19] One of his most cherished debating methods was to score points against his adversaries by citing chapter and verse from their own holy books, and by sometimes showing them that he knew their scriptures better than they did. A clear example occurred during a dinner in Paris when Hajarī sparred with a few lawyers, and talked about the two thousand pigs who threw themselves in the sea according to Mark 5:13: "They then said: 'They did not amount to the number you mentioned!' I answered: 'This is what I read!' They then brought the Gospel and found it as I mentioned it. This subject is mentioned twice in the Gospel: in the fifteenth chapter of Mark, who says: 'They were about two thousand.' Then they started to talk again, but did not find an answer."[20] He also relied on converts to Islam who wrote polemical texts: ʿAbd al-Haqq al-Islāmī, who was born a Jew,[21] and Anselm Turmeda / ʿAbd Allāh al-Turjumān al-Mayurqī, a converted Franciscan monk.[22] The latter's anti-Christian polemic influenced many Morisco authors after the expulsion.[23] Hajarī also mentions ʿAbd al-ʿAzīz al-Dinīrī (1215–97), author of a polemic against Christians.[24] He often cites the judge ʿIyād, author of an enormously successful treatise, which circulated widely among Moriscos and which to this day continues to play an important part in popular piety.[25] Hajarī quoted it in the *Supporter* and adapted parts of it in Spanish.[26]

Unsurprisingly, by depending on a bibliography and on a polemical tradition, Hajarī deploys classic themes, such as the refutation of the Trinity, the veneration of Christ as a prophet, but not as the son of God, and the attacks on the Church and the papacy, accused of changing dogmas based on whims. Even the legend of the woman named Joan who was elected pope while passing herself as a man was also told by other Morisco authors, including his friend Ahmad al-Hanafī.[27] More than once, in disputes with Erpenius and with a monk in Egypt, Hajarī argued that the Paraclete—often translated as "helper" or "advocate"—mentioned in the Gospel ("I will ask the Father, and he shall give you another Paraclete, that he will dwell with you forever"),[28] refers to Muhammad, another common theme in Muslim polemics.[29] Relying on a written tradition, Hajarī the debater essentially performs a well-known script for his adversaries and readers. The originality of his contribution thus does not lie in the content of the arguments but rather in the way he frames and presents them.

Indeed, differences in dogmas, ideas, or rituals are not the only important element in the disputes. These also prominently involve characters, and stage exchanges between Hajarī and other people—real people, not generic fictions. Some are explicitly named, and the identity of many others can be ascertained or guessed at from the context. These debaters often initiate the disputes, oppose counterarguments to the ones proffered by the author, and, most importantly, react to his responses. In these emotive confrontations, the most prominent character is Hajarī himself—not merely the individual but the authorial voice his text constructs and fashions. Urged by his ulama friends to write about these theological debates, he had to build the persona of a controversialist to prove not only his polemical skill, but more broadly, the value of his literary contribution.

Hajarī performed the defense of Islam in dramatized discussions, although in one case the controversy was written. For the most part, he recounts oral exchanges, and his reactions to his adversaries are as important as the content of his interventions. These performances elicited in him specific affects, depending on his success or failure in his task, that he described and analyzed in an illuminating passage:

> Whenever I exerted myself to refute the Christians during my disputes with them, I experienced a feeling of exaltation and exhilaration sent upon me from God, so that I was honoured in their eyes by mentioning the Unity of the Exalted God and remembering the graciousness of the Prophet—may God bless him and grant him peace!—and the nullity of the Trinity, as God has said: "Those who say: 'God is three' are infidels." Whenever I felt unable to refute them assailed by fear or worry, a feeling of shame on their part was sent down to me.[30]

By using strong emotions to mark the success or failure of his polemical encounters, Hajarī chose to stress feelings, affective responses, rather than merely the theological content of the arguments. This accords with recent turns toward the investigation of "economies of affect" that some scholars consider central to the study of religion.[31]

This self-assessment of his performance as a controversialist highlights that Hajarī understood his success as a debater and his ability to find the right arguments as an inspiration from God. More than once, the text suggests a direct divine guidance. In Paris, Hajarī, working with the French

Orientalist Étienne Hubert, read in the margin of a Quran owned by Hubert a gloss the latter had written in French about verse 2:223, which contains the following: "Your women are a tillage [fertile ground] for you, so approach your tillage as you please."[32] Hubert's gloss asserted that Muslims understand this passage as meaning that Islam authorizes the act of sodomy. Hajarī vigorously denied the claim and demanded that Hubert erase the note, to no avail. Later, the two men visited a church library. There was a book in Arabic: "I opened it to read it and the passage I found was an exegesis of the verse: 'Your women are a tillage for you.' It was unintentional on my part to look for this verse, but only as a result of Guidance from God—Praised be He!"[33] Thanks to the references and exegesis cited in the book, Hajarī convinced Hubert, who erased the offensive gloss. Many years later, a similar occurrence happened in Egypt, when, in the middle of a debate that lasted a few days, Hajarī dreamed of a Quranic verse which suggested an answer to his opponent.[34] Such direct help from God is akin to the blessings enumerated in chapter 13. Hajarī deduced from his strong emotional response that God wanted him to go to battle for Him, and used a word derived from jihad to describe this fight.[35]

In his combat against the enemies' untruths, Hajarī presented his arguments like an actor or a performer defending Islam against adversaries, and also like a diplomat speaking to foreigners. A quote from his friend Ragrāguī clarifies this mission. When time came to send an advocate to France for the robbed Moriscos, two men were considered, including Hajarī. Ragrāguī said that the other person should not be chosen because "he is an uneducated man. The priests and the Christians would doubt the sincerity of his religion. The only person who should go is you."[36] Hajarī noted in conclusion that as a result he had written this book, demonstrating again that his debating persona is strongly connected to his authorial voice. He proudly affirms that he acquitted himself beautifully as a representative and defender of Islam, drawing glowing reviews from his very adversaries, whose prejudices he unsettled. The guests at the Paris dinner told him: "We have seen men from among the adherents of your religion and we talked to them, but we never met anyone who talked or answered the way we have heard and seen you do."[37] Hajarī enjoyed these successes, and his account of the disputes consistently highlights the responses of the opponents. If his emotional responses are a vital part of his success as an apologist, the feelings of the adversaries are no less essential.

AFFECTIVE CONNECTIONS AND
THE DEFENSE OF ISLAM

Hajarī's narratives in the *Supporter* demonstrate that interaction opened the possibility for attachments, despite the religious disagreement.[38] The adversaries are often portrayed as dumbfounded, astonished, unable to answer his arguments. Maybe more surprisingly, they are also frequently pleased, and the disputes often resolve in laughter, banter, and good humor, and almost never in animosity. In most cases, the dispute is just a moment in a continuum of sociability. The narrative focuses on the debate, but the controversy itself happens against a background of social occasions, amiable exchange, and intellectual collaboration. Hajarī sparred with Hubert while they were working together on Arabic texts and visiting Parisian libraries and monasteries. Many of his French adversaries assisted him in his lawsuit. His very spirited dispute with the "judge of the Andalusians," Marc-Antoine de Gourgues, and his family and acquaintances happened during a pleasant dinner on the night of the Prophet's birthday. He brought to this occasion a surprising conclusion:

> I noticed they were glad and thankful to me, while they had only heard from me what I had related, and all that was contrary to their religion!
>
> Another day I got up and went to the judge, who handed me the papers I had asked him before, without asking me any money for it. At that occasion, the woman who had been talking with us took notice of me, while she took care that no one would see her. She gave me a lot of gold coins, due to the grace of God, my effort in defending the religion of Islam, and the blessing of the birthday of the Prophet.[39]

Far from resenting Hajarī's debating skills, the guests at the dinner felt increased friendliness toward him. Gourgues did not take money from him for his work, and Marie Tudert, his wealthy mother-in-law, rewarded him with gold. Hajarī considered that she was unwittingly doing God's work, honoring him for his combative defense of the true religion, but her gift was also a symbol of the generosity of spirit that prevailed even among adversaries. Another debater, Fayard, a member of the Bordeaux parliament, displayed the same liberality: he "used to give me a lot of advice, as he knew the Spanish Andalusian language. I owed him a lot of money and wanted to pay him, but he did not accept anything from me."[40] In fact, Hajarī's success as a debater, far from making him enemies, brought him friends: "God made me victorious over them, so that they said: "Whenever you need something of us, we will do it for you!"[41]

Hajarī as a controversialist is a combatant, but his fight is for the most part defensive, not offensive. The controversies are almost always initiated by the adversary, and his part in the dispute is in general apologetic rather than polemical. He is often prompted to protect his religion from mistaken or insulting assertions. This happens from the very first dispute with a trader in Rouen, who claimed that Islam condoned theft and adultery.[42] Even when the exchange deploys a common theme in Muslim anti-Christian polemic, such as the contradictions of the Trinity and the double nature of Jesus, Hajarī does not initiate the discussion. When he sparred about these issues with the merchant in Rouen, the latter first asserted the Christian view and challenged him to respond.[43] Twice, he had to refute the old canard that the tomb of Muhammad is suspended in the air by magnets.[44] This floating-coffin fabrication emerged in Europe in the twelfth century and was used to connect the Prophet of Islam with magic and trickery.[45] Three times, Hajarī answered questions about the Islamic representations of paradise in response to Christian debaters who expressed shock at the notion that Muslims "believe that the inhabitants of Paradise are eating and drinking and enjoying delights similar to those of this world."[46] He also compared more than once the fasts in the Islamic and Christian faiths, citing not only scripture but also sometimes the classical medical thinking of Ibn Sīnā, Hippocrates, and Galen.[47]

His adversaries' admiration for Hajarī's debating skills does not, of course, mean that he had truly convinced them of the falsity of their religion and the truth of Islam. Although a cousin of Fayard facetiously asked Hajarī to refrain from converting his elderly uncle,[48] he did not aim to effect such a drastic change. Neither did his adversaries. The debaters in a polemic, on both sides, are playing well-known parts in a familiar script on the frontier between religions. Doing so, they performed the way in which they could coexist if not in the same society, at least at the level of exchange between members of the elite. The success of Hajarī is not measured by his capacity to convert his opponents, but by his ability to lower the level of hostility against Islam. He plays the role of a diplomat rather than an antagonist, which explains why so many discussions do not look like disputes at all. The exchanges often do not focus on theological differences, and simply attempt to correct misconceptions, or even merely convey information. One of his earliest accounts of discussion with Gourgues ends with the debaters being in complete agreement: "The question he posed to me was: 'Can a good deed by anyone else reach a man after he has died?' I answered him: 'Our Prophet— may God bless him and grant him peace!—said: "When a man dies his work comes to an end, apart from three cases: an ongoing act of charity, a fruit of scholarship from which people may benefit, or a pious child who prays for him!"' He was very happy because this agreed with their own belief."[49] In some discussions, Hajarī simply teaches his interlocutors about Islam. On a boat on the Garonne River, he explained to two monks the reason for the ritual ablutions of the Muslims.[50] Later, in the Netherlands, Hajarī encountered a physician, who expressed his surprise that the Quran does not mention any miracles by Muhammad. Hajarī referred him to many books on the subject, including the treatise by the judge 'Iyād. The conversation then moved to how to distinguish authentic miracles from tricks by charlatans, and never turned to religious difference and controversy.[51] Some amicable discussions concerned the political system. Hajarī recounted in some detail conversations with Gourgues about the succession of a king,[52] and the general well-being in France, which the judge attributed to Christianity. Hajarī answered: "Your legal rules and the law of your religion were not derived from the Gospel. Your law follows the doctrine of the Heathens who were living in Rome. The books of your law have been translated from their books, like the great book entitled *Baldu,* etcetera." The judge said: "You are right!"[53] The two men might have compared the aftermath of the assassination of Henri IV on May 14, 1610, and the turmoil that followed the death of Ahmad al-Mansūr in 1603, about which Hajarī himself complained in his Paris letter. Recounting these discussions amid the more obvious controversial disputes, Hajarī situates the latter, beyond the content of the polemics and on the continuum of sociable exchange, as another level more open to emotional attachments of his interaction with Christians.

Even love and desire could interfere. Among the originalities of Hajarī's account is the inclusion of a number of disputes with women. These discussions led to the expression of stronger personal emotions than his debates with men. In his account of the May 13, 1612, banquet, Hajarī put Marie Tudert front and center in the conversation, highlighting their exchanges and emphasizing that they often tended to turn toward a discussion of the Islamic laws regulating the relations between the sexes. These themes are also central in Hajarī's account of his discussions with two young women while he was visiting a property belonging to a high-ranking official near Olonne. The first encounter is described more in terms of sexual temptation than of religious disagreement. In this episode, which offers more details about the circumstances of the encounter than is usual in Hajarī's book, the scene was dramatically set in an opulent country castle, surrounded by gardens, woods, and extensive agricultural lands. In this idyllic environment, he met a female guest. His conversations with the young woman include many flirtatious repartees. She asked him to describe the ideal of feminine beauty in his country. After he complied, "She said, 'You are right!' She said this, because she herself was white and a bit reddish. Her hair, including the hair of her eyebrows and eyelashes, was black. She had pitch-dark eyes. Among the French, the beauty of such woman was disregarded, and they used to say: 'She is black.'"[54] Her reaction suggests that, when asked to portray the most beautiful woman in his eyes, he described the one who was in front of him. Another coy exchange was disguised as mere inquiry about his culture: "The girl preened herself and asked me whether there were people in my country who were wearing clothes of silk like herself?"[55] thus attracting his attention to her attire. They were brought closer when she offered to teach him French, and their "mutual love" increased to the point that Hajarī felt the strain of temptation: "I said to myself: 'Before this you were opposing the Christians in matters of money and were engaged in the holy effort to defend your religion, but now you will have to oppose your own soul and Satan!'"[56] Hajarī connected here the two other wars he was waging: a material struggle, to obtain retribution for the robbed Moriscos, and a spiritual fight, to defend Islam against its detractors. He did not expect this new battle against his own desires in defense of his soul. This episode puts in sharp focus the importance of Hajarī's feelings in his representation of his encounters with Christians, an element that distinguishes his text from other polemical texts.

The mutual attraction between Hajarī and the brunette led him to some soul-searching, and to a meditation on the nature of temptation and the means to resist it. The reader thus might get closer to Hajarī the private man. However, his dramatization of the episode also shows that his authorial voice, so strongly linked to his performance in disputation, was also connected to his role as eminent defender of the Moriscos. In his travels in France, Hajarī was accompanied by Moriscos, and the episode with the brunette reveals that he felt that he was not simply entrusted with their legal representation but also in charge of their spiritual matters. One of his companions was surprised by his flirtation with the young woman, "as I had been admonishing them to restrain themselves from their inclination toward forbidden women."[57] Hajarī soon understood that his friend was really Satan's unwitting conduit, trying to weaken his resolve to resist temptation. His companion told him that not only was the young woman willing to engage in some more involved flirting, but that in France, no one would consider "this is misbehavior."[58] Hajarī responded that "in our religion we are forbidden to do that," and cited a verse from the very famous devotional poem "al-Burda" ("The Mantle") by Muḥammad al-Būṣīrī (1211–94), which warns that by yielding a little to temptation one does not weaken but rather strengthen it.

The attraction between him and the French woman persists, even after she learns about his wife and children, until one day they came close to acting on it. They went for a walk toward the edge of the gardens where wild trees could protect them from view: "We had a talk there and I understood the state she was in, though this was well known to me already. Then one of my friends called me from the gardens and approached me. She went away. God set me free by His grace, benevolence, protection and gracious favour. I ask God for forgiveness for the words I expressed to her and for having looked at her."[59] This elliptically reported conversation and its sudden interruption finally freed him from his forbidden attraction. When another pretty young woman came to the castle, the exchange between them is more akin to other encounters, when, untroubled by desire, he was able to effectively defend Islam again. The new visitor was initially hostile and provoked a dispute. Hajarī demonstrated to her that by rejecting images and idols Muslims obey God's commandments better than Christians do: "Looking at the other women, she told them in their language: 'He has beaten me! I do not know what to answer him.' I looked at her and noticed that she became very glad and relaxed, as if a veil had been removed from her heart. She then turned to me with nice words. The anger and the fury she had been fostering toward the Muslims had disappeared."[60] Hajarī was able to make his adversary see Islam, and Muslims, in a better light, and the discussion with the young woman then proceeded more like an amicable exchange of information instead of a contentious controversy, and she asked him questions about how Muslims count time, about women's veil, and the possibility of premarital courtship in his country. At this point, Hajarī was done with the encounter with the young woman but not with the information that he wanted to share with the reader, explaining the social interactions between unmarried men and women deemed acceptable in France and the Netherlands. Back to religious matters, he gave the list of God's commandments and continued to examine the question of idols to show that both Judaism and Christianity prohibit them but only Muslims truly obey this fundamental rule.

As a traveling debater, Hajarī was thus providing his adversaries with a better knowledge of Islam at a time when, as he was well aware, some Europeans were in the process of amassing information on the subject. He was himself gaining a broader understanding of the world through his readings and his encounters with people. Three moments in the text open to a broader representation of the world, which makes his polemics, although rooted in the Morisco experience and cultural milieu, a conduit through which he widened his intellectual horizon to a much larger stage. Among the most heavily rewritten chapters of the *Supporter,* chapter 10 narrates disputes Hajarī engaged in with Jews in Bordeaux and Amsterdam. Like the discussions with Christians, his polemic was nourished with books obtained both in Europe and the Maghrib. After his return to Marrakesh, he read the book penned by the convert from Judaism 'Abd al-Haqq al-Islāmī, which bolstered his view that the Bible announced the mission of Muhammad, a common theme in Muslim polemics, though it "never became as important for Islam as the typological and allegorical interpretation of the Hebrew Bible was for Christianity."[61] Again, Hajarī mostly took an apologetic posture, defending Islam against attacks, as when the Jewish scholar began a dispute by noting that Hagar, mother of Ismā'īl, ancestor of the Arabs, was Abraham's slave.

The chapter goes through a few other well-known topoi in Muslim-Jewish polemics, including the supposed Jewish arrogant disrespect for the prophets,[62] and the possibility of abrogation, which allows for the advent of Islam and its rejection of previous errors. Hajarī nevertheless insists that, read correctly, the Old Testament accords with Islam on the prohibition of alcohol or the condemnation of idols, both themes to which the *Supporter* returns several times. On other matters, the rabbis have abusively relaxed some biblical rules, such as the ritual washing after sex, while Muslims fastidiously preserve their purity. Hajarī brought a personal touch to age-old arguments regarding the unreliable transmission of the biblical text, suggesting that the Bible had not been preserved through the generations and might have been tampered with.[63] He compared this carelessness with the ubiquity of the Quran in all Muslim countries, and, close to his own experience, to the way Moriscos protected their Holy Book even against terrible persecution, "the severe infliction and the intense surveillance by the Infidels against those who were found to possess it, who were killed, whose properties were confiscated, and who were burnt."[64] To the already present standard themes borrowed from the polemical tradition, the Tunis rewriting of the *Supporter* also added a sizable amount of text which considerably widened the chapter's scope of meaning and put the defense of Islam on a world stage informed by cosmographical knowledge, as we shall see later in this chapter.

Another polemical encounter opens to a similar widening of vista. The first third of chapter 12, another addition made in Tunis, differs from the usual writing mode hitherto established by the text. In this case, the debate with the adversary is epistolary and more intellectual, leaving less room for the emotional exchange prevalent elsewhere. It recounts his debates in Marrakesh with a monk, whom he describes as "one of the great scholars of the Christians," who "arrived in a ship that was sailing from the Indies to the country of al-Andalus, in order to attend the assembly that was sending monks to various parts of the world."[65] Hajarī is undoubtedly talking about Christoval de Flores, Franciscan, Definitor of New Spain, and bound to attend the General Chapter, who died in captivity in 1626.[66] After his capture, the monk wrote to Hajarī, knowing that he had previously interceded for the release of Antoine de Sainte-Marie. This letter, written to solicit his help in getting ransomed, launched epistolary debates between the two men about several topics, including the difference between God's and man's attributes and the buying of indulgences. In this exchange, the adversary is the one in foreign territory, in which he found himself involuntarily, as a captive. The monk was coming from America, which might be relevant beyond the religious polemic in that Hajarī, whose interest in the wider world deeply informed his writings and his revisions of the *Supporter,* might have discussed the newly known continent with Christoval. One or both of the captive monks collaborated with Hajarī in translating books, mostly in the field of cosmography, for Mūlay Zaydān, and both are said to have had intellectual exchanges with the sultan himself.

Another episode recounted in the *Supporter,* which approaches the issue of captivity more directly than any other, also links controversy and the representation of the world. Although its ostensible content seems far from religious debates, it actually connects with it in a more circuitous way and helps us better understand how Hajarī conceived his religious role. In a number of cases, he does not limit himself to recounting his performance with adversaries but develops the themes beyond the dispute, adding supplemental information about the changes brought to dogma by the popes, or about the theological underpinnings of purity rituals. This is related to an important aspect of Morisco polemics. Critics have observed that these are not only aimed at the adversary but also, crucially, address fellow Moriscos, teaching them Islamic doctrine and practices and showing them the irrationality and falsity of the Christian beliefs in which they had been raised and to which they were attached, at least in appearance and maybe much more deeply. There are in effect two audiences to Hajarī's polemic. In his (mostly) oral performances, he staged his encounters with Christian or Jewish adversaries. In his writing, he addressed his fellow Muslims and, maybe more precisely, the Moriscos.

Fulfilling this purpose, parts of the *Supporter* are akin to the devotional and theological translations contained in the Bologna manuscript. Like them, they present similarities to the early modern transnational and transreligious production of religious manuals for the general public, as part of a phenomenon called *confessionalization*. First used to describe the crystallization of differences in rituals between Catholics and Protestants, some scholars have argued that this term can be profitably employed to describe social features and texts observed in the Ottoman Empire.[67] In the post-expulsion era, and especially in Tunis, there was a concerted effort on the part of the Morisco elite to produce texts aimed at instructing refugees in the Islamic religion, of which they might be quite ignorant since most of "the Moriscos who settled in Tunisia came from Aragón and Castile, areas where they had been deeply acculturated to Spanish society from an early date, having lost the Arabic language and the Islamic religion."[68] Hajarī participated in the pedagogical enterprise of helping them become well-adjusted subjects of an Islamic state, and the *Supporter* bears many traces of this effort. Highlighting the deep agreement between the Quran and the Gospel, when the latter is read correctly, he suggests that the Moriscos could become true Muslims without completely renouncing their attachment to the scripture they had been raised to follow.

Participating in the movement of confessionalization, parts of Hajarī's text addressed Moriscos, as people in need of Islamization or re-Islamization. A story he told about two Turkish ladies who were captured on their way to the pilgrimage in Mecca, and then brought to Paris, shows him pursuing a similar effort. Hajarī recalled this interesting encounter at the very end of the chapters devoted to France and just before he turns his attention to his trip to Holland.

> In Paris, I also saw two Turkish women, one of them an old woman, the other about forty years of age. She was occupied with beautiful work for the

Sultana. All the women marveled at her fine and elegant embroidery. The Sultana paid her a big *riyāl* every day. I asked her why she had come from the lands of the Muslims to France. She answered: "We were at sea on our way to perform the hajj, when we were captured by the Christians who took us to Venice. The ambassador of the Sultan of France wrote to inform the Sultana about our work. She wrote to him to send us to her. Then, the Sultana and the women of the notables invited her to convert to their religion which she did." . . . She told me that she belonged to the venerable household of the Sultans of Istanbul.[69]

The tale of the Turkish captives is a revealing account of the way Hajarī considered his religious mission. This lady was educated, and both she and her older companion could read Arabic. In France, they were in the service of the "Sultana," Marie de Medici, daughter of the grand duke of Tuscany, widow of King Henri IV, mother of Louis XIII, and queen regent from 1610 to 1617. They were brought to France by François Savary de Brèves, who, after twenty-two years in Istanbul, was ambassador of France in Rome until 1614, and advised Marie de Medici in her diplomatic communications with Italian courts.[70] He was known for procuring for members of the French elite artifacts and objects from the Levant, including a beautiful rug for the palace of the queen that he had ordered from Turkish craftsmen.[71] He was also on the lookout to acquire skilled Muslim captives, and he sent experienced artisans to the queen, who was a committed patron of the arts and an amateur of oriental embroidery. In 1609, he brought five female embroiderers from the eastern Mediterranean to France.[72] This number included two Turkish women, Catherine and Marie Daime or Esmain.[73] These are undoubtedly the ladies that Hajarī met in Paris.[74]

The "beautiful work" noted by Hajarī was known to the most acclaimed French poet of his time, François de Malherbe (1555–1628), who on April 6, 1614, informed his friend the French antiquarian Nicolas Fabri de Peiresc that two "Turkish ladies" were making a superb dress for the queen's favorite, the Maréchale d'Ancre, to wear at the wedding of Louis XIII and Anne of Austria.[75] The skilled embroiderers were paid more or less the level of pay of other craftsmen, and were lodged, at the queen's expense, in the convent of the Ursulines.[76] This choice of place was not fortuitous: employing and converting infidels or heretics, thus saving their souls, was a work of religion. Indeed, the two Turkish women converted to Christianity. Hajarī, however, demonstrated to the younger lady that only Islam could save her and her companion, deploying efforts that accord with his commitment to the re-Islamization of the Moriscos: "I told her the matters God had inspired me with concerning religions, and also that today no one would be rescued outside the religion of Islam. I produced to her proofs thereof."[77]

This brief summary of these religious discussions leaves one wishing for a more detailed account, since this encounter resulted in one of his most resounding victories in his defense of Islam. His arguments probably echoed passages of the *Supporter*. Hajarī's experience as a polemicist, and his intimate understanding of the thinking of those who are situated between Islam and Christianity, served him well. He convinced his interlocutor so completely that the younger lady requested his support to escape, since the queen would not let them go. Later, in the Netherlands, Hajarī activated his broad transnational political network to assist them. He met again Pieter Coy, whom he had helped release from incarceration in Marrakesh, and he promised to return the favor:

> I told him: "There are two Turkish women in France, in Paris. They happened to embrace the religion of the Christians, but they asked me to arrange their return to the lands of the Muslims. I am returning to Marrakesh in these days, the Exalted God willing. How can I still arrange their return for them?"
>
> He answered me: "Write to both of them that they should come to my house, and I will arrange their return to their country."
>
> I wrote that to them and sent the letter to an Andalusian man who conveyed it to them. The Exalted God withdrew them from the sight of people on their way from France, until they reached the Netherlands. Their case was arranged with the Prince, and he sent them to Istanbul in a ship of merchants, where they arrived safely. He did this for them after I had left that country, and I did not see them again.[78]

The story of the Turkish captives also shows how Hajarī's networks and writings connected the local and the global. If the Morisco polemic is strongly local, his intervention in this case illustrates his larger commitment to bringing back lapsed Muslims to the true faith.

Other documents help fill out details of the story and show the intervention of another important character belonging to the Mediterranean diplomatic networks. Samuel Pallache was Mūlay Zaydān's agent in the Netherlands from 1609 until his death in 1616. Hajarī probably discussed with him the fate of the Turkish ladies. A letter by Pallache dated late May or early June 1615 was addressed to the powerful Khalīl Pasha, chief admiral and later grand vizier of the Ottoman sultan, and mentioned an official, named Ismāʿīl Aga, whose sister had been captured and held in France.[79] This is undoubtedly the younger woman that Hajarī met in Paris. One of the queen's Turkish embroiderers was named "Catherine Esmain," and Esmain in early modern European texts is a very common misspelling for Ismāʿīl. The letter did not name Hajarī, and Samuel Pallache was clearly taking sole credit for her liberation.[80] Sometime after May 1616, his brother Joseph testified in front of the States General that Samuel was worried that the French ambassador in The Hague, Benjamin Aubery du Maurier (1566–1636), might try to abduct "Catherine Esmain" and her female companions.[81] In the end, on the orders of Maurits of Nassau, the Turkish captive and her retinue embarked on a Dutch ship that led them to Tunis, where she was met by an envoy of Khalīl Pasha. She arrived in Istanbul on January 5, 1616, and was "most peacefully and hospitably delivered to the authorities."[82]

The story of the French queen's Turkish embroiderers—which played out in Istanbul, Venice, Paris, the Hague, and Tunis—illustrates dramatically the large scale of Hajarī's text. Through the role of Savary de Brèves, it confirms that early modern Orientalism was connected to the wider circulation across borders, in both its positive and negative aspects, including captivity and enslavement. Hajarī's sustained collaboration with some prominent European Orientalists made him aware of these paradoxes and contributed to the way he situated Islam on a global stage. Besides, the *Supporter* does not separate Orientalism from its author's commitment to polemic and records religious exchanges with some of his learned interlocutors, especially Hubert, who also introduced him to monks with whom he debated, and Erpenius, who alluded in his correspondence to Hajarī's skill in this exercise: "We had frequent disputations about religion, but, believe me, some of their errors are not as easy to refute as many suppose."[83] If Hajarī's controversy is embedded in the specific context of Morisco anti-Christian polemics, it also belongs to a larger transcultural landscape of religious conflict and controversy to which Orientalism was connected. As seen earlier, controversy shaped the career of many native speakers or Easterners who made decisive contributions to the discipline and was an essential part of the work of many European Orientalists. Hajarī's acquaintance with those circles in Europe led him to situate his own practice of polemical exchange and writing beyond the Morisco milieu. It made him cognizant of the circulation that rendered Orientalism possible: circulation of objects and books, that he witnessed and to which he contributed, and circulation of people, like the ambassador Savary de Brèves and the Turkish captives. This awareness informed his view of the world, now known to be much larger than previously thought. Beyond any material rewards, he benefited intellectually from his collaboration with Orientalists in ways that nourished his reflections and provided him with arguments to support his conception of the worldwide eminence of the Arabic language, to which these foreigners had devoted their energies, and which occupies a strategic place in Hajarī's representation of the world.

HAJARĪ AND COSMOGRAPHY

In the *Supporter,* Hajarī presents his vision of the world in a comprehensive way, synthesizing his studies in the natural sciences and his religious thinking and interweaving his knowledge of European cosmography and the Islamic civilizational framework to which he adhered. His borrowings from the new learning devised by Flemish cartographers, Spanish astronomers, and Portuguese explorers, is not limited to discrete information that he incorporated in his picture of the regions of the world. More importantly, their study informed his cosmographic view of the world that embraced and described the world as a totality, so perfectly encapsulated in the globes he was observing in the palace of the sultan.

From Spain to the later stages in his life, Hajarī demonstrated a constant interest and involvement in cosmography and related sciences, predating his move to Morocco, and still evident when he sojourned in Cairo. In Egypt, wanting to calculate the right time to perform a ritual of the hajj, he looked for a book of astronomy titled "*Taʿdīl al-Kawākib,* from which I wanted to find out on which day the halting in ʿArafa would take place, as well as other events that fall on the days of the new moons."[84] Decades earlier, he came in contact with a study of the earth and heavens spurred by different reasons in Spain, where the colonial expansion had made the study of cosmography crucial to the culture and the state. Hajarī spent time in Seville, an important node of information exchange with the New World. At the end of the sixteenth century, most cosmographical production in Spain was not taking place in universities but in political institutions, which included in Seville the Casa de Contratación, or House of Trade, established to regulate all commerce and navigation to the Americas.[85] The Casa also held debates between pilots and cosmographers over epistemological and methodological issues. One of the most important position in the Casa was that of pilot major, whose role was to establish the officially sanctioned navigation routes to the

Americas, and to examine and license pilots. The first and maybe most famous of these pilot majors was Amerigo Vespucci.

A number of prominent authors belonging to that milieu appear in a passage of chapter 6 of the *Supporter.* All of them belonged to the "community of experts,"[86] who produced knowledge about America that found a wide European audience, and that, through Hajarī, reached North Africa. These scholars include Rodrigo Zamorano, with whom Hajarī had been acquainted to some extent.[87] This university-trained cosmographer was first appointed in the Casa de Contratación in 1575, where he fulfilled over the years all of the important positions, including professor of cosmography and pilot major. A respected author and translator, he published a Spanish version of the first six books of Euclid's *Elements,* and a navigation manual, the *Compendio de la arte de navegar* (Seville, 1581), with updated astronomical tables. Like other practitioners at the Casa, Zamorano's cosmography emphasized the mathematical aspects of the discipline over its humanistic roots. In the same passage, Hajarī referred to earlier authors, including the "astronomer Kurtish," identified by the editors of the *Supporter* as Martín Cortés de Albacar (1510–82), and author of the *Breve compendio de la esfera* (Seville, 1551), one of the most widely read navigation manuals of its time. He also mentioned a writer whose name he transcribed as "Jabbish," who has to be identified as Jeronimo de Chaves (1523–74), first professor of cosmography at the Casa and author of the bestselling *Chronographia o Repertorio de los tiempos,* first published in 1548. Hajarī's interest in Spanish, and especially Sevillan cosmography, which emphasized mathematical and theoretical over practical knowledge, is related to his propensity to provide the position of cities and regions in degrees. The passage in which these luminaries are mentioned, however, relies on the less technical contents of their contributions, since Hajarī used some of their books on chronology to point to the changes to Christian dogma brought by the popes over the centuries, which, in his mind, demonstrates that Christianity is at the mercy of the whims of the pontiffs.[88]

Kindled in Spain, Hajarī's interest in this field of knowledge did not abate when he moved to Marrakesh, where soon he began to acquaint himself with North African astronomy and astrology. He studied "*'ilm al-ahkām,*"[89] or astrology, with Ahmad al-Ma'yūb (or al-Masyūb) al-Fāsī, astrologer, and practitioner of geomancy (*al-khāṭt al-rimlī*).[90] Other sources state that Ma'yūb was also reputed for his work in astronomy. According to Ifrānī, he was a *mu'aqqit,* an astronomer who specialized in timekeeping, known for a commentary on a treatise by famed mathematician and astronomer Ibn al-Bannāʾ (1256–1321).[91] Hajarī knew that Maʿyūb held such a privileged position in Ahmad al-Mansūr's court that the sultan made available to him his rich library, which comprised thirty-two thousand volumes. However, he criticized his pretention to predict the future and his rumored interest in magic. Insisting that predictive astrology is not credible, he recalled a discussion with another of the learned men he met in his travels, the unnamed and unidentified "greatest astronomer" in Paris, who agreed with him, citing the conjectures of the constellations that could not announce the assassination of Henri IV.[92] Hajarī himself was told in Seville by "two major astrologers" that he would not live beyond forty or fifty years, and Maʿyūb forecast for him a sixty-six-year-long life. Hajarī proved them all wrong, as he was still alive and writing at age seventy-four. He might have had another reason to keep his distance from Maʿyūb, considering how the latter allegedly met his end. The unfortunate astrologer predicted to Mūlay Zaydān that he would lose an important battle. Fearing that he would spread the rumor of a coming defeat, the sultan had him strangled.[93]

Being in the service of Mūlay Zaydān as secretary and translator rather than astrologer, Hajarī presumably did not risk such a fate. His work documents that Mūlay Zaydān kept, like his father, an active patronage of astronomy, including a curiosity and awareness of European work in the domain, maybe encouraged by the number of Moriscos at the Saʿdī court. Marrakesh, during the reign of Ahmad al-Mansūr and Zaydān, followed a trend observed in European courts when "in the course of the sixteenth century there arose an entirely new kind of princely and aristocratic involvement in astronomy, an involvement in which astronomical observations, instruments, models, and ultimately world systems themselves became objects of courtly production, exchange, and competition."[94] One significant and influential result of this common interest of sultan and translator in astronomy is the Arabic version of an important early modern work, which would be studied and commented upon for centuries. It was authored by Abraham Zacuto (1450–1515), "one of the most prominent astronomers of the late Middle Ages in the Iberian Peninsula,"[95] who studied in Salamanca, and then, after the expulsion of the Jews from Spain in 1492, continued his career in Portugal, where he held the title of astronomer of the king. He moved later to the Maghrib and then to the Levant, where he spent the end of his life.[96]

Zacuto was prominent among a group of astronomers who converted the great progress made in trigonometry and astronomy in Iberia during the previous few centuries into a practical knowledge that facilitated cross-ocean travel. His most important work was the *Great Treatise,* completed in Hebrew in 1478, based on the Alfonsine Tables, and composed of sixty-five tables giving the positions of the sun, the moon, and the five planets, presented in the form of an almanac, and of canons or instructions explaining their use. It became widely influential mostly through an adaptation by one of his disciples, Joseph Vizinho, and printed in 1496 under the title *Almanach perpetuum,* both in Latin and in Spanish.[97] This almanac provided accurate tables, and thus made possible "mathematically correct predictions of the sun's seasonal position in relationship to the earth."[98] Hajarī's version of the Castilian canons, though not the only Arabic translation of the text, helped ensure that Zacuto's work would also influence Maghribi culture. Five copies of his version, known as *Zīj Zakūt* (The Astronomical Tables of Zakūt), or *al-Risāla al-Zakūtiyya* (The Epistle of Zakūt), are held in libraries in Milan, Rome, Rabat, and Cairo, and many Maghribi astronomers quoted this adaptation (see fig. 7).[99]

Other translations produced by Hajarī for Mūlay Zaydān have unfortunately not been found, but the information he provides allows us to complete our picture of his contribution to courtly cosmography in early seventeenth-century Marrakesh. One translation is of a book of geography entitled *Darān,* "after a huge mountain called by this name which is known to geographers as the hugest mountain of the world," as stated in the *Supporter.* This book was "written in the language of the Frenchmen. The author of the book was called al-Qabitān. All the countries and rivers of the world were depicted in that book, together with the breadth and length of each country. The area and place of origin of each river was specified, together with the cities lying along its banks, each of them with its name. It also contained all the seas, islands, and areas."[100]

The editors of the *Supporter* suggest that the book in question is Pierre Davity's *Les Estats et Empires du monde* (1614). However, since *Darān* is a North African name for the Atlas Mountains, a more convincing identification has been proposed by Pierre Ageron: this book is likely the *Atlas* conceived by Gerhard Mercator (1512–94), arguably the most important cartographer of the sixteenth century, and revised and augmented after his death by Jodocus Hondius (1563–1612). Several editions were published, including an in-quarto *Atlas Minor* in 1607. The in-quarto version was less cumbersome than the previous in-folio. A French translation of the *Atlas Minor,* first published in 1609, was made by Lancelot de La Popelinière. La Popelinière

FIGURE 7. Last page of a manuscript of *al-Risāla al-Zakūtiyya* (The Epistle of Zakūt). The last paragraph on the page states that Ahmad al-Hajarī translated the treatise. Hasaniyya Library, Rabat, MS 8184. By permission.

fought during the French civil wars, which might explain why he was described as the "Captain."[101] Hajarī's translation of the *Atlas Minor* predates by decades the Turkish one made in 1654 by Kātip Çelebi—with the help of Sheikh Mehmed Ikhlasī, a French convert to Islam—that is considered a watershed in the cultural relations between Islamic and European countries.[102] The pioneering role of Hajarī and of his patron Mūlay Zaydān deserves wider recognition.

Hajarī might have acquired the well-known *Atlas Minor* during his travels in Europe. However, it is possible that the book arrived in Morocco thanks to networks of scholarly and diplomatic exchange and might have been the atlas sent by Erpenius to Mūlay Zaydān in 1624, as Thomas Le Gendre recounted. Hajarī used a quote from this treatise to bolster the common argument in Islamic anti-Christian and anti-Jewish polemic that their scriptures are undermined by their geographical inaccuracies. In this case, the evidence concerned the four rivers that they claim come from paradise even though it "is known today that each of these four rivers are in different countries."[103] To counter this notion, he quotes not only Shaʿrānī (only one of the many Muslim authors who pointed to that mistake),[104] but also "al-Qabitān," who remarked: "The statement, found in our Old Testament, which says that the rivers spring from one place is false and a lie, as is confirmed by eye-witnesses."[105] This seems to paraphrase the discussion of the earthly paradise and other states in *Atlas Minor*: ". . . they used to situate the sources of these four rivers in places where they do not appear."[106]

Another of Hajarī's geographical translations has been identified as the *Tractatus de Globis et eorum usu*, first published in Latin in 1594 by Robert Hues, the English mathematician, explorer, and companion of Richard Hakluyt (d. 1616), a geographer and ardent promoter of Elizabethan overseas expansion in North America.[107] This treatise was written to explain how to use the Molyneux Globes, in all likelihood the ones that Hajarī described admiringly in chapter 13 of the *Supporter* (see figs. 8a and 8b). The work, undertaken with the help of a captive, was commissioned by the sultan, who "ordered me to translate that treatise. I told him: 'It is written in the Latin language, which I do not know!' He asked: 'Who knows Latin?' I answered: 'A monk, who is one of the captives of your sublime court.' He said: 'Let him sit with you!'"[108]

The superb Molyneux Globes, the first to be printed in England, were published in 1592 and dedicated to Elizabeth I. Although the celestial globe was not very different from the one produced in 1551 by Mercator, the terrestrial globe highlighted the recent English achievements in navigation and the power of the monarchy. Financed by a rich merchant, they were produced by Emery Molyneux (d. 1598), who hired Jodocus Hondius to draw the engravings and the cartographer, instrument maker, and mathematician Edward Wright (d. 1615) to plot the coastlines.[109] How these beautiful and prestigious objects found their way to Marrakesh is not known, although a letter sent by an English merchant established in the Saʿdī capital, and who happened to be the brother-in-law of Edward Wright, suggests one avenue. Thomas Bernhere informed his learned relative in a letter dated June 24, 1600,[110] that Ahmad al-Mansūr was sending an ambassador to London and was "much delighted in the studie of astronomie and astrologie" and keen on obtaining instruments of that field. And so were "his sonnes, who all are

FIGURES 8a and 8b. Molyneux Celestial and Terrestrial Globes, The Honourable Society of Middle Temple, London, 2022. By permission. © I thank the Masters of the Bench of the Honourable Society of the Middle Temple.

exceedingly studious of matters tending this way." Therefore, Bernhere informed his brother-in-law of an opportunity to make money: "your spheare, your watch, your mundane dial and your sextans, your new magneticall instrument for declination, or any astrolabe that hath somewhat extraordinarie in it, will be accepted; and you might sell the same at good prices." Even the sultan's secretary, who was on his way to London, had "some insight of such matters." Bernhere had arranged with friends to bring the envoy to Wright so he could show him the "varietie of instruments" that he was making in the hopes that he would buy "some for the Kings use and his owne." He was so confident that this transaction would come to fruition that he advised Wright to frame "some instruments in brasse or silver, leaving the spaces for Arabique words and figures." This business would provide Wright, whose vast learning had not brought him wealth, with much-needed income.

This fascinating letter provides rich information on the circulation of scientific artifacts between Europe and North Africa in the early modern period. It confirms the interest that the Sa'dī court held for sciences and for European work, and shows how diplomatic and trade networks facilitated the circulation of new knowledge and innovative devices. The Molyneux Globes, as well as other instruments made by European scientists and artisans, could find their way to Morocco as objects of commerce destined to a transcultural educated elite as "exchangeable objects caught up in new and highly elaborate forms of commercial transaction."[111] Hajarī mentions other texts of European geography and astronomy, though it is unclear whether he read them for his own studies or for his service to the sultan. One can surmise that his interest in Luis del Mármol Carvajal and his *Descripción general de África,* quoted in Hajarī's May 1612 letter, predated his move to Morocco.

The way that Hajarī approached cosmography, especially considering his reliance on European authors, was unusual in Morocco. As seen earlier, he was on the margins of the cultural trends of his time. Lacking mastery of prestigious fields of learning like theology or jurisprudence, his inclination led him rather to the natural sciences. These were not ignored in the Maghrib. In an important book published in 2021, Justin Stearns retraces how these sciences were practiced in seventeenth-century Morocco, usually by scholars who were also recognized for their command of jurisprudence and religious disciplines, such as theology and Quranic exegesis. He stresses, however, that their scholarship "was largely not concerned with European expansion or intellectual developments in Europe, for although they were not ignored, neither was seen as central to the main intellectual pursuits of the day."[112] Hajarī is thus out of the ordinary when he displays awareness of the European expansion, and engages with some of the intellectual production that accompanied it. To explain this unusual position, one probably has to point to his identity as a Morisco and his experiences in Spain, and maybe more precisely Seville.

In Morocco, his position in Mūlay Zaydān's *makhzan* certainly influenced his intellectual outlook. As he told his Parisian interlocutors, in order to better serve the sultan, whose chancery was bilingual, he had to study the books of the Christians, and Mūlay Zaydān had him translate a number of such texts. These assignments were all the more remarkable because the sultan was said to speak Spanish "as fluently as if he had been born in Spain."[113] Very cultured, he wrote a book of Quranic exegesis, and some poetry.[114] He was also seriously interested in European culture, especially cosmography, as Hajarī's translating activity shows and as other evidence confirms. That an atlas was among the books presented to him by Golius on behalf of Erpenius in 1624 attests that his interest in European geography was well known. Even the chronicler of the Franciscan mission who sojourned in Marrakesh a few decades later heard about his desire to explore European learning, and noted that when Mūlay Zaydān was informed that the Irish captive Antoine de Sainte-Marie owned "some curious books" in Latin, he asked him to translate them into Spanish so that Moriscos (including probably Hajarī) could produce Arabic versions.[115] The same historian asserts that Mūlay Zaydān enjoyed holding religious debates with another learned captive, Christoval de Flores.[116]

Hajarī, in the service of Mūlay Zaydān, was involved in diplomatic relations, and was also engaging with European culture, and thus a participant and an agent in these "courtly encounters." Some of his Arabic versions of European texts circulated among scholars. Others have left little or no impact, and the texts he authored were only quoted by a handful of other writers. This dissemination does not lead to the conclusion that the preoccupations of this minor author were widespread, nor that they exerted a profound and lasting influence on Maghribi culture. His work, however, confirms that some cultural expression resulted from the interaction with European powers in early modern Morocco and the Maghrib, and ignoring this reality leads to distorting the historical record. The fact that most of Hajarī's work was written in a courtly context rather than in the dominant scholarly centers of his time, such as madrasas and Sufi lodges, is probably significant. Indeed, "societies do not encounter each other in their entirety, rather they do so as fractions."[117] In this case, thanks to a series of factors, the presence of a Morisco diaspora, the intellectual interests of Mūlay Zaydān, the resources he could put toward these interests, and the personal talent of Hajarī, the latter produced a few texts that are significant in themselves, some of which, mostly his translations, were still read decades and even centuries after his death, and all deserving of close study. If "the majority of Moroccan scholars at the time paid scant attention to European powers,"[118] Hajarī was in a different position: entrusted by Mūlay Zaydān and his sons and successors with the relations of the Sa'dī court with Europeans, he had to pay attention to them, and even to study some of their intellectual culture. He included this knowledge in his own representation of the world.

HAJARĪ'S REPRESENTATION OF THE WORLD

Hajarī's interest in cosmography, and his work in that field, was not confined to his duties as a translator for Mūlay Zaydān, it also nourished his own vision of the world, expressed in coherent fashion in the *Supporter*. Like the twin globes helping to mediate the relation between the terrestrial and the celestial, his vision connects the secular and the religious, borrows from both Arabic and European traditions, and highlights how beliefs and ideologies crossed borders to delineate a global intellectual horizon. Like the Spanish *chronologias* and *chronographias* he was fond of quoting, this construction expresses a global vision that extends through time and space. Chapter 10 of the *Supporter* is the central site of the book that exposes in the most systematic manner this view of the world, and brings together threads that appear in less focused form in other parts of the text. Most of this representation is contained in pages that do not figure in the earliest version of the *Supporter* held in al-Azhar but were added when Hajarī revised his text in Tunis. Making this editorial decision years after the original compendium was written, Hajarī included crucial elements of his thinking. He drew on his lifelong study of European cosmography to fulfill this project.

Among the themes of Muslim-Jewish polemics present in Hajarī's text, the most important is undoubtedly the notion of abrogation, essential in Islamic polemics against the other revealed religions. This theme takes central stage in chapter 10, in which he quotes the scripture of the Jews to establish that they support the truth of the Quranic verse which states that "God cancels or confirms what He wants. He possesses the Original Book."[119] Polemicists before Hajarī had mined this theme in Islamic controversy. Examining 'Abd al-Haqq al-Islāmī's narrative, one of Hajarī's references, among other accounts of conversion from Judaism to Islam, Ryan Szpiech notes that their most salient aspect is their chronological linearity: "Islam is the culmination of a historical process of the clarification of truth. Muhammad's prophecy marks the final stage in a progressive sloughing off of perversion and falsification, an increasing purification of a single, unchanging message. In all three texts, the primary argument centers on a historical account of Islam's abrogation of earlier errors."[120] Hajarī followed this model in the *Supporter*. The extensive Tunis revision of chapter 10 focuses on chronology but also develops a theme absent from Islāmī's work and offers a synthetic representation of the contemporary world and of a global history. Both are couched in terms of a competition of empires, informed by a millenarianist understanding of their struggle.

In an early modern world which was "above all a patchwork of competing and intertwined empires,"[121] these realms borrowed from each other symbols, ideas, and institutions. Hajarī's text provides another example of these exchanges of images across borders, when it moves on to a long quote from the Book of Daniel, chapter 2, and its role in the representation of global history. During the captivity of the Israelites in Babylon, only Daniel was able to help Nabuchadnezzar recover and interpret a dream. The king had dreamed of a statue of a man whose head was gold, his breast and arms silver, his belly and thighs brass, his legs iron, and his feet a mix of iron and clay. Then a stone uncut by human hands crushed the statue to dust. The stone expanded until it covered the whole world. According to Daniel's interpretation, Nabuchadnezzar and his monarchy were the head of gold. After him would come successively three other monarchies signified by the other metals of the composite statue, each coming to destruction. A final kingdom would finally arise, symbolized by the stone, that would last forever.

When Hajarī offered his own political understanding of the dream, he was only a new interpreter in a very long line. The prophecy of Daniel had been used for centuries to support an important concept in Christian medieval political theory, the notion of *translatio imperii*. This tradition asserted that the vision of Daniel was about the four successive world empires: Assyro-Babylonian, Persian, Greek, and Roman. The stone was generally interpreted as the coming of Christ, especially the second coming which would usher the end of the world. This eschatological view of history was still discussed by many early modern philosophers and theologians. Although it is difficult to ascertain how aware Hajarī was of this European scholarly tradition, he had access to popular sources that attest to the widespread reliance on this biblical text to make sense of history. In Spain, he attended many sermons in which the priests "would say: 'Our Lord Jesus . . . was the one meant by this vision. His religion spread all over the world. The sultans of his religion subjugated all the sultans of the world!'"[122] As in the scholarly tradition, this interpretation conflates the mystical realm and the political dominion.

Unsurprisingly, Hajarī's interpretation is different. Perhaps surprisingly, to support it, he quotes a Moroccan author, the influential Sufi scholar Ahmad Zarrūq (1442–94), stating that the stone that crushed the statue is Islam. Although, contrary to other biblical figures, Daniel is not mentioned in the Quran, he found his way into Islamic culture through the genre called *qisas al-anbiyā*, or Tales of the Prophets. These collections include stories from the Jewish and Christian traditions, known by the generic term *Isrā'īliyyāt*, and referred to since the earliest times in Islamic theology and history.[123] Hajarī's demonstration built on views that were already circulating in Islamic countries, but he could elaborate on that basis thanks to his direct access to Christian culture, including his experience as a subject of the Spanish Empire, and his ability to read the Old Testament in a Spanish translation.

The quote by Zarrūq comments on a text of the *Isrā'īliyyāt* tradition and contains the following: "There will be no Prophet after him.... There will be no abrogation of his noble Law as long as the world remains!... He intermingled all the races and made them, notwithstanding their differences in religions and the differences of their languages, into one nation, with one language and one religion. Because all of them are reciting the Qur'an in the language of the Arabs, and in it they pray."[124] In accord with Zarrūq, Hajarī asserts that the stone in Daniel's prophecy is not Jesus, but Islam, the last revealed religion. The stone demolished the statue, like Muhammad destroyed the pagan idols in Mecca. Hajarī's demonstration continues: "Let us turn to the words of the prophet Daniel—peace be upon him—that in the days of the later sultans God will establish a sultanate that will not collapse but will last forever."[125] He then attended to the political dimension of the dream and the identification of the last monarchy. He explicitly recognized that he was going beyond what Ujhurī wanted him to do, which was "to write in this compendium only the discussions which I had with the Infidels." Hajarī decided, however, to go beyond this assignment, and "to prove here clearly and unequivocally that Islam has spread in most of the countries of the world known to the ancients." That he exceeded his respected mentor's wishes, after many years in which Hajarī could ponder the implications of the new cosmography, indicates the importance of this part of the text in his eyes. To propose his representation of the world and to situate Islam in it, he drew on cosmographical literature, one of his main fields of study and expertise. Opening it with the dream of Daniel allows him to offer a complete picture of the world and its history, connecting the religious with the profane.

Two larger framing contexts help map Hajarī's representation and imagination of the world. The first is the background of a global intellectual culture, part of the notion of connected histories made familiar by Subrahmanyam, but focusing more closely on the sphere of ideas and concepts. The history of encounters between early modern Europe and its neighbors needs to be written by attending also to the voices of the latter, including the work of Hajarī. The second framework is the related, but distinct, phenomenon analyzed by Ayesha Ramachandran, more narrowly circumscribed in time and linked to the passage to modernity. She studied a striking feature

of early European modernity that she calls "worldmaking," or "this imagina-
tive struggle to capture the world's entirety through the self-conscious efforts
of particular human makers."[126] Ramachandran wondered if this enterprise
could be documented in other parts of the world: "Is the reconception of the
world a European phenomenon, whose products were exported along with
imperialism and colonialism? Or, were there simultaneous, different versions
of worldmaking taking place across global space?"[127] She does not mention
Hajarī, whose own project of imagining the world makes him a prime example of this phenomenon occurring beyond the boundaries of Europe. Aware
of the intellectual cultures of Europe and North Africa, and making connections between them, Hajarī was well situated to engage in his own effort
toward a global representation of the world. In this added part of chapter 10,
where the term *world* (*dunyā*) appears several times, Hajarī engaged in his
own cosmographical project, drawing on his eclectic background to nourish
it, and associating a geographical depiction of the world as revealed by the
recent European navigations, with a reflection on the theological and eschatological dimensions of its extension and history. This religious dimension
explains why Daniel's interpretation of the dream was a fitting introduction
to his depiction of the world.

This choice itself shows that it would be a mistake to judge that Hajarī has
picked up the new knowledge of the world in European sources and simply
added to it elements borrowed from his Islamic faith, thus diluting with
religious views the modernity of the new cosmography. Many European
authors of the time were, like he, freely mixing the secular and the spiritual,
an operation that is documented in a number of the texts that Hajarī quotes
in his own work, such as the Spanish *chronologias* and *chronographias,* and
including one of the most famous texts he translated, the *Atlas Minor,* whose
author, Gerhard Mercator, was not seen in his time as a "mere mapmaker. He
joins the stars to the earth, combines the sacred and the profane, displays an
entire vision of the world, demarcates the boundaries of its kingdoms, and
establishes with certainty the progression of historical time."[128] By combining the religious and the scientific, these trailblazers for a new age put to the
test the "now-classic Weberian narrative of modernity and disenchant-
ment."[129] When he wove his theological views with his geographical learning,
Hajarī was no more archaic than his European counterparts.

In his representation of the world, Hajarī made liberal and knowledgeable
use of European geography, completing his readings with his own observations and information. When he speaks of Morocco and West Africa, his

knowledge might have rivaled that of many European geographers, including what Ahmad al-Manṣūr's invasion of the Songhay kingdom had revealed and changed about the sub-Saharan region. On the other hand, Hajarī borrowed many new elements from European culture, including an awareness of the wider world revealed by the voyages and the transformation of concepts devised to represent space. He adopted without reservation the notion that the earth is divided into continents. This proposition is not as straightforward as it would seem. The ancient Greeks divided the known world into three masses, Europe, Asia, and Libya (later called Africa), with unstable and contested borders. The distinction was reinforced in late antiquity when Christian writers adopted the notion that the world was divided among the descendants of Noah, Asia going to Shem, Europe to Japheth, and Africa to Ham. In the European Renaissance, thanks to the revival of classical learning, "the continental scheme became the authoritative frame of reference."[130]

On the other hand, Arabic geography had early on adopted another division, also originating in Greek culture and still accepted by the only prominent Arab geographer alluded to by Hajarī, Idrisī, for whom the earth has been conventionally divided by scholars and astronomers into seven climates, parallel to the equator, each extending from west to east. Hajarī was no stranger to this concept, as he shows when he states that The Hague is "located in the sixth climate."[131] Adopting in chapter 10 the division of the earth into continents, Hajarī was following in the footsteps of another Iberian–North African writer aware of European geography, Leo Africanus, who knew that, for Idrisī and others, African territories were distributed over four different climates.

Hajarī's global view, encompassing the world in its entirety, is summed up by his recounting of the travels of the Portuguese explorer Pedro Teixeira, who wrote a book describing his round the world voyages.[132]

He mentioned that he had embarked in the country of Portugal (which forms part of the country of al-Andalus) and sailed to the West Indies [al-hunūd al-maghribiyya]. Then he disembarked and crossed their continent. Then he mounted the ocean again sailing westwards for some time, crossing the sea between the Western Islands, until he finally arrived in the neighborhood of Baghdad. He then disembarked in the territory of the Muslims and went forth until the Mediterranean (I think he mentioned Aleppo). Then he embarked and sailed to the territory of the Christians. By completing this journey over sea and land he circled around the whole world.[133]

Summarizing the travels of Teixeira all the way from Iberia and back, Hajarī insists that they amount to a circumnavigation of the globe, a quintessentially modern adventure. As for himself, his readings and encounters helped him conceive of the world as a whole, and, even for small things, to think on a world scale. Admiring the beauty of Amsterdam, he put it on a global stage thanks to a conversation with a man who had traveled widely: "I met someone who had seen the Lands of the East, the lands of the Slavonians, Rome and other countries of the world. He told me that he had never seen a city so nicely decorated."[134]

Conversations with travelers and readings of learned men such as Teixeira made Hajarī aware that "in our time, people are better informed about the things of the world than the ancients were."[135] They enabled him to share with his readers the new European geography, including information about America. His Sevillian sojourn had likely made him appreciate the role of ocean voyages in furthering cosmographical knowledge. Years later, he was still keenly interested in navigation: in chapter 11, recounting his time in the Netherlands, he mentioned briefly having heard of the "story of the six men who came in their ship from the sea where the day lasts for six months approximately,"[136] meaning the three expeditions to the North Pole headed by the Dutch explorer Willem Barentsz (ca. 1550–97), which Hajarī described at greater length in his lost travel account.

In representing the world, he did not claim to be purely neutral. One of his aims was to prove the extent of the possessions of Muslim princes in each of the continents and the global spread of Islam. For many of these possessions in Asia, European information and books were revelatory to Hajarī. For example, he learned from European sources about the multitude of islands populated by Muslims—the confirmation of which he found in Teixeira's *Relaciones,* where he learned about the island of Java and its Muslim population. He collected information through conversations, such as when, in the college of al-Azhar in Cairo, an Indian man told him about the Mughal ruler Jalāl al-Dīn Akbar (d. 1605), who used elephants in warfare.[137] Expounding the spatial extension of Islam and its presence in the continents of Europe, Africa, and Asia, Hajarī emulated the Spanish priests whose sermons eulogized both the spread of Christianity and the dominance of Christian princes, and he focused on the Muslim power that was rivaling the Habsburgs: "Every Christian Sultan is terrified by the bellicose Sultans of Islam defending the Religion who are waging war for the sake of the Lord of the Universe, viz. the noble and great Ottoman Turkish Sultans."[138] Like other Moriscos, Hajarī counted on the Ottomans for protection, especially at the time when he was revising his text in Tunis, in an Ottoman province. He did not, however, pretend that the fourth monarchy was the Ottoman Empire, and confined his interpretation of the prophecy of Daniel to seeing Islam as the stone that would expand to cover the whole world.

Having listed the territories inhabited by the Muslims in the *oikumene* (or inhabited world), he furthered his case with his knowledge of the new cosmography that went beyond mere awareness of the travels and navigations of geographers to teaching about the lands and seas of the world. Having studied many treatises and recently drawn maps and globes, he also acquired understanding of the conceptual apparatus that undergirded these representations.

> On the maps drawn by the Christians and the terrestrial globes they make every city is indicated, together with its name and its [latitude and longitude]. The same is true for the rivers and seas. . . . One also finds on them the large [contiguous land belonging to the Muslims, starting from the Maghribi quarter and then to] the other half of the world which we already said that it is called Asia, about a hundred and forty degrees or more [of longitude]. Every degree of the earth equals fifty-two and a half miles for an average foot-traveller walking on a straight line, without climbing a mountain or descending. Every degree thus equals approximately three days' walk by an average foot-traveller, just as I calculated the length of the country of al-Andalus at thirty days' walk by an average foot-traveller, while its [longitude] is ten or eleven degrees, in accordance with the calculation of well-known travellers, viz. thirty days approximately. Thus every degree equals three days, as said earlier. Thus I calculate that the total surface of the continent inhabited by Muslims is equal to a journey of four hundred and twenty days.[139]

This important passage shows that Hajarī, thanks to his study of maps and globes, was aware of the progress of the new representation of space in European geography. This "cartographic humanism" recently studied by the cultural historian Katharina N. Piechocki, relies on arbitrary lines that promote an "outstanding impact of the map."[140] Piechocki notes the paradox of a Renaissance humanism that does not use the human body to measure space:

> It is a great paradox of Renaissance humanism that its cartographic underpinnings promoted a concept of space which, unlike its medieval counterparts (bound up with the individual experience of time and inextricably entangled with the embodied practice of travel), disengaged the human body (deemed

an unreliable yardstick to measure space), from spatial measurement; with the abstract coordinate system on the rise, the physical human presence on the ground was no longer felt to be needed as an essential element to reckon space.[141]

Hajarī's awareness of this epistemological shift shows in his study of the cartographic instruments produced by European scholars. He also clearly felt that readers might not understand the meaning of his representation of the territories possessed by Muslims in the world if he only used the vocabulary of the cartographic grid, of the degrees of latitude and longitude. He thus translated these abstract coordinates into the language of embodied travel, with space measured by time and referring to the days it takes to travel a distance.

Understanding the new cosmographic representation of space, Hajarī calculated the place of Islam in the world, measuring it both in degrees of longitude and in days of travel. This is only one way in which he showed the global power of Islam. Another is the extent of the use of Arabic in the world. The quote from Zarrūq with which Hajarī introduced his interpretation of Daniel affirmed the eminence and universality of the Arabic language, another iteration of a recurring theme in the *Supporter*. Since his childhood in Hornachos, mastering Arabic was a heroic part of Hajarī's story, closely linked to his Islamic devotion. Elsewhere, he developed the theme of the reach of Arabic in time. From the *plomos* affair, he drew the conclusion that Arabic was as old as the coming of Christ. Later, he found confirmation of even greater antiquity when, with Hubert, he visited the abbey of Saint-Denis near Paris, and saw "a big crystal goblet with an Arabic inscription, its letters had been designed and engraved in the middle of the goblet. [Hubert] said that this goblet belonged to Solomon the son of David, the prophet of God."[142] In his eyes, this inscription proved that Arabic was already spoken and written in that ancient time. The object in question is the so-called "Cup of Khosrow," or "Chosroes," now held in the Cabinet des Médailles of the Bibliothèque Nationale de France in Paris. Long believed to have belonged to King Solomon, it has been identified for more than a century as a Sassanid artifact (see fig. 9).[143] That vessel bears the marks of its successive owners, including engraved words in Arabic Kufic characters.[144] Hajarī's deeply felt response to the relics he touched, in Spain, and in France, highlights their connection: "I marvelled at what was happening to me when I took the goblet of our lord Solomon—peace be upon him—in my hands. The same

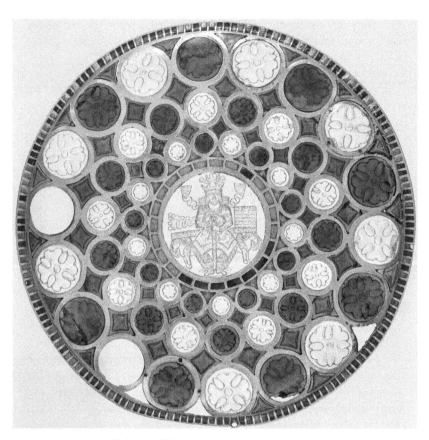

FIGURE 9. The so-called Cup of Chosroes. Ahmad al-Hajarī saw it at the abbey of Saint-Denis, and was told that it had belonged to King Solomon. Bibliothèque Nationale de France, Médailles et Antiques, ID/Cote:Camée.379, inv.56.95; Chabouillet.2538. Public domain.

occurred to me when I laid hands on the parchment, which I mentioned previously, dating back to the time of Cecilio, the secretary of Saint Mary—peace be upon her!—and when I laid hands on some books consisting of leaves of lead dating back to that time, as well. Behold how ancient Arabic is and how sacred."[145]

These venerable objects illustrated the extension of Arabic in time. In chapter 10, Hajarī used his cosmographical studies to demonstrate its extension in space. One informant who helped him make this point is the ambassador sent by the Dutch state to meet with Mūlay Zaydān, who knew Arabic and possessed Arabic books, whom Hajarī does not name, but who was clearly Albert Ruyl.[146] Hajarī asked him where he learned Arabic:

He answered: "You should know that I have stayed in one of the East Indian islands from which cinnamon, cloves and other spices are brought. These islands belong to the Muslims. There I learned to read Arabic.'

I asked him: "Are there any Muslims in those islands?"

He answered: "There are! Also, on every island there is a Muslim Sultan. On some islands there are even two!"

I was amazed by this, but he swore to me by his religion and faith that those islands encompassed in fact more than ten thousand islands belonging to the Muslims.[147]

This conversation needs to be connected with another one whose account Hajarī added in the Tunis version. When he was in Leiden in 1613, Erpenius introduced him to some scholars who brought him a book that he identified as an Arabic book on mysticism:

They were surprised and told me: "This book was brought along from such and such an island in the East Indies which is only reached by a long sea voyage, of a bit less than a year! How remarkable this is! Between your country and that island there is a very long distance but you understand the contents of the book! This means that Arabic is one, general language in every country. But our speech in this country differs from the other languages: in England there is one language, while the people of France have another language. The same holds true for al-Andalus, that has another non-Arabic language, and also in Italy, Germany, and Moscovia. Each language differs from the other. But the Arabic language we are talking about is one and the same in the whole world!"

They indeed spoke the truth in that matter, because it is a blessed language.[148]

Hajarī was happy to witness Erpenius's and his friends' interest in the Arabic language. He helped some European Orientalists in their studies of the tongue, and was rewarded by a new awareness of its place in the world—including their own somewhat exaggerated estimation of its spread. The common Orientalist theme of the eminence and extent of the Arabic language not only accorded with Hajarī's reverence for it but also helped him tie together different threads of his own intellectual trajectory, from his first valiant apprenticeship of the language in Hornachos, to his career in court as a translator, to his experience in the European Republic of Letters, to his performance as a polemicist, to his autobiographical writings, and to his role in the Arabic Republic of Letters. As a collaborator to European scholars, Hajarī gladly helped them further their knowledge of the Arabic language and of Arabic texts. What he learned from them was arguably as important.

He related this knowledge to his interest in European cartography and cosmography, which he shared with Mūlay Zaydān, to nourish his own efforts to understand and imagine the world.

. . .

Hajarī's testimony, and the connections it reveals between his own work and the European intellectual life he had experienced, suggests that early modern Orientalism can be fruitfully considered as advancing a shared global culture. Not only did many people coming from North Africa and the Middle East make important contributions to its development; some, like Hajarī, extended in their own cultural region what they learned through these collaborations. One wonders how he compared the translations of Arabic texts he read in Europe to his own work as a cultural translator who introduce European learning to the Sa'dī court for Mūlay Zaydān. Like many Orientalists, he enlisted the help of captives for understanding and translating difficult texts, or the aid of friends, such as when, in 1624, he solicited Golius's assistance for astronomical vocabulary. This collaborator of Orientalists enjoyed a long career as a translator of cultural and scientific texts. Through him, early modern Orientalism, seen as the European study of the cultural production of the neighboring Arab and Ottoman countries, found, to a more limited extent, its counterpart in North Africa.

In the Sa'dī court, Hajarī could count on the patronage of a sultan curious about cosmography and geography—and who had access through diplomatic networks to artifacts, such as the Molyneux Globes, and to books, such as the atlas sent by Thomas Erpenius. This highlights the importance of states and courts in the production of learning, especially scientific knowledge, through the desire to participate in elite networks of exchange of highly valued scientific instruments, and through large-scale technological projects focusing on infrastructure, or on warfare. Such enterprises in North Africa provide a background to the exchange of technological knowledge between Europe and the Maghrib, in which Hajarī played his own part. This will be the focus of the last chapters of this book.

PART THREE

———

Technology in the Contact Zone

THIS BOOK, INFORMED BY THE NOTION of networks, turns now to examine how the networks of Orientalism and diplomacy are imbricated within a transnational geography of technical expertise that included Europe and North Africa. Lively debates surround the long-lasting impact of important changes in military strategy and tactics that occurred in Europe in the sixteenth and seventeenth centuries. This so-called military revolution included as a central tenet the widespread use of new technology in warfare. The efficiency of artillery necessitated better fortifications, and these transformations in turn implied profound changes in the size and organization of the army, and in the forms of political power. The centrality of military technology and its early modern dissemination is well established. However, the theme of technology rarely comes into focus in recent studies of the connections between early modern Europe, North Africa, and the Middle East. Nevertheless, exchange in this domain did occur, often through the same channels that produced the currents of Orientalism. The last two chapters of this book are case studies in the circulation of such technical and scientific knowledge, an area usually ignored in the analysis of the Muslim world.

The assumption of a clear divide between Europe and the rest of the world, especially the Muslim countries, has long dominated scholarship, despite persuasive revisionist studies. One hindrance to the study of commonalities between regions is that the "history of science, even more than most historical fields, has focused on origins and producers ... we are obsessed with novelty and the places in which novelty begins."[1] The search for origins, and for originality, can obscure issues that are as—or more—illuminating. The appropriation, exchange, and expansion of technical knowledge involves not only techniques but also the cultural modes of communication, through which they are socially and politically situated: the types of written or spoken discourses, the professional paths and roles they can produce, and the modifications they entail in terms of training and acquiring skills.

Part III of this book will focus on this shared culture of technology between the shores of the Mediterranean. One particular instance of these commonalities is the emergence of a dominant new figure in the new age of warfare: the early modern engineer. This figure differs in crucial ways from his medieval predecessors, as well as from his descendants of the eighteenth century, and, even more so, of the industrial revolution. He first appears in the military context as an expert in technical, political, and military knowledge. In this role, the early modern engineer embodies a new iteration of the age-old role of advisor to the prince, thanks to empirical skill and theoretical knowledge that produce practical results, especially on the battlefield, rather than to wisdom and an understanding of ideological codes.

Hajarī played a key role in bringing together both traditional textual forms of knowledge and new works and processes linked to technology and the mechanical arts, in great part owing to his closeness with patrons at courts and political centers. His observations about and his participation in the circulation of technology yield many insights in the still understudied field of the history of material culture in North Africa and its connections to Europe. Two projects in which Hajarī was involved stand out as examples of the way technological knowledge circulated between Europe and North Africa; both projects are related to the changing environment of warfare and the military. One is the planning of a port on the Atlantic coast of Morocco. The second is the codification of knowledge on gunnery and artillery that was being strongly developed in Europe, and, to a lesser extent, in North Africa and the Middle East. The last two chapters of this book examine the two case studies using insights from science and technology studies. Taken together, both cases paint a picture of the crosscurrents in play in scientific development throughout the Mediterranean.

FIVE

———

A Harbor on the Atlantic Coast

WALĪDIYYA (OR OUALIDIA), A SMALL TOWN on the Atlantic coast of
Morocco, boasts of waves and pink flamingos that attract surfers and bird-
watchers. Visitors, seeking an escape from the tumult of Casablanca and
Marrakesh, come to taste its renowned oysters and admire the sunset on the
nearby lagoon. Tourists might also feel curious about some of the town's
venerable constructions. A now empty summer palace was built for King
Muhammad V in the 1940s. Much older are the remains of a kasbah, a fort
that was erected in 1634 on the orders of the Saʿdī Sultan Mūlay al-Walīd,
after whom the town was named. The citadel was actually a diminished version of a much more ambitious scheme envisioned by his father, Mūlay
Zaydān.

On Shaʿbān 12, 1030—during the eighth month in the Islamic calendar—
corresponding to July 2, 1621, Mūlay Zaydān signed a letter addressed to the
Dutch States General.[1] The tone was amicable, and the sultan expressed his
satisfaction with his friendly relations with the Netherlands. He also revealed
that he wanted to deepen them by a mutually profitable exchange: he was
ready to export to Holland saltpeter, an essential component of gunpowder,
and he wanted Dutch assistance in building a harbor. He expected in particular that the States General would send master stoneworkers. Interested,
the Dutch dispatched a mission to explore the feasibility of the project. An
analysis of the harbor episode helps situate technical knowledge in the context not only of Saʿdī power in the early seventeenth century, and of its relations with the Netherlands, but also of the multifarious forms of cultural
interaction between Europe and North Africa.

In addition, the diplomatic and technical mission is an episode in the
history of Orientalism, especially due to the participation of Jacob Golius.

The latter participated in the mission not as an interpreter or translator but as an engineer. Golius was not the only person related to Orientalism who was involved in this mission. Hajarī was in touch with the Dutch envoys in his capacity as translator to the sultan. Furthermore, the head of the embassy, Albert Ruyl, had a long-standing and overlooked interest in the study of oriental languages. The analysis of the role played by these three men highlights the interweaving of diplomacy and Orientalism that is a distinctive feature of the field in the early modern period and beyond.

This harbor project, and the circumstances of its abandonment, are the subject of this chapter. While the project would eventually come to naught, it serves to illustrate how knowledge about the orient circulated in seventeenth-century Europe not only in academic settings but also through channels deeply influenced by political and military circumstances. Orientalism was only one site in a larger topography of knowledge. Indeed, the coexistence of the scholarly and the practical, when it comes to technical issues, was critical to the construction of Orientalist learning itself.

MŪLAY ZAYDĀN AND THE HARBOR PROJECT: A BRIEF HISTORY

The Saʿdīs came to power after the ominous development of gunpowder technology. During that period, artillery became ascendant over defensive fortifications, as was made clear in the region by the advantage cannons gave Spain in its conquest of Granada. The century that followed witnessed, in the words of military historian Weston F. Cook, a "hundred years war" for control of Morocco, fought between local dynasties, the Iberian states, and even the Ottoman Empire.[2] The Saʿdī dynasty emerged as the eventual winner, thanks to its own "military revolution," involving the widespread use of artillery, the building of new forms of fortifications, and the deployment of larger armies. This achievement allowed Morocco to keep its independence alongside the gunpowder Islamic empires of the Ottomans in the Near East, the Safavids in Iran, and the Mughals in India.[3] The Saʿdī adoption of new forms of warfare resulted most spectacularly in the historic 1578 victory of Wādī al-Makhāzin, where the defeat of the Portuguese marked the beginning of the long and prosperous reign of Mūlay Zaydān's father, Ahmad al-Mansūr. But toward the end of Ahmad al-Mansūr's reign, a terrible epidemic of plague spread from Europe, ravaging Spain—which likely lost 10 percent of its population—and the Maghrib. This catastrophe was compounded by a long drought that provoked a famine in North Africa.[4] The Saʿdī dynasty began to break down in 1603 after Ahmad al-Mansūr died of the plague. The country then fell into a civil war among his sons.

During the destructive fratricide war, Muhammad al-Shaykh al-Maʾmūn sought the help of the Spanish against his brother Mūlay Zaydān and in exchange ceded to them control of the northern port of al-ʿArāʾish. This action diminished the legitimacy of the Saʿdī dynasty and emboldened tribal contenders and charismatic rebels, especially after Spain imposed a suffocating blockade, occupying, threatening, and harassing Moroccan ports and coasts. Mūlay Zaydān ended up winning the civil war, but he spent his reign shoring up his power against his brothers and their sons, and against agitators and tribal powers. He had to flee Marrakesh more than once, and only toward the end of 1613 would he ensure permanent control over his own capital. Once he established a precarious control of the southern part of the old Saʿdī territory, he had to contend with an uprising led by the charismatic Ibn Abī Mahallī (d. 1613), who proclaimed himself the *mahdī*, the mythical restorer of justice who would rule before the end of the world.[5] His millenarian message resonated in an apocalyptic context of war, famine, and pestilence, and while in the end, Zaydān prevailed, his power outside the city and its nearby region steadily decreased. Hajarī heard about the Ibn Abī Mahallī uprising when he was in France, and he mentioned it in his May 1612 letter to his Morisco friends who resided in Istanbul.

Until his death, Mūlay Zaydān tried to reverse or at least slow the decline of the dynasty. His resilience in the face of constant rebellions and challenges made him, in the eyes of French historian Henry de Castries, "one of the greatest princes of the Saʿdī dynasty."[6] He attempted to reinforce the military capabilities of the Saʿdī state by drawing on his dynastic history, but Mūlay Zaydān did not have the same financial and political resources as his father. Not only was his legitimacy diminished and challenged by powerful local rivals, but the territory he controlled had dwindled considerably, and the catastrophic past decade resulted in an economic and demographic collapse and thus lower tax revenues. As historian Jerome Bruce Weiner notes in his study of conflict in early modern Morocco, "The local and regional governors continued to attempt to collect taxes and maintain the sultan's authority, but with diminishing success."[7] Furthermore, firearms and artillery had spread to the challengers to his state. Nevertheless, Mūlay Zaydān, like other Moroccan powers, engaged in diplomatic and trade relations with European powers, on whom he counted to build up his defensive and offensive capabilities.

Mūlay Zaydān's efforts to acquire a fleet for military purposes were again in keeping with the history of the dynasty,[8] and among his many uphill battles was the defense of the coast of his diminishing territory. To this end, he aspired to the building of new ports, since most harbors were occupied, like al-'Arā'ish, by Spain, and threatened by the Habsburgs and other European powers. Marrakesh only controlled the port of Safi. Rabat-Salé, the best port on the Atlantic, had been settled by Moriscos who helped to rebuild the port and made it into an important center of corsair activity. Beginning in the 1620s, Rabat-Salé gave itself an independent political structure, at best only nominally connected to the Sa'dī *makhzan*.[9] It even proclaimed its independence toward the end of Mūlay Zaydān's life.

To protect the part of the coast that was still under his control, and to reinforce Sa'dī naval capabilities, Mūlay Zaydān considered building a port in the lagoon of Aier, north of Safi. He initially approached the French. In fact, a Frenchman, Antoine de Saint-Mandrier, employed as an engineer by Mūlay Zaydān, had been involved early on, and thought the removal of some reefs would make the lagoon into a viable harbor. He proposed the project to the French envoy Claude Du Mas, who arrived in Safi in January 1619, sent by Louis XIII to redeem captives. This mission went badly, since the relations between the Sa'dī *makhzan* and the French Crown had deteriorated significantly due to an event that happened in 1612. Mūlay Zaydān, fleeing the advance of Ibn Abī Mahallī, hired the French consul and ship captain Jean-Philippe de Castelane to transport to safety his personal treasure, including his beloved library. Rather than delivering the cargo, Castelane took off, maybe heading to France, but his ship was seized by a Spanish fleet, and the library ended up in the Escorial palace, where it remains to this day, or what is left of it after the great fire of 1671.[10] Informed by Saint-Mandrier of the potential of the Aier lagoon, Du Mas returned to Paris where he found financing for the project. He was accompanied by a Moroccan ambassador who was charged with demanding that the French obtain the return of the stolen library. He was never received by the French court, which infuriated Mūlay Zaydān, who decided to propose the Aier project instead to the Dutch Republic, through his agent Joseph Pallache.

As a translator for the sultan, Hajarī was involved in a minor way in the Sa'dī–Netherlands connection, since the Dutch initiated contact by sending Pieter Coy to Marrakesh in 1605. Hajarī visited the Netherlands not long after the 1610 Treaty of Friendship and Free Commerce cemented the relationship between the two states. The exchange between the Saʿdī state and the Netherlands was largely concerned with strategic materials and artefacts. In 1612, Mūlay Zaydān asked his Dutch allies' help in order to fortify the sites of Mogador and Maʿmūra, hoping to build the stronger Dutch-style fortification his envoys had seen in the Netherlands.[11] Their long war of independence from Spain gave the Dutch mastery in matters of fortifications that attracted the attention of many foreign rulers, and made possible the export of Dutch military engineering.[12] An engineer accompanied the squadron of three ships sent to defend Maʿmūra, which had become a nest of corsairs from different regions, including England and Holland. This did not prevent the seizure of the port by the Spanish in August 1614. A few years later, Hajarī figured, again as a secondary player, in the harbor venture between the Saʿdī *makhzan* and the Dutch. He did not participate in high-level negotiations, but he helped with the translation of documents, and with the reception of the Dutch representatives.

In 1622, the States General sent an embassy to Morocco on the *Overijssel,* headed by Albert Corneliszoon Ruyl, that included Jacob Golius, a student of Hajarī's friend Thomas Erpenius. The embassy was charged with delivering a warship, two frigates, and a number of bronze cannons that had been manufactured for Mūlay Zaydān in Holland. Ruyl was also entrusted with assessing the feasibility of the projected harbor, and studying the prospect of importing other commodities, especially saltpeter. The *Overijssel* arrived in Rabat-Salé on December 6, 1622, where participants talked about freeing captives with a famous Dutch renegade pirate named Jan Janszen / Murat Rais (c. 1570–c. 1641).[13] The ship reached Safi on the Moroccan Atlantic coast on December 20, 1622, and left the Moroccan port to go back to the Netherlands in June 1624. The most extensive source on the mission is the diary written by Ruyl, and presented by its author to the States General on August 5, 1624.

Their stay started badly, and Ruyl complained bitterly about food and lodging. However, the main issue that would plague his mission was that he detested his dealings with the Pallaches, members of a family of former Iberian Jews who moved to Morocco after the Spanish expulsion of Jews in 1492 and who had worked for generations for the Moroccan *makhzan*. Ruyl came to hate the Pallaches with a passion, especially Mūlay Zaydān's agent Joseph, whom he called the "old Pallache," and his nephew Moses, who held a high position in Mūlay Zaydān's *makhzan*. The stressful eighteen months that Ruyl spent in Morocco were punctuated by increasing hostility, including physical altercations. Ruyl suspected the Pallaches of sabotaging his mission, and of inciting Mūlay Zaydān against him. For their part, the Pallaches complained that Ruyl was arrogant and disrespectful, and Moses Pallache told the States General that their ambassador was inexperienced and badly advised.[14]

The envoys waited seven months in Safi before they could go to Marrakesh to meet the sultan. During this interval, the crew of the *Overijssel* revolted and demanded their immediate return to Holland. Although Ruyl ordered the return of the ship, harsh punishment was meted, including the hanging of four rebels on June 21, 1623. Then, in the middle of the crew crisis, on June 12, news arrived that a Spanish fleet was approaching the projected port, making the population very nervous about yet another attack on the Moroccan shore. Several days later, the vessels moved toward Safi, which caused an even bigger commotion. However, it soon became clear that the fourteen warships, now close to Safi, were in fact Dutch. It was the Nassau fleet, under the command of admiral Jacques L'Hermite, which was headed for Peru. He stopped at Safi in order to request that sugar, seized from just-captured Spanish ships coming from Brazil, be loaded on the *Overijssel* on its way back to Holland.[15] Some Moroccan officials still suspected that the Dutch fleet's intention was to seize Aier, or Safi itself, and kept surveilling the ships "as if they were Spanish," and Ruyl was not allowed to visit the main vessel.[16] Such suspicion illustrates that misgivings were not limited to Ruyl and the Pallaches.

Meanwhile, on May 13, 1623, Pieter van Neste, in charge of the stables of Maurits of Nassau, arrived with two small pieces of artillery as a present from the prince of Orange to Mūlay Zaydān. He was also tasked with buying horses for Maurits. The Dutch envoys left Safi for Marrakesch, where they stayed from June 28 to November 15, 1623. On August 7, Mūlay Zaydān sent superbly saddled horses to Ruyl and van Neste to bring them to his palace, and received them with great honors. The sultan was magnificently dressed, despite having just lost his mother, a mark of respect that pleased Ruyl. The ambassador presented Mūlay Zaydān with a letter from the States General, while van Neste gave him a missive from the prince of Orange. Later, the sultan offered horses from his own stables to be sent as a personal gift to Maurits of Nassau. The two diplomats were received again on November 11, and van Neste thanked the sultan in person for the horses gifted to the prince. Golius did not attend either of these two audiences with Mūlay

Zaydān. Back in Safi, the envoys stayed in the port from November 1623 to May 1624, waiting to receive the authorization to go back to Holland. Ruyl had to send several requests for permission from the sultan. The most notable was an Arabic letter sent on April 15, 1624, in all likelihood the epistle written by Golius that Thomas Le Gendre, who was in Safi at that time, mentioned in his memoir.[17] Ten days later, when van Neste went to the army camp of Mūlay Zaydān to deliver the two cannons offered by Maurits of Nassau, Ruyl requested that Golius accompany him to plead again for authorization to leave.[18] It is certainly at that time that Golius had the conversation with the sultan recounted by Le Gendre.

The mission was finally authorized to leave, and, to Ruyl's immense relief, the envoys left Safi on June 1, 1624, accompanied by Joseph Pallache and Mūlay Zaydān's ambassador Yusuf Biscaïno. On July 22, Ruyl declared to the States General that the products Morocco had to offer were of no interest to the Dutch. That was not, however, the end of Ruyl's troubles. Soon after arriving in the Netherlands, Joseph complained to the States General of Ruyl's mistreatments of his sons, which included physical violence, and so did Biscaïno, in a letter that was rendered into Dutch by Thomas Erpenius.[19] This translation is not the only connection between this embassy and Orientalism, which often developed in the shadows of state relations and political power. It is an example of one of the modalities of Orientalist learning in early seventeenth-century Morocco. While the Dutch mission had turned into a diplomatic disaster, and resulted in poisoning the Dutch-Moroccan relations for years, and hurting Ruyl's career,[20] this political failure nevertheless generated a goldmine for historians thanks to the many documents—official reports, diplomatic and personal correspondence, scholarly manuscripts— that shed a fascinating light on the interweaving of different threads in the history of the complex cultural relations between Arab countries and Europe, and on the contact zone between civilizations.

ORIENTALISM IN THE MARGINS OF THE DUTCH MISSION

Scholarship on Orientalism only allusively mentions the Dutch mission, usually to note that Golius was in Morocco to collect Arabic manuscripts. This considerably narrows the importance of this episode, in more ways than one. On the one hand, Orientalism was only a secondary part of the mission, and even of Golius's involvement. On the other hand, Hajarī and Albert Ruyl, like Golius, engaged in practices of Orientalism. These three characters embody different figures in the field: the pragmatic Orientalist, who might nevertheless seek to obtain philological respect; the learned Orientalist, in search of manuscripts of high culture; and the so-called local informant, who might also have his own research or intellectual agenda that his connections with Europeans help him fulfill. All three were also working for political powers, serving different states as diplomats, interpreters, and experts, and through this employment, they found the opportunity to connect and interact.

The head of the mission himself, Ruyl, had a strong engagement with the study of oriental languages, which is ignored by the few historians who have taken an interest in this failed venture. Ruyl probably began his career as a trader with the Dutch East Indies Company (the Vereenigde Oost-Indische Compagnie, or VOC), and "sailed to the East Indies as a junior merchant (*onderkoopman*) on the *Haerlem*."[21] During his travels, he learned Malay well enough to produce pioneering work on and in this language, which was a "lingua franca in major parts of Southeast Asia."[22] Although he never pursued an academic career, Ruyl's philological accomplishments are far from inconsiderable. He authored the first printed grammar of Malay, *Spieghel van de Maleysche tale* (Mirror of the Malay Language), including a glossary, and a translation of a summary of the teachings of the Reformed Church, published in Amsterdam in 1612, and which used Latin letters to transcribe Malay. In 1612, he completed the translation of the Gospel of Matthew into Malay, only published in 1629. These publications were financed by the VOC, and were used in the churches and in the schools sponsored by the company in Southeast Asia. The publication of the Matthew Gospel also included Malay versions of the Ten Commandments, the Apostles' Creed, a few Psalms and hymns, the Lord's Prayer, and other songs and prayers.[23] All were key elements in the Dutch Reformed church services.[24] Ruyl also made a Malay version of the Gospel of Mark. In 1651, an edition combining Ruyl's translations of these two Gospels, and the version of Luke and John and of the Acts produced by other VOC traders, was published.

Ruyl's translations were part of the evangelizing efforts financed by the VOC that were in keeping with much of early modern Orientalism. Nevertheless, Ruyl sought philological respectability, and claimed that he translated from the Greek, although historians think that his base text was the Dutch version.[25] He also chose to use, rather than the vernacular spoken forms of Malay, a higher version of the language, which he called "court Malay." However, he did not master it well enough to produce a text in "the style of the Malay literary tradition." Furthermore, he permitted himself "a number of striking liberties," borrowing terminology from other religions and coining neologisms.[26] These daring strategies were destined to influence the language used in Malay Christianity for centuries. They also occasioned him some trouble with gatekeepers, when the Church council of Amsterdam, attempting to regulate a disorderly translation field, forbade him from translating the Bible without clerical assent.[27] Its intervention points to a practice of Orientalism that developed apart from the academic world, a practice frowned upon not only on theological grounds but also for philological reasons, like when late seventeenth-century Malay specialists looked critically at Ruyl's and other VOC traders' translations and pointed out the mistakes made by these "uneducated persons."[28] This harsh judgment does not make these early Malay versions of the Bible any less historically influential, however.

Ruyl also played his part in transmitting knowledge to Hajarī, who appears several times in his diary. The ambassador described him to the States General as trustworthy and as a "man of good faith."[29] Even before the arrival of the envoys, Hajarī translated into Spanish a missive addressed by Mūlay Zaydān to the States General.[30] Later, in a report dated May 25, 1623, Ruyl stated that van Neste, who had arrived in Safi on May 13, was still waiting for a response to the letter he had sent to Hajarī, whom he called "Ehmed bin Caçim."[31] Thus, the prince of Orange's envoy contacted Hajarī, who was in Marrakesh, quite soon after his arrival. This suggests that van Neste might have heard about Hajarī prior to arriving in Morocco, and might even have met him in The Hague. Maybe because of his experience in Holland, Hajarī was also assigned by Mūlay Zaydān to prepare the reception of the envoys at court, and worked in tandem with the *qā'id* 'Ammār, whom Ruyl called the "principal person in court."[32] The Dutch met with Hajarī in the capital and enjoyed excellent relations with him, in stark contrast with their execrable dealings with the Pallaches. On August 10, Ruyl was pleasantly surprised to learn that Hajarī would be translating the letters he gave Mūlay Zaydān, rather than the dreaded Moses Pallache. He even used his relationship with Hajarī to create his own independent channel of communication with Mūlay Zaydān: on October 14, he requested Hajarī translate a Spanish memo into Arabic, and asked Golius to give it to the *qā'id* 'Ammār, because it would have been too dangerous to count on Moses.[33]

Before leaving Marrakesh, Ruyl gave Hajarī an unspecified present on November 12, 1623, for his services.[34] During his second stay in Safi, Ruyl was still in touch with Hajarī, exchanging letters with him and using him as a conduit to transmit documents sent by the States General to Mūlay Zaydān, to avoid the interference of Moses Pallache.[35] Between the Dutch envoys and Hajarī, there was a relation of trust built on the good will he had created with people from the Netherlands since Coy's embassy in 1605–9 and his own visit to Holland in 1613. Ruyl and his companions even assumed, and maybe hoped, that Hajarī would be Mūlay Zaydān's ambassador to Holland. Part of this old relationship was his connection with Erpenius. All these characters' work in Orientalism was not strictly separated from their other careers. Concerning the Ruyl mission, while Hajarī rendered in Arabic documents authored by the envoy, his friend Erpenius, who like him was employed as a diplomatic interpreter, albeit merely as a secondary career, translated several missives by Mūlay Zaydān and members of his *makhzan*.

If Ruyl mentioned Hajarī in the records of his mission, Hajarī in turn spoke of the ambassador in his book, confirming their good relation, and providing information about Ruyl that, to my knowledge, no other source mentions:

> Once, an ambassador from the Netherlands arrived at the court of Moulāy Zaydān . . . in the City of Marrakesh. His letter of credential was written in Spanish. I was ordered by the Sultan to translate it into Arabic. For that reason, the ambassador was sympathetic towards me. I saw he had books in Arabic, and that he could read and write Arabic. So I asked him: "Where did you learn that?"
>
> He answered: "You should know that I have stayed in one of the East Indian islands from which cinnamon, cloves, and other spices are brought. These islands belong to the Muslims. There I learned to read Arabic."[36]

Ruyl is ignored in histories of the learning of Arabic in early modern Europe. Scholars are however increasingly interested in the not inconsiderable number of Europeans who studied this language outside of academic settings, often as "travelers to foreign shores."[37] Hajarī was aware of both paths to Arabic learning in Europe. He came into contact with the academic, learned way, through Hubert and Erpenius, distinguished members of the Republic of Letters. He also knew about the pragmatic mode, embodied by Ruyl, and also by a French merchant he met in Marrakesh and saw again in Rouen, and who "knew Arabic very well."[38] Ruyl and the trader learned the language and the culture thanks to their interactions with people, and maybe simpler books than the treatises of exegesis, rhetoric, or science that the university professors and students were collecting and studying. We unfortunately do not know which Arabic texts Hajarī saw in the possession of Ruyl, or what Golius thought of them. Despite Ruyl's linguistic skills, he still needed professional translators, like Moses Pallache and Hajarī. Even Golius, during the last months of the Dutch stay in Morocco, only translated one official letter, although drafts of personal Arabic letters by him are extant. Hajarī's text also shows that if scholarship usually considers him as the informant of European Orientalists, from his perspective, Ruyl was his informant. Ruyl helped him complete the view of the world that he collected from his readings of European geography and travel literature, making him, in particular, more aware of the reach of Islam and Arabic.

As for the exchanges between Golius and Hajarī, a few traces remain (see fig. 10). The only extant letters between the two men date from the time that Golius and the rest of the embassy were back in Safi, which might suggest that they only began to work together during the Dutch envoys' stay in Marrakesh, which lasted from June 28 to November 15, 1623. Of course, earlier messages might have been lost. In a letter dated February 2, 1624, Hajarī described his editorial work on the copy of the *Mustaʿīnī* by Ibn Baklārish that he had procured and partly copied for Golius, collating two manuscripts (see fig. 11). He also "translated most of the names of the simple medicines into Spanish,"[39] and promised to answer a letter from Erpenius that Golius had given him. In a letter dated February 29, 1624, Hajarī commented on the news that a copy of Masʿūdī's *Murūj al-dhahab* had been stolen by highway robbers on its way to Safi, told Golius that he was still working on the *Mustaʿīnī,* and asked Golius to translate for him in Arabic or Spanish a treatise of astronomy.[40]

In his quest for books, Golius also involved other officials of Mūlay Zaydān's *makhzan.* Concerning the stolen copy of *Murūj al-dhahab,* on May 5, 1624 (dated in the Islamic calendar as 16 Rajab 1033h), he drafted a letter reminding the *qāʾid* Ibrāhīm al-Qāliʿ of a conversation they had about this issue.[41] The Dutch were in touch with this official, whom Ruyl referred to as "Alcala" in his diary.[42] But Golius's search for Arabic manuscripts goes unmentioned by Ruyl, since Golius did not participate in the mission as a scholar, nor even as an interpreter, but to help with the main goal of the mission, and his search for scholastic documents was of a private nature.

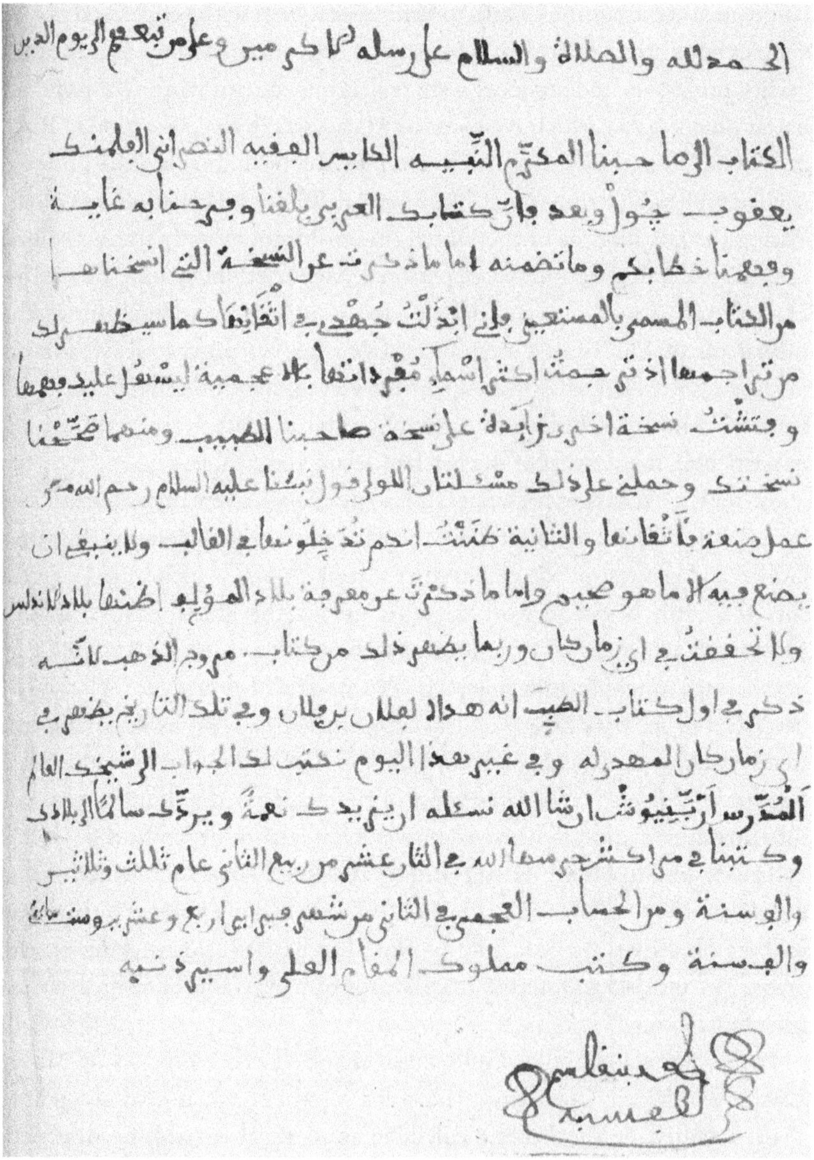
الحمد لله والصلاة والسلام على رسوله الكريم وعلى من تبعه الى يوم الدين

الكتاب الى صاحبنا المكرم النبيه الكاتب الفقيه النصراني الفلمنك
يعقوب جول وبعد فان كتابك العربي بلغنا وفرحنا به غاية
وفهمنا خطابكم وما تضمنه اما ما ذكرت عن النسخة التي انسخناها
من الكتاب المسمى بالمستعيني فاني ابذلت جهدي في اتقانها كما سيظهر لك
من تراجمها اذ ثم جملة اكثر اسمائه مفردات بالاعجمية ليشكل عليك فهمها
وبقيت نسخة اخرى زائدة على نسخة صاحبنا الطبيب ومنهما صححنا
نسختك وحملني على ذلك مسئلتان الاولى قول نبينا عليه السلام رحم الله من
عمل صنعة فاتقنها والثانية كنت اعلم انك تحب طبعها في القالب ولا ينبغي ان
يصنع فيه الا ما هو صحيح واما ما ذكرت عن معرفة بلاد المؤلف اظنها بلاد الاندلس
ولا نعرفه في اي زمان كان وربما يظهر ذلك من كتاب مروج الذهب لانه
ذكر في اول كتاب الطب انه هداه لفلان بن فلان وفي تلك التاريخ يظهر في
اي زمان كان المهدى له وفي غير هذا اليوم نكتب لك الجواب الشيخ العالم
المدرس ارتبنيوس ان شا الله نسئله ان يزيدك نعمة ويردك سالما الى بلادك
وكتبنا في مراكش حرسها الله في الثالث عشر من ربيع الثاني عام ثلاث وثلاثين
والف سنة ومن الحساب العجمي في الثاني من شهر فبراير اربع وعشرين وستمائة
والف سنة وكتب مملوك المقام العلي واسير ذنبه

FIGURE 10. Letter from Ahmad al-Hajarī to Jacob Golius, February 2,1624. University of Manchester, John Rylands Library, Persian MS 913. Creative Commons. Copyright of the University of Manchester.

FIGURE 11. A page of the manuscript of Ibn Baklārish's *Mustaʿīnī,* copied by Ahmad al-Hajarī. Leiden University Library, Manuscripts of the Middle East, Cod. Or. 15. Creative Commons (CC BY-NC-SA 4.0).

Overall, the exchanges connected to Orientalism were a marginal part of the Dutch mission in Morocco. However, the traces they left are not insignificant. Beside the *Musta'ini* and other manuscripts now held in the library of Leiden University, the few letters from Hajarī are in themselves interesting literary documents, since "examples of Arabic private correspondence of this period" are rare.[43] These letters, added to the earlier missive he sent to Erpenius when he arrived in Holland in 1613,[44] constitute a small but nevertheless noteworthy epistolary corpus by a Maghribi notable of his time. Addressed to European scholars, they attest to exchanges dominated by trust and friendship, and by the mutual benefits enjoyed by the parties in their pursuit of knowledge.

These scholarly exchanges also tell us about the informal ways in which learning, and in particular Orientalism, was constructed outside academic settings, through the practices of traders, diplomats, and translators. As historian Romain Bertrand explains: "In these early days of Orientalism, technical philological skills—the acquired ability to speak, read, write, transliterate, and translate foreign languages—were seemingly not the scholar's privilege, but rather were distributed across a large and moving social field comprising 'men of all sorts.'"[45] Proficiency in Arabic and other oriental languages developed in Europe through the personal contacts and experience of unlettered practical men, distinct from the textual study pursued by scholars looking for artifacts of the culture of the learned, such as manuscripts of respected authors. Different approaches played their part in the spread of knowledge.

Such early modern encounters, not only between Europe and North Africa but also between low and high culture, are not limited to this particular field. They figure more prominently when it comes to technical knowledge and skills, a domain that holds a crucial place in the evolution of scientific and political cultures. This aspect of the story of Aier and its Moroccan context still involves Jacob Golius, and reveals some of the commonalities between Europe and its Islamic neighbors.

KNOWLEDGE HIGH AND LOW: GOLIUS
AND THE CRAFTSMEN

When Ruyl headed to Morocco, he was carrying instructions by the States General to begin the construction of the port if it was deemed feasible, thanks to the masters and experienced workers he brought with him.[46] In the end, no work was undertaken at all. Although Ruyl did affirm his opposition to the project, providing his diary to the States General as a supporting document, it fell to Golius to author the final report which accompanied a map of Aier, signed on July 24, 1624, in The Hague.[47] This account concluded unequivocally that the construction of the port was unadvisable: "a port could never be built in Aier because there was a massive rock barrier across the entrance to the channel."[48] However, the record is actually more ambiguous than this, and close analysis of how this conclusion was reached is very revealing about the construction of technological knowledge and authority in the early seventeenth century.

Golius's report on the site of Aier is quite long and complex. It is also, with regard to the technical aspect of the project, based on hearsay and not on his own examination. In fact, neither Golius nor Ruyl visited the site on which the harbor would have been built. Only two members of the mission went to Aier when the Dutch envoys were in Marrakesh, and they are barely mentioned in Ruyl's diary: the two craftsmen, the stone mason Baerent Volmer, and his companion Isaac de Backer, who were sent on July 18, 1623, to examine the site. According to Golius's report, they "were led in great haste to flooded rocks that they had to remove. As they said it was impossible, they were sent back on the third day."[49] Golius then presented a forceful case detailing the technical impossibility of the project. He minutely described the reefs, insisting that they were a major obstacle for navigation. Moreover, removing them would be extremely difficult because of the roughness of the sea on this coast, making the rafts needed by the stone workers very unsteady and dangerous. Furthermore, even if it were possible to take off the reefs, a big sand ridge would create problems for ships.

The two stoneworkers who examined the site did not write down their own conclusions in any reports. The accounts we have on their views are not as clear-cut as Golius implied in his report, where he said that he had spoken to them and others in order to describe the site and come to his final assessment, even if Ruyl, during his stay in Marrakesh, wrote in his diary: "On Saturday 5 August [1623], I received from master Baerent Volmer, the stone mason, a letter written in Safi dated 30 July. He tells me that they had been with the qā'ids to the new port of Aier . . . which they had found to be completely different from what the Jews [i.e., the Pallaches] had described, as it is not possible to remove the reefs at the entrance of this port."[50] The same Volmer, however, would later give a quite different assessment to two Dutch officials who met with him in Amsterdam and wrote a report to the States

General dated September 13, 1624: "But, concerning the possibility to do this job, all that the said Volmer could tell us was that it should be done by the means of large vertical rammers, put on rafts and operated by seventy to eighty men. One could work only at low tide. To cut the top of the reefs little by little, six or eight men would hold and direct at them a strong iron pick that one would hammer with a mallet. He said that the stone was sandy and rather like, as far as hardness, the stone of Bentheim."[51] Not only does this report suggest that it was possible to remove the reefs that were blocking the entrance of the lagoon, it also proposes technical detail on how it could be done. In this discrepancy between Volmer's and Golius's assessments, the latter's conclusion carried the final decision. This cannot be merely attributed to privileging the university-trained mathematician's theoretical knowledge over the practical knowledge of the master craftsman. In fact, if salary is a reliable indication, the Dutch state placed a higher value on technical skill. The master stoneworker Volmer, who received a salary of sixty guilders per month, was much better paid than the engineer Golius, who received forty. The latter, however, had a higher salary than the companion stoneworker, de Backer, who was paid thirty.[52] The discrepancy in salary between Golius and Volmer is somewhat surprising, since historian Erik Swart's study of Dutch engineers indicates that "the level of pay of 'ingenieurs' in the first half of the seventeenth century corresponds to that of skilled artisans in Holland."[53] Maybe Volmer was particularly well known for his mastery and experience.

This discrepancy notwithstanding, Ruyl's diary clearly suggests that Golius was far more important to the mission than Volmer. Ruyl's assessment might have been influenced by their social difference. He talked more often in his diary about Jacob Golius, scion of a prominent family and university student, and Pieter van Neste, who was in the employ of the prince of Orange, than he did about the craftsmen. In addition, Golius often appears in the diary not in his capacity as an engineer but rather as Ruyl's close collaborator, sent to represent him in meetings, such as the one with Mūlay Zaydān in April 1624. In contrast, Volmer is only mentioned about Aier and his assessment of the site.

A close examination of Golius's report makes clear why it was given more weight than the brief testimony of Volmer. His title as engineer did not imply that his work was confined to the narrowly conceived technical part of the Aier project. His report provides a great deal of the information about the project. It began by offering a detailed narrative of how the scheme came to be. The Frenchman Saint-Mandrier was evidently a major source for the historical part of Golius's report. He learned about the site from a Morisco (probably in late 1618), was sent by the sultan to examine the lagoon, concluded that a viable harbor could be built, and, in early 1619, informed French envoy Claude Du Mas of the potentialities of the lagoon. Back in France, Du Mas and others created a society, with the goal of exploiting the port for fish, coral, salt, and other products. On his way back to Morocco, Du Mas stopped in Cádiz, and showed the plan for the site to Don Fadrico of Toledo, Spanish admiral for the Atlantic, who, according to Golius, would sometime later send a frigate to examine the site, concluding that the project was not feasible. In the meantime, the sultan had decided to propose the affair to the Dutch Republic. He ordered Saint-Mandrier to produce a drawing of the site and give it to Outger Claesz., a Dutch ship captain who was in Morocco at that time and who would carry it to the Netherlands. After this point, Golius's narrative is based on the observations made by the Dutch envoys themselves, including the long waiting time in Safi, and the turmoil provoked by the arrival of the Nassau fleet. Alarmed that the plans had been shown to the Spanish admiral, Mūlay Zaydān had Du Mas and Saint-Mandrier arrested. The latter was probably able to convince the sultan that he was not involved in Du Mas's dealings with the Spaniards, and was soon released (on September 8, 1623), but at the time that Golius was writing, the other Frenchman was still in prison.

Golius's negative evaluation of the site and its potentialities was in clear agreement with Ruyl's diary. His presentation of Volmer's technical assessment that the removal of the reefs was "impossible," and that the sandbank would make navigation difficult echoes Ruyl's summary of the letter he received from Volmer in August 1623.[54] His final advice was also based on a political estimation: this project would not be viable, given that the local population often rebelled against the sultan, and that they would never accept that a foreign power would operate the port. In fact, "several of their kings have paid such concessions with their throne and with their lives."[55] Ruyl had already made that point in a letter dated May 25, 1623, before Volmer and de Backer were even sent to the site, a letter in which he gave specific examples of such occurrences that ended with the slaying of two sultans: the alliance of Muhammad al-Mutawakkil with Portugal in the 1570s, and the cession of al-'Arā'ish to Spain in 1610 by al-Shaykh al-Ma'mūn.[56] Golius concluded that the value of the commerce of the Dutch Republic with the Saʿdī state did not necessitate a new port, especially considering all the risks and difficulties involved.

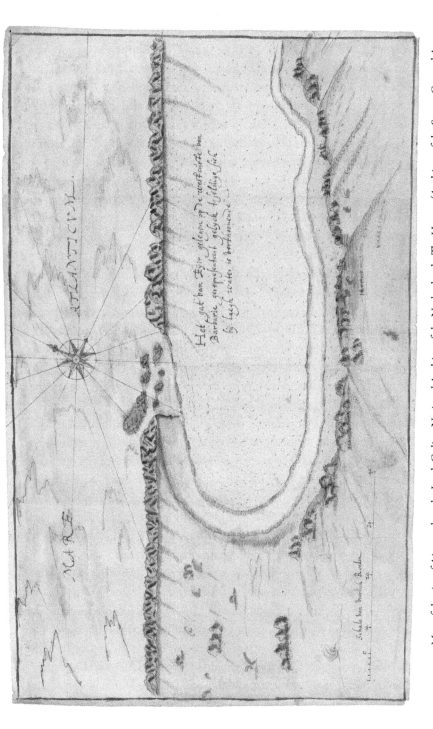

MARE

ATLANTICUM.

Het gat van Aier gelegen op De westsijde van
Barbarie geprosondeert gelijck t syllinge sich
bij laegh water is bethoonende

Schdl van twalls Roeden.

FIGURE 12. Map of the site of Aier, perhaps by Jacob Golius. National Archive of the Netherlands, The Hague. (Archives of the States-General Access code 1.01.02, inventory number 6897). By permission.

Golius's report was accompanied by a map of the lagoon, probably authored by him as well (see fig. 12). As both the cartographer and the historian of the project, he synthetized and reduced to its essentials the repetitive and cantankerous Ruyl's narrative, interpreted Volmer's estimation of the material site, evaluated the information provided by Saint-Mandrier and others, and produced an assessment that put together all the relevant concerns to the decision. In this final judgment, the physical characteristics of the place are just an element alongside the precarious hold of Mūlay Zaydān over the region, and the historical reluctance of the local population to a European and Christian presence on the coast.

EARLY MODERN ENGINEERS AND EXPERTS

Golius's task as an engineer was thus to mediate between the different stakeholders, as well as between the technical and the political, and the practical and the scholarly. During this mission, he appears to be quite similar to the "expert mediators" of Elizabethan England analyzed by historian Eric H. Ash. Ash has described the way these experts were able to use their understanding of technical matters in order to supervise projects, while at the same time using their social skills and standing to make possible a smooth communication between the technicians and the people who commission their work, in Golius's case the Dutch state.[57]

Despite the obvious anachronism, since the word *expert* does not appear in sources, Ash proposes to use the term to designate "a new concept emerging in early modern Europe, a form of knowledge that was not entirely rooted in empirical, hands-on experience, nor yet in practical mathematics, nor in a rarified natural philosophy, but arose instead from a fluid combination of these various forms of knowing."[58] It could be argued that a better choice would be to use the term employed by the sources, according to which Golius was an engineer. This designation might, however, actually compound the issue of anachronism, since what is considered an engineer today is very different from what the same term covered at that time. The word itself, coming from Latin, is quite old in European languages. It existed in French since at least the twelfth century, designating a still vague function that nevertheless gestures toward the early modern definition: "a maker of machines, but also a mechanic, an architect, someone who draws the plans for a project and directs its execution."[59] The term *engineer* begins to approach the modern definition only at the beginning of the eighteenth century.[60]

Golius, a gifted student of mathematics, was cast in the role of the expert who mediates between different observers of the situation, including the craftsmen, the diplomats, and the state, and then issues a final recommendation. His counterpart in Morocco on the Aier project was Saint-Mandrier. The reflection on the words *expert* and *engineer,* and how this position was enacted in North Africa, continues with the assessment of the part played by Saint-Mandrier, including the role of foreigners and foreign techniques, an important question exemplified by the Aier project.

Saint-Mandrier, an interesting and murky character, is a very minor figure in early modern history, although his contemporary Honoré Bouche (1599–1671) described him as being "very illustrious during his lifetime and in his death."[61] Several documents record his life and career, and help illuminate the question of technology and its circulation in the early modern Mediterranean. French historians of the colonial period have tended to paint him as an almost heroic character, a portrayal not borne out by the sources.[62] Antoine de Salettes, sieur de Saint-Mandrier (whose name appears in documents under different forms),[63] was born around 1580 in Provence, which became part of France in 1594. A member of a band of adventurers, he committed a murder in Toulon in 1611, and left France to escape justice. He was hired as a mercenary by Charles-Emmanuel I, duke of Savoy, and headed a company of about a hundred men, almost all criminals who had fled France. He obtained *lettres de marque* from the duke, giving him license to arm a ship and seize enemy vessels, and became a notorious corsair. On May 30, 1614, he captured a Dutch ship in Carthagena and headed to the Moroccan Atlantic port of Maʿmūra, at that time a refuge for mostly European pirates. When the Spanish admiral seized the port on August 3, 1614, Saint-Mandrier fled on land and was taken prisoner by the sultan's army. Thanks to his military talents and experience, he found employment in the service of Mūlay Zaydān.

Contemporary sources agree that his function was to produce and use weapons and gunpowder and to help fortify places. Jorge Mascarenhas, the governor of the Portuguese stronghold of Mazagan on the Moroccan coast, called him, in a letter dated January 1619, Mūlay Zaydān's "founder of artillery and his engineer."[64] In a letter dated May 1, 1623, Felipe IV of Spain talked about him as a "French engineer, in the service of Mūlay Zaydān."[65] Another contemporary account by the historian Cespedes (d. 1638) described him with a little more detail as "a Frenchman, and great confidant of Zaydān

... who knowing him to be conversant about fortification and foundries, spared him, and made him his favorite."[66] A few decades later, Bouche wrote that the sultan took him to his service "and used him for his wars as for infantry as well as cavalry." Bouche also remarked upon his prowess: "He had amazing success; being extremely adept in all sort of military exercise, and very knowledgeable in mathematical sciences; so much that in little time he acquired great credit in the mind of the King of Marrakesh, distributing the state positions to whom he pleased."[67] The descriptions of his capacities and of his position in the Saʿdī *makhzan* seem to get inflated with the passage of time, from being a valued employee in the sultan's army to running his government. This exaggeration of his importance continued arguably up to the twentieth century, when de Castries asserted that thanks to Saint-Mandrier, "one could see in Morocco cannon foundries and saltpeter refineries," implying that it had never happened before him, and that the presence in Morocco of this foreign engineer was proof of the absence of these productions before he introduced them.[68] In fact, both Moroccan and European sources attest unequivocally that there were foundries and refineries during the time of Mūlay Zaydān's father.[69] Furthermore, evidence of a domestic arms industry appeared in Morocco much earlier.[70] De Castries implies that there was something unique about the position of this Frenchman in the Moroccan sultan's army. In fact, recent scholarship has shown that "the employment of foreign military technicians and artisans . . . was a well-established practice all over Europe."[71]

The business in which Saint-Mandrier specialized was international. Before Morocco, he had already been employed in France and Savoy, and he tried to obtain a position in Spain. De Castries epitomizes the discrepancy that has long characterized the assessment of the presence of foreign military technicians in early modern Islamic countries, as opposed to the same phenomenon which is well attested, among others, in England and France, where many Italians and Germans made careers.[72] Interpreting Saint-Mandrier's presence in Morocco as the proof that before him, military technology was lacking, is the result of a common bias that extended far beyond de Castries's time. In the minds of many, "when experts travel from Italy to England, it is taken as a sign of openness to new ideas; when they travel from Italy to Turkey, suddenly it is a crippling dependence on foreign technology."[73] What is at stake here is not merely the irritating double standard, but also the fact that it obscures the continuities across boundaries and distorts the historical record.

Mūlay Zaydān taking Saint-Mandrier into his service was no different from the practice of other Islamic and European rulers. He aimed at taking advantage of foreign talent and maybe learning about the ways of the enemy. That Saint-Mandrier entered the sultan's service as a prisoner of war gave him only a very relative specificity, since many other military technicians were forced down the same path. In this respect, he was also similar to the collaborators of Orientalists who, like Hasan al-Wazzān / Leo Africanus and lesser-known others, were put in such a position by the hazards of war and corsair activity. However, contrary to Leo Africanus, Saint-Mandrier is not said to have converted, in contrast with the numerous "renegades" from Europe who left their Christianity behind to pursue their careers and lives in Muslim countries.[74] This resistance to whatever pressure he might have received from the sultan or others could suggest that he intended to keep all options open for his transnational career. One of the commonalities across boundaries masked by the quasi-heroic view of Saint-Mandrier presented by de Castries and Coindreau, is the fact that the French adventurer embodied a form of competence that seems to have spread during the early modern period not only in many parts of Europe but also in North Africa: that of the military expert practitioner. The meeting between Saint-Mandrier and Golius was an encounter between two experts, one in the service of the sultan, the other representing the interests of the Dutch state. Their assessments of the potentialities of Aier were very different.

As is the case for many parts of the story of Aier, the main sources concerning Saint-Mandrier's work are the writings of the Dutch envoys. The Frenchman was probably the first expert sent by the sultan to examine its potentialities for a harbor. The French company created to exploit the projected port also sent its own expert to visit the place and "ascertain if it was stone, dirt, or sand, and generally all its situation and force, this with the advice of people who understand best about fortifications."[75] When the sultan decided against the French involvement and chose to rather work with the Dutch, he instructed Saint-Mandrier to produce a drawing of the site.[76] In sum, Saint-Mandrier was the counterpart of Golius, who would also make a map and offer his own, decidedly negative, expert opinion. He thus had to undermine Saint-Mandrier's earlier, favorable estimation. According to Golius, the Frenchman's assessment was based on a superficial analysis, as he did not have a raft or a boat to sound the depths of the waters or estimate the shape of the reefs at different times of the tide. Unnamed others agreed that the site could be made into a harbor, but they knew nothing, Golius said, about sea and ports.[77]

Saint-Mandrier's experience and testimony were also relevant to another aspect of the Dutch mission, saltpeter. This substance had been used for centuries in tanning, soapmaking, metallurgy, and other industrial processes, but in the early modern period, it became overwhelmingly employed to make gunpowder, after having been refined into pure potassium nitrate. During the reign of Elizabeth, England had imported saltpeter from Morocco to that end, often in exchange for other strategic products, such as munitions and shipbuilding materials.[78] Since the early days of their alliance, the exportation of saltpeter from the Sa'dīs to the Netherlands was a crucial part of the negotiations and agreements between the governments, and Mūlay Zaydān sought to exchange this quintessential "commodity of Empire" for the States General's help with Aier.[79]

Saint-Mandrier himself supervised part of the production of saltpeter, and he provided information to the Dutch envoys. The latter were not deterred from seeking advice from him, despite his arrest that Ruyl learned about on June 16, 1623, and the obvious deterioration of his position in court.[80] He was released on September 8, and the very next day, he met with the Dutch, only one of many occasions during their time in Marrakesh, including the moment of their departure.[81] Ruyl wanted to hear from him about saltpeter production, as an expert "most competent in the matter, since he was in charge of it for three years and everything had gone through him."[82] His assessment of the low yield of the four *ingenios,* or saltpeter mills, that he had founded, helped convince Ruyl to drop that part of the project, which might have been Saint-Mandrier's goal all along. In fact, other estimations were fairly higher. These include the opinion of a Jewish concessionaire for saltpeter production who was willing to arrive at an agreement with the Dutch, and more relevantly, the assessment by Ruyl's own expert, Golius, who, accompanied by van Neste, had visited the mills. However, Ruyl concluded that the investment would not be profitable. The Aier project was thus altogether abandoned.

A less ambitious version of the port would be undertaken in 1634 by Mūlay Zaydān's son Mūlay al-Walīd, who built a fort and exploited the salines to produce salt. The Walīdiyya site was thus described to Thomas Le Gendre: "a small port for boats and midsized ships, as it has at its entrance a reef that makes it difficult, and there is just a fort and a very small town."[83] As for Saint-Mandrier, he soon made more overtures to Spain, which put him in an increasingly perilous situation in the Sa'dī court.[84] He tried to escape, was caught, and was finally executed. Despite Saint-Mandrier's end, both

Golius and Saint-Mandrier represent in the Aier project the new role of early modern engineers, one belonging to a new class of technical experts, who exercised their craft in warfare, and were needed by political powers.

The figure of the early modern engineer-expert has thus far been investigated almost exclusively in the European context. In Europe, specific schools to train engineers, first for the military and later for civil engineering, were not created before the eighteenth century. However, at least since the sixteenth century, an early form of that function, less clearly defined, and without the benefit of an elaborate and dedicated cursus of instruction, began to exist in the military context. Engineers and their schools came into existence in the Ottoman Empire in the eighteenth century—when reformist sultans proposed the example of European, especially French, institutions—and then during the following century in Egypt.[85] Little is known about the medieval or early modern figure of the engineer before the formalization of training, and before demand increased for these professionals for both military and industrial purposes. Despite the scarcity of sources, a tentative exploration of the issue yields a few provisional conclusions.

As seen earlier, European documents refer to Saint-Mandrier as an "engineer," sometimes specifying that he was a cannon founder, that he had knowledge about fortifications, or that he had a competence in mathematics or geometry. Indeed, both the military element and the connection to mathematics are defining features of the early modern engineer. The role of the engineer and his work was shaped in the early sixteenth century, a modification connected to the transformation of warfare. Military historian Steven A. Walton describes the emergence of the engineer as a military expert: "When gunpowder artillery changed the face of warfare in the sixteenth century, first seen in fortification design and then later in naval and eventually field tactics, the practitioners also changed."[86] The role of this new engineer was to help in the war effort, as cultural historian Hélène Vérin has noted: "War between kingdoms and principalities is the sphere of activity of engineers *par excellence*."[87] In Dutch, when the word *ingenieur,* borrowed from French, appeared in the mid-sixteenth century, its original meaning was "purely military," and toward the end of the century predominantly referred to "military engineers working on fortifications."[88] The transformations in offensive and defensive forms of warfare, with guns becoming more efficient, and fortifications more resilient, changed the role of the engineer in the sixteenth and seventeenth centuries, both intellectually and socially.

Applying mathematics to tasks that were the purview of craftsmen had been established long before it became prominent in the early modern period. Centuries before the birth of the early modern engineer, the exchange between mathematics, especially geometry, and the work of artisans was already explicit in the work of the philosopher Abū Nasr al-Fārābī (c. 872–c.950), whose *Ihsā' al-'Ulūm* (Enumeration of the Sciences) devotes a chapter to the discipline called *'ilm al-hiyāl*.[89] The word *'ilm* means science, and the word *hiyāl* (sing. *hīla*) can mean "tricks" but was also used to designate "industrious techniques," as well as the devices and tools they produce. The main feature of this science is that it entails "the application to natural bodies of all that has been demonstrated by mathematics."[90] This science comprised the knowledge needed by craftsmen, according to Fārābī, who recognized "three sets of procedures called *handasiyya* (geometrical)," the first being construction, the second the "processes for measuring the different sorts of bodies," and the third the fabrication of astronomical, musical and optical instruments, arms, mirrors, and automata.[91] Thus, the notion of using mathematical principles for practical purposes is not an early modern innovation. It was already part of medieval culture, both in Arabic-language writing, as well as in Europe, and these two might well be related. The Latin translation of Fārābī's treatise exerted a considerable influence in Europe, and Domenico Gundisalvi (c. 1115–c.1190) rendered *'ilm al-hiyāl* by *scientia de ingeniis,* which points to a lineage between the making of various instruments by craftsmen applying geometrical principles, and the late medieval or early modern "engineer."[92] There were thus, both in the Arab and the European cultures, a tradition of applying mathematical knowledge to the mechanical arts and crafts.

Warfare and its early modern prevalence and efficiency helped develop this connection. This makes highly significant the few mentions of Saint-Mandrier's knowledge of "geometry," in the words of Cespedes, and of "mathematical sciences," according to Bouche. This does not necessarily mean that the Frenchman was a serious student of mathematics. There is in fact no evidence that he studied in any university, and that his knowledge would be comparable to that of the other expert he encountered, Golius. The latter would soon abandon altogether any engineering career and become one of the great scholars of his time, both in mathematics and in oriental philology. More broadly, the level of proficiency of early modern engineers or "mathematical practitioners" was not necessarily very high: "their definition of being 'mathematical' was not as 'scientific' as ours."[93]

Whatever the true level of the ability of the engineer, this figure became increasingly important in European armies. The documents on Saint-Mandrier help begin an investigation on a similar evolution in North Africa. Hajarī again is a useful guide to the cultural interactions between the two regions. His work is, as far as is known, the only Arabic source to mention Saint-Mandrier. Several years after the Aier affair and the death of the Frenchman, Hajarī brought him up in the appendix to his translation of Ibrāhīm Ghānim's manual of artillery. According to Hajarī, "Captain Samandris" was a *mudāfiʿ wa muhandis,* a "gunner and engineer."[94] Hajarī described how Saint-Mandrier was able to become "a close companion" of Mūlay Zaydān by telling him "certain of the secrets of the art of gunnery." This statement is followed by a few sentences that are not translated in Harvey's version, since, as he explained in parentheses, "the Arabic text here is obscure." It is indeed, and it concerns a somewhat technical matter that Hajarī had complicated by passing over relevant information. The untranslated Arabic text mentions a conversation between Saint-Mandrier and the sultan: "I think it was about the numbered ruler that this book mentions." Hajarī refers here to chapter 31 of Ghānim's manual, which explained in detail how to make a ruler which helps calculate the weight of the balls depending on their material (lead, stone, or iron), by measuring the diameter of the cannon bore and by using different compasses. Hajarī offered only a very succinct and indeed confusing explanation before concluding: "You know the weight of any ball from the ruler. The point is that you can make the measurements and do the job thanks to the marks on the ruler."[95]

Despite its turbid brevity, this text offers a number of interesting elements concerning technical knowledge in early seventeenth-century Maghribi society. The use of the word *muhandis,* which is the modern Arabic term for engineer, is especially revealing since it was not common at that time. Some lexicographical exploration is necessary to show the extent and limits of his innovation, or, at least, of his assignation of an uncommon meaning to the word. The term comes from *handasa,* a word of Persian origins that designates the scholarly field of geometry. Fārābī, connecting artisan and scholarly knowledge, and speaking of the use in craftmanship of the principles of *handasa,* did not call *muhandis* the person who did implement this relation.

If the connection between mathematics and practical arts had had currency in Arabic texts, the authors rarely mentioned a practitioner called a *muhandis* who would enact that connection.

A few practitioners were designated by this name. Authoritative dictionaries' definitions apply the term to the person who measures subterranean water channels.[96] The word had also been sometimes used for builders and architects in Mamluk Egypt, and probably in other regions. As seen earlier, Fārābī recognized that construction necessitated geometrical (*handasiyya*) procedures. Some Mamluk chroniclers used the term *muhandis* (along with other words) to designate the person in charge of "the building of bridges, dams, canals and aqueducts,"[97] and other types of large buildings, such as madrasas or big mosques. It did not seem to designate an independent common trade (like masons, plasterers, or decorators), but was linked to an assignment by the court that commissioned those expensive buildings. In sum, when employed, which was not common, this word designated someone akin to a supervisor or a contractor of large architectural projects, who mediated between "the ruling establishment and the specialized craftsmen."[98] In the Maghrib, the word might have been even less often employed in the sense of builder, architect, or contractor. The celebrated author Ibn Khaldūn insists that parts of *handasa* or geometry are useful to some crafts such as carpentry and architecture, without using the word *muhandis* to designate the man in charge of building projects.[99]

Hajarī's use of this term to speak about a practitioner is thus remarkable, at least in Maghribi texts. Besides, the meaning he assigns to the word differs from the way it was understood by Mamluk chroniclers. His appendix to the gunnery manual applies it to Saint-Mandrier but also to another character, who had been brought to Tunis by the ruler, ". . . the Engineer Captain (*Raïs*) who in Algiers demonstrated his ability in putting the harbour in order. He brought a plenteous water-supply there and to the new edifices. This was al-Hāj Mūsā, known as Jamiro al-Andalusī al-Gharnātī. He undertook the repair of the port at Bizerta on the orders of the Dey, may Allah make him content, he also set in order everything necessary for ships and galleys to put in there and to repel the unbelievers."[100] Using in the same text, the same word *muhandis* for Hāj Mūsā and for Saint-Mandrier, Hajarī indicates that there were commonalities between the two men that could be linked to building, as some documents state that the Frenchman knew about fortifications, but also, very importantly, to their expertise in military matters.[101] In sum, its meaning is very close to that of *engineer* in European languages. One could argue that Mūsā personifies the transition between the old *muhandis,* since he was also a specialist of irrigation, and the early modern one, whose foremost domain of competence was military.

Mūsā left traces in other records. Even European writers, like the Trinitarian friar Pierre Dan, knew that Mūsā ("maistre Mousse") had built fountains in Algiers.[102] A Spaniard named Fray Melchor called Mūsā a *fontanero,* but also talked about his work on the fortifications of Algiers.[103] The mentions of Mūsā in Arabic sources show that Hajarī was seemingly the only one to describe him as a *muhandis.* The inscriptions on Algiers' monuments that Mūsā built or restored, call him a *muʿallim,* a master craftsman, or a *sāhib al-mabānī,* a master builder.[104] The chronicler Ibn Abī Dīnār (d. ca. 1690), mentioned him in his history of Tunisia as the person in charge of the building of the fortifications, and also called him a *muʿallim.*[105] He did not distinguish the function of this skilled man from that of an artisan, at least not to a degree that would warrant the usage of a different word.

The use of *muhandis* in Hajarī's text is thus unusual. Furthermore, the content he assigned to it is consistent with the contemporary, and somewhat unstable, meaning of the word engineer in European languages. This is suggested by the brief description of how Saint-Mandrier attracted the sultan's attention by employing mathematical instruments to understand artillery, indicating the connection with mathematics that is so important in the evolution of the word and of the function in Europe. The term appears again a few times in Hajarī's translation of Ibrāhīm Ghānim's text, and a brief analysis of these occurrences will help understand the oscillation of its meaning. In a few cases, it clearly designates the scholar who works in the academic field of geometry, when the text associates the *muhandis* to the astronomer, and opposes both to the craftsman.[106] On one occasion, it is, like in the description of Saint-Mandrier, connected to the use of instruments, when the text mentions differences among engineers concerning the utilization of the set square to determine the trajectory of the cannonball.[107] Early in the text, an enumeration situates the engineer between the scholars on the one hand, and the people in charge of organization in the army on the other hand, almost as an intermediary between the learned and the practitioners of warfare.[108] When Ibrāhīm Ghānim mentions the rudimentary schools of artillery that existed at the time in Spain, he says that the teacher, who held the grade of captain, had to be an accomplished gunner, as well as an engineer.[109] This usage indicates a distinction between the two functions, which is made more explicit later, when Ghānim discusses how to place guns on a battlefield field, a determination that has to be made in consultation between "gunners and engineers."[110] The function of the latter is to dig tunnels or build bridges.[111] In these last occurrences, rather than simply denoting a general knowledge and application of mathematics, the word designates more precisely the builders of constructions for warfare. In sum, except for the rare cases in which it is clearly used to designate the geometer, as the scholar in the field of geometry or *handasa,* the word *muhandis* is employed by Hajarī as essentially the equivalent of *engineer* in European languages at the time, to denote a skilled mathematical practitioner who focuses on the more technical aspects of warfare, such as the cannonball path or the design and building of constructions for the army.

How groundbreaking Hajarī's use of the word in this specific sense is can only be ascertained by a more thorough examination of a wider range of sources than what has been proposed here. What might be new at the time is the very choice of writing about these specialized workers within the military. Even the fact that Ibn Abī Dīnār in his chronicle named Mūsā, who fortified Algiers and Tunis, and not just the rulers who commissioned and paid for the work, might indicate a higher prominence of a category of technicians, whether they are called craftsmen or engineers, as was happening in Europe. The clues assembled here point again to a parallel and probably connected evolution occurring in North Africa, even if on a lesser scale. As for the Ottoman army, according to Luigi Marsigli, author of the "best treatise on the seventeenth-century and early eighteenth-century Ottoman military,"[112] it counted a corps of artificers called *mimars,* which the author translated in Italian as *ingenieri militari* and in French simply as *ingénieurs.*[113] The word *mi'mar* is connected to architecture and construction, and thus likely designates the engineers in charge of building bridges or tunnels, as Ghānim described them.

A century before the publication of Marsigli's work, Hajarī's text attests to the recognition of a similar function in the Ottoman as well as non-Ottoman Maghrib. How widespread this recognition was remains to be explored in greater detail. Hajarī was certainly, if not a pioneer, at least unusual. This points again to his perceptiveness as a witness of his time, and of the modes of cultural interaction of North Africa and Europe in the early modern period. By his choice of words and his descriptions, he testifies to an awareness in North Africa of an early modality of what would later become the profession of engineer, and of the existence of a transitory figure between the medieval builder or specialist of irrigation, and the modern engineer.

• • •

The numerous documents produced around and about the failed project by Mūlay Zaydān to build a harbor in Aier offer many clues to understanding the place of technical knowledge in the culture and politics of the early seventeenth-century Maghrib. These indications do not merely provide information about the kind of technologies that were in use, they also help understand how these technologies were situated in the interaction between Europe and North Africa. They tell us about the entanglement of several forms of exchange: political, scholarly, and personal. Golius, Hajarī, Ruyl, Mūlay Zaydān, and even Saint-Mandrier, were more or less active participants in all of these interactions. They represented divergent political interests at a time of momentous change affecting the shores of the Mediterranean, as well as southern and northern Europe. They could nevertheless also engage in associations and help the circulation of knowledge and ways of knowing between polities and regions.

The academic and pragmatic fashions in which early modern Orientalist learning was constructed in the first part of the seventeenth century confronted each other in the persons of Golius, the Leiden University student, and Ruyl, the former VOC trader, although no trace of any dialogue in which they might have compared their experiences has reached us. Beyond Orientalism, the Aier affair was the site of other exchanges not only between North Africa and Europe but also between high and low culture. Safi and Marrakesh can, in this instance, be described as the trading zones "in which learned men and artisan practitioners communicated reciprocally, exchanging knowledge."[114] Golius had to hear from Volmer the stoneworker in order to produce his final assessment on the viability of the project. As an engineer, he was embodying a renewed form of technical knowledge, combining the practical skills of craftsmen and the theoretical learning of scholars, especially in the fields of mathematics and geometry. This process in itself was not entirely new, and medieval precedents are attested. However, the more visible emergence of the figure of the technician who specialized in that connection, especially in warfare, indicates a deeper social transformation. Hajarī, and maybe others, gave to North African "mathematical practitioners," a name which drew on the previously recognized relation between geometry, *handasa,* and some crafts.

It is no coincidence that this rare (for its time) occurrence of the word *muhandis* as the equivalent of the contemporary *engineer* appeared in Hajarī's translation of Ibrāhīm Ghānim's manual of artillery. This translation, which is the subject of the next and final chapter, illustrates another early modern evolution of technical culture, well known and already studied in the European context, the writing of technical manuals, especially concerning the military arts, and the transformation of artisans' practices into learned discourses. Like the birth of the *muhandis,* such changes are attested to a lesser extent in North Africa. Through a close reading of this translation, the concluding chapter will continue the exploration of the role of the engineer in early seventeenth-century North Africa, and reflect on this evolution in the Maghrib, in the context of the exchange of knowledge practices and discourses between Europe and North Africa, between high and low culture, and between the competence of the artisan and the learning of the scholar.

SIX

———

Artillery and Practical Knowledge in North Africa

IN HIS INFLUENTIAL *Histoire de Barbarie et de ses corsaires* (1637), Pierre Dan, a friar of the order of the Holy Trinity, describes the fortress of Tunis, an imposing edifice built by Charles V after the 1535 conquest by the Habsburgs. Ottoman troops destroyed the fortress in 1574, but subsequently rebuilt and fortified it as a bastion for the defense of the capital, where, in the early seventeenth century, the Tunisians maintained "a garrison of fifty soldiers of their militia."[1] Unbeknown to Dan, this site, where conflict raged between imperial rivals of the Mediterranean world, nevertheless harbored intellectual exchanges in the region. Especially noteworthy are two treatises on artillery completed in the fortress.

In 1559, Fernández de Espinosa composed his never-published *Tratado de artillería, minas y fortificaciones,* and in 1632, Ibrāhīm Ghānim, a battle-hardened Morisco put in charge of the defense of the city, completed another Spanish-language book on the same subject. They belonged to a large early modern corpus of books on gunnery. In Europe in particular, beginning in the sixteenth century, practitioners took pen in hand to write about the craft of artillery, and pursued two closely related goals: they sought to improve their social status, and they endeavored to increase the reputation of artillery in the army. This effort first began in Italy, then moved to other regions, including Spain, France, and England, and eventually spread to the Maghrib. Ghānim's treatise is now lost, but fortunately, the Arabic version produced by Hajarī is still extant.

Hajarī undertook the translation of Ghānim's work in the later stages of his prolific career. After decades in Morocco, he headed east to perform the pilgrimage to Mecca. He sojourned in Egypt, where he wrote extensively, and finally settled in Tunis. Into his late sixties, Hajarī was still intellectually active. Beside his ongoing revisions of the *Supporter,* he was also a prolific translator from Arabic to Spanish, and vice versa. His Arabic version of Ghānim's treatise, that he titled *Kitāb al-'izz wa al-rif 'a wa al-manāfi' li l-mujāhidīn fī sabīl Allāh bi l-madāfi'* (The Book of Glory, Elevation, and Advantages of Artillery for the Righteous Warriors for God against the Infidels) is a fascinating intervention in the history of the intellectual and technical exchange between Europe and North Africa. It bears witness to the rise in Arab countries of a written middle culture alongside the rarefied and still largely dominant high scholarly production. As part of this evolution, technical knowledge was increasingly written down and codified. The translation also offers precious clues concerning the role played by patronage and state power in these changes. This text mediates not only between Europe and the Maghrib but also between high and low culture and between practical knowledge and theoretical learning, and it reveals the role of the technical expert in the societies of early seventeenth-century North Africa.[2]

GUNNERY AND PRACTICAL KNOWLEDGE

Ibrāhīm Ghānim, the author of this treatise, was known in Spanish as al-Ribāsh.[3] The only known source of information about the author's life is the text itself. The prologue informs the reader that he was born in the village of Nūlash, in the region of Granada, which he left with his family after the "distress," the repression and deportation of Moriscos that followed the second Alpujarras war, which ended in 1571. He eventually moved with his family to Seville, and became a sailor in this bustling colonial city. As a sailor, he traveled "with an army and men knowledgeable about artillery" across the Atlantic on the big fleets of galleons that transported silver from the "West Indies" (*al-hunūd al-gharbiyya*).[4] Before these long-distance travels, Ghānim attended one of the schools that trained the artillerymen needed for the fleets bound for America. These schools welcomed dozens of apprentices every year, usually sailors and soldiers but also carpenters, blacksmiths, or builders looking for a second career.[5] Ghānim admired the system, describing how students read books and practiced on a small gun: "On holidays, the artillerymen would get together and fire a gun on a white paper target the size of a shield, on a mound of dirt so that the balls don't get lost. Some would bet dirhams."[6] Naval gunners were in such high demand in Spain that in 1595 the Crown conceded important rights to them as incentives,[7] including exemption from debt prison.[8] Throughout the book, Ghānim displays great pride in his work and the privileges it bestows, and was likely pleased with his ability to read and write a long book, at a time when the percentage of gunners on the Spanish fleet who could sign their name was no higher than fifty-five.[9] He had, however, to hide his Morisco origins, since only Old Christians were admitted in the schools and on the fleet.

When the expulsion decree came, he was in jail after an altercation, but friends in high places procured his release. He then left Spain, despite, he says, being forbidden from doing so, even after he disclosed that he was a Morisco, and eventually had to bribe his way out of the country. Maybe Ghānim embellished this account to emphasize his desire to join the land of Muslims in order to make his North African readers forgive him for the years he spent serving the Spanish Crown. In any case, he left for Tunis, which had become an Ottoman province after its conquest in 1574. The ruler 'Uthmān Dey (r. 1598–1610) recognized his competence, and hired him as a corsair. Ghānim was given authority over two hundred Moriscos, provided weapons, and began to attack European vessels as a ra'īs, or ship captain. Shortly after 'Uthmān's death, he returned to Tunis with a meager bounty and an injury. When he went back to sea, his fleet encountered eleven Spanish galleys near Malaga. A bloody battle ensued, and Ghānim, wounded and captured, became a galley slave. He was ransomed after seven years, and was back in Tunis around 1617. Yūsuf Dey, who had succeeded 'Uthmān, assigned him the defense of Halq al-Wādī. Ghānim's life thus played out on the large stage of the Habsburg Empire. Before the expulsion, he participated in its Atlantic expansion. Afterward, he fought on its Mediterranean frontier and resisted European encroachments on the North African shore. In Halq al-Wādī, working with the artillery that defended the city from attacks, he furthered his knowledge of the weapons, and he read books on the subject. After fourteen years, in 1630 or 1631, he began to write his own treatise on artillery, which he completed on October 7, 1632. Hajarī finished his Arabic version on July 7, 1638.

The effort by practitioners to write about their craft, which developed in sixteenth-century Europe, was hardly confined to gunners. Other artisans began to compose texts to describe and discuss their work. This was part of a far-reaching change in the status of craftsmen in society, and illustrated the enhanced role of practical knowledge. In the Middle Ages, the social status of technical knowledge was limited in both Europe and North Africa, and the standing of people who worked with their hands was relatively low. The

Aristotelian foundations of medieval knowledge emphasized a sharp separation between theory (*episteme* or *scientia*) and practice (*praxis*). This schema assigned low prestige to technical skills (*technê*), which entailed bodily labor—skills that were further sullied by their connection to trade and money-making. On the other hand, theory was highly prized as the basis of scientific knowledge and mathematics.[10] Furthermore, technical knowledge was rarely written, and was usually not taught in schools, but handed down through apprenticeship. It was disseminated through practice and imitation, and not by the writing and study of books.

A similar antipathy for practical knowledge long prevailed in the Maghribi context as well. Ibn Khaldūn saw the social utility in the different categories of crafts (*sināʿa*), from the simple occupations that are necessary in all human societies to the arts of luxury that flourish in more advanced civilizations, but he did not ascribe to them honor or prestige, and he particularly disdained their connection to trade which, he said, favors people with unsavory character traits.[11] A few centuries later, the influential Moroccan scholar Hasan al-Yūsī (1631–91) penned a book in which he distinguished between the sciences that pertain to divine law and religion and the sciences that develop secular knowledge, knowledge he calls *falsafa*, a word derived from the Greek for *philosophy*.[12]

This secular knowledge could include prestigious disciplines such as mathematics or logic, as well as wholly practical fields. Yūsī's hierarchy of knowledge puts religious scholarship at the highest level, and the ways of knowing of the artisan at the lowest. Religious and secular domains were not, however, hermetically sealed and separated from each other. Religious scholars borrowed logic, for example, from the secular disciplines, and they helped develop some more theoretical disciplines, like astronomy or mathematics. Indeed, some scholars had an eye on the practical application of their research, as was the case in the mechanical field of weights,[13] and some even collaborated with makers of astrolabes and other instruments.[14] Even so, more practical forms of secular knowledge essentially stayed in the hands of the *ʿāmma,* the commoners or lay people, including, according to Yūsī, "farmers, builders, ship captains, magicians, geomancians, and that sort of people."[15] Overall, little deference was accorded to lay people who practiced more mundane crafts, whether related to medicine or agriculture or the mechanical arts, even if they did write about them, which remained rare. Muhammad Hajjī notes about the Moroccan author ʿAbd al-Ghānī al-Zammūrī (d. ca. 1621) that despite his authorship of books on medical remedies, "his contemporaries do not devote to him even a short biography, which is probably due to the fact that he was not also a jurist [*faqīh*] nor a belletrist [*adīb*]."[16]

The late fifteenth and the sixteenth centuries witnessed a considerable change in this order of things. In Europe, the three areas of knowledge, *episteme, praxis,* and *technê,* rather than being separate, became "linked in an entirely new way" as part of a series of transformations that renewed the approach to science and technology.[17] A decisive element of this transformation was that practical knowledge began to be written down and codified much more frequently than in earlier times. Technical literature would keep growing and influencing the work of more classically trained intellectuals, and in return, intellectuals would shape technical literature. Peter Burke argues in his *Social History of Knowledge* that "the so-called intellectual revolutions of early modern Europe—the Renaissance, the Scientific Revolution and the Enlightenment—were no more than the surfacing into visibility (and more especially into print), of certain kinds of popular or practical knowledge and their legitimation by some academic establishments."[18] This provocative statement puts in stark relief the importance of this transformation and belongs to a long-standing debate about the role that mechanical arts, carried by skilled artisans, played in helping produce these early modern transformations in European epistemologies.[19]

A somewhat analogous transformation, if not necessarily of similar scale and focus, also occurred in North Africa. In recognition of their military and civil projects in the defense and well-being of the community, skilled practitioners, like the aforementioned Mūsā, attained fame and power. A blurring of the lines separating craftsmen and intellectuals was modifying to some extent the modes of learning and writing in Arab countries. More people who were not elite scholars began to produce treatises and chronicles. Innovative studies have shown the blossoming of new writing modes, besides the production of the academic and religious elite, in seventeenth- and eighteenth-century Egypt and Syria. The elite did not cease to dominate the cultural field in terms of output and prestige, attracting the respect of rulers and population alike. Nevertheless, favorable economic conditions helped the development of a new middle-class audience, somewhat literate but not especially learned.

This new literacy influenced prose production in two ways. On the one hand, some educated academics wrote in less ornate forms, in order to reach a wider audience. An early example is the mystical writer Sha'rānī, who "specifically addressed tradesmen, craftsmen, workers, and simple people."[20] Sha'rānī was a model for Hajarī, who likely appreciated his simpler writing style. On the other hand, the increasing cultural visibility of literate though not highly learned people can be shown in the production of historical works written by the members of this new middle class. These texts often mixed the public and the private, the socially prestigious and the mundane. The Syrian notary Ibn al-Tawq (d. 1509) wrote a book that was "both a personal diary and a record of public events";[21] the barber Ahmad ibn Budayr (d. 1762) produced a chronicle of Damascus that did not record merely obituaries of prominent public figures but also those of his fellow barbers and craftsmen, and events not connected to the ruling class.[22] This increasing cultural visibility of a middle class of artisans and traders can also be seen in the work of Hannā Diyāb, who, after his time in Europe when he worked with Antoine Galland, became a cloth merchant in Aleppo. In his old age, he authored a lively memoir of his travels, which made few concessions to the forms of high culture.[23] Yūsuf al-Maghribī (d. 1610), who wrote a book on colloquial Egyptian, eventually studied in al-Azhar and became a scholar, but he "started out his life as an artisan. . . . He was familiar with the marketplace; he knew the vocabulary that was used by different craftsmen when talking about their work techniques and work tools."[24]

Scholars were also affected by this transformation. A very distinctive figure in seventeenth-century Moroccan culture, Muhammad b. Sulaymān al-Rūdānī (1627–83) studied with many prestigious scholars, from Marrakesh to Mecca, and became a famed theologian, logician, astronomer, and author of esteemed works. What set him apart was his dexterity in many crafts, including embroidery, goldsmithing, and bookbinding. When studying in Marrakesh, he paid for his expenses by making and selling shoes. Later, during his years in Arabia, he earned a living by producing astronomical instruments and metal- and glassware. His biographers memorialized his invention of a superior version of the astrolabe, of which he made and sold many copies, and wrote a treatise to explain its use.[25] The narration by the Moroccan traveler 'Ayyāshī clearly presents this innovative astrolabe as making a connection between Rūdānī's abilities as a craftsman and his scholarship as an astronomer, which helped him advance and codify technical knowledge.[26] Another later scholar interested in the mechanical arts is 'Abd al-Razzāq ibn Hamādūsh (1695–ca. 1785), whose interest in technology led him to visit the fortresses of Algiers to experiment with cannons, where he learned to shoot, to mix gunpowder, and to measure the angle of the gun, sometimes using instruments that were ascribed to "Christians," including an "English bow," or a kind of ruler "used by Christians," with no more details. He even wrote an opuscule on these issues.[27] Later, he mentions reading a European book on geometry and surveying, although he does not say if it was translated or in a foreign language.[28]

These examples illustrate the rise in Arab countries of a prose production distinct from the elite scholarly output, often written in a simpler language accessible to the less learned, and taking as its subject forms of practical knowledge ignored by most academics. These texts attest to a more sustained interaction between scholars and craftsmen, and a growing formalization of practical knowledge, echoing wider ranging and further reaching changes that were occurring in Europe. This context helps make better sense of the *Kitāb,* which, while using foreign models, should not be seen as alien in Arab culture but rather as exemplifying this larger trend. In addition to adapting European models for North African readers, the treatise made connections between high and low Maghribi cultures to produce an Arabic version of a book that took gunnery as its subject matter. Writing about the military arts presents strong specificities, given their necessary deployment in a political context, and their connection with centers of power, and with the courtly culture that develops around them.

ARTILLERY AND WRITING BETWEEN EUROPE AND NORTH AFRICA

The author and translator of the *Kitāb* did not aim at pleading for the adoption of gunpowder and artillery by Maghribi and Arab powers. At that time, these instruments of war had been for many decades already widely used in Arab and Islamic countries, and discussed in treatises.[29] As for the Maghrib, Hajarī testified in the appendix to his translation that his patron Mūlay Zaydān was able to field eighty cannons during the civil war. He also talked of the role of Saint-Mandrier, "gunner and engineer," in the sultan's army. Hajarī certainly knew about the military achievements of the Saʿdī dynasty, able to withstand decades of assaults from both the Iberians and the Ottomans thanks to their own successful deployment of firearms and artillery.[30] Evidence by contemporary authors show that other Maghribi powers were also effectively using artillery against attacks by Europeans. Pierre Dan's history of the Barbary coast and its pirates describes the many cannons that defended Algiers in the early seventeenth century.[31] As to the very place in which Ghānim and Hajarī were writing, a century before their time, Hasan al-Wazzān / Leo Africanus described how artillery repelled the 1519 assault of Pedro de Navarro on the Tunisian harbor of Mahdiyya.[32]

That does not mean that the *Kitāb* was not innovative in other ways. However, what was truly new was not the technology but the writing about it in North Africa. The writing of military treatises was a Europe-wide phenomenon, connected to the endemic state of war on the continent during the early modern period, and reaching different countries at different times. Italy witnessed the first groundbreaking work about the new forms of warfare in the early sixteenth century, at a time when the peninsula was subjected to constant invasions. Since the defensive craft of fortification needed to be rethought in light of the new efficacy of artillery, authors wrote treatises about the new forms called *trace italienne* or bastion forts that could better withstand cannon fire.[33] Practitioners composed artillery manuals, and some books explored both fortification and gunnery. Ghānim had direct access to the treatises on gunnery and fortifications written by the Spanish, who began to contribute seriously to the literature on the subject in the latter part of the sixteenth century. This flurry of texts coincided with the Eighty Years' War that began in 1568, during which the occupying Spanish army encountered grave difficulties when the Flemish rebels adopted the new style of fortifications. Spanish officers took to writing books calling for reform, and aiming at impressing upon the readers, especially the political class, the importance of the new forms of warfare and the increasing need to rely on technical knowledge.[34] Ghānim was obviously familiar with the *Plática manual de artillería* (Practical Manual of Artillery), a very influential treatise first published in Italian in 1586, then in a considerably revised Spanish edition in 1592. Its author, Luis Collado, was a master gunner and engineer of the Spanish army in Lombardy. Ghānim probably also read Cristobal Lechuga (1557–1622), one of the most important Spanish specialists of artillery in Flanders.[35] Lechuga was later sent to the North African frontier and participated in the seizure of Ma'mūra in 1614. In addition, Ghānim was likely familiar with Diego de Ufano's *Tratado dela artillería*, first published in 1612 and translated into several languages. Relying on the literature, and on his extensive experience both on ships and on land, Ghānim decided to compose his own treatise that included, like his models, many pictures of guns and tools.

To explain how he had the idea of composing this book, he provided a very informative narrative. After his release from captivity, Ghānim was assigned to the defense of Halq al-Wādī, a position he had held for fourteen years at the time he began writing. He observed how ignorant about their craft the artillerymen were that were sent to work under him. He was dismayed to note that the eight new recruits who would arrive every six months were dispatched to the job without having undergone any training, and were given the responsibility of the defense of the capital without knowing what would be expected from them. They would arrive without bringing "any of the instruments that the artilleryman needs," and did not display any care for their craft.[36] He compared this negligence with the discipline that prevailed in Spain, where he witnessed "good organization, and good care for what is needed at war for manning the guns." Working for the Spanish army, he could observe "excellent order for firearms, and numerous books by many authors that contain instruction and information for all who work in this rank, and to the gunners, and this feature is a part of their organization."[37] He described the training with which he had become familiar in the Spanish institution:

> First the members of the war council look at who deserves the rank of super-visor of gunners and who could teach the others. They only appoint one who has many years of experience in the craft. He is an engineer. He receives 30 *riyāl*s a month or thereabouts. He only answers to the head of the army, and he has the title of captain. And this pertains to places where there are foundries where they melt the metal needed to make weapons, in the coastal cities. The captain gunner is given a house or a place where he assembles some students in the craft of firearms. He sits on a high chair, and the students sit lower.[38]

Prospective students were vetted, and examined to make sure that they were healthy of body, neither weak nor disabled, nor drunkards. Their soul and their blood were also probed. Of course, no suspected heretics were admitted, and students had to produce a certification that they were Old Christians, and only from Spain or Italy, not from England, France, or Flanders. They must also be of "pure blood," that is, not descendants of Muslims or Jews. Unabashed in his admiration of the Spanish system, Ghānim, strikingly, made no effort to disguise that this institution was not only Christian but also very much beholden to the *limpieza di sangre* (pure blood) beliefs that justified the expulsion of Jews and Moriscos. Once the candidates were vet-ted as having a healthy body, a soul uncontaminated by heresy, and "pure blood," they were given a printed book that described "the good habits that the gunner must adopt concerning his manners toward his teacher and his superiors," and the knowledge of the gunnery craft expected of captains:

[He should know] the names of all the instruments that are necessary for the craft, the genres of cannons and their differences, how to measure the width and length of the ladles used to load the cannon with powder, and how to make in the presence of the captain paper templates of these ladles at the request of the master craftsman. He should have all the instruments that a gunner needs. He should draw all the kinds of cannons on paper, and the right diameter of their muzzles. He should learn how to load the cannon, and how to design the appropriate carriages to put them on, so that he can give the carpenter the right length and width.[39]

The instruction lasted up to three months. Then the student had to pass a public exam, in which he was asked questions in random order, not necessarily following the order of the book: "He stands up and takes off his hat in sign of humility and politeness. He only speaks to answer the questions directed at him. If the teacher sees that the student still has shortcomings, he tells him: 'Study more until you attain competency.' If he sees that the student has excelled, he gives him a certification (*ijāza*)."[40] The certification mentions the name of the licensed and of his father, his age, and some physical characteristics, in order to avoid fraud. It defended the rights of the trained gunner, who can see his competency recognized wherever he goes, and it helped avoid damage inflicted by the ignorant to the cannons, which were, as the text tirelessly stresses, a very expensive commodity. Ghānim also described fondly the competitive games among trainees who aimed a small cannon at a paper target, and concluded: "I wish this, or something close to it, existed in the countries of the Maghrib."[41]

The system he wanted to replicate is a sketchy, early form of the military academies that would not flourish until the eighteenth century. In Spain, rudimentary schools for gunners had existed since the sixteenth century, although only two—one in Seville, the other in Madrid—were still in place by the end of the century. Ghānim was undoubtedly trained in Seville, in the school created to staff the ships bound for America, which stayed in existence until 1681, and where training lasted two months and concluded with an exam.[42] Basically, he wanted to create in Tunis a system to train and license gunners, where he would be the first captain, and for which he wrote the manual. He was helping disseminate the Spanish model he was familiar with, which included a close interaction between the technical literature of gunnery and the programs offered in the early artillery schools that served the needs of empire.[43]

The treatise he wrote is comprised of a prologue, followed by fifty chapters, and finally the appendix by Hajarī. The largely autobiographical prologue reveals the author's credentials, details his knowledge and experience, and recounts his history with Spain, where he was born, where he served in the army, and which he fought after the expulsion on corsair ships and for the defense of Tunis. Chapter 1 deals with war in general, offers a brief history of firearms and gunpowder, explains the author's motivation and goals, and includes more autobiographical material. Chapter 2 approaches for the first time an essential theme, to which the book would often return: the instruments needed for the gunner to do his job. Then the text focuses on the three main types of cannons, how to recognize and differentiate them, how to test them to ascertain their quality, which tools are needed to operate and transport them, and how to make some of these instruments. More technical chapters are dedicated to shooting and to the calculation of distances. The text offers a variety of information, on the type of metal needed to cast guns, the best wood for their carriages, the fabrication of cartridges, grenades, and other small explosive devices, the refinery of saltpeter, and the manufacture of gunpowder. It also imparts logistical advice for the transport of artillery to distant battlefields or the building of temporary bridges, and provides tactical instruction on the positioning and aiming of guns in different circumstances. The final chapters recapitulate information concerning the instruments needed by gunners, and the manufacture of gunpowder. The last two chapters were written after the translation was completed and read by unnamed friends.

Belonging to a transnational movement of writing about artillery, the *Kitāb* presents many commonalities with other books. Like them, it seeks several audiences and has multiple goals. The prologue named the intended readers: the beginners in gunnery, and their military superiors.[44] The Spanish literature on artillery was closely linked to the rudimentary forms of instruction that gunners received at that time and that Ghānim himself had experienced. His most clearly and constantly stated goal was pedagogical: he wanted to produce a reference book for trainees. This puts in the proper perspective the decidedly practical aspect of the book and its evident lack of originality. Ghānim aimed at helping with the training of competent gunners, who would learn to manipulate and care for the cannons. He also wanted to teach them the more mathematical aspects of gunning, as well as an ethics of the artilleryman.

These potential readers are often referenced in the book. Toward the end of the book, Ghānim states: "You should know that the goal in writing this book is to teach the beginning gunners . . . it limits itself to this and it only mentions what they need to know."[45] Early on, the author stressed that ignorant gunners might break the guns, and he detailed the expense and effort needed to make and transport pieces of artillery, in order to convince readers that such a valuable commodity had to be handled with care and skill.[46] Untrained gunners could damage them even when firing them for celebrations, or simply when cleaning them. They could also break the carriages and their wheels.[47] The author wanted to protect the gunners as well as the guns. To stress the danger of guns, he recalled an accident in 1615 in the province of Valencia, when he was a captive on a Spanish ship. Cannon shots were fired to honor a grandee departing for Milan. A gunner reloaded too fast and was killed in the fire and explosion that followed. Ghānim even saw body parts flying.[48] Addressing beginners dictated authorial choices, such as the frequent repetitions: "If I say some things many times, this is for the benefit of the beginner and to impress his memory."[49] The numerous images of guns and different instruments also helped reach this pedagogical goal.

A precise analysis of the sources of the *Kitāb* is beyond the scope of this chapter, but it is important to keep in mind that Ghānim was adapting a widely disseminated discourse, and he readily acknowledged his indebtedness to predecessors. Its early date makes it an invaluable example of the ways in which not only technology but also the practices it entails, including writing, circulated between Europe and North Africa, and provides precious clues about the place of technology in Maghribi societies of its time. Writing about modern weaponry would become more prevalent in the Islamic world in the eighteenth century. Leaving aside the sizable number of Turkish treatises on mathematics and their use in war situations, other examples in Arabic can be found.[50] These include the remarkable 1779 treatise written in Belgrade by Osman Efendi, a convert to Islam, devoted to geometry and its military applications, especially to bomb throwing and mines.[51] Even before that date, Muhammad al-Aqkirmānī had produced a short Arabic treatise of surveying that could be "useful for people in everyday life and at war."[52] The production of treatises on artillery and gunpowder is also attested in the eighteenth-century Maghrib. About the time that Osman Efendi was writing, five such texts were written in Morocco during the reign of Muhammad III (r. 1757–90).[53] In that same time frame, Ibn Hamādūsh devoted a treatise to the use of cannons, after practicing in the fortresses of

Algiers. This inventory might very well be augmented by new finds in the many unpublished manuscripts of the period. It certainly attests that there was a not inconsiderable production of Arabic texts about the manufacture and use of artillery and firearms, and the application of mathematical knowledge to warfare.

THE GLORY OF GUNNERY AND A NEW
TYPE OF HEROISM

Though Hajarī came up with the Arabic title of the treatise, Ghānim had good reason to accept it, as it was very apposite to its content: *The Book of Glory, Elevation and Advantages of Artillery for the Righteous Warriors for God against the Infidels.* The most important word is *glory*. Indeed, the book attempts to impress upon its readers that artillerymen worked in a glorious craft. Insisting on the good manners expected from the students, the author aimed at instilling in beginners an ethics of their job, and to fashion a new type of soldier. This had to be forcefully stressed, as it went against long-standing traditions. In both Islamic and Christian histories, military prestige was strongly linked to horsemanship as part of mounted warfare, which is invoked by terms such as *chivalry* and, in Arabic, *furūsiyya*. These words, suffused with positive connotations, both come from the term for horse, *cheval* and *faras*. The proponents of the new forms of technical warfare, in the Maghrib and in Europe, had to insist that they too deserved honor. Ghānim and his Spanish models relied on widely disseminated tropes.

Warcraft is a noble endeavor: "The craft of war is among the most prestigious, the highest and the best of all crafts. . . . It is not confined to humans, but is attested among birds and animals."[54] The trope of the universal discord of the world was commonly used by early modern military engineers to legitimize their practice and their social role.[55] In the history of war, the invention and spread of gunpowder and firearms stands out, distinguishing two epochs of warfare. Ghānim did not tire of asserting that artillery is now, in "our time" (a phrase that echoes throughout the text) the most important and efficient corps in the army. This stark distinction between ancient times in the history of warfare, and the present, is a salient aspect of the text, that marks the author's commitment to the idea, if not the word, of modernity in the sense of a break with the past. Like many predecessors, he embodied this novelty in the legendary figure of the German monk to whom tradition ascribed the invention of gunpowder. Berthold Schwartz remains unnamed in his text, but the moment of his invention is narrated early: "Among scholars, it is generally agreed that powder only began to be used two hundred and sixty-five solar years ago. The discovery was made by a monk who studied chemistry. He wanted to distill saltpeter and sulfur with a phial and a still, and ground them in a mortar. There was a spark, and immediately the mixture took fire with power and a thrust. He was amazed as he had never seen anything like this, and had never heard of such a thing."[56] Like his predecessors, Ghānim was aware that some contend that powder was invented in China. Others asserted that the Greek mathematician and inventor Archimedes of Syracuse (287–212 B.C.E.) knew its secret but took it to his grave—a theory that Ghānim, like Collado, deemed unbelievable. Modern guns, however, could be situated in a long genealogy of ingenious devices used in combat, as is proven by the ancient war machines. These are described again and even drawn later, with Archimedes reappearing, not as the putative discoverer of gunpowder, but as the inventor of a device.[57] These gestures toward highlighting continuities across centuries and millennia do not prevent Ghānim from repeating the German monk story, and maintaining him as the figure of a new beginning, marking a sharp distinction between a before and an after gunpowder.[58] The German monk and the Greek philosopher are two contradictory and complementary figures. Both are images of technical achievement but one embodies novelty and the other continuity.

Modern times and modern warfare call for a new type of heroism. The theme of the nobility of the craft is deployed through an argument that is at the same time military, technological, and social, and that seeks to advocate for a new model for military valor. Away from the old ideal of the knight on horseback, it promotes the paradigm of the technician-warrior. Ghānim borrowed from Collado a stark symbol of this new form of military heroism, when he affirmed that losing a cannon to the enemy is worse than losing a flag. Recognizing that some dreaded the loss of a flag that the enemy would humiliate by dragging it in dirt, Ghānim concluded: "It seems to me that the loss of a cannon is worse than the loss of a flag. . . . A cannon costs a lot of money . . . and [to lose it] is a great damage to its owner."[59] This image sums up a new pragmatic, utilitarian approach to military valor, in which the notion of honor is transformed. The glory and the disgrace have to be assigned according to different criteria, and the cost of the weaponry is not to be neglected.

Starting with the first chapter, the value of the weapons helped Ghānim impress on the beginners that their job was the most important in the army, compared not only to an infantryman but also to a cavalryman, whose prestige had been established for centuries: "The soldier should take care of his rifle, the rider of his horse. As for the gunner, his responsibility is huge as it concerns the most essential feature of the army, and he should consider how expensive it is to manufacture and cast a cannon."[60] The new ethics was based on efficiency. Artillery was a "most noble of crafts," since "the craft of firearms is now the best part of all the weapons of war, and it scares away the enemy more than any other."[61] This superiority of modern weapons is extolled many times: "These weapons that use gunpowder are mightier, better, and more excellent than all those that the ancients employed in their wars." Using these expensive and efficient machines entails its own form of honor, linked to technical knowledge and care: "The shoot is the result of hard work, and who does not care for what we said does not deserve to be in this craft."[62] The modern soldier, who uses the new weapons, finds his glory not merely in courage and bravery, but in the mastery of his work. When he achieves it through practice and training, he feels "joy and happiness," while ignorance in the tenets of his art results in "shame and humiliation," and missing the aim is a source of mortification.[63]

The new soldier feels shame and pride, like his predecessor, but the proximate causes of these feelings are often mediated through instruments. Since the very first chapter, the text insists on the need for the gunner to own, sometimes make, and take care of the tools of the craft. They were needed to test, operate, clean, and repair the guns. Some were common: ropes, baskets, rags, hammers, pliers, scissors, files, and sticks are used by gunners as well as many other artisans. Others are more specific to their craft, and more complex to use: fuses, ladles to load the cannons, compasses and calipers, quadrants, plumb-lines, mirrors, gauges, and screws. Many tools are listed in chapter 2, including some needed when the gunner travels to the battlefield. Another list reminds the gunner that, if he does not have all the needed tools when he is loading, it would be a "failing and a shame."[64] Chapter 13, titled: "About measured shooting," stresses that rulers and set squares are needed for verification (tahqīq, one of the keywords in the text) to firing a precise shot by calculating distance and height. Chapter 46 recapitulates all the instruments that a gunner needs. Many pages are devoted to the making and the use of different tools, such as the ladles to load the guns, the rulers and gauges to measure the cannonballs and the interior of the cannons, and the quadrants needed to calculate the distance and trajectory of the shot. Most images in the manuscripts are of these instruments. By relentlessly stressing the importance of tools, Ghānim was attempting to develop in North African soldiers a new form of subjectivity, which has been called "the gunner's instrumental identity."[65] This subjectivity was based, not only on the soldiers' ability to defend the community against its enemies, but also on their technical proficiency, best deployed by the use of tools. Contrary to the hammer or the stick, some even required a measure of mathematical skill (see fig. 13).

This new type of soldier is distinguished from his predecessors by the knowledge he has to master. The first difficulty of his task comes from the bewildering variety of guns that are divided into three main categories (the long gun, or culverin, the medium gun, or cannon, and the bombard). The first two categories, the most common, include many subdivisions. Long guns are mostly used to defend places, and on battlefields. The medium guns are good for sieges, and some are used on warships. The less common bombards used big stone balls that efficiently attack ships. The gunner needs to recognize what kind of metal the guns are made of and the differences between them so that he can choose the right-sized cannonballs, and the adequate amount of powder to shoot them, since too much powder could break the gun and even kill the unfortunate beginner. He has to learn to maintain the ball and the powder in the right place, and to clean the guns between shots with brushes and waddings.

Precision requires more technical instruments and more skills to master them. Each gun being a unique piece, the cannoneer has to verify that it was built according to the right proportions, inside and out. The gunner measures the outside of the gun to ascertain that it was cast in conformity with its type, seeing that its different parts are in the right proportion of each other for each type of gun. This operation is called triangulation (*tathlīth* in the *Kitāb,* and *terciar* in the Spanish models), for which one used a straight-legged compass, and a curved-legged one. The cannoneer also has to make sure that the interior of the cannon was symmetrical, he inspects the inside of a gun with a mirror and a candle.[66] To give the right measurement to carpenters, he evaluates the proportions of the needed carriages and wheels for different guns, and for cranes to move heavy cannons. He also learns to manufacture gunpowder, in case he finds himself isolated in a fortress, for which recipes are provided in the last few chapters.

This part of the work of the gunners calls for calculations, and if not scientific in the modern sense, it is at least measured, what the text calls *bi al-qiyās.* "Measured shooting" necessitates instruments to calculate distances. The artilleryman as a technician uses the most effective weapons, and

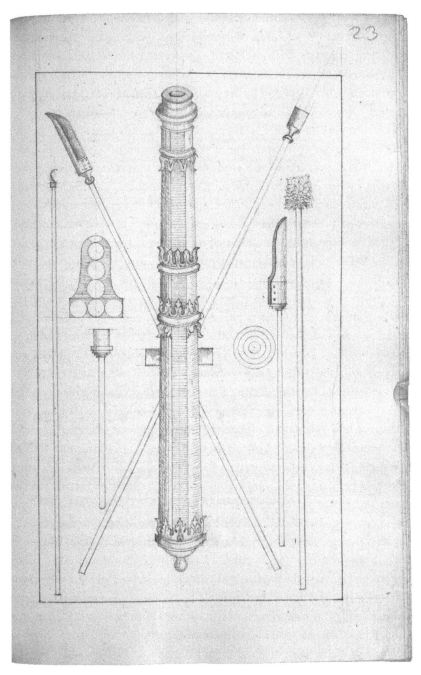

FIGURE 13. Page of manuscript of the *Kitāb al-'izz,* by Ibrāhīm Ghānim, translated into Arabic by Ahmad al-Hajarī. The instruments needed by the gunner. Österreichische Nationalbibliothek, ÖNB/Wien, Cod. A. F. 8. Creative Commons.

relies on venerable fields. He needs to have notions of three sciences: *handasa, bunyān, hisāb,* geometry, architecture, arithmetic.[67] This knowledge will help him calculate the right elevation angle of the gun on its axis to reach the target and build temporary bridges to cross rivers when moving to the battlefield. This mastery of instruments is the hallmark of the artilleryman, and marks his value and modernity as compared to less-skilled soldiers.

THE RHETORIC OF TECHNICAL EXPERTISE

The insistence by early modern military writers on their instruments is a testimony to their usefulness, but also a rhetorical device to impress on the reader their degree of dexterity and knowledge.[68] The technicity of this job and the mastery it implied help produce this important early modern figure, the technical expert. The *Kitāb* addresses, along with beginners, those in charge of the army, and tries to convince this parallel audience that a high degree of skill and knowledge is involved in the craft of gunnery, and thus that great respect is due to whomever can train and command the artillerymen. This other audience is sometimes conjured rhetorically, like in the prologue, where the foreign rulers who honor practitioners and reward writers are represented in the text as meriting the respect due to this essential part of warfare. They themselves are following the example of the ancient Romans, a bellicose nation, who "honored scholars, engineers and war leaders [*'ulamā', muhandisīn,* and *ahl al-tadābīr li al-harb*]."[69] These examples, ancient and modern, are part of Ghānim's effort to establish experience as a valuable form of knowledge in warfare.

The same chapter describes more explicitly the role that he hoped for himself and his peers: "The leaders need to listen to the opinion of the experienced warriors."[70] Other passages suggest that Ghānim aimed at influencing the organization of artillery within the army, maybe as an advisor. He certainly believed that the information he was disseminating would help recruit the right people: "The sultans and princes who own firearms should employ someone who knows the contents of our book, and who could thus make sure that the soldiers in this craft are knowledgeable and can provide good advice, and they should give high positions and ranks to those deserving of these distinctions."[71] The necessity for leaders to consult gunners is particularly acute when it comes to sending an army to a distant battlefield: "The heavy artillery is moved with difficulty and pain, and the judgment about this should be made by gunners with the person in charge [*sāhib al-amr*] so he can order that everything needed is supplied."[72] The key matter of logistics is explored further. Ghānim describes how the "chief foreman" (*al-rayyis al-muqaddam*) for artillery had to keep a big register noting everything he needs to move heavy pieces: "He should consult with veteran gunners and shooters who are battle hardened, because he can benefit from their advice given their experience, and they might mention an important thing he omitted."[73] Besides, "the person in charge of artillery and firearms" should require all and everybody that is needed by the artillery section of the army, including blacksmiths and carpenters—Ghānim adds that the Christians also enlist cannon casters in long campaigns.[74] Finally, at the very end of the text, Ghānim returns to emphasizing the necessity for the "person in charge to have knowledgeable gunners," insisting that he "did not doubt that there were in the Maghribi kingdoms intelligent and noble men and powerful leaders who could have an impact in this craft, but they need someone who would show them its secrets, advantages and utility."[75]

In sum, the book also aims at impressing on the political class the necessity of taking advice from experienced artillerymen, who would know how to train new recruits, and how to organize this part of the army, defensively in fortresses and castles, and offensively on the battlefield. To achieve these objectives, Ghānim advocated giving an official position to the most experienced and most dedicated gunners, which would be akin to what had already been in place in European armies since the sixteenth century. This position, which he calls "foreman," mediates between the state and the soldiers. The ideal person for such a post would be someone very much like him, who would master the contents of his book. This treatise is not only a textbook formalizing the training of beginners in the craft, but also a plea to institutionalize the place of artillery in the army. This, to a large extent, depended on raising the profile of the master gunner, as a category of soldier worthy of a higher esteem.

The people in charge, who could help create the position of the expert, had to be impressed by the deployment of technical knowledge of the skilled artilleryman, and his ability to handle an equipment. About the master gunner in the English army of the time of Elizabeth, Steven Walton notes: "In this sense, he is one of the first classes of soldier to be acknowledged for his expertise rather than simply for his corporeality."[76] The instruments that the gunner masters and often makes are crucial to his practice, and the insistence on them is a rhetorical device, only one of many that a technical writer has to display, especially when he is illustrating a genre new in his time and place. The most obvious of these devices, paradoxically, is the insistence that he is not using any rhetoric at all. An unusual type of author, he had to contrast himself from other more established and prestigious writers. "I request the reader of this book to not pay attention to my writing style, because I am no scholar nor belletrist [*'ālim* or *adīb*]. However, due to the hardships that I went through, I attained a degree of experience [*tajrīb*] since I practiced this craft [*sinā'a*] for about thirty years at sea. I was passionate about its secrets, and I was keeping company with skilled people of this art [*fann*] to benefit from them."[77] Ghānim was not a writer by education or profession, he did not achieve prominence in the fields of theoretical knowledge and stylistic prowess, and, to establish his authority, he did not rely on his own or on borrowed stylistic or rhetorical mastery: "I wrote without gathering scholars to improve my style."[78] He counted on the usefulness of the knowledge he was imparting, and that he acquired through readings or in conversations with practitioners. Most importantly, he learned by his own experience, as he forcefully underlines.

Like his predecessors who sought to raise the profile of the gunner in the army and in society, Ghānim deploys two main strategies which might at first glance look contradictory, but which are complementary. On the one hand, the authors insist on experience, through which they acquired their expertise. On the other hand, they stress that their work is based to some extent on the application of mathematical principles, and highlight the most complex instruments used by artillerymen. Some authors of gunnery treatises go even further in establishing their interest in mathematics and their application to their craft. Ghānim, who manifested an even stronger commitment to the primacy of experience and practice than his main model, Collado, refuted the importance of theoretical knowledge, while, nevertheless, displaying his understanding of it. The only time he named authors of treatises, quoting a trio of references, is significant. This takes place in the discussion of the range of a cannonball's trajectory depending on the position of the gun. Among the authors who discussed this topic, are "Rujilli and Tartali and al-Catani, who based their principles on *falsafa*."[79] The three authors are mentioned by Collado, who speaks of "Nicolao Tartalla, Geronimo Rucelli, y el Cataneo," whom he presents as "hombres mathematicos, y en otras artes instruydos, que no de platicos del exercito del Artilleria, y de sus effectos."[80] Collado was scathingly critical of the contributions of these Italian authors. The polymath Girolamo Ruscelli (ca. 1518–66), today a relatively obscure writer, was "a well-known humanist in the sixteenth century,"[81] who wrote on a variety of subjects, including commentaries on Boccaccio and Petrarch. His text on military matters contains many recipes for fireworks and tips on the use of guns.[82] Collado dismissed him as an academic who should have contented himself with writing about scholastic subjects, rather than relying on flawed secondhand information on the practice of artillery. As for Girolamo Cattaneo (ca.1540–84), who led a solid career in building and writing about fortifications, Collado judged his opinions on artillery confused and irrelevant.

More significant is the mention of Niccoló Tartaglia (ca. 1500–1557), the most important author on ballistics before Galileo, and indeed the first scholar to "claim that the mathematical study of gunshot could yield a science."[83] His *Nova Scientia* (1537) "established the modern science of ballistics, as characterized by the search for a mathematical understanding of the trajectory of projectiles."[84] However, the reason behind the writing of this text was eminently practical. Tartaglia began to ponder these issues when a gunner asked him at which angle the barrel of a cannon should be raised in order to achieve the longest possible shot. Even though Tartaglia's book is theoretical, it was intensely discussed by practitioners of artillery, including Collado, who recused some of Tartaglia's conclusions based on his own experience.[85] Lumping together Ruscelli and Cattaneo with Tartaglia might surprise the modern reader in light of the importance of the latter in the history of science, an importance the first two do not approach. It made sense for Collado, who affirmed the primacy of practice and experience over a theoretical approach. This opposition also helped Collado assert his authority as an expert practitioner.

It is not certain that Ghānim had firsthand knowledge of the three authors Ruscelli, Cattaneo, and Tartaglia, though he might have known of their views through Collado and other writers.[86] When Ghānim stated that the greatest shooting range is achieved when the piece of artillery is raised at forty-five degrees, he was certainly aware that Tartaglia was widely credited for having demonstrated this fact.[87] It is indeed now considered that this was "from a perspective confined to the development of ballistics . . . Tartaglia's principal scientific achievement."[88] Ghānim adopted Collado's disdain for more theoretical authors without engaging, like the Spanish author did sometimes, in detailed critiques of their approach. He thus tends to transform their rejection into an almost purely rhetorical posture. Advocating an eminently practical, applied, even hybrid form of mathematical knowledge, useful for gunners, he refuses a purely deductive approach to warfare, unchecked by concrete experience, through trial and error. His great commitment to experience is highlighted when he expresses the wish that he could afford to buy a gun so that he could try all degrees on the quadrant to measure more precisely the range of different shooting points.[89]

In Hajarī's translation, the word designating the approach that Ghānim attributed to the cited authors is *falsafa,* a term already encountered in Yūsī's text, in which it means secular philosophical and scientific knowledge as opposed to divine theological knowledge. In Ghānim's text, this notion is mostly opposed to *tajrīb,* experience, and should thus be understood as "theory." In the same chapter, he mentions *mujarribūn,* a word from the same root as *tajrīb,* as the men who do and try things, the practitioners. The figures that best embody the commitment to experience that he advocates, in opposition to the authors who write about practices they had not mastered, are the "Tudescos," the Germans, already prominent in Collado's text. Ghānim, as seen earlier, told more than once the story of the German monk credited with the invention of gunpowder. When he repeats this foundation myth, he puts its hero among the Tudescos, described as "knowledgeable and noble master craftsmen" (*muʿallimūn nujabāʾ ʿārifūn*), who make the best guns, since they have empirically verified which proportions are the best, and tested which quantity of metal is needed to minimize the risk of breaking. They also know the best way to build carriages and wheels, having "experimented with their hands."[90] The Tudescos are the rhetorical figure for the primacy of hands-on experience over academic credentials to produce practical knowledge. They aid in extolling the nobility and excellence of craftsmanship as such. The technical expert, such as Ghānim, does not disdain mathematical knowledge, but does not pursue it for its own sake. Like a craftsman, he seeks concrete results in the material realm. His authority rests on the knowledge he wants to transmit by advising rulers and instructing beginners, and which he attained partly thanks to his mastery of mathematical operations and instruments, and mostly thanks to years of practice. This practical knowledge, now being formalized and institutionalized, can aspire to social and political recognition, and aims at the cultural respectability of the written text.

Ghānim was thus attempting to introduce or at least formalize in North Africa cultural practices surrounding this more recent war technology, such as the training in artillery schools, and the writing of books to sustain this instruction. These practices would not only produce a competency, but also new forms of subjectivity, including a new type of soldier as technical practitioner who masters the tools of the trade, and a modern version of the old figure of the advisor to the ruler, now reborn as technical expert to serve the needs of the state. They also comprise the practitioner as author, a producer of written knowledge, which could be shared and disseminated beyond the age-old exclusively oral way in which craftmanship was usually handed from master to apprentice.

RELOCATING A TECHNICAL TEXT

Hajarī began to work on the translation shortly after moving to Tunis. One passage in the *Supporter* suggests he had a personal interest in the mechanical arts—when he asked Hubert to show him the water pump of a Parisian monastery[91]—and he had long been an avid reader of astronomy and cosmography. He was thus relatively well equipped to undertake the translation of Ghānim's book. But this new project was daunting, because it tackled a new subject, and because technical knowledge, connected to craftsmanship, was still rarely written down. He did not know any equivalent in Arabic that he could have used as a model; and when technology spreads, the culture that accompanies it has to be translated as well. Through translation, texts are literally relocated: "'*translatio*' implies 'carrying across' linguistic and conceptual schemes or boundaries."[92] So, Hajarī's task was not only to translate the text but also to relocate the practice of writing about artillery in a culture that was not accustomed to it. His translation was thus dual.

As experienced as Hajarī was, he felt in the beginning that he was not up to the task. A particular challenge was coming up with terms for the tools and guns. After a few days working on a book he believed to be the first in Arabic on this art, "I gave up because, concerning the names of the guns and of what was connected to them, no Arabic words existed for them." But he returned to his work: "If I ever met a difficulty, I would ask the author the captain, and he would give me a clear answer to all my queries. I thus understood everything he mentioned in the book, by his words and deeds."[93] The Arabic version was the result of a close collaboration between author and translator. The former even changed his text to make the translation easier: after describing the different types of shots, Ghānim concluded: "I have shortened as much as I could so that it would not be difficult to translate from Spanish to Arabic."[94]

Hajarī did finish the translation, and was able to produce the necessary conceptual vocabulary to describe the technical processes at the center of Ghānim's text (such as *tadbīr, tajrīb, qiyās, tahqīq*) by researching them with the help of the author. Strategies to reach this goal, embedded in the translation itself, concerned the passage from Spanish to Arabic, but also between levels of Arabic, since those technical processes also mediated between craftsmanship and applied mathematics. Working with the author, and sometimes seemingly relying on other books and maybe learned friends, Hajarī produced a translation that transmitted to an Arab readership the early fruits of the formalization of artillery that was occurring in Europe.

Arabizing the text, Hajarī put his own mark on the *Kitāb* by intervening directly. In order to shift and adapt the meaning of the text, he used, like many other translators, "literary accretions" (prefaces, marginalia, footnotes, commentary, appendices).[95] Such additional material that frames the reception of a text and orients its reading has been famously baptized as *paratext* by the literary theorist Gérard Genette. In a later period, a translator would have consigned some of these direct interventions to footnotes.

The first element in his own paratext is the all-important title. Hajarī attests that he came up with it, and that the author agreed to it, thus indicating that the translator had made a serious change to the unknown original title. He proposed a rhyming title, as was often the case for premodern Arabic high cultural texts, which helps acclimate the book to an elite readership. The use of the word *glory* is essential, emphasizing that prestige should be attached to artillery. Its dignity derived in large part from the advantages it brings, another word used in the title. Then Hajarī added information about "the captain (*ra'īs*) Ibrāhīm ibn Ahmad Ghānim ibn Muhammad ibn Zakariyā al-Andalusī, who wrote it in Spanish, then it was translated into Arabic by the translator for the sultans of Marrakesh Ahmad ibn Qāsim ibn Ahmad ibn al-faqīh Qāsim ibn al-Shaykh al-Hajarī al-Andalusī." This highlights the Andalusian origins of both author and translator and their credentials, with Hajarī proudly drawing attention to his career in the Saʿdī court. As for the author's position as captain, it insists on his role in the defense of Muslims, a *jihād* that was already present in the main title in its cognate *mujāhidīn*.

After Hajarī's title, the manuscript presents a table of contents, which lists the fifty chapters, introduced as follows: "Here is the plan of this book, comprised of fifty chapters, with a preface by the author about his travels, and an appendix by the translator from Spanish to Arabic concerning his travels, the

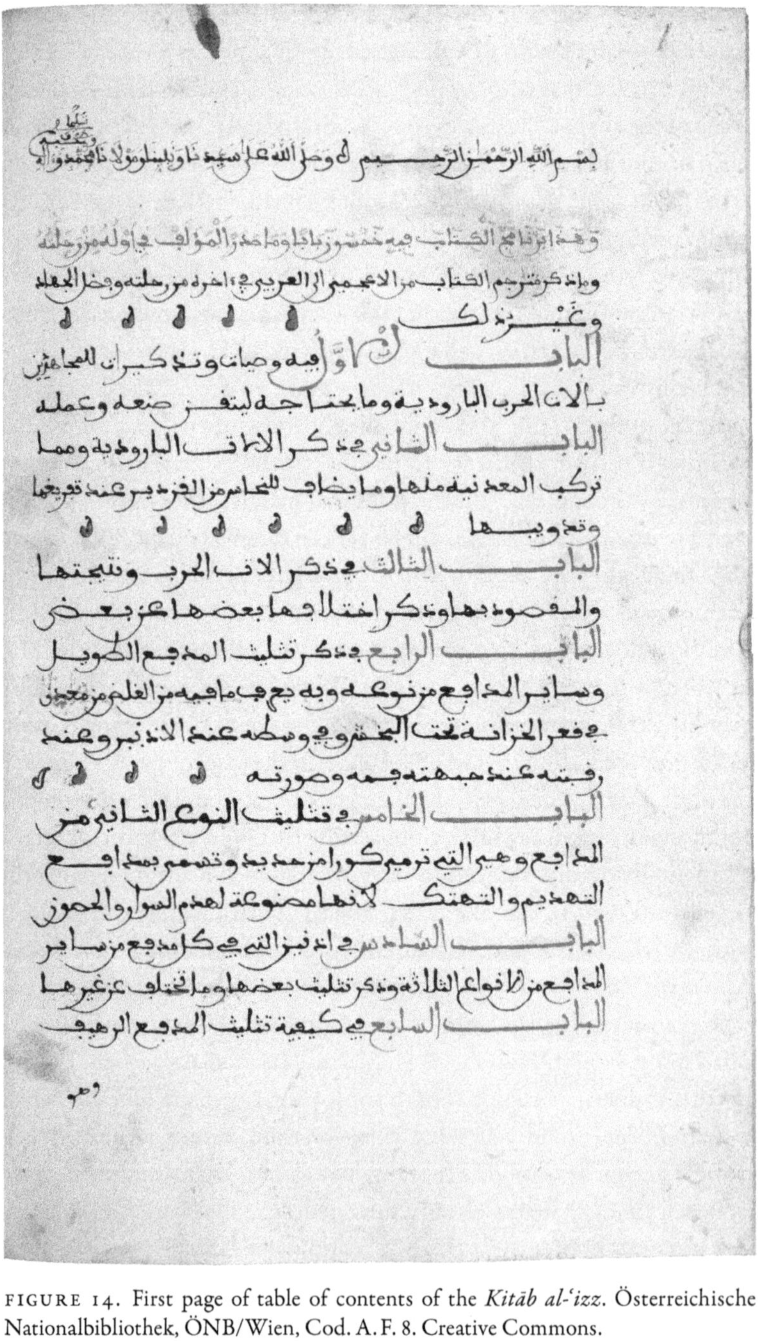

بسم الله الرحمن الرحيم وصلى الله على سيدنا محمد وآله وسلم ...

وهذا فهرست الكتاب ... بين تمت وزياته وما عمده المؤلف ... أول ... مرتبة

وإنا ذكرنا في الكتاب من الأعجم العربي ... أخرى من رتبته وفظ الجعله

وغيرنا لك

الباب ... وأربعة وحياة وتذكيران للمحاربين

بالآت الحرب البارودية وما يحتاج إليه في صنعه وعمله

الباب الثاني في ذكر الآلات البارودية ومما

تركب المعدنية منها وما يضاف للخامس من الغزو عند تفريغها

وتخويها

الباب الثالث في ذكر الآلات الحرب وتلبيتها

والفصوص بها وذكر اختلاف أحدها بعضها عن بعض

الباب الرابع وذكر تثليث المدفع الطويل

وسائر المدافع من نوعه وفيه يجمع ما فيه من العلم من معين

في عمل الخزانة لفت البخور ومحله عند الأنبوبة وصنع

فتته عند حبته جسمه وصورته

الباب الخامس في تثليث النوع الثاني من

المدافع وهي التي ترميها وكذا رامها عد به وتسمى بمدافع

التهديم والتهتك لأنها مصنوعة لهدم السور والحصون

الباب السادس في ذكر فيزا التي هي كل مدفع من سائر

المدافع من الأنواع الثلاثة وذكر تثليث بعضها وما اختلاف عن غيرها

الباب السابع في كيفية تثليث المدفع الرهيف

وصل

FIGURE 14. First page of table of contents of the *Kitāb al-ʿizz*. Österreichische Nationalbibliothek, ÖNB/Wien, Cod. A. F. 8. Creative Commons.

excellence of *jihād*, and more,"[96] thus paralleling Ghānim's preface with Hajarī's appendix (see fig. 14).

Hajarī's translating strategies are quite common, explicating words, geographical names, or philosophical concepts. He used his life experiences and readings to provide geographical and even conceptual background. In a few passages, his studies of European geography and his work with Orientalists informed his translation. When the word *Ūrubbā*, "Europe," came up, he interrupted the text: "The translator of this book says: this word designates the quarter of the world in the northern region, which comprises many sultanates belonging to Christian sultans, including the sultanate of al-Andalus [Spain], which is the best of all in what is called Europe by all foreigners. In this part, there is also the greatest city in the whole world which is the great Constantinople [*al-Qustantīniyya al-ʿudhmā*] . . . the end."[97] As he does in the *Supporter*, Hajarī informs the North African reader of the different concepts used in European geographical texts, such as the division and names of continents. Hajarī relates these to the European Muslim or formerly Muslim territories, in Spain and in the Eastern Mediterranean. He draws again on this knowledge when "Almāniya," Germany, is mentioned: "The translator of this book says: this is a country of the Grandee of the Christians whom they call *Imbiradur* [Imperator], which means the sultan of their sultans. . . . It is likely the country of the people that the history books of the Muslims call *Saqāliba*, and I think that in the lands of the Turks they call it the lands of the *Majar*. The end."[98] However, in this explanation, it appears he confused the Germans with the Slavs and the Magyars or Hungarians.

In the absence of established counterparts for Spanish terms, he transliterated them, searched for equivalents, or paraphrased them, often combining these approaches. Frequently the term is both explained and transliterated, for example, when Ghānim recalls his travels to the Americas, "on the large ships they call *ghalyūniya* [*galeón*] in Spanish."[99] Elsewhere, the text mentions the "*bunbāsh* [*bombas*], which means incendiary devices."[100] Certain transliterated words designating guns are accompanied with information about the category of guns they belong to, their size, or their common use. This is the case for the small gun called *ashmarīl* (*esmeril*). Interestingly, Hajarī sometimes provides both an Arabic equivalent and a Spanish transliteration, for example to name guns, such as the mortar, in Spanish *trabucco*, and in Arabic *mihras*; as well as common objects, such as rags or baskets; and most often tools, such as the *cabria*, or screw.[101]

The textual presence of the translator is sometimes more obvious, and offers a glimpse into Hajarī's thought process. He often relied on the etymology of the Spanish word to give names to some guns, thus explaining that "the *doble* means *al-matwī* as derived from the meaning of the Spanish word," the "*bashtardu* [*bastardo*] means *zanīm*," and the *volante*, "referring to its etymology, is called *al-ṭayyār*."[102] When he speaks of the first category of artillery, "the long guns called in Spanish *qulbrinat* [culverins]," he states that "there is no word in Arabic." A few pages later, however, he adds that this word is "derived from the name of a snake, because of the length" of the gun.[103] Elsewhere, he tentatively proposes a translation: "a gun called in Spanish *falconetto,* the meaning of which is *bāz* but God knows best."[104]

Some direct interventions were inspired by Hajarī's readings. He thus speaks of a gun "called in Spanish *bashilishqu* and I named it in Arabic the 'killer by a glance.' The Spanish say there is a small animal which can kill whatever it sees just by its glance, and they named this gun after it. I don't know its name in Arabic, I have never seen this animal, and I wish to never see it."[105] Hajarī probably read accounts of the lethal reptile called basilisk in European texts, which in the early modern period still spread its ancient legend. In another passage, readers are reminded that, before the invention of gunpowder, "the ancients used to throw huge balls with a bow, and I think it is called the *manjanīq*." Later he is more assured: "As for the *balishtar* [*balista*] the Arabs used to call it the *manjanīq*."[106] In other cases, he simply asserts his choice. When talking about the "ruler with which one weighs any cannonball, called in Spanish *culibr* and I will call it in Arabic the ruler for balls [*mistarat al-kuwar*]." He wavered on the translation, since in some manuscripts the instrument is also called *mistarat al-ʿadad,* the numbered ruler.[107]

Some passages show him mediating between two ways of writing (learned and practical), and between two social categories (scholar and craftsman). To make sure the proportions of a culverin are right, the text recommends: "measure with a compass the width of the muzzle of the gun, and this is called diameter [*qutr*] in the books of geometry."[108] Applying a term of geometry to the gunner's concrete operations, Hajarī makes more explicit their mathematical underpinnings, and provides support for the practitioners' effort to acquire social and epistemological respectability. Elsewhere, he explicitly mediates between vernacular and classical, and between artisans and scholars, by showing that similar instruments could bear different names. The "geometers and astronomers call [the plumb-line] *shāqūl,* while carpenters call it *wazna*."[109] On the contrary, the same word can have different meanings. After giving in steps (*khutwa*) the measure of the reach of the cannonball, the text specifies: "The steps we are talking about... are the common steps [*ʿammya*] not the steps mentioned in geometry. The common step is three feet long... while the steps for the geometers are five feet long." Just a few pages later, the text gives both the numbers of steps according to the popular understanding and to the geometers.[110] This indicates that the book wanted to reach two different readerships: the "common people," artisans or craftsmen who would be training to become efficient gunners, and a more educated constituency, maybe among the higher echelons of the army or in courts. The latter might call an underground vault or tunnel a *khattāra*, while the common people, or *ʿamma*, would call them *dāmis*.[111]

Hajarī also mediates between local forms of Arabic, thanks to his experiences in both Morocco and Tunisia. In a chapter devoted to incendiary devices thrown by hand, one type comprises "the ones that are thrown in the days of celebration and festivals, and they ascend in the sky. They are called *anfāt* in Tunis, and *samāwiyāt* in Morocco."[112] Hajarī added more linguistic information in the following chapter: "One makes wheels or crowns and the devices that fly in the sky during the days of celebrations. They call them *anfāt* in Tunisia, and this word *anfāt* designates in Marrakesh and in all of Morocco artillery guns [*madāfiʿ*], while *madāfiʿ* designates rifles in Morocco. As for the devices used for celebrations and in festivals, they are called *samāwiyāt* in Morocco because they ascend in the sky, and in Spanish they are called *quhit* [*cohete*]."[113]

This intervention by Hajarī is noteworthy beyond merely linguistic characteristics. Like many early modern treatises on gunnery, Ghānim's book considers gunpowder devices in their important role in celebrations, especially in courts. The very first reason the author gave to advocate for a certification is the mistakes made by inexperienced gunners "during every holiday, when cannons are detonated in sign of celebration and they break despite being made of metal."[114] Just like artillery to which they were closely linked, fireworks helped develop connections between artisans, natural philosophers, and political powers.[115] Gunners sometimes presented this craft in specific texts, although most often, like Collado, they devoted chapters to the manufacture and use of fireworks in artillery books. Ghānim says little about fireworks, not even devoting a whole chapter to them, which makes Hajarī's intervention all the more intriguing. Beyond its linguistic information, it may suggest that his court experiences in Marrakesh made him aware of the worthiness of such details (see fig. 15).

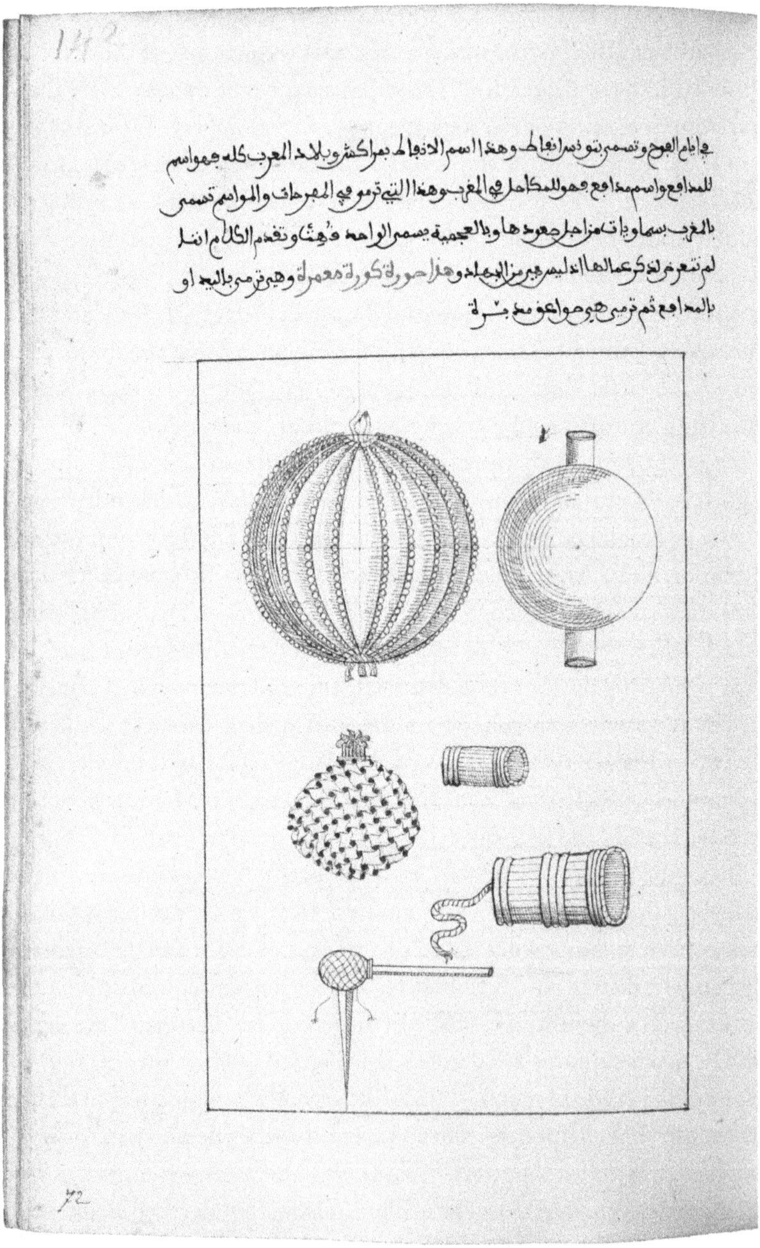

Hajarī also more than once supplemented Ghānim's text with information beyond strict linguistic equivalences. In a rare passage in which Ghānim engaged with issues of natural philosophy, he recalled that philosophers and sages (*falāsifa* and *hukamā*), trying to explain why powder produces explosions and noise, pondered the nature of its components. In Spain, he attended many debates where discussants confronted theories about how hot or cold, dry or humid these elements were. As to how to ascertain their qualities, one sentence is clearly an intervention by Hajarī, who quotes the book on simples or medicinal herbs that he had procured for Jacob Golius more than a decade earlier: "One knows the natural qualities of simples by putting them on one's tongue, as is mentioned in *al-Mustaʿīnī.*"[116]

Ghānim also contributed what is arguably another paratext, at the end of the text. Early on, he had identified two groups of potential readers (or listeners) to the book, the beginners, and their hierarchical superiors. In the last two chapters, the latter group makes its final appearance, among the first readers of his work. Chapter 48 ends this way: "This book was begun in Halq al -Wādī . . . in the year 1040, and was finished on the 22nd of Rabīʿ I in the year 1042 [October 10, 1632]. Its translation into Arabic was completed on the 13th of Rabīʿ I in the year 1048 [July 25, 1638]."[117] However, the book is not finished yet. Ghānim explains the reason for this belated writing: "I have talked about the purification of saltpeter, without mentioning how to make it and extract it from dirt, because I wanted to be brief. . . . After the book was translated into Arabic and copied and before it was bound, some smart people read it, and they liked it. . . . This reinforced my intention to add this chapter on the fabrication of saltpeter, and its manufacturing from dirt, since it is the most essential feature of this craft."[118] These two chapters on the fabrication of saltpeter and gunpowder complete previously provided information.

The last two substantial chapters resulted from a discussion with the first readers of the book, who were probably officers in the dey's army. The addition suggests that the making of this book involved to an extent a community of experts, whose opinion was sought and valued by the author. It is noteworthy that Ghānim was again emulating the practices of some Spanish authors-soldiers, such as Lechuga, who "carried his manuscript with him on campaign to gain the opinions and comments of his fellow officers."[119] Ghānim insists not only on his technical knowledge, but also on his desire to foster a culture of exchange. This quasi paratext thus tends to bolster his image as an expert, and sketches some of the ideal readers of the text.

The paratext of the *Kitāb* is particularly rich: Hajarī and Ghānim both contributed to it, and enlisted the help of others. Ghānim always intended, since its inception, that the treatise be translated into Arabic. Hajarī, who was already a skillful translator and an accomplished writer, and who had exhibited interest in less than academic forms of knowledge, including geography and mechanical devices, took the project on once he had moved from Cairo to Tunis. Beyond specific technical or scientific content, close attention has to be paid to the practice of translation itself, which "involves often very substantial epistemological, authorial, and literary shifts across cultures, and over time." As translator and as author, he learned to navigate the cultural and social codes of court life and of learned writing, conjuring different readers as a part of his effort to position the *Kitāb al-'izz* in North African written culture.

TECHNICAL EXPERTISE AND POLITICAL POWER

I have examined the prologue in search of biographical information about the author, his life as a Morisco in Spain, his career as a sailor, his theoretical and practical study of gunnery, his relocation to Tunis after the expulsion, his service to the deys at sea and his capture, his work in the fortress of Halq al-Wādī, and finally his motivation for writing the book. In this section, I will analyze the appendix, using the Vienna text, published and translated by the historian of Muslim Spain L. P. Harvey, rather than refer to the edition of the *Kitāb* in which the appendix is inexplicably truncated.

Hajarī's appendix is a lengthy and highly elaborate document that reprises the role played by Moriscos in the defense of North Africa, the jihad fought on the frontier between Christendom and Islam, and even the story of the translator himself, placing his translating work into his own intellectual trajectory and biography. While barely touching upon the contents of the book, this appendix offers valuable information about Morocco and Tunisia in the early seventeenth century, and skillfully deploys Hajarī's strategies to situate the work within a Maghribi political context.

This complex text includes a discourse about the excellence of the war against the infidels, which mainly consists of a series of hadith invoking the Prophet Muhammad's example that Hajarī found in the voluminous collection *Mishkāt al-masābih,* by al-Khātib al-Tabrīzī (d. 1340), enough of these to fill out a few pages.[120] These references to the Prophet Muhammad can be compared to the way in which Europeans in the sixteenth century legiti-mized the use of technology in state building by presenting it as an innova-tion, that, however, was not a complete break of the order of things, and by referring to classical antiquity: "It will thus be considered as the expression of a restart. It is the mythical time of the imitation of the Ancients, which knew a lively revival throughout the century."[121] Similarly, the mention of Muhammad in Hajarī's appendix situates new technical modes in the mythi-cal time of early Islam, equivalent to Renaissance Europe's invocation of classical antiquity.[122] This is not to downplay the religious reference in Hajarī's text, considering his deeply sincere devotion, and the role of Islam in legitimizing political power in seventeenth-century North Africa in its bat-tles against powerful and threatening Christian neighbors. Nevertheless, rushing to religion as an explanation for all or most cultural and political developments in Islamic countries obscures more complex historical evolu-tions, hides commonalities with their neighbors, and promotes a simplistic reading or even hasty dismissal of too many documents.

The appendix was also firmly situated in the place in which Hajarī had recently relocated after his stay in Egypt, and which he seemed to know well enough to navigate its politics and culture. In this Ottoman province, Hajarī offers fulsome praise of Sultan Murād IV (1623–40), extolling his vast realm and highlighting the Christian fear of the Turks he knew about thanks to the unfulfilled prophecies of doom that circulated in Europe about the Muslim enemy. He then turned to the Tunis of the deys, military rulers who still recognized the sovereignty of Istanbul but were moving toward greater autonomy.[123] Several pages praise the accomplishments of Ustā Murād, dey from 1637 to his death in 1640. This Genoese convert championed Islam against internal and external enemies; he closed the many taverns of Tunis and forbade children from disrupting the sermons in the capital's Zaytūna mosque with their loud play. Most important, he protected the country from Christian enemies. Before becoming dey, Murād defended the community as a corsair and ship captain. Hajarī recalls one of his triumphs when, in 1625, Murād, heading a small squadron of ships, got chased by Maltese ships and engaged in a fierce battle. Victorious, Murād and his men seized two enemy galleys and released five hundred Muslim captives.[124]

As dey, Murād rebuilt the port of Bizerte, reinforced the defenses of Tunis, and erected the fortress of Ghār al-Malh, to protect the lives and prop-erty of the population against Christian attacks. Hajarī frames his narrative of the great deeds of the dey with his own contribution to the defense of

Tunis and North Africa, beginning: "I began this translation after ... Murād Dey ... came to power," and ending: "Among all his other benefactions is that I have been able to finish the translation of this book."[125] These passages suggest that the dey might have sponsored Hajarī's work, by encouraging it and maybe even paying for it. In addition to portraying Murād as a model, Hajarī's extols Ghānim, as a ship captain and warrior, and Hāj Mūsā, the Morisco architect brought from Algiers to reinforce old fortresses and build new ones, drawing attention to the contributions of exiles from Spain. Even though Hajarī elsewhere had stated that the refugees had been very well received in Tunisia, he evidently felt the need to highlight their contributions. In the same text, he also defended his (and Ghānim's) perfect command of Spanish against distrustful observers.

Hajarī was indeed a superlatively competent translator, thanks to his linguistic mastery and because he could understand the importance of the book and situate it in the cultural and political landscape. The parallel between Ghānim's and Hāj Mūsā's contributions highlights their Morisco origins, but also stresses that both are associated with the defense of the realm, as masters of technical skill in military domains. Hajarī clearly grasped the reciprocal relation between the expert and the state, each legitimizing the other. His appendix presents Murād as a patron of a work that could help fight the foes of the state and the community. By enlisting Hāj Mūsā to shore up the defenses of Tunisia, Murād was reinforcing his own power and legitimacy. Although not identical in scale to what was happening in Habsburg Spain, or in the France of Louis XIII and Richelieu, where "scientific and technical experts ... were deployed to meet a wide variety of challenges from navigation to mining, fortification to land drainage,"[126] Hajarī's appendix attests that similar processes occurred in the Ottoman province of Tunisia.

By the same token, Ghānim was certainly also trying to raise his own professional profile, like his Spanish models, by borrowing the prestige of written culture, and seeking social and political recognition of his skills. To help Ghānim reach his goals, Hajarī could use his experience and observations in Marrakesh. Starting with the title, he insists on his career in the Saʿdī court. In fact, his "friend and brother" Ghānim asked him to translate his book "because he knew that ... I had been interpreter for many years to Muley Zaidan."[127] During this time, he could witness how Saint-Mandrier's technical expertise won him a career not only in the army but also at court. The unfortunate Frenchman appears as another figure of the relation between political power and technical mastery that this appendix analyzes.

Ghānim, in the body of the text, and in the quasi paratext constituted by the two last chapters, addresses an audience of army veterans, who could pinpoint precise shortcomings to be addressed. Hajarī's appendix aims at reaching a readership closer to the higher levels of power, probably including the dey himself. This explains the bifurcated aspect of this book, which conveys a technical content written in simple, unadorned Middle Arabic, easy to understand by the presumably barely literate gunners to whom it would be read, but which is also framed to reach a more elite audience. This ambiguity between practical goal and courtly value is another commonality between the Maghribi and the European cultures of gunnery. The early modern artillerymen's instruments that have survived in Europe are often beautiful and expensive items made with care and art, that could not have been in the possession of the ordinary gunner, but that would rather have enhanced the prestige of the captain or even the ruler who owned them.[128] The status of these instruments and of the treatises on gunnery, oscillates between "a practical science and a polite science, an art of the court and an art of war, a support for action and a support for rhetoric."[129] This oscillation is present in the *Kitāb,* with Ghānim focusing more clearly on the practical purpose, and with Hajarī aiming at locating the treatise in a courtly culture in which power drew its legitimacy from religion, but also from a high culture of refinement and scholarly achievement.

When he enlisted Hajarī's help, Ghānim might have been counting not only on his fellow Morisco's linguistic mastery, but also on his political and scholarly networks, that would add social and cultural authority to the text. Although he had recently relocated to Tunis, Hajarī could, and did, boast of his previous and prestigious position in the court of Marrakesh. In the appendix, he proudly mentions his acquaintance in Cairo with ʿAlī al-Ujhurī, and in Marrakesh with the judge al-Saktī (or al-Suktānī), both already featured in the *Supporter.* As a further mark of his familiarity with high culture, he refers to the "illustrious scholar Ahmad al-Maqqarī" (1577–1632),[130] who led a career as a religious appointee and as a man of letters in Morocco, which he left after falling out of grace with Mūlay Zaydān. In Cairo and Damascus, he wrote a monumental history of al-Andalus considered a high point in Arab seventeenth-century literature.[131] Hajarī read it in Cairo not long after its completion, and his appendix to the *Kitāb* contains an early reference to it.

Beyond establishing his status as an acquaintance and reader of prestigious scholars, Hajarī could also count on his eminence among the Morisco diaspora. In the closing of the appendix, other learned friends helped him frame the *Kitāb*'s contribution to high culture, in a particularly noteworthy hybridization of cultural practices of Spain and North Africa. Among the well-connected people that Hajarī knew in Tunis was the Morisco Ahmad al-Hanafī, who taught at the prestigious Shammāʿiyya madrasa and authored many books. He contributed a short passage to the *Kitāb,* attesting that he had read the treatise at the request of Hajarī, and concluding that he found it "of great use to Muslims, and a guide to men of learning and to Muslim students of artillery and gunnery."[132] By asking this religious scholar to vouch for the usefulness of the text, Hajarī was to an extent emulating the Spanish system of precensure of books, and did the same for his revisions of the *Supporter.*[133] The appendix echoes another Spanish (and more generally European) cultural practice by including at its very end a poem, written by the otherwise unknown ʿAbd al-Rahmān Masʿūd al-Jabālī, and singing the praises of Ghānim as heroic defender of the community and as author.[134]

Hanafī and Jabālī, the religious scholar and the poet, represent a class of potential readers or patrons close to the courts and the political class, while Ghānim addresses master gunners and officers. The effort to reach a double audience, common in the early modern culture of military treatises, is also evident in the work of the makers of the *Kitāb*—not only the author and the translator, but also the scribe of many of the extant contemporary manuscripts, Hajarī's son Muhammad Khūja, who produced beautifully executed copies, often lavishly illustrated. Ghānim expressed more than once his strong desire to disseminate his work beyond Tunis, and to see that "copies are made and sent God willing to some places in the lands of Muslims" to help the gunners who work in "the service of Muslim rulers."[135] Elsewhere he states: "I ask God . . . that this book becomes well known and I don't disallow whomever wants to copy or read it (in public)."[136] Toward the end of the text, he confirms his desire to divulge in this book the "secrets, advantages and utility" of gunnery, and to see it sent to "all Islamic countries in which artillery is in use."[137] This was not mere rhetoric, and he worked seriously at disseminating his book. Of the many extant manuscripts, six were executed by Khūja for the author. Several copies were made in later decades, up to the late eighteenth century, and even in the nineteenth century (see fig. 16).[138]

More studies are needed to measure the forms and modalities of its influence, including on some of the Arabic texts about the tools and practice of warfare that were written during the seventeenth and eighteenth centuries, and maybe beyond this field. Decades ago, Manūnī noted that the first evocation by Ghānim of the invention of gunpowder by the German monk was

والتعليم من اهل صناعة المطابع و روات المسلمين الفقراء المشربين الشريف احمة الحنفي عامله الله بلطفه الخفي بمنه وكرمه الحمد لله و ممالله العبد الفقير الى الله تعالى عبده الرصاص بن مسعود الجبار عبار في هذه الكتاب على الجملة الوضع شهيد هذا

هذا العبد واذا اما مساوئ ك ا ... من العبد واذا اما مساوئ ك ا
اهذا الساحكما قاعد لملتنا ... نهج الحروب على شكر وما احمدا
من المطابع فلا من ابنتنا ... بل سافها اظران بعد الساع ه ا
وهاك همنه في السهو ظاهرة ... تمشي العليل بعز النجم و الرشا
مزد وومنتشبه رافت عكفون ه ... فا سقر حيت محاكات لها عد دا
هو المعلم ابراهيم الا نه لسمي ... اور مر الرمات و بعد العصر جتهه ا
انظر لخط امام سيد روي ش ... معزا الى نظام لفهم آسمه العرمه ح ا
لا زام تقيا نجم البلاد ع ه ما ... فاست لعديه على علوم الدرس واجتهها
ثم الصلاة على جمله و على ... مركاز نادئه ابهرالنار شهد ا
وهو المطابع عنادكر مهلكة ... من العبد واذا اما مساوئ ك ا
قمت النصفة المباركة لهذا الكتاب في الشاءا مريعشي مزه ذي القعدة كسام خمسون والف على يد العبد المنة نه الراني عفو الله و عفر انه محمد خوجه بن احمد المترجم للكتاب بن قاسم بن احمد بن الفقيه فا هم بن الشيخ الحجري الا نه لمر كنبه في مدينة تونس مو سط الله الربيس الموالف للكتاب تقبل الله منه و حل الله على ميرنا ومولانا عمرو على النوجه و سلم تسليما

quoted in a text about the judicial practice in Fez by 'Abd al-Rahmān al-Fāsī (1631–85).[139] More interesting than the quote itself is the personality of the author, a renowned writer who belonged to a "very illustrious and scholarly family."[140] The fact that such a respected citizen of the Arabic Republic of Letters quoted the *Kitāb* indicates that it did reach some readers beyond the professionals for whom Ghānim wrote. It also shows that Fāsī was not as strictly confined by the academic standards of his time as one would think for such a consummate member of the ulama class. Beside his widely read and commented treatise on judicial practice, this very prolific author also wrote a still-in-manuscript mnemonic poem on the classification of the sciences, at about the same time that Yūsī was writing his *Qānūn*.[141] Contrary to the latter, Fāsī was among the scholars who displayed interest in technical matters, and his poem features descriptions of astrolabes, solar quadrants, and of irrigation techniques.[142] It is noteworthy that Ibn Hamādūsh, the Algerian scholar who enjoyed studying technical matters and instruments, referred to Fāsī when, describing his experiments with cannons, he spoke about the measurement of the angle of the gun, suggesting that Fāsī, decades after his death, was still reputed among those who were interested in these questions, and not merely in theology and law. His example has to be added to the list of Maghribi scholars who were relatively open to technical issues during the seventeenth and eighteenth centuries. The mastery of artillery and, more generally, of technical expertise, was situated in a new form of relation between technology and the state, where practical knowledge directly serves the needs of political power. This connection was being negotiated in early modern Europe, in ways that were different from but nonetheless comparable to what was happening in North Africa.

. . .

The number of extant manuscripts, many completed during the lifetime of the author and/or translator, attests to the success of the book. Some scholars have analyzed the *Kitāb* in the context of early modern translations into Arabic or of Morisco cultural production.[143] Other critics have situated Ghānim's treatise in the much larger historical background of two grand and interrelated narratives, the story of the rise of the West, and the story of the decline of Islamic cultures. The first narrative is encapsulated in the resilient mythology of the Scientific Revolution.[144] It draws "on the nineteenth-century belief in a historical European exceptionalism," and its flipside concerning the Islamic countries was that they had been for centuries "intellectually dormant."[145] This latter view assigns a specific role to translation. According to a well-worn account, the movement of translation of Greek, Indian, and Persian texts in the eighth to tenth centuries helped usher a golden era of Arabic science, philosophy, and literature, which came to an end in the thirteenth century. This era was, it is said, followed by a dark age marked by a lack of innovation, an abandonment of scientific inquiry, and a complete lack of interest for other civilizations, especially a resurgent Europe. According to this view, only in the nineteenth century did the Arab world begin to revive and revitalize its culture, and its science, in a reawakening spurred in large part by a new movement of translation of European texts.

Such an account considers Ghānim's manual an anomaly, since it is both an adaptation of European models and a translation into Arabic created at a time when, according to the narrative, such cultural productions were nonexistent. As a consequence, some historians have tended to reduce or dismiss the significance of the *Kitāb*, painting it as an inconsequential curiosity that does not truly belong to North African culture.[146] The historian of Islamic manuscripts David James forcefully sums up this perspective when he even invented a Spanish title, *Manual de artillería* (Artillery Manual), rather than use the only attested title, the Arabic *Kitāb al-'izz,* thus highlighting the Europeanness of the treatise. Indeed, he considered that it was "unlike anything written in the Arab world" before the nineteenth century, and even asserted that the quotes of hadith in Hajarī's appendix were justifications for the study of what James termed confusingly "Christian" technology, thus implying a religiously motivated failure to acclimate the text in the Maghrib.[147] This argument in turn built on an essential feature of the narrative of the Scientific Revolution, the "notion that the wrong kind of religion blocked rational thought and historical progress."[148] This interpretation asserts that the *Kitāb* has nothing positive to reveal about the culture in which it was produced, only negatively testifying to its incapacity to transform itself. The present study argues that, on the contrary, this book provides important insights on the cultural processes, and the social and discursive practices, through which technology spread in the early modern Western Mediterranean. It also illustrates the rise of a "middle" culture between the scholarly elite and the popular classes, and the ascent of a less educated category of writers and readers who nevertheless sought entrance on the intellectual scene.

The *Kitāb al-'izz* is a remarkable document that reveals the still obscure history of the technical and material culture in the early modern Maghrib, and how their study and practice were considered and connected to other forms of knowledge. It offers information about the modernization of weaponry, and the challenges the adoption of artillery presented, in terms of training and of the organization of the armed forces. New weapons and the social evolution they brought helped introduce the idea of a break with the past—a notion that is clearly present in Ghānim's text, and, interestingly, reprised by Fāsī in his brief citation. This study, however, refrains from analyzing the *Kitāb* solely in terms of its inability to usher in a wholescale transformation of the forms of culture and power in North Africa. It has also tried to avoid the teleological trap of simply assessing how people, events, and texts fit in the grand narratives of the rise of the West and the decline of Islamic countries.

This book has operated under the belief that to consider this text against more modest backgrounds can further our understanding of the historical trajectory of North Africa, and reconstruct the culture of the people who lived in that region in the early seventeenth century. Ghānim and Hajarī set out to produce and adapt a text to the society in which they had chosen to live, and they fulfilled their ambition. Ghānim wrote a well thought-out adaptation of Spanish treatises. Despite his lack of familiarity with the subject matter, and the absence of models to which he could refer, Hajarī made an Arabic version that is striking in the cogency of its technical and conceptual vocabulary. Both author and translator worked hard to precisely situate the work in its new environment. Ghānim consulted with other professionals before adding more information. Hajarī's decades-long experience in Maghribi court and intellectual life enabled him to ensure that the text was not read only by gunners. The number and the quality of the manuscripts executed by his son and, later, others suggest that the reception of the treatise was far from narrow. This relative success might be explained by the fact that, rather than being a completely anomalous document, it was situated in the gradual development of a middle culture, between the erudite elite and the popular forms of the illiterate, which included modes of historical writing not focused merely on the ruling class or the aristocracy of learning, and comprised new formalizations of artisan knowledge, sometimes thanks to a blurring of the lines that separated scholars and practitioners.

Hajarī's work on Ghānim's treatise shows him to be not only a skilled translator but also an astute observer of his time, able to compare and connect different phenomena, such as the role of Saint-Mandrier in the court of Mūlay Zaydān, the work of Hāj Mūsā in Algiers and Tunisia, and the forms of knowledge that Ghānim was working at spreading in Ottoman Tunis and beyond. This alertness might be due to his dual situation, both as an insider, who lived for many years as a courtier, and as a friend of prominent scholars, and as an outsider, given his background as a Morisco and as an exile. Thanks to this complex identity, Hajarī was able to play a major role in a field of scientific and technical literature that developed in the early modern period and which connected Europe and its Muslim neighbors. This field included translations and adaptations, that often blended the new material found in European texts with Arabic or Turkish productions, and creating what has been termed Euro-Islamic hybrids in different domains of knowledge.[149] In the Maghrib, Moriscos, who mastered Spanish and had direct access to European books, played a paramount role in transmitting and adapting texts in the fields of geography, astronomy, medicine, and mathematics.[150] The study of Hajarī and Ghānim's contributions helps revise and amend the familiar narrative of the ignorance of European culture in the premodern Islamic world. They attest that the Arab world was less introverted during these centuries than was long assumed, and that it was an active participant in the connected intellectual history of the early modern Mediterranean.

Conclusion

AMONG THE MANY BLESSINGS GOD bestowed on him during his long and productive life, Hajarī counted his relationships with "the kings and scholars of the two religions."[1] He viewed his political and learned networks as signs of the divine benevolence that had accompanied him from childhood to old age. Hajarī considered himself privileged and even empowered as a result of his frequent crossing of geographical, political, and cultural boundaries, and indeed it is these cross-boundary exchanges that make his work so compelling. They dominated his life experiences as a significant figure that made connections between Republics of Letters, and shaped his intellectual output, from his early involvement in the syncretic corpus of the Lead Books, to his translations and autobiographical writings, and in his work with European Orientalists.

In his cross-border work with Orientalists, Hajarī provided a model for mediating between diverse cultures and communities. Within Orientalism and beyond, Hajarī constantly mediated between European and Arab spheres of knowledge, between Islam and Christendom, and between religions. Working with Hubert, Erpenius, and others in Europe, and with Golius in Morocco, Hajarī, like many other subjects of Muslim countries, made clear that Orientalism itself was the product of transnational connections. His career also shows that cultural practices commonly ascribed to early modern Orientalism were also present in the Islamic countries of the early modern age.

Beyond European Orientalism, Hajarī extended his intellectual reach toward the Arabic Republic of Letters. As he readily recognized, he never attained the high status of the ulama, a status that could have guaranteed him a religious or legal appointment. He was nevertheless able to attract the interest of friends belonging to that rarefied company through his experience as a religious controversialist, one who used the deep understanding of Christianity that he acquired in Spain and his close study of the Bible to defend Islam. His familiarity with the literature produced by Muslim polemicists and converts to Islam also facilitated his success in disputes.

As an apologist for Islam, Hajarī borrowed from easily recognized themes and tropes and looked for commonalities between religions, an effort accentuated by his friendships and alliances with religious adversaries—friendships that flourished despite, or maybe even thanks to, the rhetorical confrontations. His arguments often sought to uncover similarities between the three revealed religions—Judaism, Christianity, and Islam—and concluded that these were better preserved and defended in Islam, as Judaism and Christianity were predecessors to the Prophet Muhammad. Though these themes were present in earlier polemical literature, he might have accentuated them because of his paramount concern for bringing converts back to Islam, rather than convincing infidels of the falsity of their beliefs.

Hajarī placed a high premium on his performance in controversy, and his writing extensively documented it. His able defense of the faith earned him the respect and esteem of the learned that he admired so much. His most influential work was, however, produced within a system of patronage in the Saʿdī court, and in milieus close to the dey of Tunis. Judging by the number of extant manuscripts, his output as translator of Zacuto and Vizinho's *Almanach Perpetuum* and of Ghānim's artillery book circulated far more widely than his work as an author and a controversialist. These two translations illustrated the formalization and circulation of scientific and technical knowledge, produced thanks to political sponsorship, and aiming at enhancing the power of the state. These evolutions of knowledge were an important feature of early modern Europe, and Hajarī was both a witness and a participant in their spread in North Africa, where new modes of technical practices, including writing about these topics, were also adopted, often in direct connection with European forms.

Beyond the translations and his autobiographical writing, other documents, including correspondence and the testimonies of the Orientalist contemporaries with whom he worked, show that Hajarī's work helped put oriental studies into a larger context of intellectual and social exchange. These connections allowed people of different cultures to engage in practices of knowledge that borrowed from their diverse backgrounds. These are the networks connecting Europe and its Islamic neighbors in which Hajarī's work was but one among many nodes. Early modern Orientalism was a result of this interaction. These associations also made possible some cultural productions in Muslim countries, often the work of people situated, like Hajarī, between cultures, as Moriscos or as converts. Although they could be seen as marginal, or minor, actors in the cultural fields, it would be a mistake to diminish their significance. Through the work of individuals such as Hajarī, we have a better sense of a lively written middle culture, less beholden to the higher forms, and more attuned to the life experiences of a literate though not deeply learned constituency. This culture was not the work solely of those in contact with Europe. It was also the output of other constituents of society, whose efforts created a new kind of literacy beyond the customary written academic modes.

Hajarī was located at the point of encounter of European and Muslim regions, like other participants in Orientalism hailing from Ottoman and Arab countries. He was situated at the point of encounter between the high cultural spheres, where many of his respected friends and mentors belonged, and this middle culture of diplomats, soldiers, and technical experts. He participated in these new written forms, employing language that did not rely on classical norms, a language that linguists term "Middle Arabic," often used to include experience not focused on the scholarly elite. Connected to court culture, he also understood the interest that rulers increasingly felt for technical issues, in part because of the prestige attached to the possession of beautiful instruments, such as the Molyneux Globes, and in part because of the real advantage expertise could bring in new forms of warfare and statecraft.

His successful career was dependent primarily on his mastery of Spanish, which opened a path for him as a courtier, which found him patrons, who, like Mūlay Zaydān, sponsored his translating work, and which eased his communications with Europeans. He states as much in the appendix to the *Kitāb al-ʿizz,* after reflecting in the *Supporter* on the many diverse threads of his personal and intellectual trajectories. This self-conscious interweaving may be a hallmark of his work. As compelling as it seems, it should not obscure the fact that his career is only one of many that were made possible in North Africa for those who connected cultural and civilizational spheres, and for those who illustrated a nascent nonacademic writing production.

The study of his work offers an entry to better understand the cultural forms produced in the contact zone between Europe and North Africa and West Asia, marked not only by political and military confrontations but also by more intense diplomatic relations, in the sixteenth and especially the seventeenth centuries. At this time, when Orientalism was developing in

Europe, the production of a corpus of translations, hybridizations, adaptations in Arabic of European texts was facilitated by the rise of a middle culture. This new literary culture of the middle class favored simpler writing, addressed a public beyond the academic, and produced new authors who did not go necessarily down the usual scholarly path. These could adapt and translate technical treatises, and they could write chronicles and autobiographies. Hajarī's career draws its significance from his ability to embody these different threads and trends, to connect them, and to reflect on them, beyond his testimony on Morisco history, beyond the polemical literature to which he is mostly associated, and beyond Orientalism.

NOTES

INTRODUCTION

1. The States General (Staten-Generaal), assembly of the provincial states of the Netherlands.

2. "En l'année 1622, vint à Maroc un ambassadeur de Messieurs les Estats, un escuyer du prince d'Orange, & un disciple de Harpinius, professeur ès langues orientales et etrangeres à Leyden, tous deux avec des presens qui furent bien agreables au roi Mouley Zidant, mais principalement celuy d'Harpinius, qui estoit un atlas et un Nouveau Testament en arabe; & il nous fut rapporté par les eunuques que le Roy ne cessoit de lire dans le Nouveau Testament. Or comme l'Ambassadeur s'ennuyoit de ce qu'on ne luy donnoit point son expedition, il fut conseillé de presenter au Roy une peticion ou requeste, laquelle fut faite par ce disciple d'Harpinius, nommé Golius, en écriture et langue arabesque, & en stile chrestien. Ce roy demeura estonné de la beauté de cette requeste, tant pour l'écriture, pour le langage que pour le stile extraordinaire en ce païs-là. Il manda aussitost ses talips ou écrivains, leur montra cette requeste qu'ils admirerent. Il fit venir l'Ambassadeur, auquel il demanda qui l'avoit faite. Il luy répondit que c'étoit Golius, disciple et envoyé d'Harpinius. Le Roy le voulut voir, luy parla en arabe. Ce disciple répondit en espagnol qu'il entendoit fort bien tout de ce que Sa Majesté luy disoit, mais qu'il ne pouvoit luy répondre en la mesme langue, parce que la gorge ne luy aidoit point (car il faut autan parler de la gorge que de la langue); ce que le Roy, qui entendoit bien l'espagnol, trouva fort bon; & accordant les fins de la requeste, fit donner à l'Ambassadeur les expeditions pour son retour. Et aujourd'huy ce Golius est à Leyden, professeur ès langues orientales & étrangeres, au lieu et place d'Harpinius, qui est mort," *Sources inédites de l'histoire du Maroc* (henceforth *SIHM*), Archives et Bibliothèques de France, Série Saadienne, vol. 3, Henry de Castries, ed., Paris, Ernest Leroux, 1911, 731–32.

3. On Erpenius and Golius, see Arnoud Vrolijk and Richard van Leeuwen, *Arabic Studies in the Netherlands: A Short History in Portraits, 1580–1950*, trans. Alastair Hamilton, Leiden, Brill, 2014, 31–48.

4. As will be shown below, other names were also given to him by himself and others, as was the case for many Arab premodern figures. This book will follow the scholarly convention of calling him Ahmad ibn Qāsim al-Hajarī, shortened to Hajarī.

5. Paul Colomiès, *Mélanges historiques,* Orange, J. Rousseau, 1675, 75–78.

6. Edward H. Said, *Orientalism,* London, Penguin Books, 2003 (1st ed., 1978).

7. Sanjay Subrahmanyam, *Courtly Encounters: Translating Courtliness and Violence in Early Modern Eurasia,* Cambridge, MA, Harvard University Press, 2012, 30.

8. *SIHM,* Archives et Bibliothèques des Pays-Bas, vol. 3, Henry de Castries, ed., Paris, The Hague, Leroux and Martinus Nijhoff, 1912, 571–85.

9. Fokko Jan Dijksterhuis, "The Mutual Making of Sciences and Humanities: Willebrord Snellius, Jacob Golius, and the Early Modern Entanglement of Mathematics and Philology," in Rens Bod, Jaap Maat, and Thijs Weststeijn, eds., *The Making of the Humanities,* vol. 3, *From Early Modern to Modern Disciplines,* Amsterdam, Amsterdam University Press, 2012, 73–92.

10. See the informative review of Eric R. Dursteler, "On Bazaars and Battlefields: Recent Scholarship on Mediterranean Cultural Contacts," *Journal of Early Modern History* 15 (2011), 413–34; see also Brian A. Catlos and Sharon Kinoshita, eds., *Can We Talk Mediterranean? Conversations on an Emerging Field in Medieval and Early Modern Studies,* Cham, Palgrave-McMillan, 2017.

11. Tijana Krstic, "Islam and Muslims in Europe," in *The Oxford Handbook of Early Modern European History, 1350–1750,* vol. 1, *Peoples and Place,* Hamish Scott, ed., Oxford, Oxford University Press, 2015, 20; see also Nabil Matar, *Britain and Barbary, 1589–1689,* Gainesville, University Press of Florida, 2005; Jocelyne Dakhlia and Bernard Vincent, eds., *Les Musulmans dans l'histoire de l'Europe,* vol. 1, *Une intégration invisible,* Paris, Albin Michel, 2011; Jocelyne Dakhlia and Wolfgang Kaiser, eds., *Les Musulmans dans l'histoire de l'Europe,* vol. 2, *Passages et contacts en Méditerranée,* Paris, Albin Michel, 2013.

12. Said, *Orientalism,* 2.

13. These present "Orientalism [as] a style of thought based upon an ontological and epistemological distinction made between 'the Orient' and (most of the time) 'the Occident'," so broadly defined that it "can accommodate Aeschylus, say, and Victor Hugo, Dante and Karl Marx." Most famously, Said describes the Orientalism he sees beginning roughly in the late eighteenth century, as "a Western style for dominating, restructuring, and having authority over the Orient" (*Orientalism,* 3).

14. Peter N. Miller, *Peiresc's Mediterranean World,* Cambridge, MA, Harvard University Press, 2015, 60.

15. Adrian Parr, ed., *The Deleuze Dictionary,* New York, Columbia Unversity Press, 2005, 13; Gilles Deleuze and Félix Guattari, *Kafka: Toward a Minor Literature,* trans. Dana Polan, Minneapolis, University of Minnesota Press, 1986; henceforth *Kafka.*

16. On this notion, see *Osiris* 2:25 (2010), issue titled *Expertise: Practical Knowledge and the Early Modern State,* Eric H. Ash, ed.

PART ONE. A CONNECTED REPUBLIC OF LETTERS

1. Anthony Grafton, *Worlds Made by Words: Scholarship and Community in the Modern West,* Cambridge, MA, Harvard University Press, 2009, 7. The notion was recently extended to other periods by an influential book by Pascale Casanova (*The World Republic of Letters,* trans. M. B. DeBevoise, Cambridge, MA, Harvard University Press, 2004).

2. Alastair Hamilton, Maurits H. van den Boogert, and Bart Westerweel, eds., *The Republic of Letters and the Levant,* Leiden, Brill, 2005; Sonja Brentjes, "The Interests of the Republic of Letters in the Middle East, 1550–1700," *Travellers from Europe in the Ottoman and Safavid Empires, 16th–17th Centuries: Seeking, Transforming, Discarding Knowledge,* Farnham, Ashgate-Variorum, 2010, 435–68; Alexander Bevilacqua, *The Republic of Arabic Letters: Islam and the European Enlightenment,* Cambridge, MA, Harvard University Press, 2018.

3. Muhsin J. al-Musawi, *The Medieval Islamic Republic of Letters: Arabic Knowledge Construction,* Notre Dame, IN, University of Notre Dame Press, 2015; Ilker Evrim Binbas, *Intellectual Networks in Timurid Iran: Sharaf al-Dīn ʿAlī Yazdī and the Islamicate Republic of Letters,* Cambridge, Cambridge University Press, 2016.

4. Paul Babinski, "Ottoman Philology and the Origins of Persian Studies in Western Europe: The *Gulistān*'s Orientalist Readers," *Lias* 46:2 (2019), 233–315, 237.

5. E. Natalie Rothman, "Dragomans and 'Turkish Literature': The Making of a Field of Inquiry," *Oriente Moderno,* new series 93:2 (2013), 390–421, 392.

6. As noted in the case of Morocco by Yasser Benhima, "Le Maroc à l'heure du monde (XVᵉ–XVIIᵉ siècle): Bilan clinique d'une histoire (dé)connectée," *L'Année du Maghreb* 10 (2014), 255–66.

CHAPTER 1. AHMAD AL-HAJARĪ:
TRAJECTORIES OF EXILE

1. *The Supporter of Religion against the Infidels,* rev. ed., trans., and presentation by P. S. van Koningsveld, Q. al-Samarrai, and G. A. Wiegers, Madrid, CISC, 2015 (1st ed., 1997). Henceforth *Supporter.* In this study, the page numbers followed by "e" will refer to the English translation, and the numbers followed by "a" to the Arabic text. My biographical account relies partly on the general introduction of this 2nd edition.

2. On this manuscript, see Juan Penella Roma, "Introduction au manuscrit D. 565 de la Bibliothèque Universitaire de Bologne," in Mikel de Epalza and Ramon Petit, eds, *Recueil d'études sur les moriscos andalous en Tunisie,* Madrid and Tunis, Dirección General de Relaciones Culturales, Instituto Hispano-Árabe de Cultura; Société Tunisienne de Diffusion, 1973, 258–63.

3. The letter has been published by Jaime Oliver Asín, "Noticias de Bejarano en Granada," *Conferencias y apuntes inéditos,* Madrid, Agencia Española de Cooperación Internacional, 1996, 145–50, and translated into English by Gerard Wiegers,

A Learned Muslim Acquaintance of Erpenius and Golius: Ahmad b. Kāsim al-Andalusī and Arabic Studies in the Netherlands, Leiden, Documentatiebureau Islam-Christendom, 1988, 33–44.

4. Ibrāhīm ibn Ahmad Ghānim al-Andalusī, *Kitāb al-'izz wa al-rif 'a wa al-manāfi' li l-mujāhidīn fī sabīli Allāh bi l-madāfi',* trans. Ahmad al-Hajarī, Ihsān Hindī, ed., Damascus, Markaz al-dirāsāt al-'askariyya, 1995.

5. This appendix has been first published and translated into English by L. P. Harvey, "The Morisco Who Was Muley Zaidan's Spanish Interpreter," *Miscelanea de Estudios Arabes y Hebraicos* 8:1 (1959), 67–97.

6. *Supporter,* introduction, 74e / 7a.

7. Francisco Núñez Muley, *A Memorandum for the President of the Royal Audiencia and Chancery of the City and Kingdom of Granada,* Vincent Barletta, ed. and trans., Chicago, University of Chicago Press, 2007, 73.

8. Harvey, *Muslims in Spain, 1500 to 1614,* Chicago, University of Chicago Press, 2005, 205–6.

9. Harvey, *Muslims in Spain,* ch. 12, "Hornachos: a Special Case," 369.

10. Bernard Vincent, "Les Morisques d'Estrémadure au XVIᵉ siècle," *Annales de Démographie Historique* (1974), 431–48.

11. Claire M. Gilbert, *In Good Faith: Arabic Translation and Translators in Early Modern Spain,* Philadelphia, University of Pennsylvania Press, 2020, 6.

12. Mercedes García-Arenal and Fernando Rodríguez Mediano, *The Orient in Spain. Converted Muslims, the Forged Lead Books of Granada, and the Rise of Orientalism,* trans. Consuelo Lópe-Morillas, Leiden, Brill, 2013, 150. Henceforth *Orient.*

13. *Supporter,* ch. 1, 87e / 23a.

14. *Supporter,* general introduction, 35–36.

15. See Isabel Boyano Guerra, "Al-Hayarī y su traducción del pergamino de la Torre Turpiana," in Manuel Barrios Aguilera and Mercedes García-Arenal, eds, *¿La historia inventada? Los Libros Plúmbeos y el legado sacromontano,* Granada, Editorial Universidad de Granada, 2008, 137–58.

16. García-Arenal and Mediano even suggest that he might have helped with some of the forgeries (García-Arenal and Rodríguez Mediano, *Orient,* 147).

17. A. Katie Harris, *From Muslim to Christian Granada: Inventing a City's Past in Early Modern Spain,* Baltimore, Johns Hopkins University Press, 2007, xv.

18. *Supporter,* ch. 13, 264e / 286a.

19. Ibn Tūda was so well known that the famous playwright Lope de Vega (1562–1635) made him a character named Albacarin in *La tragedia del Rey Don Sebastián y Bautismo del Principe de Marruecos.* This play centers around the disastrous defeat met by the King Sebastian of Portugal when he attempted to invade Morocco in 1578, which resulted in his death on the battlefield and the annexation of Portugal by Spain for sixty years. Another consequence was the exile of Mūlay al-Shaykh, young son of Muhammad al-Mutawakkil (d. 1578), dethroned sultan of Morocco and ally of Portugal. Ibn Tūda was among his companions of exile. In the play, upon learning of the Moroccan prince's intention to convert to Christianity, Albacarin tries in vain to poison him. On these events and the play, see Jaime Oliver

Asín, *Vida de Don Felipe de Africa, Principe de Fez y Marruecos (1566–1621),* Granada, Editorial Universidad de Granada, 1955, esp. 100–122.

20. García-Arenal and Rodríguez Mediano, *Orient,* 140.

21. Harvey, "The Morisco," 95 (82 for Arabic.)

22. Wiegers, *Learned Muslim,* 34; *Supporter,* ch. 2, 109e, 53a.

23. García-Arenal and Rodríguez Mediano, *Orient,* 142.

24. Translated by Harvey as "Private Secretary" for Spanish, "The Morisco," 86.

25. See Muhammad Jādūr, *The Institution of the Makhzan in Moroccan History* (in Arabic), Casablanca, Fondation du Roi Abdul-Aziz, 2009, 126.

26. See Jacques Caillé, "La mission à Marrakech du Hollandais Pieter Maertensz. Coy," *Revue d'Histoire Diplomatique* 86 (1972), 97–123; and Erica Heinsen-Roach, *Consuls and Captives: Dutch-North African Diplomacy in the Early Modern Mediterranean,* Rochester, University of Rochester Press, 2019, 24–27.

27. *Supporter,* ch. 11, 231–35e / 235–40a.

28. Cardinal de Richelieu, quoted in Youssef El Alaoui, "The Moriscos in France after the Expulsion: Notes for the History of a Minority," in Mercedes García-Arenal and Gerard Wiegers, eds., *The Expulsion of the Moriscos from Spain: A Mediterranean Diaspora,* trans. Consuelo López-Morillas and Martin Beagles, Leiden, Brill, 2014, 239–68, 240. Henceforth *Expulsion.*

29. Louis Cardaillac, "Le passage des Morisques en Languedoc," *Annales du Midi,* 5:83 (1971), 259–98; Pierre Santoni, "Le passage des Morisques en Provence (1610–1613)," *Provence Historique* 185 (1996), 333–83.

30. Cardaillac, "Le passage," 276–82.

31. For a Tunisian case, see Pierre Grandchamp, *La France en Tunisie au début du XVIIe siècle (1601–1610),* vol. 2, Tunis, Société Anonyme de l'Imprimerie Rapide, 1921, 185–90.

32. See Francisque Michel, *Histoire des races maudites de la France et de l'Espagne,* Paris, Franck, 1847, 2:92.

33. For a useful overview of medicine in Morocco at the time of Ahmad al-Mansūr, see Justin Stearns, *Revealed Sciences: The Natural Sciences in Islam in Seventeenth-Century Morocco,* Cambridge, Cambridge University Press, 2021, 200–202.

34. Wiegers, *Learned Muslim,* 40.

35. *Supporter,* ch. 5, 131e / 79a.

36. *The Correspondence of Joseph Justus Scaliger,* Paul Botley and Dirk van Miert, eds., Geneva, Droz, 2012, 7:396.

37. Apart from Hajarī, Hubert was also in touch with another official working for Mūlay Zaydān, named Khalīl, who translated between Arabic and Dutch (*SIHM,* Pays-Bas, 2:749).

38. *Supporter,* ch. 7, 152e / 113a.

39. *Supporter,* ch. 13, 258–59e / 276–79a.

40. Robert Jones, *Learning Arabic in Renaissance Europe (1505–1624),* Leiden, Brill, 2020, 84; the book (Res FOL.T. 29.5) is held in the BNF (Bibliothèque Nationale de France). Henceforth *Learning.*

41. Arabe 4348, BNF; see ff. 1r, 140v, 146r, 151v, 182v.

42. BNF, Arabe 4213, 29 v.

43. Muhammad ibn Sulaymān al-Jazūlī (d. 1465), *Dalā'il al-khayrāt,* Arabe 1181, BNF, 99v.

44. On Savary's career as ambassador and Orientalist, see Gérald Duverdier, "Savary de Brèves et Ibrahim Müteferrika: Deux drogmans culturels à l'origine de l'imprimerie turque," *Bulletin du Bibliophile* 3 (1987), 322–59; Guy Thuilier, "'Un 'politique' au XVIIᵉ siècle: Savary de Brèves (1560–1628)," *La Revue Administrative* (2009) 62:68, 124–29; Alastair Hamilton, "François Savary de Brèves," in David Thomas and John Chesworth, eds., *Christian-Muslim Relations: A Bibliographical History,* vol. 9, *Western and Southern Europe (1600–1700),* Leiden, Brill, 2017, 417–22.

45. This information is only found in the Paris manuscript. See *Supporter,* ch. 13, 276e, n115 / 307a, n3.

46. For his acute criticism of poetry, see *Scaligerana, Thuana, Perroniana, Pithoeana, et Colomesiana, ou Remarques historiques, critiques, morales et littéraires,* vol. 1, Amsterdam, 1740, 391–97. For a rare modern study of his poetry, see A. Kibédi Varga, "Enfin Du Perron vint. Malherbe ou le sens de la publicité," *Revue d'Histoire Littéraire de la France* 67:1 (1967), 1–17.

47. *Index Latinarum Vocum ex dictionario Arabolatino,* Arabe 4338, BNF, 997–98. The two Maronites are Nasrallah Shalaq al-'Āqurī / Victorius Scialac Accurrensis (d. 1635), and Jibrā'īl al-Sahyūnī / Gabriel Sionita (1577?–1648).

48. For the English translation of the relevant parts of the letter, see Jones, *Learning,* 77–78. On Casaubon and his connection with Erpenius, see Alastair Hamilton, "Isaac Casaubon the Arabist: 'Video Longum Esse Ite,'" *Journal of the Warburg and Courtauld Institutes* 72 (2009), 143–68.

49. The letter is translated into English in Jones, *Learning,* 90–91.

50. Wiegers, *Learned Muslim,* 42.

51. Wiegers, "Managing Disaster: Networks of the Moriscos during the Process of the Expulsion from the Iberian Peninsula around 1609," *Journal of Medieval Religious Cultures* 36:2 (2010), 141–68. The networks connecting Spain, France, and North Africa, which helped some Moriscos to save their lives and at least part of their wealth at the time of expulsion have been sketched by Jorge Gil Herrera and Luis F. Barnabé Pons, "The Moriscos outside Spain. Routes and Financing," in García-Arenal and Wiegers, eds., *Expulsion,* 219–38.

52. Herrera and Barnabé Pons, "The Moriscos outside Spain," in García-Arenal and Wiegers, eds., *Expulsion,* 220–21.

53. Wiegers, *Learned Muslim,* 40.

54. *Supporter,* general introduction, 48.

55. Wiegers, *Learned Muslim,* 38.

56. *Supporter,* general introduction, 49.

57. Tijana Krstic, "The Elusive Intermediaries: Moriscos in Ottoman and Western European Diplomatic Sources from Constantinople, 1560s–1630s," *Journal of Early Modern History* 19 (2015), 129–51, 141.

58. Wiegers, "Managing Disaster," 158.

59. García-Arenal and Rodríguez Mediano, *Orient*, 150.

60. This poem is included in a manuscript of Muhammad ibn Mālik's *Lāmiyyat al-af'āl* copied by Hajarī for Hubert, and held in the Bibliothèque Nationale de France (Arabe 4119, fol. 26r).

61. The document concerning this incident had been published by Francisque Michel, *Histoire des races maudites,* vol. 2, 92, and cited in *Supporter,* general introduction, 51n.

62. See Dast Le Vacher de Boisville, *Liste générale et alphabétique des membres du Parlement de Bordeaux*, Bordeaux, Gounouilhou,1896, 30. A number of councilors of the parliament of Bordeaux were named Fayard, included one Antoine Fayard who was appointed on April 14, 1598. This might be the person mentioned by Hajarī.

63. Wiegers, "The Expulsion of 1609–1614 and the Polemical Writings of the Moriscos Living in the Diaspora," in García-Arenal and Wiegers, eds., *Expulsion,* 389–412, 396.

64. Herrera and Barnabé Pons, "The Moriscos outside Spain," in García-Arenal and Wiegers, eds., *Expulsion,* 231. See also García-Arenal, who cites a document mentioning how wealthy Moriscos had collected "certain sums of money which were sent to Toulouse to a safebox in Chapiz's power": "The Moriscos in Morocco," in García-Arenal and Wiegers, eds., *Expulsion,* 286–328, 303.

65. *Supporter,* ch. 10, 215e / 205–6a.

66. M. Th. Houtsma, "Uit de Oostersche correspondentie van Th. Erpenius, Jac. Golius en Lev. Warner, eene bijdrage tot de geschiedenis van de beofening der oosterche letteren in Nederland," *Verhandelingen der Koninklijke Akademie van wetenschappen,* Amsterdam, Johnnes Müller, 1888, 1–116, 20–24.

67. *Supporter,* ch. 11, 221e / 217a.

68. *Supporter,* appendix 2, 295, and 300 for the English translation.

69. Jones, *Learning,* 89. The manuscript is a commentary by 'Abd al-Rahmān al-Makkudī on Ibn Mālik's *Alfiyya* held in Cambridge University Library, Mm.6.23..

70. *Supporter,* general introduction, 53. The manuscript is Cod. Or. 154 of the Stadtbibliothek Hamburg. On Erpenius's edition of the proverbs, see Vrolijk, "The Prince of Arabists and His Many Errors: Thomas Erpenius's Image of Joseph Scaliger and the Edition of the 'Proverbia Arabica' (1614)," *Journal of the Warburg and Courtauld Institutes* 73 (2010), 297–325.

71. *Supporter,* Introduction, 53–54; the volume is held in the Bodleian, call number MS Pococke 434.

72. *Supporter,* ch. 11, 221e / 217a.

73. Gilbert, *In Good Faith,* 128.

74. Mercedes García-Arenal, Fernando Rodríguez Mediano, and Rachid Al Hour eds., *Cartas marruecas,* Madrid, CSIC, 2002, 337–39, 367–76, for the original documents and Hajarī's translations.

75. Gilbert, *In Good Faith,* 127–35.

76. Gilbert, *In Good Faith,* 132.

77. *Supporter,* ch. 12, 237–38e / 242a; see Francisco Del Puerto, *Mission historial de Marruecos,* Seville, Francisco Garay, 1708, 162. Antoine de Sainte-Marie was charged by captives to deliver a letter to the king of France written on December 4, 1622. See *SIHM,* Série Saadienne, France, 3:88.

78. *SIHM,* Pays-Bas, 3:107–8.

79. Houtsma, "Oosterche correspondentie," 24–25 and 28–29.

80. Jones, *Learning,* 15.

81. As shown by Jan Just Witkam, "The Leiden Manuscript of the *Kitāb al-Mustaʿīnī,*" in Charles Burnett, ed., *Ibn Baklarish's Book of Simples: Medical Remedies between Three Faiths in Twelfth-Century Spain,* London and Oxford, Arcadian Library and Oxford University Press, 2008, 75–94.

82. Witkam, "Leiden Manuscript", 78–79.

83. University of Manchester, John Rylands Library, Persian MS 91, 87a and 88a. Its contents are briefly described by Jan Schmidt, "An Ostrich Egg for Golius: The John Rylands Library MS Persian 913 and the History of the Early Modern Contacts between the Dutch Republic and the Islamic World," *The Joys of Philology: Studies in Ottoman Literature, History, and Orientalism (1500–1923),* vol. 2, Istanbul, Isis Press, 2002, 9–74, 17.

84. *Orationes tres de Linguarum Ebraeae, atque Arabicae dignitate,* Leiden, 1621.

85. For examples of letters from Mūlay Zaydān translated by Erpenius, see *SIHM,* Pays-Bas, vol. 3, 250–54, 480–86, and 495–98, 562–65; the notes provide information about Erpenius's translations.

86. Witkam, "Leiden Manuscript," 80.

87. *SIHM,* Série Saadienne, France, vol. 3, 451, 458, 464, 465, 466.

88. *Supporter,* general introduction, 58.

89. About Tunisia and the Moriscos, see *Recueil d'études;* Olatz Villanueva Zubizarreta, "The Moriscos in Tunisia," in García-Arenal and Wiegers, eds., *Expulsion,* 357–88.

90. *Supporter,* 295–305, for the Spanish text and an English translation.

91. Harvey, "The Morisco," 96 (83 for Arabic)..

92. See Alexander Bevilacqua, *The Republic of Arabic Letters: Islam and the European Enlightenment,* Cambridge, MA, Harvard University Press, 2018, ch. 4, "D'Herbelot's Oriental Garden."

93. Here is the complete text of the entry devoted to al-Hajarī: "AHMED Ben Cassem Al-Andalousi More de Grenade, qui vivoit l'an de J.C. 1599, cite un manuscrit Arabe de saint Cœcilius Archevêque de Grenade, qui fut trouvé avec seize lames de plomb gravées en caracteres Arabes, dans une grotte proche de la même ville. Don Petro de Castro y Quinones Archevêque pour lors de la même Ville, en a rendu luy-même témoignage. Ces lames de plomb que l'on appelle de Grenade ont été depuis portées à Rome, où, après un examen qui a duré plusieurs années, elles ont été enfin condamnées comme Apocryphes, sous le Pontificat d'Alexandre Septième. Elles contiennent plusieurs histoires fabuleuses touchant l'enfance et l'éducation de JESUS-CHRIST, & la vie de la sainte Vierge. Il y a entr'autres choses que JESUS-CHRIST étant encore enfant, & apprenant à l'école l'alphabet Arabique, il interro-

geoit son maître sur la signification de chaque lettre; & qu'après en avoir apprins de lui le sens & la signification Grammaticale, il luy enseignoit le sens mystique de chacune de ces lettres. Ce Manuscrit est dans la Bibliotheque du Roy n°. 1043," *Bibliothèque orientale,* Paris, Compagnie des Libraires, 1687, 73. And here is the relevant passage in the entry "Gharnatah": "Ahmed Ben Cassem Al Andalousi écrit qu'en l'an 1008. de l'Heg. de J.C. 1599. l'on trouva proche de Grenade dans un lieu nommé Khandax algennat, seize lames de cuivres et de plomb de la grandeur de la main, que l'on prétendoit avoir été enterrées par Saint Cœcilius Archevêque de Grenade, où la predication de la foy Chrêtienne étoit décrite en langue Arabique, mêlée de plusieurs contes fabuleux. Ces lames furent portées à Rome, & ont été condamnées à Rome depuis peu d'années. *Voyez dans la Bibliothèque du Roy n. 1043." Bibliothèque orientale,* 360.

94. Muhammad ibn al-'Ayyāshī, *Zahr al-bustān,* Ahmad Qaddūr, ed., Rabat, Rabat-Net, 2013, 159–62.

95. *Nuzhat al-Hādī,* A. al-Shadilī, ed., Casablanca, al-Najah, 1998, 195–96.

96. For a presentation of this genre in the early modern Moroccan context, see Stearns, *Revealed Sciences,* 46–48.

97. Ifrānī, *Safwat man intashar min akhbār sulahā' al-qarn al-hādi 'ashar,* 'Abd al-Majīd Khayālī, ed., Casablanca, Markaz al-turāth al-thaqafī al-maghribī, 2004, 45.

98. *Safwat,* 46. This story is summarized by Ahmad al-Nāsirī (1834–97), *Kitāb al-istiqsā,* vol. 5, Muhammad Hajjī, Ibrāhīm Abū Tālib, and Ahmad al-Tawfiq, eds., Casablanca, Ministry of Culture, 2001, 206.

99. *Safwat,* 229.

100. The entire Azhar manuscript, which is an early version of the text, is reproduced in the 2015 edition of the *Supporter.*

101. On 'Attār's life and works, see Peter Gran, *The Islamic Roots of Capitalism: Egypt, 1760–1840,* Syracuse, NY, Syracuse University Press, 1998 (2nd ed.); and Shaden M. Tageldin, *Disarming Words: Empire and the Seductions of Translation in Egypt,* Berkeley, University of California Press, 2011, ch. 2.

102. *Supporter,* notes on 36a and 207a.

103. Eduardo Saavedra, "Índice general de la literature aljamiada," *Memorias de la Real Academia Española* 6 (1889), 237–320, 287–89.

104. Jaime Oliver Asín, *Vida de Don Felipe de Africa,* 101, and *Conferencias,* "Ahmad al-Hajarī Bejarano. Apuntes biograficos de un Morisco notable residente en Marruecos," 151–64.

105. "The Morisco."

106. This fragment is since 1980 held in the Bibliothèque Nationale de France, and is the manuscript S used by the editors of the *Supporter.*

107. Muhammad al-Fāsī, Moroccan Travelers and Their Work," (in Arabic) *Da'wat al-Haqq,* 2:3 (1958), 19–23.

108. "The Phenomenon of Translation into Arabic in Sa'dī Morocco," (in Arabic) *Da'wat al-Haqq* 10:3, 74–91.

109. Fu'ād Sayyid, *Fihrist al-makhtūtāt,* vol. 2, Cairo, Dār al-kutub, 1963, 147.

110. These studies by Clelia Sarnelli Cerqua include: "La fuga in Marocco di al-Shihāb Ahmad al-Andalusī," *Studi Magrebini* I (1966), 2145–229; "Lo scrittore ispano-marochino al-Hajarī e il suo *Kitāb Nāsir al-Dīn," Atti del III Congresso di Studi Arabici e Islamici,* Ravello, Istituto Universitario Orientale, 1966, 597–614; "Al-Hajarī in Andalusia," *Studi Magrebini* 3 (1970), 161–203.

111. *Nāsir al-Dīn ʿalā al-qawm al-kāfirīn,* Muhammad Razzūq, ed., Casablanca, Publications of the Faculty of Letters and Human Sciences, 1987.

112. Jones, *Learning.*

113. Gerard Wiegers, *Learned Muslim.*

114. See ʿAbd al-Majīd al-Qaddūrī, *Moroccan Ambassadors in Europe, 1922–1610* (in Arabic), Rabat, Publications of the Faculty of Letters and Human Sciences, 1995, 11–21; Nabil Matar, *In the Lands of the Christians,* which contains translated parts of the *Supporter,* New York, Routledge, 2003, 5–44; Jonathan Burton, *Traffic and Turning: Islam and English Drama 1579–1624,* Newark, University of Delaware Press, 2005 (esp. chapter 6 "'Bondslaves and Pagans Shall Our Statesemen Be': *Othello,* Leo Africanus, and Muslim Ambassadors to Europe"); Oumelbanine Zhiri, "Voyages d'Orient et d'Occident: Jean Léon l'Africain et Ahmad al-Hajarī dans la littérature de voyage," *Arborescences* 2 (2012), 1–15; Rashā' al-Khātib, *Ahmad ibn Qāsim al-Hajarī al-Andalusī, the Translator, Traveler and Diplomat* (in Arabic), Beirut and Abū Dhabī, al-Muʾassasa al-ʿarabiyya li al-dirasāt wa al-nashr, 2018. See also the novel by ʿAbd al-Wāhid Brāhim titled *Taghribat Ahmad al-Hajarī (The Exile of Ahmad al-Hajarī),* Cologne and Baghdad, Manshurat al-jamal, 2006.

115. See Muhammad Razzūq, *The Andalusians and Their Emigration to Morocco, 16–17th centuries* (in Arabic), Casablanca, Afrique-Orient, 1997; and Houssem Eddine Chachia (Husām al-Dīn Shāshya), *The Sephardim and the Moriscos: Their Emigration and Settlement in the Maghrib (1492–1756)* (in Arabic), Abū Dhabī-Beirut, al-Muʾassasa al-ʿarabiyya li al-dirasāt wa al-nashr, 2015, "The Moment of Choice: The Moriscos on the Border of Christianity and Islam," in Claire Norton, ed., *Conversion and Islam in the Early Modern Mediterranean, The Lure of the Other,* New York, Routledge, 2017, 129–54, and "The Morisco Ahmad ibn Qāsim al-Hajarī and the Egyptian Manuscript of his *Nāsir al-Dīn ʿalā qawm al-kāfirīn (*The Triumph of Faith over the Nation of Unbelievers)," *Kodex. Jahrbuch des Internationalen Buchwissenschaftlichen Gesellschaft* 8 (2018), 57–71.

CHAPTER 2. NETWORKS OF ORIENTALISM:
OUT OF THE SHADOWS

1. Wiegers, *Learned Muslim,* 41–42.
2. As noted by Aurélien Girard, "Introduction," *Dix-Septième Siècle* 67:2 (2015), 385–92, 387.
3. Sonja Brentjes, introduction to *Travellers,* xxviii.
4. Brentjes, "Interests," in *Travellers,* 465.

5. Charles Burnett, "The Coherence of the Arabic-Latin Translation Program in Toledo in the Twelfth Century," *Science in Context* 14:1–2, 249–88, 249.

6. See Fernando Rodríguez Mediano, "Fragmentos de orientalismo español del s. XVII," *Hispania* (2006), 243–76; and García-Arenal and Rodríguez Mediano, *Orient.*

7. Claire Gilbert has shown how translation between Arabic and Spanish also played a crucial role in local governmental, administrative, and legal contexts following the fall of Granada. See *In Good Faith.*

8. Harvey, *Muslims in Spain,* 14.

9. Ugo Monneret de Villard, *Lo studio dell' Islam in Europa nel XII e nel XIII secolo,* Vatican City, Biblioteca Apostolica Vaticana, 1944, 35–59.

10. Quoted in Jesse D. Mann, "Throwing the Book at Them: Juan de Segovia's Use of the Qur'ān," *Revista Española de Filosofía Medieval* 26: 1 (2019), 79–96, 80.

11. See Gerard Wiegers, *Islamic Literature in Spanish and Aljamiado: Yça of Segovia (fl. 1450), His Antecedents and Successors,* Leiden, Brill, 1994; Anne Marie Wolf, *Juan de Segovia and the Fight for Peace: Christians and Muslims in the Fifteenth Century,* Notre Dame, IN, University of Notre Dame Press, 2014; Ulli Roth, "Juan of Segovia's Translation of the Qur'ān," *Al-Qantara* 35:2 (2014), 555–78.

12. Scholars however debate whether a 1606 manuscript of a complete Castilian translation of the Quran is a copy of 'Īsā ibn Jābir's translation. See Consuelo López-Morillas, "Lost and Found? Yça de Segovia and the Qur'ān among the Mudejars and Moriscos," *Journal of Islamic Studies* 10:3 (1999), 277–92.

13. Mercedes García-Arenal, "The Religious Identity of the Arabic Language and the Affair of the Lead Books of the Sacromonte," *Arabica* 56 (2009), 495–528, 501–2.

14. Quoted in Henry Kamen, *The Spanish Inquisition: A Historical Revision,* 4th ed., New Haven, CT, Yale University Press, 2014, 81.

15. Pedro de Alcala, *Vocabulista aravigo in letra castellana,* Granada, Juan Varela de Salamanca,1505; *Arte para ligeramente saber la lengua araviga,* Granada, Juan Varela de Salamanca, 1505.

16. Teresa Soto and Katarzyna Starcweska, "Authority, Philology, and Conversion under the Aegis of Martín García," in Mercedes García-Arenal, ed., *After Conversion: Iberia and the Emergence of Modernity,* Leiden, Brill, 2016, 199–228, 223.

17. Elisa Ruiz García and Isabel García-Monge, eds., *Confusión o confutación de la secta Mahomética y del Alcorán,* Mérida, Editora regional de Extremadura, 2003 (first published in 1515).

18. Quoted and translated in Ryan Szpiech, *Conversion and Narrative: Reading and Religious Authority in Medieval Polemic,* Philadelphia, University of Pennsylvania Press, 2013, 33.

19. Szpiech, *Conversion and Narrative,* 34.

20. See Szpiech, "A Witness of Their Own Nation: On the Influence of Juan Andrés," in Mercedes García-Arenal, ed., *After Conversion,* 174–98, 180.

21. Consuelo López-Morillas, "The Genealogy of the Spanish Qur'ān," *Journal of Islamic Studies* 17:3 (2006), 255–94, 276–78.

22. Mercedes García-Arenal and Katarzyna Starczewska, "'The Law of Abraham the Catholic': Juan Gabriel as Qur'ān Translator for Martín de Figuerola and Egidio da Viterbo," *Al-Qantara* 35:2 (2014), 409–59. The authors propose as a "working hypothesis" that "the text attributed to Juan Andrés was not in its entirety authored by him" and argue that "it was created in the circle of Martín García and was put together by different authors and in different hands" (436).

23. Soto and Starcweska, "Authority, Philology, and Conversion," 224.

24. García-Arenal and Rodríguez Mediano, *Orient,* 302.

25. Pier Mattia Tommasino, "Textual Agnogenesis and the Polysemy of the Reader: Early Modern European Readings of Qur'ānic Embryology," in Mercedes García-Arenal, ed., *After Conversion,* 155–73, 172.

26. Jacob Golius prepared a never completed Latin edition. See Harmut Bobzin, "Juan Andrés und sein Buch *Confusion del secta mahomatica* (1515)," *Festgabe für Hans-Rudolf Singer,* Frankfurt, Peter Lang, 1991, 534–35; Wiegers, "Polemical Transfers: Iberian Muslim Polemics and their Impact in Northern Europe in the Seventeenth Century," in Mercedes García-Arenal, ed., *After Conversion,* 229–48, 242.

27. "Toda la ley de los moros," in Ruiz García and García-Monge, eds., *Confusión,* 91.

28. François Secret, *Les kabbalistes chrétiens de la Renaissance,* Paris, Dunod, 1963.

29. *De Orbis terræ concordia,* Basel, 1544, 157 and 154–55; cf. Ruiz García and García-Monge, eds., *Confusión,* 184. See Secret, "Guillaume Postel et les études arabes à la Renaissance," *Arabica* 9 (1962), 21–36, 31, and Bobzin, "Juan Andrés," 530.

30. Secret, *L'Ésotérisme de Guy Le Fèvre de La Boderie,* Geneva, Droz, 1969. Le Fèvre's French translation was published under the title *Confusion de la secte de Muhamed,* Paris, Martin Le Jeune, 1574.

31. "J'estime que nous avons aujourd'huy la despouille non seulement des Latins et des Grecs . . . mais aussi des Perses, Arabes, Caldez, Egyptiens, & Hebrieux."

32. As demonstrated by Maurice Olender, *Les Langues du Paradis, Aryens et Sémites, un couple providentiel,* Paris, Gallimard-Le Seuil, 1989.

33. See William J. Bouwsma, "Postel and the Significance of Renaissance Cabalism," *Journal of the History of Ideas* 15:2 (1954), 218–32.

34. *Thresor de l'histoire des langues de cest univers* (1613), Geneva, Slatkine Reprints, 1972, 402.

35. On the history of the original lost manuscript and its remaining copies, see García-Arenal and Starczewska, "Law of Abraham"; and Starcweska, ed., *Latin Translation of the Qur'ān (1518/1621) Commissioned by Egidio da Viterbo: Critical Edition and Case Study,* Wiesbaden, Harrassowitz Verlag, 2018.

36. Thomas E. Burman, *Reading the Qur'ān in Latin Christendom, 1140–1560,* Philadelphia, University of Pennsylvania Press, 2007, 156.

37. See Dario Cabanelas, *El Morisco Granadino Alonso del Castillo,* Granada, Patronato de la Alhambra, 1965; and García-Arenal and Rodríguez Mediano, *Orient,* ch. 4.

38. García-Arenal and Rodríguez Mediano, *Orient,* 97.

39. For an analysis of his performance as official translator see Gilbert, *In Good Faith,* 51–56 and 111–17.

40. Barbara Fuchs, *Exotic Nation: Maurophilia and the Construction of Early Modern Spain,* Philadelphia, University of Pennsylvania Press, 2009, 49.

41. Daniel Hershenzon, "Doing Things with Arabic in the Seventeenth-Century Escorial," *Philological Encounters* 4 (2019), 159–81, 162.

42. Cabanelas, *El Morisco,* 126.

43. The German Orientalist Christian Ravius republished it in his *Tredecim Partium Alcorani Arabico-Latini* (1646) and the Swiss Hottinger added it as an appendix to his *Promptuarium sive Bibliotheca orientalis* (1658); see Jan Loop, *Johann Heinrich Hottinger: Arabic and Islamic Studies in the Seventeenth Century,* Oxford, Oxford University Press, 2013, 169n.

44. See García-Arenal and Rodríguez Mediano, *Orient,* ch. 7.

45. The first part was published in 1592, and the second in 1600. See on this text Francisco Marquez Villanueva, "La voluntad de leyenda de Miguel de Luna," *Nueva Revista de Filología Hispánica* 30:2 (1981), 359–95.

46. Gioia Marie Kerlin, "A True Mirror of Princes: Defining the Good Governor in Miguel de Luna's *Historia verdadera del Rey Rodrigo,*" *Hispanófila* 156, 13–28; Gilbert, *In Good Faith,* 216–24.

47. Robert Ashley, *Almansor the Learned and Victorious King That Conquered Spain,* London, Parker, 1627; on Ashley, see Virgil Heltzel, "Robert Ashley, Elizabethan Man of Letters," *Huntington Library Quarterly* 10:4 (1947), 349–63.

48. *Histoire de la conquête d'Espagne par les Mores,* Paris, Barbin, 1680, 1:175.

49. Deborah Root, "Speaking Christian: Orthodoxy and Difference in Sixteenth-Century Spain," *Representations* 23 (1988), 118–34, 130.

50. Barbara Fuchs, *Mimesis and Empire: The New World, Islam, and European Identities,* Cambridge, Cambridge University Press, 2004, 101.

51. Harvey, *Muslims in Spain,* 287.

52. Francis Javier Martínez Medina, "La inmaculada concepción en los libros plúmbeos de Granada: Su influjo en el catolicismo contrarreformista," *Magallánica: Revista de Historia Moderna* 3:5 (2016), 6–47, 19.

53. Quoted in Nabil Matar, *Mediterranean Captivity through Arab Eyes, 1517–1798,* Leiden, Brill, 2020, 82.

54. This collaboration ended tragically nine years later, when, after an altercation between the two men, the slave hung himself. See Norman Daniel, *Islam and the West: The Making of an Image,* Oxford, Oneworld, 1993, 141; and David Wacks, *Medieval Iberian Crusade Culture and the Mediterranean World,* Toronto, University of Toronto Press, 2019, 99 and 194n55.

55. Daniel Hershenzon, *The Captive Sea: Slavery, Communication, and Commerce in Early Modern Spain and the Mediterranean,* Philadelphia, University of Pennsylvania Press, 2018, 142 and 9.

56. After Louis Massignon's pioneering and still useful study (*Le Maroc dans les premières années du XVIème siècle, Tableau géographique d'après Léon l'Africain,* Algiers, Adolphe Jourdan, 1906), see Muhammad al-Hajwī, *The Life and Works of al-Wazzān al-Fāsī* (in Arabic), Rabat, al-Matbaʿa al-iqtisādiya, 1935; Zhiri, *L'Afrique au miroir de l'Europe, fortunes de Jean Léon l'Africain à la Renaissance,* Geneva, Droz, 1991, and *Les Sillages de Léon l'Africain, du XVIème au XXème siècle,* Casablanca, Wallada, 1996; Dietriech Rauchenberger, *Leo der Afrikaner,* Wiesbaden, Harrassowitz Verlag, 1999; Natalie Zemon Davis, *Trickster Travels: A Sixteenth-Century Muslim between Worlds,* New York, Hill and Wang, 2006; François Pouillon, ed., *Léon l'Africain,* Paris, Karthala—IISMM, 2009.

57. On the Italian milieu of Wazzān/Leo, see Davis, *Trickster,* ch. 2.

58. Giorgio Levi della Vida, *Ricerche sulla formazione del più antico fondo dei manoscritti orientali della Biblioteca Vaticana,* Vatican City, Biblioteca Apostolica Vaticana, 1939, 103–8. Henceforth *Ricerche.*

59. See Jacques de Chaufepié, *Nouveau dictionnaire historique et critique pour server de supplement ou de continuation au Dictionnaire historique et critique de Pierre Bayle,* vol. 3, Amsterdam, Pierre de Hondt, 1753, 221n, and Levi della Vida, *Ricerche,* 311. Only the part that Leo devoted to poetic meter has survived. Angela Codazzi has edited this short treatise in "Il trattato dell'arte metrica di Giovanni Leone Africano," *Studi orientalistici in onore di Giorgio Levi della Vida,* vol. 1, Rome, Istituto per l'Oriente, 1956.

60. As it is called in the body of the untitled only surviving manuscript (VE 953, Biblioteca Nazionale Centrale, Rome). Its first editor, Gian Battista Ramusio, named it *Descrittione dell'Affrica* (Description of Africa), and showcased it in his widely influential collection of travel accounts (*Delle Navigationi e Viaggi,* Venice, Giunti, 1550.)

61. G. J. Toomer, *Eastern Wisdom and Learning: The Study of Arabic in Seventeenth-Century England,* Oxford, Clarendon Press, 1996, 21.

62. Zhiri, "Turcs et Mores: Monarques musulmans dans les *Histoires tragiques* de Boaistuau et Belleforest," *L'Esprit créateur* 53:4 (2013), 33–45.

63. VE 953, 34r.

64. Zhiri, "Lecteur d'Ibn Khaldoun," in *Léon l'Africain,* 211–36.

65. Translated into English by Robert Jones, "Thomas Erpenius (1584–1624) on the Value of the Arabic Language," *Manuscripts of the Middle East* 1 (1986), 16–25.

66. Under the title *Libellus de Viris quibusdam illustribus apud Arabes* (*Short Treatise of Illustrious Men among Arabs*) in his *Bibliothecarius Quadripartitus,* Zurich, Melchior Stauffacher, 1664. See Loop, *Johann Heinrich Hottinger,* ch. 4. Leo's text circulated earlier in manuscript, and was quoted by the polymath Johannes Gerard Vossius (*De Philosophia et Philosophorum Sectis, Libri II,* The Hague, Adrian Vlacq, 1658, ch. 14). It has been recently edited with a French translation (Jean-Léon l'Africain, *De quelques hommes illustres chez les Arabes et les Hébreux,* ed. and trans. Jean-Louis Déclais and Houari Touati, Paris, Les Belles-Lettres, 2020).

67. Loop, *Johann Heinrich Hottinger,* 132.

68. Nicholas Dew, *Orientalism in Louis XIV's France,* Oxford, Oxford University Press, 2009, ch. 4; Bevilacqua, *Republic of Arabic Letters,* ch. 4, and "How to Organize the Orient: D'Herbelot and the *Bibliothèque Orientale," Journal of the Warburg and Courtauld Institutes,* 79 (2016), 213–29.

69. Cl. Gilliot, et al., s.v., "'Ulamā'," in *Encyclopaedia of Islam,* 2nd ed., ed. P. Bearman et al., Leiden, Brill, 2012.

70. Levi della Vida, *Ricerche,* 100.

71. A Saʿdī prince enlisted his help in "Ileusugaghen" around 1514 because there was "no jurist nor scholar" in his retinue ("ne iudece né docto alcuno," VE 953, 50r). In "Semede," Hasan decided litigations, and even wrote down contracts as a notary "because there was no one who could write two words." ("non ce'ra Persona alcuna che sapesse comporre due parole," VE 953, 77v–78r.) He also adjudicated differences in Mazuna (in modern-day Algeria), where the population stopped "any foreigner with some knowledge of letters" ("qualche forestero che ha qualche cognitione de lettere," VE 953, 294r). On retellings and interpretations by Guillaume Bouchet and Montaigne of some of these episodes and others where Leo describes his experiences in rendering and observing the administration of justice in the Maghrib, see Zhiri, "'Sauvages et Mahométans,'" *Esculape et Dionysos: Mélanges en l'honneur de Jean Céard,* Geneva, Droz, 2008, 1125–39.

72. See for example Thomas d'Arcos, *Lettres inédites à Peiresc,* Philippe Tamizey de Larroque, ed., *Revue africaine* 32:189 (1888),161–95, 179.

73. The first part was published in 1573, the second in 1599.

74. Pieter van Koningsveld, "'Mon Kharuf': Quelques remarques sur le maître tunisien du premier arabisant néerlandais, Nicolas Clénard (1493–1542)," in Abdelmejid Temimi, ed., *Nouvelles approches des relations islamo-chrétiennes à l'époque de la Renaissance,* Zaghouan, FTERSI, 2000.

75. On his life, see Victor Chauvin and Alphonse Roersch, *Étude sur la vie et les travaux de Nicolas Clénard,* Brussels, Hayez, 1900.

76. Nicolas Clénard [Cleynaerts], *Correspondance,* 3 vols., ed. and trans. from Latin into French by Alphonse Roersch, Brussels, Palais des Académies, 1941, 3:168.

77. *Correspondance,* 3:95 and 133.

78. *Correspondance,* 3:145.

79. *Correspondance,* 3:111.

80. *Correspondance,* 3:112.

81. *Correspondance,* 3:113 and 148.

82. *Correspondance,* 3:130.

83. Ahmad al-Manjūr, *Fihris,* Muhammad Hajjī, ed., Rabat, Dār al-Maghrib, 1976, 69–71.

84. *Correspondance,* 3:189.

85. Khalid El-Rouayheb, *Islamic Intellectual History in the Seventeenth Century: Scholarly Currents in the Ottoman Empire and the Maghreb,* Cambridge, Cambridge University Press, 2015, 148–49.

86. Muhammad Amīn al-Muhibbī (d. 1699), *Khulāsat al-athar,* 4 vols., Cairo, al-Matbaʿa al-wahbiyya, 1867–68, 4:121.

87. ʿAbd al-ʿAzīz al-Fishtālī, *Manāhil al-safā*, ʿAbd al-Karīm Kurayyim, ed., Rabat, Jamʿiyāt al-muʾarikhīn al-maghāriba, 2005, 229–31.

88. Ahmad ibn al-Qāḍī, *al-Muntaqā al-Maqsūr*, ed. and presented by Muhammad Razzūq, Rabat, Maktaba al-maʿārif, 1986, 307. For mentions of other texts he lost at that time, including poems written by him and others and correspondence with scholars, see also 246, 375–76, 676, 747–49, 765, 871.

89. Robert Jones, "Piracy, War, and the Acquisition of Arabic Manuscripts in Renaissance Europe," *Manuscripts of the Middle East* 2 (1987), 96–110.

90. In *al-Muntaqā*, 695–96; in his biographical dictionaries *Durrāt al-hijāl*, Mustafa ʿAbd al-Qādir ʿAtā, ed., Beirut, Dār al-kutub al-ʿilmiyya, 2002, 236, and *Jadwat al-iqtibās*, Rabat, Dār al-Mansūr, 1974, 322–23.

91. Alberto Tinto, *La tipografia medicea orientale*, Lucca, Fazzi, 1987; Caren Reimann, "Ferdinando de Medici and the *Typographia Medicea*," in Nina Lamal, Jamie Cumby, and Helmer J. Helmers, eds., *Print and Power in Early Modern Europe (1500–1800)*, Leiden, Brill, 2021.

92. Robert Jones, ""The Medici Oriental Press (Rome 1584–1614) and the Impact of its Arabic Publications on Northern Europe," in G. A. Russell, ed., *The "Arabick" Interest of the Natural Philosophers in Seventeenth-Century England*, Leiden, Brill, 1994, 88–108.

93. See Levi della Vida, *Ricerche*, 405–10; and Jones, *Learning*, 66–70. These contributors include Paulo Orsino (d. 1600), a Turk from Istanbul who was an interpreter, and a member of the committee that published in 1591 a bilingual Arabic-Latin Gospel, and, in 1593, Ibn Sīnā's *Canon;* Guglielmo Africano (d. 1594), who came from Tunis, also copied Arabic manuscripts, as did Clemente Urbino, and Domenico Sirleto Africano who came from the island of Djerba.

94. *Introductio in linguam Arabicam*, Frankfurt, Andreas Eichorn, 1592.

95. Claudia Römer, "An Ottoman Copyist Working for Sebastian Tengnagel, Librarian at the Vienna Hoftbibliothek, 1608–1636," *Archiv Orientální* 7 (1998), 331–50, 343. See also *Learning*, 74–85. Tengnagel also employed another Muslim scribe named as-Shuwaikh Abū Al-Hasan ʿAlī al-Daqqāq, about whom nothing is known.

96. Jones, *Learning*, 71 ("retiré des gardes du Roy").

97. *Voyages d'Afrique*, Paris, Nicolas Traboulliet, 1631; on the missions of Razilly, see Oumelbanine Zhiri, "Les corps, les âmes et le droit: Isaac de Razilly et les captifs français du Maroc au XVIIème siècle," in Nicolas Lombard and Clotilde Jacquelard, eds., *Les Nouveaux mondes juridiques du Moyen Âge au XVIIème siècle*," Paris, Classiques Garnier, 2015, 227–51.

98. See also Sonja Brentjes, "Peiresc's Interest in the Middle East and Northern Africa in Respect to Geography and Cartography," in *Travellers*, 1–56.

99. Miller, *Peiresc's Mediterranean*, 213; see also 342, 345.

100. Peter N. Miller, "Peiresc and the Study of Islamic Coins in the Early Seventeenth Century," reprint in *Peiresc's Orient: Antiquarianism as Cultural History in the Seventeenth Century*, Farnham, Ashgate-Variorum, 2012, 103–57, 146.

101. Peiresc, *Lettres inédites à Thomas* d'Arcos, ed. Fauris de Saint-Vincens, Paris, J-B. Sajou, 1815, 10 ("qui avoit force livres curieux, et qui avoit lu dans leurs histoires").

102. Miller, *Peiresc's Mediterranean*, 277.

103. Loop, *Johann Heinrich Hottinger*, 86, 154–56, 164–65. See Hottinger, *Historia Orientalis*, Zurich, J.J. Bodmer, 1660, 505–6.

104. Houtsma, "Oosterche correspondentie," 34–47; and Schmidt, "Ostrich Egg," 2:20–27.

105. Tommasino, "Lire et traduire le Coran dans le grand-duché de Toscane," *Dix-Septième siècle* 268 (2015), 459–80, 475–79, and "Bulghaith al-Darawi and Bar-thélemy d'Herbelot: Readers of the Qur'ān in Seventeenth Century Tuscany," *Journal of Qur'ānic Studies* 20:3 (2018), 94–120. The freedom of Abū al-Ghayth was negotiated by a Jesuit Father, himself a former Muslim captive, who claimed, maybe falsely, to be a Moroccan prince. On him and for a bibliography about him, see Emanuele Colombo, "A Muslim Turned Jesuit: Baldassare Loyola Mandes (1631–1667)," *Journal of Early Modern History* 17 (2013), 479–504. Colombo thinks that this prince was of the Saʿdī dynasty. However, Henry de Castries was convinced that he was a grand-son of Sīdī Muhammad al-Hāj (1589–1671), the ruler of the powerful independent principality of Dilāʾ; see *SIHM*, Série Filalienne, Archives et Bibliothèques de France, vol. 1, Henry de Castries, ed., Paris, Leroux, 1922, 203–8. For his part, Muhammad Hajjī suggested that Mandes was an impostor, since the Moroccan sources, even written by the many enemies of the Dilāʾites, say nothing of a member of the ruling dynasty who was captured and converted to Christianity. See *The Zāwiya of Dilāʾ and Its Religious, Cultural, and Political Role* (in Arabic), Casablanca, Matbaʿat al-najah al-jadīda, 1988, 221–26.

106. His Arabic name was Muhammad ibn ʿAbd Allāh al-Saʿīdī al-ʿAdawī; see Samir Khalil Samir, "Un Imam égyptien copiste au Vatican, Clemente Caraccioli, 1670–1721," *Parole de l'Orient* 21 (1996), 111–54.

107. Quoted by Gérald Duverdier, "Du livre religieux à l'orientalisme: Gibra'īl al Sahyūnī et François Savary de Brèves," in Camille Aboussouan, ed., *Le Livre et le Liban jusqu'à 1900*, Paris, UNESCO, 1982, 159–74, 164 ("deux ou trois autres des prisons de Malte ou de celles de Monsieur le grand duc"), and 165 ("acheter à Malte et à Livourne deux Turcs et deux Persiens").

108. Giovanni Giovannozzi, "La versione Borelliana di Apollonio," *Memorie della Pontifica Accademia Romana dei Nuovi Lincei* 2:2 (1916), 1–31, 5.

109. See Bernard Heyberger, *Les Chrétiens du Proche-Orient au temps de la Réforme catholique,* Rome, École Française de Rome, 1994; Aurélien Girard, "Entre croisade et politique culturelle au Levant: Rome et l'union des chrétiens syriens (première moitié du XVIIᵉ siècle)," in M. A. Visceglia, ed., *Papato e politica internazionale nella prima età moderna*, Rome, Viella, 2013, 419–37.

110. Kamal S. Salibi, "The Maronites of Lebanon under Frankish and Mamluk Rule," *Arabica* 4 (1957), 288–303.

111. Robert J. Wilkinson, *Orientalism, Aramaic, and Kabbalah in the Catholic Reformation: The First Printing of the Syriac New Testament,* Leiden, Brill, 2007, 11–28; Levi della Vida, *Ricerche,* 103–8 and 133–36.

112. Wilkinson, *Orientalism,* 22.

113. Teseo Ambrogio, *Introductio in Chaldaicam linguam, Syriacam, atque Armenicam & decem alias linguas,* [Pavia], Giovanni Maria Simoneta,1539.

114. Wilkinson, *Orientalism,* 74.

115. Levi della Vida, *Ricerche,* 141.

116. To Widmanstetter and to Postel's Flemish friend, Andreas Maesius (1514– 73). See Wilkinson, *The Kabbalist Scholars of the Antwerp Polyglot Bible,* Leiden, Brill, 2007, 41; Muriel Debié, "La grammaire syriaque d'Ecchellensis en context," in Bernard Heyberger, ed., *Orientalisme, science et controverse: Abraham Ecchellensis (1605–1664),* Turnhout, Brepols, 2010, 99–117; Levi della Vida, *Ricerche,* 205–13. For a list of manuscripts copied by Moses, see Pier Giorgio Borbone, "'Monsignore Vescovo di Soria,' also Known as Moses of Mardin, Scribe and Books Collector," *Christian Orient* 8:14 (2017), 79–114.

117. Giovanni Pizzorusso, "Tra cultura e missione: La congregazione de *Propaganda* fide e le scuole di lingua araba nel XVII secolo," in Antonella Romano, ed., *Rome et la science moderne,* Rome, École Française, 2008, 121–52; Aurélien Girard, "Teaching and Learning Arabic in Early Modern Rome: Shaping a Missionary Language," in Jan Loop, Alastair Hamilton, and Charles Burnett, eds., *The Teaching and Learning of Arabic in Early Modern Europe,* Leiden, Brill, 2017, 189–212.

118. Pierre Raphael, *Le Rôle du collège maronite romain dans l'orientalisme aux XVIIe et XVIIIe siècles,* Beirut, Presses de l'Université Saint Joseph, 1950; Nasser Gemayel, *Les Échanges culturels entre les Maronites et l'Europe, du collège maronite de Rome (1584) au collège de 'Ayn-Warqa (1789),* 2 vols., Beirut, Gemayel, 1984; Aurélien Girard and Giovanni Pizzorusso, "The Maronite College in Early Modern Rome: Between the Ottoman Empire and the Republic of Letters," in Liam Chambers and Thomas O'Connor, eds., *College Communities Abroad: Education, Migration, and Catholicism in Early Modern Europe,* Manchester, Manchester University Press, 2018, 174–97.

119. The typographer Ya'qūb ibn Hilāl / Jacob Luna worked there, and later became the head of his own press which published books in Syriac.

120. This is the case of Sarkīs al-Rizzi / Sergio Rizzi, and later, of the al-Sim'ānī / Assemani family who worked in the Vatican Library during the eighteenth and nineteenth centuries.

121. Giovanni Pizzorusso, "Les écoles de langue arabe et le milieu ontaliste," in Heyberger, ed., *Orientalisme,* 59–80.

122. Jirjīs 'Amīra / Georges Amira (c. 1573–1644) published *Grammatica syriaca, sive chaldaica* (1596); Ishāq al-Shidrāwī / Isaac Sciadrensis, *Syriacae linguae rudimentum* (1618), and *Grammatica linguae syriacae* (1636); Butrus al-Matushī / Peter Metoscita, *Institutiones linguae arabicae* (1624).

123. Sionita collaborated with Nasrallah Shalaq al-'Āqurī / Victorius Scialac Accurrensis (d. 1635), with whom he also produced devotional works.

124. Alastair Hamilton and Francis Richard, *André du Ryer and Oriental Studies in Seventeenth-Century France,* London, Arcadian Library and Oxford University Press, 2004, 45–46.

125. Peter N. Miller, "Making the Paris Polyglot Bible: Humanism and Orientalism in the Early Seventeenth Century," Herbert Jaumann, ed., *Die europäische Gelehrtenrepublik im Zeitalter des Konfessionalismus,* Wiesbaden, Harrassowitz Verlag, 2001, 59–85.

126. Other Polyglot Bibles were published in Alcalá (1522), Antwerp (1572), and London (1657).

127. *Brevis Institutio Linguae arabicae* (1628), and *Linguæ Syriacæ, sive Chadaicæ* (1628).

128. Bernard Heyberger, "Abraham Ecchellensis dans la République des Lettres," in Heyberger, ed., *Orientalisme,* 9–51.

129. Daniel Stolzenberg, "Une collaboration dans la *cosmopolis* catholique: Abraham Ecchellensis et Athanasius Kircher," in Heyberger, ed., *Orientalisme.* Ecchellensis also took part in commercial enterprises, and between 1628 and 1633 became a business and political partner of the Druze emir Fakhr al-Dīn (1572–1635), who rebelled against the Ottomans, sought refuge in Tuscany in 1613, and spent a few years in Italy. See Kamal S. Salibi, "The Secret of the House of Ma'n," *International Journal of Middle East Studies* 4 (1973), 272–87; Albrecht Fuess, "An Instructive Experience: Fakhr al-Dīn's Journey to Italy, 1613–18," in Bernard Heyberger and Carsten-Michael Walbiner, eds., *Les Européens vus par les Libanais à l'époque ottomane,* Beirut, Ergon Verlag, 2002, 23–42. Ecchellensis even got involved in the Mediterranean slave redemption trade, and for that work traveled to Tunis, where he met Thomas-Osman d'Arcos; see d'Arcos, *Lettres inédites,* 181.

130. Hélène Bellosta and Bernard Heyberger, "Abraham Ecchellensis et les *Coniques* d'Apollonius: Les enjeux d'une traduction," in Heyberger, ed., *Orientalisme,* 191–201.

131. Including Hottinger: see Bernard Heyberger, "L'Islam et les Arabes chez un érudit maronite au service de l'Église catholique (Abraham Ecchellensis)," *Al-Qantara* 31:2 (2010), 481–512, 495–96; and John Selden (1584–1654): see Alastair Hamilton, *The Copts and the West, 1430–1822: The European Discovery of the Egyptian Church,* Oxford, Oxford University Press, 2006, 138.

132. Pieter J.A.N. Rietbergen, "A Maronite Mediator between Seventeenth-Century Mediterranean Cultures: Ibrāhīm al-Hākilānī, or Abraham Ecchellense (1605–1664) between Christendom and Islam," *LIAS* 16:1 (1989), 13–41, 35.

133. Girard, "Quand les Maronites écrivaient en latin: Fauste Nairon et la République des Lettres (seconde moitié du XVIIᵉ siècle," in Mireille Issa, ed., *Le Latin des Maronites,* Paris, Geuthner, 2017, 45–76; Girard, "Was an Eastern Scholar Necessarily a Cultural Broker in Early Modern Europe? Faustus Naironus (1628–1711), the Christian East, and Oriental Studies," in N. Hardy and D. Levitin, eds., *Faith and History: Confessionalisation and Erudition in Early Modern Europe,* Oxford, Oxford University Press, 2019, 240–63.

134. Before obtaining that prestigious position, Sergius sojourned in southern France, staying a while with the ubiquitous Peiresc, and teaching Arabic in Aix to a Capuchin. See Miller, *Peiresc's Mediterranean,* 274.

135. Levi della Vida, *Ricerche,* 280–87; García-Arenal and Rodríguez Mediano, *Orient,* ch. 11.

136. Alastair Hamilton, "An Egyptian Traveller in the Republic of Letters: Joseph Barbatus or Abudacnus the Copt," *Journal of the Warburg and Courtauld Institutes* 57 (1994), 123–50, and *Copts and the West,* 127–36.

137. *Historia Jacobitarum, seu Coptorum (The History of the Jacobites or Copts),* first published in 1675.

138. John-Paul Ghobrial, "Archives of Orientalism and its Keepers: Re-imagining the Histories of Arabic manuscripts in Early Modern Europe," *Past and Present* Supplement 11 (2016), 90–111, 98.

139. Hamilton, "Abraham Ecchellensis et son *Nomenclator Arabico-Latinus,*" in Heyberger, ed., *Orientalisme,* 95.

140. Dorrit van Dalen, "Johannes Theunisz and 'Abd al-'Azīz: A Friendship in Arabic Studies in Amsterdam, 1609–1610," *Lias* 43:1 (2016), 161–89.

141. Elio Brancaforte, *Visions of Persia: Mapping the Travels of Adam Olearius,* Cambridge, MA, Harvard University Press, 2003, 67, 70–71, 195; Babinski, "Ottoman Philology," 249–55.

142. Houtsma, "Oosterche correspondentie," 75–79; Schmidt, "An Ostrich," 51–53.

143. Schmidt, "An Ostrich," 27. He might have been one of Golius's copyists and buyers during his time in Morocco in 1622–24. See Houtsma, "Oosterche correspondentie," 28–33.

144. Loop, *Hottinger,* 13–14.

145. Peter T. van Rooden, *Theology, Biblical Scholarship, and Rabbinical Studies in the Seventeenth Century,* Leiden, Brill, 1989, 198.

146. Houtsma, "Oosterche correspondentie," 62–65; Schmidt, "An Ostrich," 32–39.

147. García-Arenal and Wiegers, *A Man of Three Worlds: Samuel Pallache, a Moroccan Jew in Catholic and Protestant Europe,* trans. Martin Beagles, Baltimore, Johns Hopkins University Press, 1999, 119–25. He might also be the same Isaac Pallache who was known as a bookseller in Amsterdam; see Schmidt, "An Ostrich," 21n.

148. *Vers l'Orient . . .* (catalog of an exhibition), Paris, Bibliothèque Nationale, 1983, 40 (n° 82).

149. Jones, *Learning,* 92–94.

150. Letter of January 31, 1608, *The Correspondence of Joseph Justus Scaliger,* vol. 7, 398. For more information on his help to Hubert, see same reference, 642.

151. Hilary Kilpatrick and Gerald J. Toomer, "Niqūlāwus al-Halabī (c. 1611–1661): A Greek Orthodox Syrian Copyist and His Letters to Pococke and Golius," *Lias* 43:1 (2016), 1–159.

152. On Ravius's time in the Ottoman Empire, see Gerald J. Toomer, "Ravius in the East," in Jan Loop and Jill Kraye, eds., *Scholarship between Europe and the Levant: Essays in Honour of Alastair Hamilton,* Leiden, Brill, 2020, 110–27.

153. See Toomer, *Eastern Wisdom*. Pococke sojourned in Aleppo from 1630 to 1637, and in Istanbul from 1637 to 1640.

154. See Jan Schmidt, "Between Author and Library Shelf: The Intriguing History of Some Middle Eastern Manuscripts Acquired by Public Collections in the Netherlands Prior to 1800," in Alastair Hamilton, Maurits H. van den Boogert, and Bart Westerweel, eds., *The Republic of Letters and the Levant,* Leiden, Brill, 2005, 27–51, 37–39.

155. Houtsma, "Oosterche correspondentie," 65–75; Schmidt, "An Ostrich," 53–59; Schmidt, "Between Author," 38–40.

156. Schmidt, "Between Author," 39. See an example in Houtsma, "Oosterche correspondentie," 69–70.

157. Quoted by García-Arenal and Rodriguez Mediano, *Orient,* 324.

158. L. P. Harvey, "A Second Morisco Manuscript at Wadham College, Oxford: A 18.15," *Al-Qantara* 10 (1989), 257–72; Gerard Wiegers, "The Andalusī Heritage in the Maghrib: The Polemical Works of Muhammad Alguazir (fl. 1610)," in Otto Zwartjes, Geert Jan van Gelder, and Ed de Moor, eds., *Poetry, Politics, and Polemics: Cultural Transfers between the Iberian Peninsula and North Africa,* Amsterdam, Rodopi, 1996, 107–32.

159. It circulated in Spain, and is one source for Marcos Dobelio's still unpublished manuscript treatise on the Lead Books (García-Arenal and Rodriguez Mediano, *Orient,* 292).

160. Wiegers, "Polemical Transfers."

161. Justin Champion, "'I Remember a Mahometan Story of Ahmed Ben Idris': Freethinking Uses of Islam from Stubbe to Toland," *Al-Qantara* 31:2 (2010), 443–80; Martin Mulsow, "Socinianism, Islam, and the Radical Uses of Arabic Scholarship," *Al-Qantara* 31:2 (2010), 549–86.

162. Bernard Heyberger, "Chrétiens orientaux dans l'Europe catholique (XVIIᵉ-XVIIIᵉ siècles)," in Bernard Heyberger and Chantal Verdeil, eds., *Hommes de l'entre-deux: Parcours individuels et portraits de groupes sur la frontière de la Méditerranée (XVIe–XXe siècle),* Paris, Indes Savantes, 2009, 61–93.

163. Solomon Negri, *Memoria negriana,* Halle, 1764. See Ghobrial, "The Life and Hard Times of Solomon Negri: An Arabic Teacher in Early Modern Europe," in Loop, Hamilton, and Burnett, eds., *Teaching and Learning*, 310–32; and Paula Manstetten, "Solomon Negri: The Self-Fashioning of an Arab Christian in Early Modern Europe," in Cornel Zwirlein, ed., *The Power of the Dispersed: Early Modern Global Travelers beyond Integration,* Leiden, Brill, 2021, 240–82.

164. Paulo Lemos Horta, *Marvellous Thieves: Secret Authors of the Arabian Nights,* Cambridge, MA, Harvard University Press, 2017, 2.

165. See Hanna Dyāb, *D'Alep à Paris, Les pérégrinations d'un jeune Syrien au temps de Louis XIV,* trans. Paule Fahmé-Thierry, Paris, Actes-Sud, 2015; *Min Halab ilā Bāris,* Muhammad Mustafā al-Jārūsh and Abū Shahlā Jibrān, eds., Beirut-Baghdād, Manshūrāt al-jamal, 2017; *The Book of Travels,* 2 vols., Arabic text ed. Johannes Stephan, English trans. Elias Muhanna, and foreword by Yasmine Beale, New York, New York University Press, 2021.

166. He procured for Golius books and manuscripts in Greek, Arabic, Persian, and Turkish; see Houtsma, "Oosterche correspondentie," 58–60; Schmidt, "An Ostrich," 40.

167. He looked for manuscripts for Edward Pococke; see Hilary Kilpatrick, "Arabic Private Correspondence from Seventeenth-Century Syria: The Letters to Edward Pococke," *Bodleian Library Record* 23:1 (2010), 20–40, 25–27 and 35.

168. Schmidt, "An Ostrich," 32–34; "Between Author," 33–34. Golius even proposed to the Syrian scholar an unrealized collaboration: he suggested that Yūhannā write an appendix to the historical treatise by al-Qazwīnī (d. 1542), *Lubb al-Tawārikh*. This complementary text would have covered events until the present day, 1649. He gave instructions as to where to look for information, in books and by approaching scholars and contemporary witnesses.

169. See Sonja Brentjes, "Early Modern Western European Travellers in the Middle East and Their Reports about the Sciences," in *Travellers*, 379–420, esp. 407–11.

170. Schmidt, "An Ostrich," 40n; Muhibbī, *Khulāsat*, 3:474; Kilpatrick and Toomer, "Niqūlāwus," 8.

171. Houtsma, "Oosterche correspondentie," 100–102; Kilpatrick and Toomer, "Niqūlāwus," 132–33.

172. Houtsma, "Oosterche correspondentie," 56–57; Muhibbī, *Khulāsat*, 3:366–75.

173. These include Abū al-Wafāʾ al-ʿUrdī (1585–1660), a Sufi, poet, historian, and *muftī* in Aleppo (see Muhibbī, *Khulāsat*, 1:148–52), and his brother Muhammad al-ʿUrdī (1617–69), who bought from the estate of Kātip Çelebi six manuscripts for Warner, and for himself a book written by his own grandfather (see Houtsma, "Oosterche correspondentie," 108–11). Muhammad was a prominent religious scholar, who succeeded his brother as *muftī*, and also wrote profane literature, including homoerotic verse (see Muhibbī, *Khulāsat*, 4:89–104). Some manuscripts held in Leiden bear his handwriting (see Schmidt, *Catalogue of Turkish Manuscripts in the Library of Leiden University and Other Collections on the Netherlands: Minor Collections*, Leiden, Brill, 2012, 221). Sālih al-ʿUrdī, probably of the same family, worked with Warner (see Schmidt, "An Ostrich," 41).

174. Simon Mills, "Learning Arabic in the Overseas Factories: The Case of the English," in *Teaching and Learning*, 272–93, 280, and *A Commerce of Knowledge: Trade, Religion, and Scholarship between England and the Ottoman Empire, c. 1600–1760*, Oxford, Oxford University Press, 2020, 74–89.

175. Miller, *Peiresc's Mediterranean*, 137.

176. Miller, *Peiresc's Mediterranean*, 137.

177. Kilpatrick, "Arabic Private Correspondence," 31.

178. *Correspondance de Peiresc avec plusieurs missionaires et religieux de l'ordre des Capucins, 1631–37*, ed. Apollinaire de Valence, Paris, Alphonse Picard, 1892, 155.

179. Muhibbī, *Khulāsat*, 4:304–6.

180. Kilpatrick, "Arabic Private Correspondence," 22. Pieter Golius called Taqwā "a werewoolf, and a fraud" (Miller, *Peiresc's Mediterranean*, 137).

181. Pieter Golius was well aware of Ahmad's interest in geography; see Miller, *Peiresc's Mediterranean*, 504 n471.

182. It is signed by al-Ḥāj Muḥammad b. Saʿīd al-Andalusī; see Schmidt, "An Ostrich," 28. The envoy was Cornelis Pynacker (1570–1645), who was in Tunisia from October 28 to December 4, 1622, and then again in fall 1626; see Gérard van Krieken, *Corsaires et marchands: Les relations entre Alger et les Pays-Bas, 1604–1830*, Paris, Bouchêne, 2002, 33 and 42.

183. It is signed by ʿAlī Ibrāhīm al-Ṭālib al-Antāsī; see Schmidt, "An Ostrich," 30.

184. The name of this correspondent is al-Ḥāj Ibrāhīm b. al-Ḥāj ʿAlī; see Schmidt, "An Ostrich," 29. Some letters to Golius, by al-Ḥāj ʿAbdallāh b. al-Ḥusayn al-Fāsī, or ʿAlī b. Muḥammad al-Andalusī al-Gharnatī al-Murrākushī, might be from booksellers.

185. Ghobrial, "Archives," 97.

PART TWO. AHMAD AL-HAJARĪ: BECOMING
AN ARAB WRITER

1. Besides the cases cited above, other examples are found in Iran, where, in 1623, an imam asked Carmelites for books in Greek, Arabic-Latin dictionaries, and for a Bible in Arabic. See Brentjes, "Early Modern Western European Travellers in the Middle East and Their Reports about the Sciences," in *Travellers*, 379–420, 409.

CHAPTER 3. HAJARĪ: A MORISCO WRITER IN
THE ARABIC REPUBLIC OF LETTERS

1. Muhammad ibn Mālik, *Lāmiyyat al-afʿāl*, with commentary by his son Badr al-Dīn ibn Mālik, Bibliothèque Nationale de France, Arabe 4119.

2. Antoinette Molinié, "Les deux corps de la Reine et ses substituts: La souveraineté d'une Vierge andalouse," *Archives de Sciences Sociales de la Religion* 161 (2013), 269–91, 273.

3. MS D 565, Bologna, University Library, 117r.

4. MS D 565, 118v–119v. Jaime Oliver Asín edited the poem in "Ahmad al-Hayarī Bejarano: Apuntes biográphicos de un morisco notable residente en Marruecos," in *Conferencias y apuntes inéditos*, 161–62. The marginal Arabic notes are omitted, however.

5. Translated by Harvey, "The Morisco," 95 (82 for Arabic).

6. For examples and references, see Thomas E. Case, "The Significance of Morisco Speech in Lope's Plays," *Hispania* 65:4 (1982), 594–600.

7. Translated by David James, "The '*Manual de artillería*' of al-Raʾīs Ibrāhīm b. Ahmad al-Andalusī with Particular References to Its Illustrations and Their

Sources," *Bulletin of the School of Oriental and African Studies* 41:2 (1978), 237–57, 251.

8. Harvey, "The Morisco," 96 (83 for Arabic).

9. Jaime Oliver Asín, "Un Morisco de Tùnez, admirador de Lope," *Al-Andalus* 1:2 (1933), 409–50.

10. On these complex issues, see Naima Boussofora-Omar, s.v. "Diglossia," and Jérôme Lentin, s.v. "Middle Arabic," in Kees Versteegh, ed., *Encyclopedia of Arabic Language and Linguistics,* 5 vols., Leiden, Brill, 2006–11; Gunvor Mejdell, "Changing Norms, Concepts, and Practices of Written Arabic: A 'Long Distance' Perspective," in Jacob Høigilt and Gunvor Mejdell, eds., *The Politics of Written Language in the Arab World: Writing Change,* Leiden, Brill, 2017, 68–89.

11. In a letter to Isaac Casaubon; see Jones, *Learning,* 78.

12. Jérôme Lentin, "Unité and diversité du moyen arabe au Machreq et au Maghreb: Quelques données d'après des textes d'époque tardive (16ème–19ème siècles)," in Jérôme Lentin and Jacques Grand'Henry, eds., *Moyen arabe et variétés mixtes de l'arabe à travers l'histoire,* Louvain, Université Catholique, 2008, 305–19.

13. See Houtsma, "Oosterche correspondentie," 28, 31–32, 40.

14. Gilles Deleuze and Félix Guattari, *A Thousand Plateaus: Capitalism and Schizophrenia,* trans. Brian Massumi, 2nd ed., Minneapolis, University of Minnesota Press, 1987.

15. Simone Aurora, "Territory and Subjectivity: The Philosophical Nomadism of Deleuze and Canetti," *Minerva: An Open Access Journal of Philosophy* 18 (2014), 1–26, 7.

16. Ronald Bogue writes on this issue: "When language users subvert standard pronunciations, syntactic structures or meanings, they 'deterritorialize' the language, in that they detach it from its clearly delineated, regularly gridded territory of conventions, codes, labels, labels and markers. Conversely, when users reinforce linguistic norms, they 'territorialize' and 'reterritorialize' the language. The processes of deterritorialization and reterritorialization go on perpetually within every language, as standard linguistic practices are either transformed and set in disequilibrium or repeated and perpetuated" ("The Minor," in Charles J. Stivale, ed., *Gilles Deleuze: Key Concepts,* Montreal, McGill-Queen's University Press, 2005, 111–12).

17. Nelly Hanna, *Ottoman Egypt and the Emergence of the Modern World, 1500–1800,* Cairo, American University in Cairo Press, 2014, 51–52.

18. *Supporter,* ch. 13, 255e / 271a. I have modified the English translation: "He created in me the love to learn the Qur'an in Arabic." However, the word Quran does not appear in the Arabic text, which only contains the word *qirā'a,* which simply denotes reading.

19. *Supporter,* ch. 13, 256e / 272a.

20. Nelly Hanna, *In Praise of Books: A Cultural History of Cairo's Middle Class, Sixteenth to the Eighteenth Century,* Syracuse, NY, Syracuse University Press, 2003, esp. 128–36. See also Hanna, *Ottoman Egypt,* esp. chapter 3.

21. Hanna, *Ottoman Egypt,* 45–46.

22. Hanna, *Ottoman Egypt,* 55.

23. *Supporter,* ch. 7, 155e / 118a. The bracketed word "religious" is added by the translation. The Arabic text only bears *'ulūm,* sciences.

24. For a foundational study on early modern Moroccan scholarly world, see Muhammad Hajjī, *Intellectual Trends in Sa'dī Morocco* (in Arabic), 2 vols., Rabat, Dār al-Maghrib, 1976–78. For an excellent and more recent overview focused on the natural sciences, see Stearns, *Revealed Sciences,* esp. 46–67.

25. Stearns, *Revealed Sciences,* 61.

26. Stearns, *Revealed Sciences,* 56.

27. Hajjī, *Intellectual Trends,* 2:389.

28. Ibn al-Qāḍī, *Durrat al-Hijāl,* 248.

29. *Supporter,* ch. 13, 274e / 305a. On this author, whose full name is Abū Mahdī 'Īsā ibn 'Abd al-Rahmān al-Suktānī, see the copious introduction to his collection of legal opinions *Ajwibat al-bādiya,* Yūsuf Amāl, ed., Beirut, Dār al-kutub al-'ilmiyya, 2015.

30. Timothy Cleaveland, "Ahmad Baba al-Timbukti and his Islamic Critique of Racial Slavery in the Maghrib," *Journal of North African Studies* 20:1 (2015), 42–64, 48.

31. Mahmoud A. Zouber, *Ahmad Bābā de Tombouctou (1556–1627): Sa vie et son œuvre,* Paris, Maisonneuve et Larose, 1977, 70.

32. *Supporter,* introduction, 77e / 10a.

33. Dwight F. Reynolds, ed., *Interpreting the Self: Autobiography in the Arabic Literary Tradition,* Berkeley, University of California Press, 2001, 61. Henceforth *Self.*

34. *Supporter,* ch. 13, 271e / 300a.

35. *Supporter,* ch. 13, 272e / 300a. The English translation of Ahmad Bābā's treatise can be found in Aziz A. Betran, *Tobacco Smoking under Islamic Law,* Belstville, Amana Publications, 2003, 169–90. The text ends with Bābā mentioning that he just heard the call for prayer, but he does not explicitly conclude, as Hajarī alleges, that this was an auspicious sign.

36. *Supporter,* ch. 13, 272e / 301a.

37. For a useful overview, see Nile Green, "The Religious and Cultural Roles of Dreams and Visions in Islam," *Journal of the Royal Asiatic Society* 13:3 (2003), 287–313.

38. *Self,* 88–93.

39. On Targhī, see Hajjī, *Intellectual Trends,* 2:380.

40. *Supporter,* introduction, 78e / 10a.

41. *Self,* 19.

42. *Self,* 66–68.

43. *Supporter,* ch. 13, 253e / 268a.

44. *Supporter,* ch. 13, 254e / 269a.

45. *Supporter,* ch. 13, 254e / 269–70a.

46. For a succinct history of this use, see *Self,* 61–64.

47. Sha'rānī wrote a lengthy and idiosyncratic autobiography, the title of which translates as *The Book of Gracious Merits and Virtues Bestowed on Me by God and the*

Absolute Obligation of Recounting His Blessings, which Hajarī cites as an example (*Supporter,* ch. 13, 274e / 304a.). The widely influential and prolific Suyūṭī named his book *Speaking of God's Blessings.*

48. *Supporter,* ch. 13, 258e / 276a.

49. On "angelic companions" in Islam, see S. R. Burge, *Angels in Islam: Jalāl al-Dīn al-Suyūṭī's al-Ḥabā'ik fī akhbār al-malā'ik,* London, Routledge, 2012, 70–87.

50. The word "better" was omitted in the *Supporter.*

51. *Supporter,* ch. 13, 273–74e / 304–5a.

52. See an analysis and an English translation of that preface in Dwight F. Reynolds, "Shaykh ʿAbd al-Wahhāb al-Shaʿrānī's Sixteenth-Century Defense of Autobiography," *Harvard Middle Eastern and Islamic Review* 4:1–2 (1997–98), 122–37. On this author, see Michael Winter, *Society and Religion in Early Ottoman Egypt: Studies in the Writings of ʿAbd al-Wahhāb al-Shaʿrānī,* New Brunswick, NJ, Transaction Publishers, 2007 (1st ed., 1982).

53. Deleuze and Guattari, *Kafka,* 16.

CHAPTER 4. HAJARĪ IN THE WORLD

1. *Supporter,* ch. 13, 261e / 281–82a.

2. Wiegers, "Polemical Transfers" in García-Arenal, ed., *After Conversion,* 231.

3. Wiegers, "The Expulsion of 1609–1614," in García-Arenal and Wiegers, eds., *Expulsion,* 390.

4. Brian A. Catlos, *Muslims of Medieval Latin Christendom, c. 1050–1614,* Cambridge, Cambridge University Press, 2014, 324.

5. The foundational study on this literature is Louis Cardaillac, *Morisques et chrétiens: Un affrontement polémique (1492–1640),* Paris, Klincksieck, 1977.

6. Wiegers, "The Expulsion of 1609–1614," in García-Arenal and Wiegers, eds., *Expulsion,* 400–401.

7. The Lead Books are part of an ensemble of religious texts authored by Moriscos, which include pseudo-apocryphal Christian texts such as the so-called *Gospel of Barnabas;* see Mikel de Epalza, "Le milieu hispano-moresque de l'Évangile islamisant de Barnabé (XVIᵉ–XVIIᵉ siècle)," *Islamochristiana* 8 (1982), 159–83.

8. Van Koningsveld and Wiegers, "The Parchment of the 'Torre Turpiana': The Original Document and Its Early Interpreters," *Al-Qantara* 24:2 (2003), 327–58, 333.

9. *Supporter,* ch. 1, 97e / 38a.

10. *Supporter,* 279–94e / 310–35a.

11. *SIHM,* Pays-Bas, 4:285.

12. *Supporter,* ch. 1, 98–99e / 40–41a.

13. *Supporter,* general introduction, 39–40.

14. *Supporter,* ch. 1, 94e / 33a.

15. Seth Kimmel, *Parables of Coercion: Conversion and Knowledge at the End of Islamic Spain,* Chicago, University of Chicago Press, 2015, 105 and 97.

16. *Supporter,* ch. 1, 96e / 36a.

17. *Supporter,* ch. 1, 103e (n104) / 46a (n4)

18. Kimmel, *Parables,* 105.

19. *Supporter,* ch. 10, 275e / 306a. Cipriano de Valera produced a revised version (published in Amsterdam in 1602) of Cassiodoro de Reina's translation of 1569. On Valera and his work, see A. Gordon Kinder, "Religious Literature as an Offensive Weapon: Cipriano de Valera's Part in England's War with Spain," *Sixteenth-Century Journal* 19:2 (1988), 223–35.

20. *Supporter,* ch. 7, 157e / 121a.

21. *Al-Sayf al-mamdūd fī al-radd ʿalā akhbār al-yahūd* (The Outstretched Sword in Refutation of the Jewish Sages), ed. and Spanish trans. by Esperanza Alfonso, Madrid, CSIC, 1998.

22. *Fray Anselm Turmeda (ʿAbdallāh al-Tarjumān) y su polémica islamo-cristiana: Edición, traducción y studio de la Tuhfa.* Mikel de Epalza, ed., Madrid, Hiperión, 1994.

23. Cardaillac, *Morisques et Chrétiens,* 217–18.

24. *Irshād al-hayāra fī al-radd ʿalā al-nasāra* (Guide to Those Who Need Help to Respond to the Christians).

25. *Kitāb al-shifāʾ bi-taʿrīf huqūq al-Mustafāʾ* (The Book of Healing by the Recognition of the Rights of the Envoy of God).

26. Luis Bernabé Pons, "El Qādī ʿIyād en la literature aljamiado-morisca," *Sharq al-Andalus* 14–15 (1997–98), 201–18. See also Cardaillac, *Morisques et Chrétiens,* 215–16.

27. Cardaillac, *Morisques et Chrétiens,* 189–90. On the stubborn legend of the woman pope, see Thomas F. X. Noble, "Why Pope Joan?" *Catholic Historical Review* 49:2 (2013), 219–38.

28. John 14:16, Douay-Rheims Bible.

29. Cardaillac, *Morisques et Chrétiens,* 383–84.

30. *Supporter,* ch. 5, 134–35e / 85a.

31. See Donovan O. Schaefer, *Religious Affects: Animality, Evolution, and Power,* Durham, NC, Duke University Press, 2015.

32. *Supporter,* ch. 5, 131e / 80a.

33. *Supporter,* ch. 5, 132e / 81a.

34. *Supporter,* ch. 12, 245e / 254a.

35. *Supporter,* ch. 5, 86a.

36. This passage figures only in the Paris manuscript. See notes in *Supporter,* ch. 13, 273e / 303a.

37. *Supporter,* ch. 7, 155e / 117a.

38. Indeed, theorists contend that "affect marks a body's belonging to a world of encounters;" Gregory J. Seigworth and Melissa Gregg, "An Inventory of Shimmers," in G. J. Seigworth and M. Gregg, eds., *Affect Theory Reader,* Durham, NC, Duke University Press, 2010, 1–25, 2.

39. *Supporter,* ch. 7, 158e / 121a.

40. *Supporter,* ch. 9, 176e / 145a.

41. *Supporter,* ch. 5, 135e / 86a.

42. *Supporter,* ch. 3, 123–24e / 71a.

43. *Supporter,* ch. 3, 124e / 71–72a.

44. Against Gourgues, and against Fayard.

45. On the long multicultural history of "static levitation," see Dunstan Lowe, "Suspending Disbelief: Magnetic and Miraculous Levitation from Antiquity to the Middle Ages," *Classical Antiquity* 35:2, 247–78; see 265–69 on the legend surrounding the tomb of Muhammad.

46. As stated by Fayard in Bordeaux (ch. 9, 177e / 147a). Another discussion on the same theme with two monks occurred in the same city (ch. 9, 173e / 140a), and a third one took place in Egypt with a monk (ch. 12, 242e / 250a).

47. *Supporter,* ch. 7, 152–53e / 112–13a.

48. *Supporter,* ch. 9, 181e / 153a.

49. *Supporter,* ch. 4, 126e / 75a.

50. *Supporter,* ch. 9, 184–85e / 158–59a.

51. *Supporter,* ch. 11, 221–23e /219–22a. The editors suggest that Hajarī's interlocutor might be Petrus Pauw (d. 1617).

52. *Supporter,* ch. 4, 126e / 75a.

53. *Supporter,* ch. 6, 141e / 95a. The editors suggest that *Baldu* might be identified as the French jurist François Baudouin (1520–73). However, Hajarī might be referring to the Italian jurist Baldus de Ubaldis (1327–1400), who left voluminous commentaries on Roman law and the Codex Justinianus.

54. *Supporter,* ch. 8, 161e / 125a. Hajarī might have heard the young woman described as a "noiraude."

55. *Supporter,* ch. 8, 162e /125a.

56. *Supporter,* ch. 8, 162e /125a.

57. *Supporter,* ch. 8, 162–63e / 126a.

58. *Supporter,* ch. 8, 163e / 127a.

59. *Supporter,* ch. 8, 164e / 129a.

60. *Supporter,* ch. 8,166e /132a.

61. Hava Lazarus-Yafeh, *Intertwined Worlds: Medieval Islam and Bible Criticism,* Princeton, NJ, Princeton University Press, 1992, 47; see also 76–110.

62. Lazarus-Yafeh, *Intertwined Worlds,* 32.

63. See Lazarus-Yafeh, *Intertwined Worlds,* 41–44.

64. *Supporter,* ch. 10, 211e / 199a.

65. *Supporter,* ch. 12, 237e / 241a.

66. Francisco del Puerto, *Mission historial de Marruecos,* 163–64.

67. Tijana Krstic, *Contested Conversions to Islam: Narratives of Religious Change in Early Modern Europe,* Palo Alto, CA, Stanford University Press, 2011; Derin Terzioglu, "Where *'Ilm-I Hāl* Meets Catechism: Islamic Manuals of Religious Instruction in the Ottoman Empire in the Age of Confessionalization," *Past and Present* 220 (2013): 79–114.

68. Villanueva, "The Moriscos in Tunisia," in García-Arenal and Wiegers, eds., *Expulsion,* 369.

69. *Supporter,* ch. 10, 217–18e / 211–12a.

70. Bénédicte Lecarpentier, "La Reine diplomate: Marie de Médicis et les cours italiennes," in Isabelle Poutrin and Marie-Karine Schaub, eds., *Femmes et pouvoir politique: Les princesses d'Europe XVe–XVIIIe siècle,* Rosny-sous-Bois, Éditions Bréal, 2007, 182–92.

71. Louis Batiffol, *La Vie intime d'une reine de France au XVIIe siècle: Marie de Médicis,* Paris, Calmann-Lévy, 1906, I, 71.

72. Jean-François Dubost, *Marie de Médicis: La reine dévoilée,* Paris, Payot, 2009, 244.

73. Or "Catherine Esmain and Marie Esme": see Louis Batiffol, "Marie de Médicis et les arts—deuxième et dernier article," *La Gazette des Beaux-Arts* 35:3 (1859), 221–43, 242.

74. Their story echoes an earlier example of two young Turkish women who were "offered" in 1557 to Catherine de Medici, while their mother kept requesting their return from the sultan, an insistence that affected the diplomatic relations between the kingdom and the Ottoman empire for decades; see Frédéric Hitzel, "Turcs et turqueries à la cour de Catherine de Médicis," in Jocelyne Dakhlia and Bernard Vincent, eds., *Les Musulmans dans l'histoire de l'Europe,* vol. 1, 33–54.

75. He talks about a "robe qui se fait à l'hôtel du Luxembourg par des Turques . . . et dit-on que c'est la chose du monde la plus belle," *Œuvres,* Paris, Hachette, 1863, 3:413.

76. Dubost, *Marie de Médicis,* 245.

77. *Supporter,* ch. 10, 218e / 212a.

78. *Supporter,* ch. 11, 228–29e / 230–32a.

79. ". . . il est arrivé ici un nommé Abdallah, de la part de l'honorable Ismaïl Aga, pour obtenir la mise en liberté d'une sœur dudit Ismaïl Aga, laquelle était esclave en France. . . . j'ai fait tout mon possible pour arracher cette esclave des mains des Français; je l'ai reçue chez moi, je lui ai donné tous les témoignages d'honneur et d'amitié, et je l'ai ensuite conduite chez Son Excellence le comte Maurice, qui était disposé à profiter de quelque navire en partance pour la renvoyer.

L'ambassadeur de France résidant aux Pays-Bas a fait traîner quelque temps cette affaire, craignant que ce départ ne fût contraire à la volonté de son roi. Mais moi, votre esclave, et Son Excellence le comte Maurice, nous avons arrangé l'affaire et usé de toute notre influence, si bien que cette femme est partie saine et sauve." *SIHM,* Pays-Bas, 2:580–81. This is a French translation by Henry de Castries of the Dutch translation of this letter held in the archives.

80. That may stem from the situation of Pallache, who was at that time in rather bad standing in the eyes of both the Dutch and the sultan, was in precarious financial shape, and was apparently thinking of finding new employment in the Ottoman court; see García-Arenal and Wiegers, *Man of Three Worlds,* 95–96.

81. A. H. De Groot, *The Ottoman Empire and the Dutch Republic: A History of the Earliest Diplomatic Relations, 1610–1630,* Leiden, Nederlands Historisch-Archaeologisch Instituut, 1978, 146–47. According to Cornelis Haga (1578–1654), Dutch ambassador in Istanbul, who was informed by the "Turk" who brought the

Turkish ladies from France (it might the Morisco sent by Hajarī), they were accompanied by two French women. One "turned Turk," that is converted to Islam, and stayed in Istanbul. The other, who was chambermaid of the wife of the superintendent of finances Pierre Jeannin (1540–1622), refused to do so (or changed her mind), and took refuge in the house of the French ambassador Achille Harlay de Sancy. See *SIHM,* Pays-Bas, 2:655–58.

82. De Groot, *Ottoman Empire,*145.

83. Jones, *Learning,* 78.

84. *Supporter,* ch. 12, 242e / 249–50a.

85. María M. Portundo, "Cosmography at the *Casa, Consejo,* and *Corte* During the Century of Discovery," in Daniela Bleichmar et al., eds., *Science in the Spanish and Portuguese Empires, 1500–1800,* Palo Alto, CA, Stanford University Press, 2009, 57–77, 57. For the more general context of scientific development in early modern Spain, see María M. Portundo, *Spanish Cosmography and the New World,* Chicago, University of Chicago Press, 2009.

86. Antonio Barrera-Osorio, *Experiencing Nature. The Spanish American Empire and the Early Scientific Revolution,* Austin, University of Texas Press, 2006, 130.

87. "Samurānū [Zamorano] from Seville, whom I knew in the City of Seville by name and personally," *Supporter,* 142e / 96a.

88. See Chaves, *Chronographia o Repertorio de los tiempos,* Lisbon, 1576, ff. 45b–47b, and Zamorano, *Cronologia y repertorio de la razon de los tiempos,* Seville, 1594, "Catalogo de los sumos pontifices", ff. 354–74. There is no chapter on the succession of popes in Cortés's *Breve compendio.*

89. *Supporter,* 207a; in 216e, the phrase is rendered as "science of the *ahkam.*" *'Ilm* (or *ṣinā'at) ahkām al-nujūm,* "the science (or art) of the judgements of the stars," is the equivalent of "astrology." See Charles Burnett, s.v. "Astrology," in Kate Fleet et al., eds., *Encyclopaedia of Islam,* 3rd ed., Leiden-Boston, Brill, 2007.

90. Hajjī, *Intellectual Trends,* 1:158 and 2:393.

91. Ifrānī, *Safwat,* 194.

92. *Supporter,* ch. 10, 215e / 206a.

93. Ifrānī, *Safwat,* 194.

94. Nicholas Jardine, "The Places of Astronomy in Early-Modern Culture," *Journal for the History of Astronomy* 29 (1998), 49–62, 51.

95. Emilia Calvo, s.v. "Zacuto, Abraham," in Thomas Glick et al., eds., *Medieval Science, Technology, and Medicine, An Encyclopedia,* London, Routledge, 2005, 525–26.

96. His fame was such that his figure was manipulated by the Portuguese chronicler Correia in his account of Asia. See Maurice Kriegel and Sanjay Subrahmanyam, "The Unity of Opposites: Abraham Zacut, Vasco de Gama and the Chronicler Gaspar Correia," in A. Disney and E. Booth, eds., *Vasco de Gama and the Linking of Europe and Asia,* Oxford, Oxford University Press, 2000, 48–71; Subrahmanyam, "Intertwined Histories: 'Crónica' and 'Tāʾrīkh' in the Sixteenth-Century Indian Ocean World," *History and Theory* 49: 4 (2010), 118–45, 131.

97. José Chabas and Bernard R. Goldstein, "Astronomy in the Iberian Peninsula: Abraham Zacut and the Transition from Manuscript to Print," *Transactions of the American Philosophical Society* (2000) 90:2, 1–196.

98. Pat Seed, "Celestial Navigation: The First Translational Science," in Patrick Manning and Abigail Owen, eds., *Knowledge in Translation: Global Patterns of Scientific Exchange, 1000–1800 ce*, Pittsburgh, University of Pittsburgh Press, 2018, 275–91, 285.

99. Manūnī, "Phenomenon of Translation," 85–88; Julio Samsó, "Abraham Zacut and José Vizinho's *Almanach Perpetuum* in Arabic (16th–19th c.)," *Centaurus* 46 (2004), 82–97. María José Parra Pérez studied Hajarī's translation in her dissertation "Estudio y edición de las traducciones al árabe del Almanach perpetuum de Abraham Zacuto," PhD diss., Department of Semitic Philology, University of Barcelona, 2013, 155–275.

100. *Supporter,* ch. 9, 175e / 143a.

101. Pierre Ageron, "Exemples précoces de traductions scientifiques vers l'arabe en Afrique du Nord," in Mahdi Abdeljaouad and Hmida Hedfi, eds., *Actes du XIIIe colloque maghrébin sur l'histoire des mathématiques arabes,* Tunis, Association Tunisienne des Sciences Mathématiques, 2019, p. 93–116. See also J. Keuning, "The History of an Atlas: Mercator-Hondius," *Imago Mundi* 4 (1947), 37–62.

102. Feza Günergun, "Ottoman Encounters with European Science: Sixteenth- and Seventeenth-century Translations into Turkish," in Peter Burke and R. Po-chia Hsia, eds., *Cultural Translation in Early Modern Europe,* Cambridge, Cambridge University Press, 2007, 192–211, 202–3; P. Ageron, "Le rôle des 'renégats' occidentaux dans le transfert des sciences modernes aux pays d'Islam," in Thomas Preveraud, ed., *Circulations savantes entre l'Europe et le monde XVIIe–XXe siècle,* Rennes, Presses Universitaires de Rennes, 2017, 36–37.

103. *Supporter,* ch. 9, 174e / 142a.

104. See Lazarus-Yafeh, *Intertwined Worlds,* on Ibn Hazm, 28.

105. *Supporter,* ch. 9, 175–76e / 144a.

106. ". . . on nous metoit ces 4 testes de fleuves en lieu auquel ils n'apparoissent," Gerhard Mercator and Jodocus Hondius, *Atlas Minor,* French trans. by Lancelot Voisin de La Popelinière, Amsterdam, Jean Jansson, 1619, 642.

107. Ageron, "Exemples précoces," 97–98.

108. *Supporter,* ch. 13, 261e / 282a.

109. Sylvia Sumira, *Globes: 400 Years of Exploration, Navigation, and Power,* Chicago, University of Chicago Press, 2014, 64–73.

110. *SIHM,* Henry de Castries, ed., Paris, Geuthner, and London, Luzac, 1925, Angleterre, 2:168–70.

111. Jerry Brotton, *Trading Territories: Mapping the Early Modern World,* Ithaca, NY, Cornell University Press, 1997, 25.

112. Stearns, *Revealed Sciences,* 31.

113. Gilbert, *In Good Faith,* who quotes an archival record (129, 273).

114. Ifranī, *Nuzhat,* 349, which cites some of his poetry.

115. Del Puerto, *Mission historial,* 162 ("Tuvo el Rey, la noticia, y hallandose con algunos libros curiosos, y siendo este Rey, llamado *Muley Zydan,* Padre de el que nos

recibiò à nosotros, menos ignorante, y mas aficionado á las letras, que los de este tiempo, le encargò, que aquellos libros los traduxesse en nuestro Castellano vulgar, para que algunos Renegados Españoles los boviessen en el Arabe").

116. *Mission historial,* 164. This well-known interest of Mūlay Zaydān for European learning and his sponsorship of translations, could explain a curious incident that happened in Safi, the closest port to Marrakesh under Saʿdī control: in July 1623, a Dutch pirate sold twelve hundred Latin books stolen from a captured ship. One wonders if the buyer might have been one of Mūlay Zaydān's *qāʾid*s, or officials, who acquired those Latin books for the sultan (*SIHM,* Pays-Bas, 3:405–6 and 414–15). In any case, this is another evidence to add to the ones collected by J. Dakhlia in "Une bibliothèque en filigrane? Eléments de réflexion sur la circulation écrite des langues européennes au Maghreb (XVIᵉ–XVIIIᵉ siècle)," in M. Meouak, P. Sanchez, and A. Vicente, eds., *De los manuscritos medievales a internet: La presencia del arabe vernaculo en las fuentes escritas,* Zaragoza, University of Zaragoza, 2012, 153–75.

117. Subrahmanyam, *Courtly Encounters,* 212.

118. Stearns, *Revealed Sciences,* 45.

119. *Supporter,* ch. 10, 192e / 170a; Quran 13:39.

120. Ryan Szpiech, *Conversion and Narrative: Reading and Religious Authority in Medieval Polemic,* 199.

121. Sanjay Subrahmanyam, *Empires between Islam and Christianity, 1500–1800,* Albany, State University of New York Press, 2019, 113.

122. *Supporter,* ch. 10, 201e / 184a.

123. See Razali et al., "The Fourth Source: *Isrāʾīliyyāt* and the Use of the Bible in Muslim scholarship," in Daniel J. Crowther et al., eds., *Reading the Bible in Islamic Context. Qurʾanic Conversations,* London, Routledge, 2018, 103–115.

124. *Supporter,* ch. 10, 201e / 183–84a.

125. *Supporter,* ch. 10, 202e / 185a.

126. Ayesha Ramachandran, *The Worldmakers: Global Imagining in Early Modern Europe,* Chicago, University of Chicago Press, 2015, 3–4.

127. Ayesha Ramachandran, "A War of Worlds: Becoming 'Early Modern' and the Challenge of Comparison," in David Porter, ed., *Comparative Early Modernities, 1100–1800,* New York, Palgrave-Macmillan, 2012, 15–46, 21.

128. Ramachandran, *Worldmakers,* 60.

129. Ramachandran, *Worldmakers,* 14.

130. Martin W. Lewis and Karen E. Wigen, *The Myth of Continents: A Critique of Metageography,* Berkeley, University of California Press, 1997, 24.

131. *Supporter,* ch. 11, 229e / 232a.

132. *Relaciones del origen, descendencia y succession de los reyes de Persia y de Harmuz, y de un viage,* Antwerp, H. Verdussen, 1610.

133. *Supporter,* ch. 10, 207e / 192–93a.

134. *Supporter,* ch. 11, 219e / 215a.

135. *Supporter,* ch. 10, 204e / 189a.

136. *Supporter,* ch. 11, 229–30e /233a.

137. *Supporter,* ch. 10, 205e / 190a.

138. *Supporter,* ch. 10, 208e / 194a.

139. *Supporter,* ch. 10, 205–6e / 190–91a. The technical aspect of Hajarī's approach has been somewhat blunted in the published English version. In this specific instance, this excellent translation lacks the precision at which Hajarī was aiming when representing the place of Islam in the world. I have indicated by brackets my modifications of the translation, and have used the words "latitude" and "longitude" rather than "breadth" and "length" when it seemed clear that Hajarī meant the technical geographical concepts. I rendered as "contiguous land belonging to the Muslims," what is translated in a confusing manner by "the large continent attached to the land of the Muslims."

140. Katharina N. Piechocki, *Cartographic Humanism: The Making of Early Modern Europe,* Chicago, University of Chicago Press, 2019, 5.

141. Piechocki, *Cartographic Humanism,* 16–17.

142. *Supporter,* ch. 7, 158e / 122a.

143. Ernest Babelon noted in his catalog: "Avant la Révolution on conservait dans le Trésor de l'Abbaye de Saint-Denis, sous le nom de *Tasse de Salomon,* la précieuse coupe sassanide que nous venons de décrire" (*Catalogue des camées antiques et modernes de la Bibliothèque Nationale,* Paris, Ernest Leroux, 1897, n° 379, 215).

144. János Harmatta described the inscriptions on the cup, which include some of the names of God in Arabic, as mentioned by Hajarī; see "La coupe de Xusrō et l'origine de la légende du Graal," *Selected Writings: West and East in the Unity of the Ancient World,* Debrecen, Kossuth Egy. K., 2002, 94–110,109.

145. *Supporter,* ch.7, 158–59e / 123a.

146. Michael Laffan identifies this ambassador as Pieter Coy, "dispatched to Marrakesh in 1607 by virtue of his having learned enough Arabic when he was in the Moluccas" (*The Makings of Indonesian Islam: Orientalism and the Narration of a Sufi Past,* Princeton, NJ, Princeton University Press, 2011, 72). However, there is no evidence that Coy traveled to the Moluccas. On the same page, Laffan mentions Albert Ruyl, as a "trader in Ambon," an Indonesian island, who was known for having "completed a translation of Matthew's gospel into Malay." Ruyl headed the 1622–24 Dutch embassy to Morocco, during which he was acquainted with Hajarī. Ruyl is certainly the envoy whom the latter mentions as having picked up Arabic during his time in Asia.

147. *Supporter,* ch. 10, 206e / 191–92a.

148. *Supporter,* ch. 11, 223–24e / 222–24a.

PART THREE. TECHNOLOGY IN THE CONTACT ZONE

1. James Secord, "Knowledge in Transit," *Isis* 95:4 (2004), 654–72, 662.

1. *SIHM,* Pays-Bas, 3:168–74.

2. Weston F. Cook, *The Hundred Years War for Morocco: Gunpowder and the Military Revolution in the Early Modern Muslim World,* Boulder, CO, Westview Press, 1994.

3. The rise of three of the most prominent early modern Muslim powers, the Ottomans, the Safavids, and the Mughals, led renowned world historians Marshall Hodgson and William McNeil to coin the famous and controversial phrase "gunpowder empires" to describe them.

4. Bernard Rosenberger and Hamid Triki, "Famines et épidémies au Maroc aux XVIᵉ et XVIIᵉ siècles" (part 1), *Hespéris-Tamuda* 14 (1973), 109–75, esp. 157–75.

5. See Mercedes García-Arenal, *Messianism and Puritanical Reform: Mahdīs of the Muslim West,* trans. Martin Beagles, Leiden, Brill, 2006, ch. 12.

6. *SIHM,* Pays-Bas, 1:xix.

7. Jerome Bruce Weiner, "Fitna, Corsairs, and Diplomacy: Morocco and the Maritime States of Western Europe, 1603–1672," PhD diss., Deparment of Political Science, Columbia University, 1976, 52.

8. Andrzej Dziubinski, "L'armée et la flotte de guerre marocaines à l'époque des sultans de la dynastie saadienne," *Hespéris-Tamuda* 13 (1972), 61–94; 'Abd al-Karīm Kurayyīm, *Morocco under the Saʿdī Dynasty* (in Arabic), 2nd ed., Rabat, Jamʿiyat al-muʾarikhīn al-maghāriba, 2006, 244. One might wonder if Mūlay Zaydān's commission of the translation by Hajarī of Zacuto and Vizino's *Almanach* was connected to his naval ambitions, since this text was not a purely theoretical treatise of astronomy, but rather a well-known example of the "translation of elite astronomical and trigonometric knowledge into the practical methods of navigation" (Seed, "Celestial Navigation," 279).

9. On the history of the corsairs of Rabat-Salé, see Leila Meziane, *Salé et ses corsaires, 1666–1727: Un port de course marocain au XVIIe siècle,* Caen, Presses Universitaires, 2007; Hossain Bouzineb, *La Alcazaba del Buregreg,* Rabat, Ministry of Culture, 2006.

10. Daniel Hershenzon, "The Arabic Manuscripts of Muley Zidan and the Escorial Libraries," *Journal of Early Modern History* 18 (2014), 1–24; and Oumelbanine Zhiri, "A Captive Library between Morocco and Spain," in Marcus Keller and Javier Irigoyen-García, eds., *Dialectics of Orientalism in Early Modern Europe,* London, Palgrave Macmillan, 2018, 17–31.

11. Weiner, *Fitna,* 258.

12. Eric Swart, "'Qualifications, Knowledge, and Courage': Dutch Military Engineers, c. 1550–c. 1660," in Bruce P. Lenman, ed., *Military Engineers and the Development of the Early-Modern State,* Dundee, Dundee University Press, 2013, 47–70, 66.

13. *SIHM,* Pays-Bas, 3:266 ff.

14. *SIHM,* Pays-Bas, 3:499–502.

15. Peter T. Bradley, *The Lure of Peru: Maritime Intrusion into the South Sea, 1598–1701.,* New York, Palgrave Macmillan, 1989, 53–54.

16. *SIHM,* Pays-Bas, 3:318n3.

17. It is unfortunately not extant, although the Dutch original is recorded by Ruyl in his diary. (*SIHM,* Pays-Bas, 3:548; see 523–24 for French translation.)

18. *SIHM,* Pays-Bas, 3:526.

19. *SIHM,* Pays-Bas, 3:564n.

20. García-Arenal and Wiegers, *Man of Three Worlds,* 106–13.

21. Arnoud Vrolijk, "Scaliger and the Dutch Expansion in Asia: An Arabic Translation for an Early Voyage to the East Indies (1600)," *Journal of the Warburg and Courtauld Institutes* 78 (2015), 277–309, 284.

22. Daud Soesilo, "Celebrating 400 years of Ruyl's Malay Translation of Matthew's Gospel," *Bible Translator* 64:2 (2013), 173–84, 175.

23. Soesilo, "Celebrating," 176.

24. Lourens de Vries, "Iang Evangelium Ul-Kadus Menjurat kapada Marcum: The First Malay Gospel of Mark (1629–1630) and the Agama Kumpeni," *Bijdragen tot de Taal-, Land- en Volkendunde* 174:1 (2018), 47–79, 54.

25. Soesilo, "Celebrating," 177.

26. De Vries, "First Malay Gospel," 63 and 65.

27. Romain Bertrand, "The Making of a 'Malay Text': Peter Floris, Erpenius, and Textual Transmission in and out of the Malay World at the Turn of the 17th Century," *Quaderni Storici* 48:142–41 (2013), 141–65, 148.

28. De Vries, "First Malay Gospel", 64.

29. *SIHM,* Pays-Bas, 3:411.

30. *SIHM,* Pays-Bas, 3:107–8.

31. *SIHM,* Pays-Bas, 3:305n.

32. *SIHM,* Pays-Bas, 3:298n1.

33. *SIHM,* Pays-Bas, 3:423; see also 430–31, and 435.

34. *SIHM,* Pays-Bas, 3:438.

35. *SIHM,* Pays-Bas, 3:506, 510, 516, 519.

36. *Supporter,* ch. 10, 206e / 191a. "Netherlands" translates "Bilād Flamink."

37. Sonja Brentjes, "Learning to Write, Read, and Speak Arabic outside of Early Modern Universities," in Loop, Hamilton, and Burnett, eds., *Teaching and Learning of Arabic,* 252–71, 252.

38. *Supporter,* ch. 4, 123e / 71a.

39. Witkam, "Leiden Manuscript," 78.

40. Witkam, "Leiden Manuscript," for the edition and translation of the two letters.

41. Boris Liebrenz, "Golius and Tychsen and their Quest for Manuscripts: Three Arabic Letters," *Journal of Islamic Manuscripts* 8 (2017), 218–39.

42. On May 3, al-Qāliʿ arrived in Safi to inquire about money issues, and probably discussed at that time the theft of the books with Golius. After going to the army camp to view the recently delivered cannons, he was back again in Safi on May 26 (*SIHM,* Pays-Bas, 3:528 and 531).

43. Kilpatrick and Toomer, "Niqūlāwus al-Halabī," 4.

44. Houtsma, "Oosterche correspondentie," 20–21, for the Arabic letter and a Dutch translation.

45. Bertrand, "Making of a 'Malay Text,'" 145.

46. In the original Dutch, *meesters ofte ervaren personen*, *SIHM*, Pays-Bas, 3:224.

47. *SIHM*, Pays-Bas, 3:571–85.

48. García-Arenal and Wiegers, *Man of Three Worlds*, 108.

49. *SIHM*, Pays-Bas, 3:575. For Golius's report, Ruyl's diary, and other Dutch records, the page numbers refer to de Castries's French translations of the documents, which are followed by the originals. My translations are made from the French.

50. *SIHM*, Pays-Bas, 3:407–8.

51. *SIHM*, Pays-Bas, 4:23.

52. *SIHM*, Pays-Bas, 3:208n. As far as is known, there is no record of de Backer's assessment of the site of Aier, although the two Dutch officials who took Volmer's testimony had suggested that the States General listen to him in person as he resided in The Hague; *SIHM*, Pays-Bas, 4:22.

53. Swart, "Qualifications," 62.

54. *SIHM*, Pays-Bas, 3:575 and 407–8.

55. *SIHM*, Pays-Bas, 3:578.

56. *SIHM*, Pays-Bas, 3:247–48.

57. Eric H. Ash, *Power, Knowledge, and Expertise in Elizabethan England,* Baltimore, Johns Hopkins University, 2004.

58. "By Any Other Name: Early Modern Expertise and the Problem of Anachronism," *History and Technology* 35:1 (2019), 3–30, 9–10.

59. Hélène Vérin, *La Gloire des ingénieurs: L'intelligence technique du XVIe au XVIIIe siècle,* Paris, Albin-Michel, 1993, 23.

60. Vérin, *Gloire*, 31.

61. *La Chorographie ou description de Provence, et l'histoire Chronologique du mesme pays,* Aix, C. David, 1664, 2:869.

62. *SIHM*, France, Série Saadienne, 3:xxxix–xlvii; Roger Coindreau, "Antoine de Salettes, sieur de Saint-Mandrier: Gentilhomme provençal et aventurier au Maroc," *Hespéris*, 34 (1947), 339–73.

63. Including Savaleta, Samandris, Samadris, San Manrique, and Suma Andrea, as well as others.

64. *SIHM*, France, 3:32 ("seu fundidor da artelharia e seu engenheiro").

65. *SIHM*, Angleterre, 2:553 ("Monsieur de San Manrrique, ingeniero frances, que sirve a Muley Cidan").

66. Gonzalo de Cespedes y Meneses, *Primera parte de la historia de D. Felipe IV Rey de las Españas,* Lisbon, Craesbeeck, 1631, 345 ("un Frances, gran confidente del Cidan . . . que conociendole por platico de fortificacion y fundiciones, de Geometria, y otras cosas, le hizo merced, y su valido").

67. "le Roy . . . l'employa en ses guerres, tant pour l'infanterie que pour la cavalerie; en quoy il reüssit merveilleusement bien: estant extrement addroit en toute

sorte d'exercise militaire, & tres-sçavant aux sciences Mathematiques; si bien que dans peu de temps il acquit grand credit dans l'esprit du Roy de Maroc; faisant donner les Charges de l'Etat à qui bon luy sembloit," *Chorographie,* 869.

68. *SIHM,* France, 3:xlii ("Grâce à lui on vit au Maroc des fonderies de canons et des raffineries de salpêtre").

69. António Saldanha, *Crónica de Almançor, sultão de Marrocos (1578–1603),* António Dias Farinha, ed. and trans. into French, Lisbon, 1997, 80–81, 142–43, and 'Abd al-'Azīz al-Fishtālī, *Manāhil al-safā,* 210.

70. Cook mentioned manufacture of firearms in the 1530s (*Hundred Years War,* 181; see also 197 about a "small but robust Sa'adian arms industry" in Marrakesh decades before Ahmad al-Mansūr). A more recent study shows that an arms industry was present in Morocco even earlier (Muhammad al-Mahnāwī, "Firearms in Morocco under the Wattāsī Dynasty," in Muhammad Istītū, ed., *Morocco under the Wattāsī Dynasty According to Hasan al-Wazzān's "Description of Africa"* (in Arabic), Rabat, Jam'iya Hasan al-Wazzān, 2011, 151–60, esp. 157–60). For an overview of Moroccan sources on arms manufacture in premodern Morocco over the centuries, see Muhammad al-Manūnī, "The Production of Firearms in Morocco," *Selected Studies* (in Arabic), Rabat, Ministry of Culture, 2000, 245–56.

71. Gábor Ágoston, "Behind the Turkish War Machine: Gunpowder Technology and War Industry in the Ottoman Empire, 1450–1700," in Brett D. Steele and Tamera Dorland, eds., *The Heirs of Archimedes: Science and the Art of War through the Age of Enlightenment,* Cambridge, MA, MIT Press, 2005, 101–34, 106.

72. Steven A. Walton, "State Building through Building for the State: Foreign and Domestic Expertise in Tudor Fortification," *Osiris* 2:25 (2010), 66–84; Frederic J. Baumgartner, "The French Reluctance to Adopt Firearms Technology in the Early Modern Period," in Steele and Dorland, eds., *Heirs of Archimedes,* 73–86.

73. Kenneth Chase, *Firearms. A Global History to 1700,* Cambridge, Cambridge University Press, 2003, 97–98.

74. See Bartholomé Benassar and Lucille Benassar, *Les Chrétiens d'Allah: L'histoire extraordinaire des renégats, XVIe–XVIIe siècles,* Paris, Perrin, 1989; and Tobias Graf, *The Sultan's Renegades: Christian-European Converts to Islam and the Making of the Ottoman Elite, 1575–1610,* Oxford, Oxford University Press, 2017.

75. *SIHM,* France, 3:56 ("pour scavoir sy c'est pierre, terre ou sable, et generallement toute son assiette et force, le tout avec l'advis de ceux qui sont les plus entenduz aux fortiffications").

76. See *SIHM,* France, 3:xlvi.

77. *SIHM,* Pays-Bas, 3:572.

78. E. W. Bovill, "Queen's Elizabeth's Gunpowder," *Mariner's Mirror* 33:3 (1947), 179–86.

79. Brenda J. Buchanan, "Salpetre: A Commodity of Empire," in B. Buchanan, ed., *Gunpowder, Explosives, and the State. A Technological History,* Aldershot, Ashgate, 2006, 67–90.

80. *SIHM,* Pays-Bas, 3:319.

81. *SIHM,* Pays-Bas, 3:412, 432, 438.

82. *SIHM,* Pays-Bas, 3:415.

83. *SIHM,* France, 3:738 ("La Houladilla, petit port à barques ou moyens navires, y ayant à l'entrée une roche qui la rend difficile & n'y a là qu'un chasteau et petite villette").

84. Cespedes, *Primera parte,* 413–14.

85. See Stéphane Yerasimos, "Les ingénieurs ottomans," in Élisabeth Longuenesse, ed., *Bâtisseurs et bureaucrates: Ingénieurs et société au Maghreb et au Moyen-Orient,* Lyon, Maison de l'Orient, 1990, 47–63; and Ghislaine Alleaume, "Les ingénieurs en Égypte au XIXᵉ siècle, 1820–1020, éléments pour un débat," in Élisabeth Longuenesse, ed., *Bâtisseurs et bureaucrates,* 65–80.

86. Steven A. Walton, "Technologies of Pow(d)er: Military Mathematical Practitioners' Strategies and Self-Presentation," in Lesley B. Cormack, Steven A. Walton, and John A. Schuster, eds., *Mathematical Practitioners and the Transformation of Natural Knowledge in Early Modern Europe,* Cham, Springer, 2017, 87–113, 90.

87. Vérin, *Gloire,* 76 ("La guerre, celle qui règne entre les royaumes, les principautés, est la sphère d'activité par excellence des ingénieurs").

88. Swart, "Qualifications," 49 and 55.

89. Abū Nasr al-Fārābī, *Ihsā' al-'Ulūm,* 'Uthmān Muhammad Amīn, ed., Cairo, Matba'at al-Khanjī, 1965, 49.

90. Jean Jolivet, "Classifications of the Sciences," in Roshdi Rashed and Régis Morelon eds., *Encyclopedia of the History of Arabic Science,* vol. 3, London, Routledge, 1996, 1008–25, 1013.

91. Sonja Brentjes, *Teaching and Learning the Sciences in Islamicate Societies (800–1700),* Turnhout, Brepols, 2018, 198.

92. Vérin, *Gloire,* 72.

93. Walton, "Technologies of Pow(d)er," 104.

94. Harvey, "The Morisco," 95 (82 for Arabic).

95. Harvey, "The Morisco," 82.

96. See *Lisān al-'Arab* by Ibn Mandhūr (1232–1311), and *Tāj al-'Arūs* by Muhammad Murtada al-Zabīdī (d. 1790).

97. Doris Behrens-Abouseif, "*Muhandis, Shād, Mu'allim:* Notes on the Building Craft in the Mamluk Period," *Der Islam* 72 (1995), 293–309, 294.

98. Behrens-Abouseif, "*Muhandis,*" 309. See also Nasser Rabbat, "Architects and Artists in Mamluk Society: The Perspective from the Sources," *Journal of Architectural Education* 52:1 (1998), 30–37.

99. *The Muqaddimah: An Introduction to History; The Classic Islamic History of the World,* trans. and introduced by Franz Rosenthal, abridged and ed. by N.J. Dawood, with an introduction by Bruce Laurence, Princeton, NJ, Princeton University Press, 2005, 478–79, and 557. See the Arabic text in *al-Muqaddima,* 3 vols., 'Abd al-Salām al-Shaddādī, ed., Casablanca, Bayt al-funūn wa al-'ulūm wa al-adab, 2005, 2:298–300, and 3:86. One should note that the English version sometimes translates *handasa* by "geometry," and sometimes by "geometry and engineering" (478). In a rare occurrence, Ibn Khaldūn employs the term *muhandis* to clearly

designate the scholar of geometry, and not a practitioner (*al-Muqaddima*, 2:300; *The Muqaddimah* translates the word as "geometrician", 479)

100. Harvey, "The Morisco," 89–90, and 78 for the Arabic text.

101. This differs from the examples given by Behrens-Abouseif ("*Muhandis*"), which all concern civil buildings.

102. *Histoire de Barbarie et de ses corsaires*, Paris, Pierre Rocolet, 1637, 100. First published in 1637, a second edition in 1649 and many imitators attest to the success of this book.

103. Archival document cited by Sakina Missoum, "Andalusi Immigration and Urban Development in Algiers (Sixteenth and Seventeenth Centuries)," in *Expulsion*, 329–56, 342n55.

104. Gabriel Colin, *Corpus des inscriptions arabes et turques de l'Algérie*, Paris, Leroux, 1901, 35, 38, 40, 42.

105. *Al-Mu'nis fī akhbār Ifrīqiyā wa Tūnis*, Muhammad Shammām, ed., Tunis, al-Maktaba al-ʿatīqa, 1967, 210.

106. Ghānim, *Kitāb al-ʿizz*, Ihsān Hindī, ed., ch. 22, 228. Henceforth *Kitāb*.

107. *Kitāb*, ch. 22, 228.

108. *Kitāb*, ch. 1, 84. The three groups are thus designated: *ʿulamāʾ*, *muhandisīn*, and *ahl al-tadābīr li al-harb*.

109. *Kitāb*, ch. 1, 87.

110. *Kitāb*, ch. 40, 365.

111. *Kitāb*, ch. 42, 371, and ch. 45. 383.

112. Ágoston, *Guns for the Sultan: Military Power and the Weapons Industry in the Ottoman Empire*, Cambridge, Cambridge University Press, 2005, 127.

113. Marsigli, *L'État militaire de l'empire ottoman*, The Hague, 1732, 79.

114. Pamela O. Long, *Openness, Secrecy, Authorship: Technical Arts and the Culture of Knowledge from Antiquity to the Renaissance*, Baltimore, Johns Hopkins University Press, 2001, 15.

CHAPTER 6. ARTILLERY AND PRACTICAL KNOWLEDGE
IN NORTH AFRICA

1. *Histoire de Barbarie*, 149.

2. The Arabic version of the work consists of fifty chapters, preceded by a prologue by Ghānim and followed by an appendix by the translator, Hajarī. Several extant manuscripts are held in European, Turkish, and North African libraries. This study will use mainly the useful although flawed edition by Ihsān Hindī. The notes will refer to the printed text, still the most easily accessible, and will add corrections and comparisons with the Algiers and Vienna manuscripts if they offer a different reading. Hindī's edition (henceforth *Kitāb*) is mostly based on the following manuscripts: 87 ج in the Maktaba Wataniyya of Morocco, and 2642 in the Hasaniyya Library in Rabat. The editor also consulted other copies for the numerous illustrations, which are at different stages of completion depending on the manuscript. The

different manuscripts bear slightly different titles. Useful for its linguistic and technical notes, this edition is unfortunately marred by some inexplicably misplaced or missing passages in the last few chapters and in the appendix to the text, as well as some misread words. Alongside this edition, I also consulted digital copies of MS 1511 of the Maktaba Wataniyya in Algiers, which might contain the best and more complete illustrations of any copy, and of Ms. 1412, in the Österreichische Nationalbibliothek in Vienna. The translations are mine, except when indicated otherwise.

3. Spelled "al-Rayyāsh" in the printed edition of the *Kitāb*.

4. *Kitāb*, prologue, 77.

5. See Brice Cossart, "Traités d'artillerie et écoles d'artilleurs: interactions entre pratiques d'enseignement et livres techniques à l'époque de Philippe II d'Espagne," in Liliane Hilaire-Pérez et al., eds., *Le Livre technique avant le XXe siècle à l'échelle du monde,* Paris, CNRS Éditions, 2017, 341–53, 344.

6. *Kitāb,* ch. 1, 89.

7. Pablo E. Pérez-Mallaína, *Spain's Men of the Sea: Daily Life on the Indies Fleets in the Sixteenth Century,* trans. Carla Rahn Phillips, Baltimore, Johns Hopkins University, 1998, 44, does not mention prison but states that, among other privileges afforded gunners, "in case of a lawsuit for debt, their salary could not be embargoed."

8. *Kitāb,* ch. 1, 88.

9. Pérez-Mallaína, *Spain's Men of the Sea,* 230.

10. According to Pamela H. Smith, "Theory (*episteme* or *scientia*) was certain knowledge based on logical syllogism and geometrical demonstration. Practice (*praxis* or *experientia*), on the other hand, could be of two kinds—things done and things made. Things done were comprised of human knowledge such as history, politics, ethics, and economics. *Praxis* was studied in the particular (by collection of experiences): it could not be formed into a deductive system, and thus was not as certain as theory. The other type of practice was comprised of things made, or *technê*, that involved bodily labor. *Technê* had nothing to do with certainty but instead was the lowly knowledge of how to make things or produce effects, practiced by animals, slaves, and craftspeople." *The Body of the Artisan: Art and Experience in the Scientific Revolution,* Chicago, University of Chicago Press, 2004, 17.

11. Ibn Khaldūn, *The Muqaddimah,* 467.

12. Al-Yūsī, *Al-Qānūn,* Hamîd Hamânî, ed., Rabat, Matba'a Shâla, 1998, 146 ff. About this text see Jacques Berque, *L'Intérieur du Maghreb XVe–XIXe siècle,* Paris, Gallimard, 1978, ch. 11; Justin Stearns, "Science, Secondary Causation, and Reason in the Early Modern Ottoman Empire and Morocco: Al-Yūsī and His Students," *Proceedings of the International Congress on the Maghreb and the Western Mediterranean in the Ottoman Era,* Istanbul, IRCICA, 2013, 43–52; Stearns, *Revealed Sciences,* 82–94.

13. See Mohammed Abattouy, "The Arabic Science of Weights (*'Ilm al-Athqāl*): Textual Tradition and Significance in the History of Mechanics," in Emilia Calvo et al., eds., *A Shared Legacy: Islamic Science East and West,* Barcelona, Presses of the University of Barcelona, 2008, 83–114.

14. George Saliba, "Artisans and Mathematicians in Medieval Islam," *Journal of the American Oriental Society* 119:4 (1999), 637–45.

15. Yūsī, *Qānūn,* 176. It is crucial to underline that the distinction between the knowledge produced by scholars and by the *ʿāmma* or commoners, is not coterminous with the opposition between religious and secular knowledge. Neither should it be confused with a distinction between the licit and the illicit. Not only are they all permissible, but Yūsī also stressed that all knowledge is "food for the mind," and "pleasure for the soul," and an attribute of perfection. He also defined "all sciences that benefited the Muslim community as religiously sanctioned" (Stearns, *Revealed Sciences,* 76).

16. Hajjī, *Intellectual Trends,* 394. On this author, and on writing on medicine in Morocco in the seventeenth century, see Stearns, *Revealed Sciences,* 200–213.

17. Smith, *Body of the Artisan,* 18.

18. Peter Burke, *A Social History of Knowledge from Gutenberg to Diderot,* Cambridge and Oxford, Polity with Balckwell, 2004, 14–15.

19. See Pamela O. Long, *Artisans/Practitioners and the Rise of the New Sciences, 1400–1600,* Corvallis, Oregon University Press, 2011, ch. 1.

20. Hanna, *In Praise of Books,* 112.

21. Hanna, *Ottoman Egypt,* 45–46.

22. Dana Sajdi, *The Barber of Damascus: Nouveau Literacy in the Eighteenth-Century Ottoman Levant,* Stanford, CA, Stanford University Press, 2013, which also analyzes the works of a number of Syrian historians who did not belong to the academic elite.

23. See the informative introductions by Heyberger and Lentin to the French translation, Dyāb, *D'Alep à Paris.*

24. Hanna, *Ottoman Egypt,* 52. At the same time, another artisan wrote a book about crafts. See Doris Behrens-Abouseif, "Une polémique anti-ottomane par un artisan au Caire du XVIIᵉ siècle," in Brigitte Marino, ed., *Études sur les villes du Proche-Orient XVIe-XIXe siècles,* Damascus, Institut Français d'Études Arabes, 2001, 55–63.

25. Muhibbī, *Khulāsat,* 4:205–6; Abū Sālim al-ʿAyyāshī (1628–79), *Māʾ al-mawāʾīd,* Ahmad Mazīdī, ed., Beirut, Dār al-kutub al-ʿilmiyya, 2011, 2:91–92; on Rūdānī and his work, see El-Rouayheb, *Islamic Intellectual History,* 160–70; Stearns, *Revealed sciences,* 183–93.

26. On Rūdānī's treatise on his improved astrolabe, see Charles Pellat's edition ("al-Naquʾa ʿalā al-āla al-jāmiʾa li-l-Rūdānī," *Bulletin d'Études Orientales* 26 (1973): 7–82, and his French translation in "L'astrolabe sphérique d'ar-Rūdānī," *Bulletin d'Études Orientales* 28 (1975): 83–165. Earlier Moroccan examples of scholars writing about craftsmanship include Ibn ʿAradūn (d. 1584) who wrote a didactic poem on the art of bookbindery (Manūnī, *History of Moroccan Bookmaking* (in Arabic), Rabat, Press of Muhammad V University, 1991, 86), and Ahmad al-Sufyānī, a master binder of Fez and *faqīh* who penned a treatise on the same subject (*Sināʿat tasfīr al-kutub,* P. Ricard, ed., Paris, Geuthner, 1925).

27. Ibn Hamādūsh, *Rihla,* Abū al-Qāsim Saʿd Allāh, ed., Algiers, al-Muʾassasa al-wataniya li al-funūn al-matbaʿiyya, 1983, 253–54.

28. Ibn Hamādūsh, *Rihla,* 265. It might be the treatise on the sextant by John Hadley (1682–1744), of which exists an Arabic translation. See Muhammad al-'Arbī al-Khattābī, *The Catalogues of the Hasaniyya Library* (in Arabic), Rabat, Hasaniyya Library, 1983, 3:416–17.

29. For early examples, see Ahmad al-Hassan, "Gunpowder Composition for Rockets and Cannon in Arabic Military Treatises in the Thirteenth and Fourteenth Centuries," *Icon* 9 (2003), 1–30.

30. Cook, *Hundred Years' War for Morocco.*

31. *Histoire de Barbarie,* 101–2.

32. "E nel tempo moderno andó el conte Pietro Navarro con 9 ligni pensado de potere pigliare la dca terra, ma fu ben defesa con la artigliaria allo intrare del porto, . . . in l'anno 1519," MS VE 953, 332v.

33. For a discussion on the role of the new fortifications in the changes in European warfare, see Mahinder S. Kingra, "The *Trace Italienne* and the Military Revolution during the Eighty-Years' War, 1567–1648," *Journal of Military History* 57:3 (1993), 431–46.

34. For an overview and analysis of the genre among Spanish writers, see Fernando González de León, "'Doctors of the Military Discipline': Technical Expertise and the Paradigm of the Spanish Soldier in the Early Modern Period," *Sixteenth Century Journal* 37:1 (1996), 61–95, and *The Road to Rocroi: Class, Culture, and Command in the Spanish Army of Flanders, 1567–1659,* Leiden, Brill, 2009, part 1, ch. 4.

35. Cristobal Lechuga, *Discurso en que trata de la artillería,* Milan, Marco Tulio Malatesta, 1611.

36. *Kitāb,* ch.1, 86.

37. *Kitāb,* ch.1, 87.

38. *Kitāb,* ch.1, 87.

39. *Kitāb,* ch. 1, 88.

40. *Kitāb,* ch. 1, 88.

41. *Kitāb,* ch. 1, 89.

42. Leoncio Verdera Franco, "La evolución de la artillería en los siglos XVII y XVIII," in Alicia Cámara, ed., *Los ingenieros militares de la monarquía hispánica en los siglos XVII y XVIII,* Madrid, Ministerio de Defensa; Asociación Española de Amigos de los Castillos; Centro de Estudios Europa Hispánica, 2005, 113–30, 121. On the Spanish schools of artillery, see Brice Cossart, *Les Artilleurs et la monarchie hispanique (1560–1610),* Paris, Classiques Garnier, 2021, part 2.

43. Cossart, "Traités d'artillerie," and *Artilleurs,* part 3.

44. *Kitāb,* 79.

45. *Kitāb,* ch. 49, 405.

46. *Kitāb,* ch. 1, 85–86.

47. *Kitāb,* ch. 3, 98.

48. *Kitāb,* ch. 20, 216.

49. *Kitāb,* ch. 6, 114.

50. Mahdi Abdeljaouad, Pierre Ageron, and Mahmoud Shahidy, "Émergence d'un savoir mathématique euro-islamique: *L'Offrande du converti pour ranimer la flamme éteinte*," *Philosophia Scientiae* 20:2 (2016), 7–32, 16.

51. Like the *Kitāb,* it adapted European manuals, and was "not a plain compilation of European books, but a fascinating witness to an attempt at creating a Euro-Islamic hybrid knowledge." Abdeljaouad and Ageron, "Eastern and Western Instruments in Osman Efendi's *Hadiyyat al-Muhtadī* (The Gift of the Convert)," in Neil Brown, Silke Ackermann, and Feza Günergun, eds., *Scientific Instruments between East and West,* Leiden, Brill, 2019, 16–38, 37. This book met with success, and eleven copies, containing images, are extant.

52. Cited in Abdeljaouad, Ageron, and Shahidy, "Émergence," 15.

53. They are described by Manūnī, "Production of Firearms in Morocco," 252–54.

54. *Kitāb,* ch. 1, 81.

55. Vérin, *Gloire,* 76–77.

56. *Kitāb,* ch. 1, 82.

57. *Kitāb,* ch. 1, 83–84.

58. *Kitāb,* ch. 11, 137.

59. *Kitāb,* ch. 19, 211. Cf. Luis Collado, *Plática manual de artillería,* Milan, Pablo Gotardo Poncio,1592, 94v.

60. *Kitāb,* ch. 1, 85.

61. *Kitāb,* ch. 49, 405, and ch. 2, 93.

62. *Kitāb,* ch. 24, 288.

63. *Kitāb,* ch. 12, 158, ch. 21, 219, and ch. 26, 308.

64. *Kitāb,* ch. 12, 158.

65. Steven Walton, "Mathematical Instruments and the Creation of the Scientific Military Gentleman," in Steven A. Walton, ed., *Instrumental at War. Science, Research, and Instruments between Knowledge and the World,* Leiden, Brill, 2005, 17–46, 42.

66. *Kitāb,* ch. 12, 159, and ch. 24, 274.

67. *Kitāb,* ch.13, 163.

68. Walton, "Mathematical Instruments"; and Pascal Brioist, "L'artillerie à la Renaissance," *Nouvelle Revue du XVIe siècle* 20:1 (2002), 79–95.

69. *Kitāb,* ch. 1, 84.

70. *Kitāb,* ch. 1, 85.

71. *Kitāb,* ch. 24, 282; see also ch. 24, 273.

72. *Kitāb,* ch. 44, 379.

73. *Kitāb,* ch. 45, 397.

74. *Kitāb,* ch. 48, 400.

75. Vienna ch. 48, 156, and Algiers ch. 48, 114v and 115r. In the printed edition of the *Kitāb,* this quote is in ch. 50, 415.

76. Steven A. Walton, "The Art of Gunnery in Renaissance England," PhD diss., Institute for the History and Philosophy of Science and Technology, University of Toronto, 1999, 185.

77. *Kitāb,* ch. 1, 89.

78. *Kitāb,* ch. 50, 415; Vienna, ch. 48, 156.

79. *Kitāb,* ch. 10, 135.

80. Collado, *Plática manual,* 7v.

81. William Eamon and Françoise Paheau, "The *Accademia segreta* of Girolamo Ruscelli: A Sixteenth-Century Italian Scientific Society," *Isis* 75:2 (1984), 327–42, 329.

82. Girolamo Ruscelli, *Precetti della Militia Moderna,* Venice, Heredi di Marchio Seffa, 1568.

83. Mary J. Henninger-Voss, "How the 'New Science' of Cannons Shook Up the Aristotelian Cosmos," *Journal of the History of Ideas* 63:3 (2002), 371–97, 375. See also Serafina Cuomo, "Shooting by the Book: Notes on Niccolò Tartaglia's *Nova Scientia,*" *History of Science* 35:2, 1997, 155–88.

84. Matteo Valleriani, *Metallurgy, Ballistics and Epistemic Instruments: The Nova scientia of Niccolò Tartaglia; A New Edition,* Matteo Valleriani, ed., Edition Open Access, Berlin, Max Planck Institute for the History of Science, 2017, 5.

85. See Brioist, "L'artillerie," 92–94.

86. In the same passage, it seems that he also alluded to the *El perfecto capitán instruido en la disciplina militar y nueva ciencia de la artilleria* (1590) by Diego de Álava y Viamont (1557-?), calling him elliptically "the great Captain." Álava's book begins with a chapter of praise for mathematics, and contains critical discussions of Tartaglia's propositions.

87. *Kitāb,* ch. 24, 290, and ch. 30, 323.

88. Valleriani, *Metallurgy,* 5.

89. *Kitāb,* ch. 22, 235.

90. *Kitāb,* ch. 11, 137 and 139; ch. 23, 241; ch. 15. 187.

91. *Supporter,* ch. 5, 135e and 86a.

92. Marwa S. Elshakry, "Knowledge in Motion: The Cultural Politics of Modern Science Translations in Arabic," *Isis* 99:4 (2008), 701–31, 704.

93. *Kitāb,* appendix, 421–22.

94. *Kitāb,* ch. 26, 312.

95. Elshakry, "Knowledge in Motion," 704.

96. *Kitāb,* 69.

97. *Kitāb,* ch. 1, 86–87. There are slight differences in Vienna 12 and Algiers 8v that do not alter the meaning.

98. *Kitāb,* ch. 16, 195.

99. *Kitāb,* prologue, 77.

100. *Kitāb,* ch. 2, 93.

101. *Kitāb,* ch. 2, 92–93, and ch. 43, 375.

102. *Kitāb,* ch. 10, 131, ch. 22, 232.

103. *Kitāb,* ch. 3, 95, and ch. 4, 99.

104. *Kitāb,* ch. 22, 232.

105. *Kitāb,* ch. 10, 131, which mistakenly reads *bashilishfu;* see Algiers 22r, and Vienna 36.

106. *Kitāb,* ch. 23, 249 and 264.

107. *Kitāb,* ch. 2, 93; Vienna, 17, and Algiers 12v use the second translation. This is the caliper, an instrument called *colibre* by Collado, *Plática manual,* 69r.

108. *Kitāb,* ch. 4, 99.

109. *Kitāb,* ch. 22, 228.

110. *Kitāb,* ch. 22, 231 and 234.

111. *Kitāb,* ch. 32, 333.

112. *Kitāb,* ch. 38, 351.

113. *Kitāb,* ch. 39, 359, where *quhit* is spelled *fuhit.* See Vienna 142, and Algiers 100r.

114. *Kitāb,* ch. 1, 89.

115. See Simon Werrett, *Fireworks: Pyrotechnic Arts and Sciences in European History,* Chicago, University of Chicago Press, 2010. For examples of the use of fireworks in the Saʿdī court, see *SIHM,* Pays-Bas, 4:595 and 632.

116. *Kitāb,* ch. 47, 393, which mistakenly reads "Mustaʿīn"; see Algiers 108v, and Vienna 152, which both read "Mustaʿīnī."

117. Vienna ch. 48, 156. This passage was moved by the editor of the *Kitāb* to ch. 50, 416.

118. *Kitāb,* ch. 49, 405.

119. González de León, "Technical Expertise," 80.

120. Harvey, "The Morisco," 80–81 (Arabic text) and 91–94 (English translation). Hajarī also quotes Ibn ʿAtāʾ Allāh al-Iskandarī (1259–1310), for a maxim erroneously attributed by Harvey to the Prophet (see 76 for Arabic, and 88 for English).

121. Vérin, *Gloire,* 83 ("[la technique] sera donc considérée comme l'expression d'un recommencement. C'est le temps mythique de l'imitation des Anciens, qui connaît un vif regain pendant tout le siècle").

122. The reference to the classics is actually present in Ghānim's text, borrowed from his Spanish models, when he praises Archimedes, and when he mentions Pliny, about the invention of catapults. "Bliniu" in ch. 23 (Vienna, 95, and Algiers, 66v). The printed text misspells the word as "Blinthī," 260.

123. See Jamil M. Abun-Nasr, "The Beylicate in Seventeenth-Century Tunisia," *International Journal of Middle East Studies* 6:1 (1975), 70–93.

124. On this victory, see also Ibn Abī Dīnār, *Muʾnis,* 208.

125. Harvey, "The Morisco," 77 and 79 (Arabic), 89 and 90 (English).

126. Ash, "Expertise and the Early Modern State," *Osiris* 25 (2010), 1–24, 13.

127. Harvey, "The Morisco," 75 (Arabic), 86 (English).

128. See Jim Bennet and Stephen Johnston, *The Geometry of War, 1500–1750,* Oxford, Museum of the History of Science, 1996.

129. Brioist, "L'Artillerie" ("une science pratique et une science polie, un art de cour et un art de guerre, un support de l'action et un support de la rhétorique"), 86.

130. Harvey, "The Morisco," 83 and 80 (Arabic), 96 and 92 (English).

131. For recent overviews of this text, see Ralf Elger, "*Adab* and Historical Memory. The Andalusian Poet/Politician Ibn al-Khatīb as Presented in Ahmad

al-Maqqarī (986/1577–1041/1632), *Nafḥ at-Ṭīb*," *Die Welt des Islams* 42:3 (2002), 289–306; and Mourad Kacimi, "Análisi crítico sobre el *Nafḥ al-Ṭīb min gusn al-Andalus al-ratib* de al-Maqqarī," *Revista Argelina* 7 (2018), 25–48.

132. Harvey, "The Morisco," 84 (Arabic), 97 (English.)

133. "It was read by the great scholar and muftī, the imam of the Mosque of the Turks, al-Sharīf Ahmad al-Hanafī," *Supporter,* ch. 13, 271e n91 / 299a.

134. "The Morisco," 84. It is not included in the English translation.

135. *Kitāb,* prologue, 79.

136. *Kitāb,* ch. 26, 312.

137. Vienna ch. 48, 156, and Algiers ch. 48, 114v and 115r. In the print edition, this quote is in ch. 50, 415.

138. On the manuscripts, see *Supporter,* general introduction, 63, m. 168. Here is a list of the known copies:

1. A copy by Khūja, April 1639 (see *Catalogue of Manuscripts in the Koprülü Library,* Istanbul, Research Centre for Islamic History, Art and Culture, 1986, 1:574).

2. A copy by Khūja with autograph notes by Hajarī (Maktaba Wataniyya of Rabat, call number ح 87, described by Manūnī, "The Phenomenon,", 81–85).

3. A copy by Khūja,1641, in Österreichische Nationalbibliothek in Vienna, call number 1412, consulted in this study (see Gustav Flügel, *Die arabischen, persischen und türkischen Handschriften,* vol. 2, Vienna, Kaiserlich-Königliche Hofbibliothek, 1867, 2:477–80).

4. A copy by Khūja, 1641, Maktaba Wataniyya in Algiers, call number 1511, consulted in this study (see Ernest Fagnan, *Catalogue général des bibliothèques publiques de France,* Paris, Plon, 1893, 18:416–17).

5. A copy by Khūja, 1641, Maktaba Wataniyya of Tunis (call number 18488).

6. A copy by Khūja, 1651, Chester Beatty Library in Dublin (call number 4107).

7. An undated incomplete copy held in Maktaba Wataniyya in Rabat (call number 1342); see Manūnī, "The Phenomenon", 81.

8. A copy dated 1653 in Cairo's Dār al-Kutub, call number Furūsiyya 97 (see James, "The *Manual,*" 238).

9. An undated, probably seventeenth-century copy, Maktaba Wataniyya of Tunis 3433 (see James, "The *Manual,*" 238).

10. A fragmentary undated copy, ca. 1700, Dublin Chester Beatty, call number 4568 (see James,"The *Manual,*" 238).

11. A copy of 1783–84 held in Maktaba Wataniyya of Algiers, call number 1512 (see Fagnan, *Catalogue,* 18:417).

12. A copy of 1783, held in Dār al-Kutub of Cairo, call number Furūsiya 86 (see James, "The *Manual,*" 238).

13. An undated copy held in the Hasaniyya Library in Rabat, call number 2646 (see Muhammad al-'Arbī al-Khattābī, *Catalogues of the Hasaniyya Library* (in Arabic), Rabat, Hasaniyya Library, 1985, 4:118).

14. A copy made in 1838, held in Tunis, Maktaba al-Qawmyya, call number 1407 (see 'Abd al-Majīd al-Turkī, "Documents of the Last Morisco Emigration to Tunisia" [in Arabic], *Hawliyyāt al-jāmi'a al-tunsiyya* 4 [1967], 23–82, 64–69). Finally, according to Manūnī, there was a copy in the Qarawiyīn Library in Fez, now lost.

139. "There was no mention of firearms by old authors . . . according to a book about *jihād* and the use of artillery against the enemy, this was invented by a philosopher [*hakīm*] who was studying chemistry. He saw an explosion, he kept working and it happened again, and he was amazed. He invented gunpowder in the foreign year of 1366, which is the Arab year of 768." 'Abd al-Rahmān al-Fāsī, *Al-'Amāl al-fāsī* (The Judicial Practice of Fez), with a commentary by Muhammad al-Sijilmāsī (d. 1800), Fez, 1899 (?), 2:325–26. See Manūnī, "The Phenomenon," 85.

140. Henry Toledano, "Sijilmāsī's Manual of Maghribī *'Amal, al-'Amal al-mutlāq*: A Preliminary Examination," *International Journal of Middle East Studies* 5:4 (1974), 484–96, 485n1.

141. *Al-Uqnūm fī mabādi' al-'ulūm* (The Substance of the Principles of the Sciences), Hasaniyya Library of Rabat, 6585.

142. On *Uqnūm* see Jacques Berque, *Ulémas, fondateurs, insurgés du Maghreb. XVIIe siècle*, Paris, Sindbad, 1982, ch. 5, and Stearns, *Revealed Sciences*, 94–95, and 242–45.

143. Manūnī, "The Phenomenon"; Muhammad 'Abd Allāh 'Inān, "From the Legacy of Andalusian and Morisco Literature" (in Arabic), *Ma'had* 16 (1971), 11–19.

144. Thus described by Katherine Park and Lorraine Daston: "It is a genuine mythology, which means it expresses in condensed and sometimes emblematic forms themes too deep to be unsettled by mere facts, however plentiful and persuasive. The Scientific Revolution is a myth about the inevitable rise to global domination of the West, whose cultural superiority is inferred from its cultivation of the values of inquiry that, unfettered by religion or tradition, allegedly produced the sixteenth- and seventeenth-century 'breakthrough to modern science', which holds both proponents and opponents in its thrall." "Introduction: The Age of the New," in Katherine Park and Lorraine Daston, eds., *The Cambridge History of Science*, vol. 3, *Early Modern Science*, Cambridge, Cambridge University Press, 2008, 1–17, 15.

145. Stearns, *Revealed Sciences*, 3–4.

146. Harvey, "The Morisco," 74; James, *"Manual de Artillería,"* and "Al-Andalus in Africa: Some Notes on the Transfer of Technology by the 17th Century Spanish Morisco Refugees to North Africa and the Sahel," *Manuscripta Orientalia* 17:2 (2011), 28–32; Nabil Matar, "Confronting Decline in Early Modern Arabic Thought," *Journal of Early Modern History* 9, 1–2, 51–78, esp. 63–71; Matar, *Europe through Arab Eyes, 1578–1727*, New York, Columbia University Press, 2009, 125–32.

147. *"Manual de Artillería,"* 255, 245.

148. Stearns, *Revealed Sciences,* 3

149. For examples of this trend, see Feza Günergun, "Ottoman Encounters with European Sciences"; Abdeljaouad, Ageron, and Shahidy, "Émergence"; Abdeljaouad and Ageron, "Eastern and Western Instruments"; Ageron, "Mathématiques de la guerre souterraine: Bélidor dans l'Empire ottoman," in E. Barbin, D. Bénard and G. Moussard, eds, *Les mathématiques et le réel,* Rennes, Presses Universitaires de Rennes, 2018, 211–24.

150. On the role of Moriscos and Sephardim, see Oumelbanine Zhiri, "The Task of the Morisco Translator in the Early Modern Maghreb," *Expressions Maghrébines* 15:1 (2016), 11–27. The Moriscos' contributions include a translation of a treatise of arithmetic that some scholars mistakenly attributed to Hajarī; see Pierre Ageron and Hmida Hedfi, "Ibrāhīm al-Balīshtār's Book of Arithmetic (*ca.* 1575); "Hybridizing Spanish Mathematical Treatises with the Arabic Scientific Tradition," *Historia Mathematica* 52 (2020), 26–50.

CONCLUSION

1. *Supporter,* ch. 13, 266e / 291a.

BIBLIOGRAPHY

PRIMARY SOURCES

Manuscripts

Arabe 4213 (untitled), Bibliothèque Nationale de France (BNF).

Duval, Jean-Baptiste, Victor Scialac Accurrensis, and Gabriel Sionita, *Index Latinarum Vocum ex dictionario Arabolatino,* Arabe 4338, BNF.

al-Fāsī, 'Abd al-Rahmān, *al-Uqnūm fī mabādī' al-'ulūm* (The Substance of the Principles of the Sciences), Hasaniyya Library of Rabat, MS 6585.

Ghānim al-Andalusī, Ibrāhīm ibn Ahmad, *Kitāb al-'izz wa al-manāfi' li l-mujāhidīn fī sabīl Allāh bi l-madāfi',* trans. Ahmad al-Hajarī, Algiers, Maktaba Wataniyya, MS 1511.

——, *Kitāb al-'izz wa al-manāfi' li l-mujāhidīn fī sabīl Allāh bi l-madāfi',* trans. Ahmad al-Hajarī, Vienna, Österreichische Nationalbibliothek, MS 1412.

al-Hajarī, Ahmad ibn Qāsim al-Andalusī Afuqay, *Nāsir al-dīn 'alā al-qawm al-kāfirīn* (fragment), BNF, Arabe 7024.

——, letter to Jacob Golius, in MS Persian 913, John Rylands Library, University of Manchester.

——, letter to Thomas Erpenius, in MS Persian 913, John Rylands Library, University of Manchester.

—— et alii, MS D. 565, University of Bologna.

Hubert, Étienne, *Dictionnaire arabic-Latin,* BNF, Arabe 4348.

Ibn Mālik, Muhammad, *Lāmiyyat al-af'āl,* with commentary by Badr al-Dīn ibn Mālik, BNF, Arabe 4119.

al-Jazūlī, Muhammad ibn Sulaymān, *Dalā'il al-khayrāt,* BNF, Arabe 1181.

Leo Africanus / Hasan al-Wazzān, *Libro della cosmographia dell'Affrica,* VE 953, Biblioteca Nazionale Centrale, Rome.

Zacuto, Abraham, and José Vizinho, *al-Risāla al-Zakūtiyya,* trans. Ahmad al-Hajarī, in untitled collection, MS 8184, Hasaniyya Library, Rabat.

Printed Sources

Álava y Viamont, Diego de, *El perfecto capitán instruido en la disciplina militar y nueva ciencia de la artillería,* Madrid, Pedro Madrigal, 1590.

Alcala, Pedro de, *Arte para ligeramente saber la lengua araviga,* Granada, Juan Varela de Salamanca, 1505.

———, *Vocabulista aravigo in letra castellana,* Granada, Juan Varela de Salamanca, 1505.

Ambrogio, Teseo, *Introductio in Chaldaicam linguam, Syriacam, atque Armenicam & decem a-lias linguas,* [Pavia], Giovanni Maria Simoneta, 1539.

Arcos, Thomas d', *Lettres inédites à Peiresc,* Philippe Tamizey de Larroque, ed., *Revue africaine,* 32:189 (1888), 161–95.

al-ʿAyyāshī, Abū Sālim, *Māʾ al-mawāʾīd,* 2 vols., Ahmad Mazīdī ed., Beirut, Dār al-kutub al-ʿilmiyya, 2011.

Bobovius, Albertus, *Topkapi. Relation du sérail du Grand Seigneur,* Annie Berthier and Stéphane Yerasimos, eds., Paris, Sindbad/Actes Sud, 1999.

Bouche, Honoré, *La Chorographie ou description de Provence, et l'histoire chronologique du mesme pays,* vol. 2, Aix, C. David, 1664.

Cespedes y Meneses, Gonzalo de, *Primera parte de la historia de D. Felipe IV Rey de las Españas,* Lisbon, Pedro Craesbeeck, 1631.

Chaufepié, Jacques de, *Nouveau dictionnaire historique et critique pour server de supplement ou de continuation au Dictionnaire historique et critique de Pierre Bayle,* vol. 3, Amsterdam, Pierre de Hondt, 1753.

Chaves, Jeronimo de, *Chronographia o Repertorio de los tiempos,* Lisbon, 1576.

Clénard [Cleynaerts], Nicolas, *Correspondance,* 3 vols., ed. and trans. from Latin into French by Alphonse Roersch, Brussels, Palais des Académies, 1941.

Codazzi, Angela, "Il trattato dell'arte metrica di Giovanni Leone Africano," *Studi orientalistici in onore di Giorgio Levi della Vida,* vol. 1, Rome, Istituto per l'Oriente, 1956.

Collado, Luis, *Plática manual de artillería,* Milan, Pablo Gotardo Poncio, 1592.

Colomiès, Paul, *Mélanges historiques,* Orange, J. Rousseau, 1675.

Cortés de Albacar, Martín, *Breve compendio de la esfera,* Seville, Antón Álvarez, 1551.

Dan, Pierre, *Histoire de Barbarie et de ses corsaires,* Paris, Pierre Rocolet, 1637.

Del Puerto, Francisco, *Mission historial de Marruecos,* Seville, Francisco Garay, 1708.

Duret, Claude, *Thresor de l'histoire des langues de cest univers* (1613), Geneva, Slatkine Reprints, 1972.

Dyāb, Hanna, *D'Alep à Paris, Les pérégrinations d'un jeune Syrien au temps de Louis XIV,* trans. Paule Fahmé-Thierry, Paris, Actes-Sud, 2015.

———, *Min Halab ilā Bāris,* Muhammad Mustafā al-Jārūsh and Abū Shahlā Jibrān, eds., Beirut-Baghdād, Manshūrāt al-jamal, 2017.

——— (Diyāb), *The Book of Travels,* 2 vols., Arabic text ed. Johannes Stephan, English trans. Elias Muhanna, and foreword by Yasmine Beale, New York, New York University Press, 2021.

Erpenius, Thomas, *Orationes tres de Linguarum Ebraeae, atque Arabicae dignitate,* Leiden, 1621.

al-Fārābī, Abū Nasr, *Ihsā' al-'ulūm,* 'Uthmān Muhammad Amīn, ed., Cairo, Matba'at al-Khanjī, 1965.

al-Fāsī, 'Abd al-Rahmān, *al-'Amāl al-fāsī* (The Judicial Practice of Fez), with a commentary by Muhammad al-Sijilmāsī (d. 1800), Fez, 1899(?).

al-Fishtālī, 'Abd al-'Azīz, *Manāhil al-safā,* 'Abd al-Karīm Kurayyim, ed., Rabat, Jam'iyat al-mu'arikhīn al-maghāriba, 2005.

García-Arenal, Mercedes, Fernando Rodríguez Mediano, and Rachid Al Hour, eds., *Cartas marruecas,* Madrid, CSIC, 2002.

Ghānim al-Andalusī, Ibrāhīm ibn Ahmad, *Kitāb al-'izz wa al-rif'a wa al-manāfi'li l-mujāhidīn fī sabīl Allāh bi l-madāfi',* trans. Ahmad al-Hajarī, Ihsān Hindī, ed., Damascus, Markaz al-dirāsāt al-'askariyya, 1995.

al-Hajarī, Ahmad ibn Qāsim al-Andalusī Afuqay, *Nāsir al-dīn 'alā al-qawm al-kāfirīn,* Muhammad Razzūq, ed., Casablanca, Publications of the Faculty of Letters and Human Sciences, 1987.

———, *The Supporter of Religion against the Infidels,* rev. ed., trans., and presentation by P. S. van Koningsveld, Q. al-Samarrai, and G. A. Wiegers, Madrid, CISC, 2015 (1st ed., 1997).

d'Herbelot, Barthélemy, *Bibliothèque orientale,* Paris, Compagnie des Libraires, 1697.

Hottinger, Johann Heinrich, *Bibliothecarius Quadripartitus,* Zurich, Melchior Stauffacher, 1664.

———, *Historia Orientalis,* Zurich, J. J. Bodmer, 1660.

Houtsma, M. Th., "Uit de Oosterche correspondentie van Th. Erpenius, Jac. Golius en Lev. Warner, eene bijdrage tot de geschiedenis van de beofening der oosterche letteren in Nederland," *Verhandelingen der Koninklijke Akademie van wetenschappen,* Amsterdam, Johnnes Müller, 1888, 1–116.

Hues, Robert de, *Tractatus de Globis et eorum usu,* London, T. Dawson, 1594.

Ibn Abī Dinār, *Al-Mu'nis fī akhbār Ifriqiyā wa Tūnis,* Muhammad Shammām, ed., Tunis, al-Maktaba al-'atīqa, 1967.

Ibn al-'Ayyāshī, Muhammad, *Zahr al-bustān,* Ahmad Qaddūr, ed., Rabat, Rabat-Net, 2013.

Ibn al-Qādī, Ahmad, *Durrāt al-hijāl,* Mustafa 'Abd al-Qādir 'Atā, ed., Beirut, Dār al-kutub al-'ilmiyya, 2002.

———, *Jadwat al-iqtibās,* Rabat, Dār al-Mansūr, 1974.

———, *al-Muntaqā al-maqsūr,* ed. and presented by Muhammad Razzūq, Rabat, Maktaba al-ma'ārif, 1986.

Ibn Hamādūsh, 'Abd al-Razzāq, *Rihla,* Abū al-Qāsim Sa'd Allāh, ed., Algiers, al-Mu'assasa al-wataniya li al-funūn al-matba'iyya, 1983.

Ibn Khaldūn, 'Abd al-Rahmān, *al-Muqaddima,* 3 vols., 'Abd al-Salām al-Shaddādī, ed., Casablanca, Bayt al-funūn wa al-'ulūm wa al-adab, 2005.

———, *The Muqaddimah: An Introduction to History; The Classic Islamic History of the World,* trans. and introduced by Franz Rosenthal, abridged and ed. by N. J.

Dawood, with an introduction by Bruce Laurence, Princeton, NJ, Princeton University Press, 2005.

al-Ifrānī, Muhammad, *Nuzhat al-hādī,* A. al-Shadilī, ed., Casablanca, al-Najah, 1998.

———, *Safwat man intashar min akhbār sulaha' al-qarn al-hādi 'ashar,* 'Abd al-Majīd Khayālī, ed., Casablanca, Markaz al-turāth al-thaqafī al-maghribī, 2004.

al-Islāmī, 'Abd al-Haqq, *al-Sayf al-mamdūd fī al-radd 'alā akhbār al-yahūd* (The Outstretched Sword in Refutation of the Jewish Sages), ed. and Spanish trans. by Esperanza Alfonso, Madrid, CSIC, 1998.

Jean Armand Mustapha, *Voyages d'Afrique,* Paris, Nicolas Traboulliet, 1631.

Juan Andrés, *Confusión o confutación de la secta Mahomética y del Alcorán,* Elisa Ruiz García and Isabel García-Monge, eds., Mérida, Editora regional de Extremadura, 2003 (first published in 1515).

———, *Confusion de la secte de Muhamed,* Paris, Martin Le Jeune, 1574 (French trans. by Guy Le Fèvre de la Boderie, of the Italian version of Domingo de Gaztelu).

Kilpatrick, Hilary, and Gerald J. Toomer, eds., "Niqūlāwus al-Halabī (c. 1611–1661): A Greek Orthodox Syrian Copyist and his Letters to Pococke and Golius," *Lias* 43:1 (2016), 1–159.

Lechuga, Cristobal, *Discurso en que trata de la artillería,* Milan, Marco Tulio Malatesta, 1611.

Leo Africanus / Hasan al-Wazzān, *De quelques hommes illustres chez les Arabes et les Hébreux,* ed. and trans. Jean-Louis Déclais and Houari Touati, Paris, Les Belles-Lettres, 2020.

———, "Libellus de Viris quibusdam illustribus apud Arabes," in J. H. Hottinger, ed., *Bibliothecarius Quadripartitus,* Zurich, Melchior Stauffacher, 1664.

Luna, Miguel de, *Almansor the Learned and Victorious King That Conquered Spain,* trans. Robert Ashley, London, Parker, 1627.

———, *Histoire de la conquête d'Espagne par les Mores,* trans. Le Roux, Paris, L. Billaine, 1680.

———, *Historia Verdadera del Rey Don Rodrigo,* Granada, René Rabut, 1592 (part 1) and Granada, Sebastián de Mena, 1600 (part 2).

Malherbe, François de, *Œuvres,* vol. 3, Paris, Hachette, 1863.

al-Manjūr, Ahmad, *Fihris,* Muhammad Hajjī, ed., Rabat, Dār al-Maghrib, 1976.

Mármol Carvajal, Luis del, *Primera parte de la descripción general de Áffrica*, Granada, René Rabut, 1573.

———, *Libro tercero, y segvndo volvmen de la primera parte de la descripción general de Áffrica,* Granada, René Rabut, 1573.

———, *Segvnda parte y libro séptimo de la descripción general de Áffrica,* Málaga, Juan René, 1599.

Marsigli, Luigi, *L'État militaire de l'empire ottoman,* The Hague, Pierre Gosse, Jean Neaulme, De Hondt & Moetjens, 1732.

Mercator, Gerhard, and Jodocus Hondius, *Atlas Minor,* French trans. by Lancelot Voisin de La Popelinière, Amsterdam, Jean Jansson, 1619.

al-Muhibbī, Muhammad Amīn, *Khulāsat al-athar,* 4 vols., Cairo, al-Matbaʻa al-wahbiyya, 1867–68.

Negri, Solomon, *Memoria negriana,* Halle, Impensis Orphanotrophei, 1764.

Núñez Muley, Francisco, *A Memorandum for the President of the Royal Audiencia and Chancery of the City and Kingdom of Granada,* Vincent Barletta, ed. and trans., Chicago, University of Chicago Press, 2007.

Peiresc, Nicolas, *Correspondance de Peiresc avec plusieurs missionaires et religieux de l'ordre des Capucins, 1631–37,* Apollinaire de Valence, ed, Paris, Alphonse Picard, 1892.

———, *Lettres inédites à Thomas d'Arcos,* Fauris de Saint-Vincens, ed., Paris, J-B. Sajou, 1815.

Pellat, Charles, ed., "al-Naquʼa ʻalā al-āla al-jāmiʻa li-l-Rūdānī," *Bulletin d'études orientales* 26 (1973): 7–82.

———, ed. and trans., "L'astrolabe sphérique d'ar-Rūdānī," *Bulletin d'études orientales* 28 (1975): 83–165.

Postel, Guillaume, *De Orbis terræ concordia,* Basel, J. Oporinus, 1544.

Radtmann, Bartholomeus, *Introductio in linguam Arabicam,* Frankfurt, Andreas Eichorn, 1592.

Ramusio, Gian Battista, ed., *Delle Navigationi e Viaggi,* Venice, Giunti, 1550.

Ruscelli, Girolamo, *Precetti della Militia Moderna,* Venice, Heredi di Marchio Seffa, 1568.

Scaliger, Joseph Justus, *The Correspondence of Joseph Justus Scaliger,* vol. 7, Paul Botley and Dirk van Miert, eds., Geneva, Droz, 2012.

Scaligerana, Thuana, Perroniana, Pithoeana, et Colomesiana, ou Remarques historiques, critiques, morales et littéraires, vol. 1, Amsterdam, Covens & Mortier, 1740.

SIHM (Sources inédites de l'histoire du Maroc), Henry de Castries, ed., Archives et Bibliothèques d'Angleterre, vol. 2, Paris and London, Geuthner, and Luzac, 1925.

———, Série Saadienne, Archives et Bibliothèques de France, vol. 3, Henry de Castries, ed., Paris, Leroux, 1911.

———, Série Filalienne, Archives et Bibliothèques de France, vol. 1, Henry de Castries ed., Paris, Leroux, 1922.

———, Archives et Bibliothèques des Pays-Bas, vol. 2, Henry de Castries, ed., Paris, The Hague, Leroux and Martinus Nijhoff, 1907.

———, Archives et Bibliothèques des Pays-Bas, vol. 3, Henry de Castries, ed., Paris, The Hague, Leroux and Martinus Nijhoff, 1912.

———, Archives et Bibliothèques des Pays-Bas, vol. 4, Henry de Castries, ed., Paris, The Hague, Leroux and Martinus Nijhoff, 1913.

Saldanha, António, *Crónica de Almançor, sultão de Marrocos (1578–1603),* António Dias Farinha, ed. and trans. into French, Lisbon, Instituto Inverstigaçào Científica Tropical, 1997.

Sionita, Gabriel [Jibrāʼīl al-Sahyūnī], and Johannes Hesronita [Yūhannā al-Hasrūnī], *Geographia Nubiensis,* Paris, Blageart, 1619.

———, *Grammatica Arabica Maronitarum,* Paris, Blageart, 1616.

Starcweska, Katarzyna, ed., *Latin Translation of the Qur'ān (1518/1621) Commissioned by Egidio da Viterbo: Critical Edition and Case Study,* Wiesbaden, Harrassowitz Verlag, 2018.

al-Sufyānī, Ahmad, *Sinā'at tasfīr al-kutub,* P. Ricard, ed., Paris, Geuthner, 1925.

al-Suktānī, 'Īsā, *Ajwibat al-bādiya,* Yūsuf Amāl, ed., Beirut, Dār al-kutub al-'ilmiyya, 2015.

al-Tarjumān al-Mayurqī, 'Abd Allāh / Anselm Turmeda, *Fray Anselm Turmeda ('Abdallāh al-Tarjumān) y su polémica islamo-cristiana: Edición, traducción y studio de la Tuhfa.* Mikel de Epalza, ed., Madrid, Hiperión, 1994.

Tartaglia, Niccolò, *Metallurgy, Ballistics and Epistemic Instruments: The Nova scientia of Niccolò Tartaglia; A New Edition,* Matteo Valleriani, ed., Edition Open Access, Berlin, Max Planck Institute for the History of Science, 2017.

Teixeira, Pedro, *Relaciones del origen, descendencia y succession de los reyes de Persia y de Harmuz, y de un viage,* Antwerp, H. Verdussen, 1610.

Ufano, Diego de, *Tratado dela artillería,* Brussels, Juan Momarte, 1612.

Vossius, Johannes Gerard, *De Philosophia et Philosophorum Sectis, Libri II,* The Hague, Adrian Vlacq, 1658.

al-Yūsī, Hasan, *Al-Qānūn,* Hamīd Hamānī, ed., Rabat, Matba'a Shāla, 1998.

Zamorano, Rodrigo, *Compendio de la arte de navegar,* Seville, Alonso de la Barrera, 1581.

———, *Cronologia y repertorio de la razon de los tiempos,* Seville, R. de Cabrera, 1594.

Secondary Literature

Abattouy, Mohammed, "The Arabic Science of Weights (*'Ilm al-Athqāl*): Textual Tradition and Significance in the History of Mechanics," in Emilia Calvo et al., eds., *A Shared Legacy: Islamic Science East and West,* Barcelona, Presses of the University of Barcelona, 2008, 83–114.

Abdeljaouad, Mahdi, and Pierre Ageron, "Eastern and Western Instruments in Osman Efendi's *Hadiyyat al-Muhtadī* (The Gift of the Convert)," in Neil Brown, Silke Ackermann, and Feza Günergun, eds., *Scientific Instruments between East and West,* Leiden, Brill, 2019, 16–38.

Abdeljaouad, Mahdi, Pierre Ageron, and Mahmoud Shahidy, "Émergence d'un savoir mathématique euro-islamique: *L'Offrande du converti pour ranimer la flamme éteinte,*" *Philosophia scientiae,* 20:2 (2016), 7–32.

Abun-Nasr, Jamil M., "The Beylicate in Seventeenth-Century Tunisia," *International Journal of Middle East Studies* 6:1 (1975), 70–93.

Ageron, Pierre, "Exemples précoces de traductions scientifiques vers l'arabe en Afrique du Nord," in Mahdi Abdeljaouad and Hmida Hedfi, eds., *Actes du XIIIe colloque maghrébin sur l'histoire des mathématiques arabes,* Tunis, Association Tunisienne des Sciences Mathématiques, 2019, 93–116.

———, "Mathématiques de la guerre souterraine: Bélidor dans l'Empire ottoman," in E. Barbin, D. Bénard, and G. Moussard, eds, *Les mathématiques et le réel,* Rennes, Presses Universitaires de Rennes, 2018, 211–24.

————, "Le rôle des 'renégats' occidentaux dans le transfert des sciences modernes aux pays d'Islam," in Thomas Preveraud, ed., *Circulations savantes entre l'Europe et le monde XVIIe–XXe siècle,* Rennes, Presses Universitaires de Rennes, 2017, 31–58.

Ageron, Pierre, and Hmida Hedfi, "Ibrāhīm al-Balīshtār's Book of Arithmetic (*ca.* 1575): Hybridizing Spanish Mathematical Treatises with the Arabic Scientific Tradition," *Historia mathematica* 52 (2020), 26–50.

Ágoston, Gábor, "Behind the Turkish War Machine: Gunpowder Technology and War Industry in the Ottoman Empire, 1450–1700," in Brett D. Steele and Tamera Dorland, eds., *The Heirs of Archimedes: Science and the Art of War through the Age of Enlightenment,* Cambridge, MA, MIT Press, 2005, 101–33.

————, *Guns for the Sultan: Military Power and the Weapons Industry in the Ottoman Empire,* Cambridge, Cambridge University Press, 2005.

Alleaume, Ghislaine, "Les ingénieurs en Égypte au XIXe siècle, 1820–1020, éléments pour un débat," in Élisabeth Longuenesse, ed., *Bâtisseurs et bureaucrates: Ingénieurs et société au Maghreb et au Moyen-Orient,* Lyon, Maison de l'Orient, 1990, 65–80.

Ash, Eric H., "By Any Other Name: Early Modern Expertise and the Problem of Anachronism," *History and Technology* 35:1 (2019), 3–30.

————, "Expertise and the Early Modern State," *Osiris* 25 (2010), 1–24.

————, ed., *Expertise: Practical Knowledge and the Early Modern State, Osiris* 2:25 (2010).

————, *Power, Knowledge, and Expertise in Elizabethan England,* Baltimore, Johns Hopkins University, 2004.

Aurora, Simone, "Territory and Subjectivity: The Philosophical Nomadism of Deleuze and Canetti," *Minerva: An Open Access Journal of Philosophy* 18 (2014), 1–26.

Babelon, Ernest, *Catalogue des camées antiques et modernes de la Bibliothèque Nationale,* Paris, Leroux, 1897.

Babinski, Paul, "Ottoman Philology and the Origins of Persian Studies in Western Europe: The *Gulistān*'s Orientalist Readers," *Lias* 46:2 (2019), 233–315.

Barrera-Osorio, Antonio, *Experiencing Nature. The Spanish American Empire and the Early Scientific Revolution,* Austin, University of Texas Press, 2006.

Batiffol, Louis, *La Vie intime d'une reine de France au XVIIe siècle: Marie de Médicis,* Paris, Calmann-Lévy, 1906.

————, "Marie de Médicis et les arts—deuxième et dernier article," *La Gazette des beaux-arts* 35:3 (1859), 221–43.

Baumgartner, Frederic J., "The French Reluctance to Adopt Firearms Technology in the Early Modern Period," in Brett D. Steele and Tamera Dorland, eds., *The Heirs of Archimedes: Science and the Art of War through the Age of Enlightenment,* Cambridge, MA, MIT Press, 2005, 73–85.

Behrens-Abouseif, Doris, "*Muhandis, Shād, Mu'allim:* Notes on the Building Craft in the Mamluk Period," *Der Islam* 72 (1995), 293–309.

————, "Une polémique anti-ottomane par un artisan au Caire du XVIIe siècle," in Brigitte Marino, ed., *Études sur les villes du Proche-Orient XVIe-XIXe siècles,* Damascus, Institut Français d'Études Arabes, 2001, 55–63.

Bellosta, Hélène, and Bernard Heyberger, "Abraham Ecchellensis et les *Coniques* d'Apollonius: Les enjeux d'une traduction," in Bernard Heyberger, ed., *Orientalisme, science et controverse: Abraham Ecchellensis (1605–1664),* Turnhout, Brepols, 2010, 191–201.

Benassar, Bartholomé, and Lucille Benassar, *Les Chrétiens d'Allah: L'histoire extraordinaire des renégats, XVIe–XVIIe siècles,* Paris, Perrin, 1989.

Benhima, Yasser, "Le Maroc à l'heure du monde (XVᵉ–XVIIᵉ siècle). Bilan clinique d'une histoire (dé)connectée," *L'Année du Maghreb* 10 (2014), 255–66.

Bennet, Jim, and Stephen Johnston, *The Geometry of War, 1500–1750,* Oxford, Museum of the History of Science, 1996.

Bernabé Pons, Luis, "El Qāḍī 'Iyāḍ en la literature aljamiado-morisca," *Sharq al-Andalus* 14–15 (1997–98), 201–18.

Berque, Jacques, *L'Intérieur du Maghreb XVe–XIXe siècle,* Paris, Gallimard, 1978.

———, *Ulémas, fondateurs, insurgés du Maghreb, XVIIe siècle,* Paris, Sindbad, 1982.

Bertrand, Romain, "The Making of a 'Malay Text': Peter Floris, Erpenius, and Textual Transmission in and out of the Malay World at the Turn of the 17ᵗʰ Century," *Quaderni Storici* 48:142–41 (2013), 141–65.

Betran, Aziz A., *Tobacco Smoking under Islamic Law,* Belstville, Amana Publications, 2003.

Bevilacqua, Alexander, "How to Organize the Orient: D'Herbelot and the *Bibliothèque Orientale,*" *Journal of the Warburg and Courtauld Institutes* 79 (2016), 213–29.

———, *The Republic of Arabic Letters: Islam and the European Enlightenment,* Cambridge, MA, Harvard University Press, 2018.

Binbas, Ilker Evrim, *Intellectual Networks in Timurid Iran: Sharaf al-Dīn 'Alī Yazdī and the Islamicate Republic of Letters,* Cambridge, Cambridge University Press, 2016.

Bobzin, Harmut, "Juan Andrés und sein Buch *Confusion del secta mahomatica* (1515)," *Festgabe für Hans-Rudolf Singer,* Frankfurt, Peter Lang, 1991, 529–48.

Borbone, Pier Giorgio, "'Monsignore Vescovo di Soria,' also Known as Moses of Mardin, Scribe and Books Collector," *Christian Orient* 8:14 (2017), 79–114.

Bouwsma, William J., "Postel and the Significance of Renaissance Cabalism," *Journal of the History of Ideas* 15:2 (1954), 218–32.

Bouzineb, Hossain, *La Alcazaba del Buregreg,* Rabat, Ministry of Culture, 2006.

Bovill, E. W., "Queen's Elizabeth's Gunpowder," *Mariner's Mirror* 33:3 (1947), 179–86.

Boyano Guerra, Isabel, "Al-Hayarī y su traducción del pergamino de la Torre Turpiana," in Manuel Barrios Aguilera and Mercedes García-Arenal, eds, *¿La historia inventada? Los Libros Plúmbeos y el legado sacromontano,* Granada, Editorial Universidad de Granada, 2008, 137–58.

Bradley, Peter T., *The Lure of Peru: Maritime Intrusion into the South Sea, 1598–1701.,* New York, Palgrave Macmillan, 1989.

Brāhim, 'Abd al-Wāhid, *Taghribat Ahmad al-Hajarī (The Exile of Ahmad al-Hajarī),* Cologne and Baghdad, Manshurat al-jamal, 2006.

Brancaforte, Elio, *Visions of Persia: Mapping the Travels of Adam Olearius,* Cambridge, MA, Harvard University Press, 2003.

Brentjes, Sonja, "Early Modern Western European Travellers in the Middle East and Their Reports about the Sciences," in *Travellers from Europe in the Ottoman and Safavid Empires, 16th–17th Centuries: Seeking, Transforming, Discarding Knowledge,* Farnham, Ashgate-Variorum, 2010, 379–420.

———, "The Interests of the Republic of Letters in the Middle East, 1550–1700," *Travellers from Europe in the Ottoman and Safavid Empires, 16th–17th Centuries: Seeking, Transforming, Discarding Knowledge,* Farnham, Ashgate-Variorum, 2010, 435–68.

———, "Learning to Write, Read, and Speak Arabic outside of Early Modern Universities," in Jan Loop, Alastair Hamilton, and Charles Burnett, eds., *The Teaching and Learning of Arabic in Early Modern Europe,* Leiden, Brill, 2017, 252–71.

———, "Peiresc's Interest in the Middle East and Northern Africa in Respect to Geography and Cartography," in *Travellers from Europe in the Ottoman and Safavid Empires, 16th–17th Centuries: Seeking, Transforming, Discarding Knowledge,* Farnham, Ashgate-Variorum, 2010, 1–56.

———, *Teaching and Learning the Sciences in Islamicate Societies (800–1700),* Turnhout, Brepols, 2018.

———, *Travellers from Europe in the Ottoman and Safavid Empires, 16th–17th Centuries: Seeking, Transforming, Discarding Knowledge,* Farnham, Ashgate-Variorum, 2010.

Brioist, Pascal, "L'artillerie à la Renaissance," *Nouvelle revue du XVIe siècle* 20:1 (2002), 79–95.

Brotton, Jerry, *Trading Territories: Mapping the Early Modern World,* Ithaca, NY, Cornell University Press, 1997.

Buchanan, Brenda J., "Salpetre: A Commodity of Empire," in B. Buchanan, ed., *Gunpowder, Explosives, and the State. A Technological History,* Aldershot, Ashgate, 2006, 67–90.

Burge, S. R., *Angels in Islam: Jalāl al-Dīn al-Suyūṭī's al-Habā'ik fī akhbār al-malā'ik,* London, Routledge, 2012.

Burke, Peter, *A Social History of Knowledge from Gutenberg to Diderot,* Cambridge and Oxford, Polity with Blackwell, 2004.

Burman, Thomas E., *Reading the Qur'ān in Latin Christendom, 1140–1560,* Philadelphia, University of Pennsylvania Press, 2007.

Burnett, Charles, s.v. "Astrology," in Kate Fleet et al., eds., *Encyclopaedia of Islam,* 3rd ed., Leiden-Boston, Brill, 2007.

———, "The Coherence of the Arabic-Latin Translation Program in Toledo in the Twelfth Century," *Science in Context* 14:1–2, 249–88.

Burton, Jonathan, *Traffic and Turning: Islam and English Drama, 1579–1624,* Newark, University of Delaware Press, 2005.

Cabanelas, Dario, "El caid marroqui 'Abd al-Karīm ibn Tūda, refugiado en la España de Felipe II," *Miscellanea de estudios arabes y hebraicos,* 12 (1963–64), 75–88.

———, *El Morisco Granadino Alonso del Castillo,* Granada, Patronato de la Alhambra, 1965.

Caillé, Jacques, "La mission à Marrakech du Hollandais Pieter Maertensz. Coy," *Revue d'histoire diplomatique* 86 (1972), 97–123.

Calvo, Emilia, s.v. "Zacuto, Abraham," in Thomas Glick et al., eds., *Medieval Science, Technology, and Medicine, An Encyclopedia,* London, Routledge, 2005, 525–26.

Cardaillac, Louis, "Le passage des Morisques en Languedoc," *Annales du Midi* 5:83 (1971), 259–98.

———, *Morisques et chrétiens: Un affrontement polémique (1492–1640),* Paris, Klincksieck, 1977.

Case, Thomas E., "The Significance of Morisco Speech in Lope's Plays," *Hispania* 65:4 (1982), 594–600.

Catalogue of Manuscripts in the Koprülü Library, vol. 1, Istanbul, Research Centre for Islamic History, Art and Culture, 1986.

Catlos, Brian A., *Muslims of Medieval Latin Christendom, c. 1050–1614,* Cambridge, Cambridge University Press, 2014.

Catlos, Brian A., and Sharon Kinoshita, eds., *Can We Talk Mediterranean? Conversations on an Emerging Field in Medieval and Early Modern Studies,* Cham, Palgrave-Macmillan, 2017.

Casanova, Pascale, *The World Republic of Letters,* trans. M. B. DeBevoise, Cambridge, MA, Harvard University Press, 2004.

Chabas, José, and Bernard R. Goldstein, "Astronomy in the Iberian Peninsula: Abraham Zacut and the Transition from Manuscript to Print," *Transactions of the American Philosophical Society* (2000) 90:2, 1–196.

Chachia, Houssem Eddine, "The Moment of Choice: The Moriscos on the Border of Christianity and Islam," in Claire Norton, ed., *Conversion and Islam in the Early Modern Mediterranean, The Lure of the Other,* New York, Routledge, 2017, 129–54.

———, "The Morisco Ahmad ibn Qāsim al-Hajarī and the Egyptian Manuscript of his *Nāsir al-Dīn ʿalā qawm al-kāfirīn (*The Triumph of Faith over the Nation of Unbelievers)," *Kodex: Jahrbuch des Internationalen Buchwissenschaftlichen Gesellschaft* 8 (2018), 57–71.

———, *The Sephardim and the Moriscos: Their Emigration and Settlement in the Maghrib (1492–1756)* (in Arabic), Abū Dhabī-Beirut, al-Muʾassasa al-ʿarabiyya li al-dirasāt wa al-nashr, 2015.

Champion, Justin, "'I Remember a Mahometan Story of Ahmed Ben Idris': Freethinking Uses of Islam from Stubbe to Toland," *Al-Qantara* 31:2 (2010), 443–80.

Chase, Kenneth, *Firearms. A Global History to 1700,* Cambridge, Cambridge University Press, 2003.

Chauvin, Victor, and Alphonse Roersch, *Étude sur la vie et les travaux de Nicolas Clénard,* Brussels, Hayez, 1900.

Cleaveland, Timothy, "Ahmad Baba al-Timbukti and his Islamic Critique of Racial Slavery in the Maghrib," *Journal of North African Studies* 20:1 (2015), 42–64.

Cockle, Maurice J. D., *A Bibliography of Military Books up to 1642*, London, Holland Press, 1957 (1st ed., 1900).

Coindreau, Roger, "Antoine de Salettes, sieur de Saint-Mandrier: Gentilhomme provençal et aventurier au Maroc," *Hespéris,* 34 (1947), 339–73.

Colin, Gabriel, *Corpus des inscriptions arabes et turques de l'Algérie,* Paris, Leroux, 1901.

Colombo, Emanuele, "A Muslim Turned Jesuit: Baldassare Loyola Mandes (1631–1667)," *Journal of Early Modern History* 17 (2013), 479–504.

Cook, Weston F., *The Hundred Years War for Morocco: Gunpowder and the Military Revolution in the Early Modern Muslim World,* Boulder, CO, Westview Press, 1994.

Cossart, Brice, *Les Artilleurs et la monarchie hispanique (1560–1610),* Paris, Classiques Garnier, 2021.

———, "Traités d'artillerie et écoles d'artilleurs: Interactions entre pratiques d'enseignement et livres techniques à l'époque de Philippe II d'Espagne," in Liliane Hilaire-Pérez et al., eds., *Le Livre technique avant le XXe siècle à l'échelle du monde,* Paris, CNRS Éditions, 2017, 344–53.

Cuomo, Serafina, "Shooting by the Book: Notes on Niccolò Tartaglia's *Nova Scientia,*" *History of Science* 35:2, 1997, 155–88.

Dakhlia, Jocelyne, "Une bibliothèque en filigrane? Eléments de réflexion sur la circulation écrite des langues européennes au Maghreb (XVIe–XVIIIe siècle)," in M. Meouak, P. Sanchez, and A. Vicente, eds., *De los manuscritos medievales a internet: La presencia del arabe vernaculo en las fuentes escritas,* Zaragoza, University of Zaragoza, 2012, 153–75.

Dakhlia, Jocelyne, and Bernard Vincent, eds., *Les Musulmans dans l'histoire de l'Europe,* vol. 1, *Une intégration invisible,* Paris, Albin Michel, 2011.

Dakhlia, Jocelyne, and Wolfgang Kaiser, eds., *Les Musulmans dans l'histoire de l'Europe,* vol. 2, *Passages et contacts en Méditerranée,* Paris, Albin Michel, 2013.

Dalen, Dorrit van, "Johannes Theunisz and 'Abd al-'Azīz: A Friendship in Arabic Studies in Amsterdam, 1609–1610," *Lias* 43:1 (2016), 161–89.

Daniel, Norman, *Islam and the West: The Making of an Image,* Oxford, Oneworld, 1993.

Davis, Natalie Zemon, *Trickster Travels: A Sixteenth-Century Muslim between Worlds,* New York, Hill and Wang, 2006.

Debié, Muriel, "La grammaire syriaque d'Ecchellensis en context," in Bernard Heyberger ed., *Orientalisme, science et controverse: Abraham Ecchellensis (1605–1664),* Turnhout, Brepols, 2010, 99–117.

de Vries, Lourens, "Iang Evangelium Ul-Kadus Menjurat kapada Marcum: The First Malay Gospel of Mark (1629–1630) and the Agama Kumpeni," *Bijdragen tot de Taal-, Land- en Volkendunde* 174:1 (2018), 47–79.

De Groot, A. H., *The Ottoman Empire and the Dutch Republic: A History of the Earliest Diplomatic Relations, 1610–1630,* Leiden, Nederlands Historisch-Archaeologisch Instituut, 1978.

Deleuze, Gilles, and Félix Guattari, *Kafka: Toward a Minor Literature,* trans. Dana Polan, Minneapolis, University of Minnesota Press, 1986.

———, *A Thousand Plateaus: Capitalism and Schizophrenia,* trans. Brian Massumi, 2nd ed., Minneapolis, University of Minnesota Press, 1987.

Dew, Nicholas, *Orientalism in Louis XIV's France,* Oxford, Oxford University Press, 2009.

Dijksterhuis, Fokko Jan, "The Mutual Making of Sciences and Humanities: Willebrord Snellius, Jacob Golius, and the Early Modern Entanglement of Mathematics and Philology," in Rens Bod, Jaap Maat, and Thijs Weststeijn, eds., *The Making of the Humanities,* vol. 3, *From Early Modern to Modern Disciplines,* Amsterdam, Amsterdam University Press, 2012, 73–92.

Dubost, Jean-François, *Marie de Médicis: La reine dévoilée,* Paris, Payot, 2009.

Dursteler, Eric R., "On Bazaars and Battlefields: Recent Scholarship on Mediterranean Cultural Contacts," *Journal of Early Modern History* 15 (2011), 413–34.

Duverdier, Gérald, "Du livre religieux à l'orientalisme: Gibra'īl al Sahyūnī et François Savary de Brèves," in Camille Aboussouan, ed., *Le Livre et le Liban jusqu'à 1900,* Paris, UNESCO, 1982, 159–74.

———, "Savary de Brèves et Ibrahim Müteferrika: Deux drogmans culturels à l'origine de l'imprimerie turque," *Bulletin du Bibliophile* 3 (1987), 322–59.

Dziubinski, Andrzej, "L'armée et la flotte de guerre marocaines à l'époque des sultans de la dynastie saadienne," *Hespéris-Tamuda* 13 (1972), 61–94.

Eamon, William, and Françoise Paheau, "The *Accademia segreta* of Girolamo Ruscelli. A Sixteenth-Century Italian Scientific Society," *Isis* 75:2 (1984), 327–42.

El Alaoui, Youssef, "The Moriscos in France after the Expulsion: Notes for the History of a Minority," in Mercedes García-Arenal and Gerard Wiegers, eds., *The Expulsion of the Moriscos from Spain: A Mediterranean Diaspora,* trans. Consuelo López-Morillas and Martin Beagles, Leiden, Brill, 2014, 239–68.

Elger, Ralf, "Adab and Historical Memory. The Andalusian Poet/Politician Ibn al-Khatīb as Presented in Ahmad al-Maqqarī (986/1577–1041/1632), *Nafh at-Tīb,*" *Die Welt des Islams* 42:3 (2002), 289–306.

El-Rouayheb, Khaled, *Islamic Intellectual History in the Seventeenth Century: Scholarly Currents in the Ottoman Empire and the Maghreb,* Cambridge, Cambridge University Press, 2015.

Elshakry, Marwa S., "Knowledge in Motion: The Cultural Politics of Modern Science Translations in Arabic," *Isis* 99:4 (2008), 701–31.

Epalza, Mikel de, "Le milieu hispano-moresque de l'Évangile islamisant de Barnabé (XVIᵉ–XVIIᵉ siècle)," *Islamochristiana* 8 (1982), 159–83.

Epalza, Mikel de, and Ramon Petit, eds., *Recueil d'études sur les moriscos andalous en Tunisie,* Madrid and Tunis, Dirección General de Relaciones Culturales, Instituto Hispano-Árabe de Cultura; Société Tunisienne de Diffusion, 1973.

Fagnan, Ernest, *Catalogue général des bibliothèques publiques de France,* vol. 18, Paris, Plon, 1893.

al-Fāsī, Muhammad, "Moroccan Travelers and Their Work," *Daʿwat al-Haqq* 2:3 (1958), 19–23 (in Arabic).

Flügel, Gustav, *Die arabischen, persischen und türkischen Handschriften,* vol. 2, Vienna, Kaiserlich-Königliche Hofbibliothek, 1867.

Fuchs, Barbara, *Exotic Nation: Maurophilia and the Construction of Early Modern Spain,* Philadelphia, University of Pennsylvania Press, 2009.

———, *Mimesis and Empire: The New World, Islam, and European Identities,* Cambridge, Cambridge University Press, 2004.

Fuess, Albrecht, "An Instructive Experience: Fakhr al-Dīn's Journey to Italy, 1613–18," in Bernard Heyberger and Carsten-Michael Walbiner, eds., *Les Européens vus par les Libanais à l'époque ottomane,* Beirut, Ergon Verlag, 2002, 23–42.

García-Arenal, Mercedes, ed., *After Conversion: Iberia and the Emergence of Modernity,* Leiden, Brill, 2016.

———, *Messianism and Puritanical Reform: Mahdīs of the Muslim West,* trans. Martin Beagles, Leiden, Brill, 2006.

———, "The Moriscos in Morocco," in Mercedes García-Arenal and Gerard Wiegers, eds., *The Expulsion of the Moriscos from Spain: A Mediterranean Diaspora,* trans. Consuelo López-Morillas and Martin Beagles, Leiden, Brill, 2014, 286–328.

———, "The Religious Identity of the Arabic Language and the Affair of the Lead Books of the Sacromonte," *Arabica* 56 (2009), 495–528.

García-Arenal, Mercedes, and Fernando Rodríguez Mediano, *The Orient in Spain. Converted Muslims, the Forged Lead Books of Granada, and the Rise of Orientalism,* trans. Consuelo Lópe-Morillas, Leiden, Brill, 2013.

García-Arenal, Mercedes, and Katarzyna Starczewska, "'The Law of Abraham the Catholic': Juan Gabriel as Qur'ān Translator for Martín de Figuerola and Egidio da Viterbo," *Al-Qantara* 35:2 (2014), 409–59.

García-Arenal, Mercedes, and Gerard Wiegers, eds., *The Expulsion of the Moriscos from Spain: A Mediterranean Diaspora,* trans. Consuelo López-Morillas and Martin Beagles, Leiden, Brill, 2014.

———, *A Man of Three Worlds: Samuel Pallache, a Moroccan Jew in Catholic and Protestant Europe,* trans. Martin Beagles, Baltimore, Johns Hopkins University Press, 1999.

Gemayel, Nasser, *Les Échanges culturels entre les Maronites et l'Europe, du collège maronite de Rome (1584) au collège de 'Ayn-Warqa (1789),* 2 vols., Beirut, Gemayel, 1984.

Ghobrial, John-Paul, "Archives of Orientalism and its Keepers: Re-imagining the Histories of Arabic manuscripts in Early Modern Europe," *Past and Present* Supplement 11 (2016), 90–111.

———, "The Life and Hard Times of Solomon Negri: An Arabic Teacher in Early Modern Europe," in Jan Loop, Alastair Hamilton, and Charles Burnett, eds., *The Teaching and Learning of Arabic in Early Modern Europe,* Leiden, Brill, 2017, 310–32.

Gilbert, Claire M., *In Good Faith: Arabic Translation and Translators in Early Modern Spain,* Philadelphia, University of Pennsylvania Press, 2020.

Gilliot, Cl., et al., s.v. "'Ulamā'," in P. Bearman et al., eds., *Encyclopaedia of Islam,* 2nd ed., Leiden, Brill, 2012.

Giovannozzi, Giovanni, "La versione borelliana di Apollonio," *Memorie della Pontifica Accademia Romana dei Nuovi Lincei* 2:2 (1916), 1–31.

Girard, Aurélien, "Entre croisade et politique culturelle au Levant: Rome et l'union des chrétiens syriens (première moitié du XVIIe siècle)," in M. A. Visceglia, ed., *Papato e politica internazionale nella prima età moderna,* Rome, Viella, 2013, 419–37.

———, "Introduction," *Dix-Septième Siècle* 67:2 (2015), 385–92.

———, "Quand les Maronites écrivaient en latin: Fauste Nairon et la République des Lettres (seconde moitié du XVIIe siècle)," in Mireille Issa, ed., *Le Latin des Maronites,* Paris, Geuthner, 2017, 45–76.

———, "Teaching and Learning Arabic in Early Modern Rome: Shaping a Missionary Language," in Jan Loop, Alastair Hamilton, and Charles Burnett eds., *The Teaching and Learning of Arabic in Early Modern Europe,* Leiden, Brill, 2017, 189–212.

———, "Was an Eastern Scholar Necessarily a Cultural Broker in Early Modern Europe? Faustus Naironus (1628–1711), the Christian East, and Oriental Studies," in N. Hardy and D. Levitin, eds., *Faith and History: Confessionalisation and Erudition in Early Modern Europe,* Oxford, Oxford University Press, 2019, 240–63.

Girard, Aurélien, and Giovanni Pizzorusso, "The Maronite College in Early Modern Rome: Between the Ottoman Empire and the Republic of Letters," in Liam Chambers and Thomas O'Connor, eds., *College Communities Abroad: Education, Migration, and Catholicism in Early Modern Europe,* Manchester, Manchester University Press, 2018, 174–97.

González de León, Fernando, "'Doctors of the Military Discipline': Technical Expertise and the Paradigm of the Spanish Soldier in the Early Modern Period," *Sixteenth Century Journal* 37:1 (1996), 61–95.

———, *The Road to Rocroi: Class, Culture, and Command in the Spanish Army of Flanders, 1567–1659,* Leiden, Brill, 2009.

Graf, Tobias, *The Sultan's Renegades: Christian-European Converts to Islam and the Making of the Ottoman Elite, 1575–1610,* Oxford, Oxford University Press, 2017.

Grafton, Anthony, *Worlds Made by Words: Scholarship and Community in the Modern West,* Cambridge, MA, Harvard University Press, 2009.

Gran, Peter, *The Islamic Roots of Capitalism: Egypt, 1760–1840,* 2nd ed., Syracuse, NY, Syracuse University Press, 1998.

Grandchamp, Pierre, *La France en Tunisie au début du XVIIe siècle (1601–1610),* vol. 2, Tunis, Société Anonyme de l'Imprimerie Rapide, 1921.

Green, Nile, "The Religious and Cultural Roles of Dreams and Visions in Islam," *Journal of the Royal Asiatic Society* 13:3 (2003), 287–313.

Günergun, Feza, "Ottoman Encounters with European Science: Sixteenth- and Seventeenth-century Translations into Turkish," in Peter Burke and R. Po-chia Hsia, eds., *Cultural Translation in Early Modern Europe,* Cambridge, Cambridge University Press, 2007, 192–211.

Hajjī, Muhammad, *Intellectual Trends in Saʿdī Morocco* (in Arabic), 2 vols., Rabat, Dār al-Maghrib, 1976–78.

———, *The Zāwiya of Dilāʾ and Its Religious, Cultural, and Political Role* (in Arabic), Casablanca, Matbaʿa al-najah al-jadīda, 1988.

al-Hajwī, Muhammad, *The Life and Works of al-Wazzān al-Fāsī* (in Arabic), Rabat, al-Matbaʿa al-iqtisādiya, 1935.

Hamilton, Alastair, "Abraham Ecchellensis et son *Nomenclator Arabico-Latinus*," in Bernard Heyberger, ed., *Orientalisme, science et controverse: Abraham Ecchellensis (1605–1664)*, Turnhout, Brepols, 2010, 89–98.

———, *The Copts and the West, 1430–1822: The European Discovery of the Egyptian Church,* Oxford, Oxford University Press, 2006.

———, "An Egyptian Traveller in the Republic of Letters: Joseph Barbatus or Abudacnus the Copt," *Journal of the Warburg and Courtauld Institutes* 57 (1994), 123–50.

———, "François Savary de Brèves," in David Thomas and John Chesworth, eds., *Christian-Muslim Relations: A Bibliographical History,* vol. 9, *Western and Southern Europe (1600–1700),* Leiden, Brill, 2017, 417–22.

———, "Isaac Casaubon the Arabist: '*Video Longum Esse Ite,*'" *Journal of the Warburg and Courtauld Institutes* 72 (2009), 143–68.

Hamilton, Alastair, and Francis Richard, *André du Ryer and Oriental Studies in Seventeenth-Century France,* London, Arcadian Library and Oxford University Press, 2004.

Hamilton, Alastair, Maurits H. van den Boogert, and Bart Westerweel, eds., *The Republic of Letters and the Levant,* Leiden, Brill, 2005.

Hanna, Nelly, *In Praise of Books: A Cultural History of Cairo's Middle Class, Sixteenth to the Eighteenth Century,* Syracuse, NY, Syracuse University Press, 2003.

———, *Ottoman Egypt and the Emergence of the Modern World, 1500–1800*, Cairo, American University in Cairo Press, 2014.

Harmatta, János, "La coupe de Xusrō et l'origine de la légende du Graal," *Selected Writings: West and East in the Unity of the Ancient World,* Debrecen, Kossuth Egy. K., 2002, 94–110.

Harris, A. Katie, *From Muslim to Christian Granada: Inventing a City's Past in Early Modern Spain,* Baltimore, Johns Hopkins University Press, 2007.

Harvey, L. P., trans., "The Morisco Who Was Muley Zaidan's Spanish Interpreter," *Miscelanea de Estudios Arabes y Hebraicos,* 8:1 (1959), 67–97.

———, *Muslims in Spain, 1500 to 1614,* Chicago, University of Chicago Press, 2005.

———, "A Second Morisco Manuscript at Wadham College, Oxford: A 18.15," *Al-Qantara* 10 (1989), 257–72.

al-Hassan, Ahmad, "Gunpowder Composition for Rockets and Cannon in Arabic Military Treatises in the Thirteenth and Fourteenth Centuries," *Icon* 9 (2003), 1–30.

Heinsen-Roach, Erica, *Consuls and Captives: Dutch-North African Diplomacy in the Early Modern Mediterranean,* Rochester, University of Rochester Press, 2019.

Heltzel, Virgil, "Robert Ashley, Elizabethan Man of Letters," *Huntington Library Quarterly* 10:4 (1947), 349–63.

Henninger-Voss, Mary J., "How the 'New Science' of Cannons Shook up the Aristotelian Cosmos," *Journal of the History of Ideas* 63:3 (2002), 371–97.

Herrera, Jorge Gil, and Luis F. Barnabé Pons, "The Moriscos outside Spain: Routes and Financing," in Mercedes García-Arenal and Gerard Wiegers, eds., *The Expulsion of the Moriscos from Spain: A Mediterranean Diaspora,* trans. Consuelo López-Morillas and Martin Beagles, Leiden, Brill, 2014, 219–38.

Hershenzon, Daniel, *The Captive Sea: Slavery, Communication, and Commerce in Early Modern Spain and the Mediterranean,* Philadelphia, University of Pennsylvania Press, 2018.

———, "Doing Things with Arabic in the Seventeenth-Century Escorial," *Philological Encounters* 4 (2019), 159–81.

———, "Traveling Libraries: The Arabic Manuscripts of Muley Zidan and the Escorial Libraries," *Journal of Early Modern History* 18 (2014), 1–24.

Heyberger, Bernard, "Abraham Ecchellensis dans la République des Lettres," in Bernard Heyberger, ed., *Orientalisme, science et controverse: Abraham Ecchellensis (1605–1664),* Turnhout, Brepols, 2010.

———, *Les Chrétiens du Proche-Orient au temps de la Réforme catholique,* Rome, École Française de Rome, 1994.

———, "Chrétiens orientaux dans l'Europe catholique (XVIIᵉ-XVIIIᵉ siècles)," in Bernard Heyberger and Chantal Verdeil, eds., *Hommes de l'entre-deux: Parcours individuels et portraits de groupes sur la frontière de la Méditerranée (XVIe–XXe siècle),* Paris, Indes Savantes, 2009, 61–93.

———, "L'Islam et les Arabes chez un érudit maronite au service de l'Église catholique (Abraham Ecchellensis)," *Al-Qantara* 31:2 (2010), 481–512.

———, ed., *Orientalisme, science et controverse: Abraham Ecchellensis (1605–1664),* Turnhout, Brepols, 2010.

Hitzel, Frédéric, "Turcs et turqueries à la cour de Catherine de Médicis," in Jocelyne Dakhlia and Bernard Vincent, eds., *Les Musulmans dans l'histoire de l'Europe,* vol. 1, *Une intégration invisible,* Paris, Albin Michel, 2011, 33–54.

'Inān, Muhammad 'Abd Allāh, "From the Legacy of Andalusian and Morisco Literature" (in Arabic), *Ma'had* 16 (1971), 11–19.

Jādūr, Muhammad, *The Institution of the Makhzan in Moroccan History* (in Arabic), Casablanca, Fondation du Roi Abdul-Aziz, 2009.

James, David, "Al-Andalus in Africa. Some Notes on the Transfer of Technology by the 17ᵗʰ Century Spanish Morisco Refugees to North Africa and the Sahel," *Manuscripta Orientalia* 17:2 (2011), 28–32.

———, "The '*Manual de artillería*' of al-Ra'īs Ibrāhīm b. Ahmad al-Andalusī with Particular References to Its Illustrations and Their Sources," *Bulletin of the School of Oriental and African Studies* 41:2 (1978), 237–57.

Jardine, Nicholas, "The Places of Astronomy in Early-Modern Culture," *Journal for the History of Astronomy* 29 (1998), 49–62.

Jolivet, Jean, "Classifications of the Sciences," in Roshdi Rashed and Régis Morelon, eds., *Encyclopedia of the History of Arabic Science,* vol. 3, London, Routledge, 1996, 1008–25.

Jones, Robert, *Learning Arabic in Renaissance Europe (1505–1624)*, Leiden, Brill, 2020.

———, "The Medici Oriental Press (Rome 1584–1614) and the Impact of its Arabic Publications on Northern Europe," in G. A. Russell, ed., *The "Arabick" Interest of the Natural Philosophers in Seventeenth-Century England*, Leiden, Brill, 1994, 88–108.

———, "Piracy, War, and the Acquisition of Arabic Manuscripts in Renaissance Europe," *Manuscripts of the Middle East* 2 (1987), 96–110.

———, "Thomas Erpenius (1584–1624) on the Value of the Arabic Language," *Manuscripts of the Middle East* 1 (1986), 16–25.

Kacimi, Mourad, "Análisi crítico sobre el *Nafh al-Ṭīb min gusn al-Andalus al-ratib* de al-Maqqarī," *Revista Argelina* 7 (2018), 25–48.

Kamen, Henry, *The Spanish Inquisition: A Historical Revision*, 4th ed., New Haven, CT, Yale Unniversity Press, 2014.

Kerlin, Gioia Marie, "A True Mirror of Princes: Defining the Good Governor in Miguel de Luna's *Historia verdadera del Rey Rodrigo*," *Hispanófila* 156 (2009), 13–28.

Keuning, J., "The History of an Atlas: Mercator-Hondius," *Imago Mundi* 4 (1947), 37–62.

Khalil Samir, Samir, "Un Imam égyptien copiste au Vatican, Clemente Caraccioli, 1670–1721," *Parole de l'Orient* 21 (1996), 111–54.

al-Khāṭib, Rashā', *Ahmad ibn Qāsim al-Hajarī al-Andalusī, the Translator, Traveler and Diplomat* (in Arabic), Beirut and Abū Dhabī, al-Mu'assasa al-ʿarabiyya li al-dirasāt wa al-nashr, 2018.

al-Khattābī, Muhammad al-ʿArbī, *Catalogues of the Hasaniyya Library* (in Arabic), vol. 3, Rabat, Hasaniyya Library, 1983.

———, *Catalogues of the Hasaniyya Library* (in Arabic), vol. 4, Rabat, Hasaniyya Library, 1985.

Khayati, Loubna, "Usages de l'œuvre d'Abraham Ecchellensis dans la seconde moitié du XVIIᵉ siècle: Controverses religieuses et histoire critique," in Bernard Heyberger, ed., *Orientalisme, science et controverse: Abraham Ecchellensis (1605–1664)*, Turnhout, Brepols, 2010, 203–13.

Kibédi Varga, A., "Enfin Du Perron vint. Malherbe ou le sens de la publicité," *Revue d'Histoire Littéraire de la France* 67:1 (1967), 1–17.

Kilpatrick, Hilary, "Arabic Private Correspondence from Seventeenth-Century Syria: The Letters to Edward Pococke," *Bodleian Library Record* 23:1 (2010), 20–40.

Kimmel, Seth, *Parables of Coercion: Conversion and Knowledge at the End of Islamic Spain*, Chicago, University of Chicago Press, 2015.

Kinder, A. Gordon, "Religious Literature as an Offensive Weapon: Cipriano de Valera's Part in England's War with Spain," *Sixteenth-Century Journal* 19:2 (1988), 223–35.

Kingra, Mahinder S., "The *Trace Italienne* and the Military Revolution during the Eighty-Years' War, 1567–1648," *Journal of Military History* 57:3 (1993), 431–46.

Koningsveld, Pieter van, "'Mon Kharuf': Quelques remarques sur le maître tunisien du premier arabisant néerlandais, Nicolas Clénard (1493–1542)," in Abdelmejid Temimi, ed., *Nouvelles approches des relations islamo-chrétiennes à l'époque de la Renaissance,* Zaghouan, FTERSI, 2000, 123–41.

Koningsveld, Pieter van, and Gerald Wiegers, "The Parchment of the 'Torre Turpiana': The Original Document and Its Early Interpreters," Al-Qantara 24:2 (2003), 327–58.

Kriegel, Maurice, and Sanjay Subrahmanyam, "The Unity of Opposites: Abraham Zacut, Vasco de Gama and the Chronicler Gaspar Correia," in A. Disney and E. Booth, eds., *Vasco de Gama and the Linking of Europe and Asia,* Oxford, Oxford University Press, 2000, 48–71.

Krieken, Gérard van, *Corsaires et marchands: Les relations entre Alger et les Pays-Bas 1604–1830,* Paris, Bouchêne, 2002.

Krstic, Tijana, *Contested Conversions to Islam: Narratives of Religious Change in Early Modern Europe,* Palo Alto, CA, Stanford University Press, 2011.

———, "The Elusive Intermediaries: Moriscos in Ottoman and Western European Diplomatic Sources from Constantinople, 1560s–1630s," *Journal of Early Modern History* 19 (2015), 129–51.

———, "Islam and Muslims in Europe," in *The Oxford Handbook of Early Modern European History, 1350–1750,* vol. 1, *Peoples and Place,* Hamish Scott, ed., Oxford, Oxford University Press, 2015.

Kurayyim, 'Abd al-Karīm, *Morocco under the Sa'dī Dynasty* (in Arabic), 2nd ed., Rabat, Jam'iya al-mu'arikhīn al-maghāriba, 2006.

Laffan, Michael, *The Makings of Indonesian Islam: Orientalism and the Narration of a Sufi Past,* Princeton, NJ, Princeton University Press, 2011.

Lazarus-Yafeh, Hava, *Intertwined Worlds: Medieval Islam and Bible Criticism,* Princeton, NJ, Princeton University Press, 1992.

Lecarpentier, Bénédicte, "La Reine diplomate: Marie de Médicis et les cours italiennes," in Isabelle Poutrin and Marie-Karine Schaub, eds., *Femmes et pouvoir politique: Les princesses d'Europe XVe–XVIIIe siècle,* Rosny-sous-Bois, Éditions Bréal, 2007, 182–92.

Lemos Horta, Paulo, *Marvellous Thieves. Secret Authors of the Arabian Nights,* Cambridge, MA, Harvard University Press, 2017.

Lentin, Jérôme, "Unité and diversité du moyen arabe au Machreq et au Maghreb: Quelques données d'après des textes d'époque tardive (16ème–19ème siècles)," in Jérôme Lentin and Jacques Grand'Henry, eds., *Moyen arabe et variétés mixtes de l'arabe à travers l'histoire,* Louvain, Université Catholique, 2008, 305–19.

Le Vacher de Boisville, Dast, *Liste générale et alphabétique des membres du Parlement de Bordeaux,* Bordeaux, Gounouilhou, 1896.

Levi della Vida, Giorgio, *Ricerche sulla formazione del più antico fondo dei manoscritti orientali della Biblioteca Vaticana,* Vatican City, Biblioteca Apostolica Vaticana, 1939.

Lewis, Martin W., and Karen E. Wigen, *The Myth of Continents: A Critique of Metageography,* Berkeley, University of California Press, 1997.

Liebrenz, Boris, "Golius and Tychsen and their Quest for Manuscripts: Three Arabic Letters," *Journal of Islamic Manuscripts* 8 (2017), 218–39.

Long, Pamela O., *Artisans/Practitioners and the Rise of the New Sciences, 1400–1600,* Corvallis, Oregon University Press, 2011.

———, *Openness, Secrecy, Authorship: Technical Arts and the Culture of Knowledge from Antiquity to the Renaissance,* Baltimore, Johns Hopkins University Press, 2001.

Longuenesse, Élisabeth, ed., *Bâtisseurs et bureaucrates: Ingénieurs et société au Maghreb et au Moyen-Orient,* Lyon, Maison de l'Orient, 1990.

Loop, Jan, *Johann Heinrich Hottinger: Arabic and Islamic Studies in the Seventeenth Century,* Oxford, Oxford University Press, 2013.

Loop, Jan, Alastair Hamilton, and Charles Burnett, eds., *The Teaching and Learning of Arabic in Early Modern Europe,* Leiden, Brill, 2017.

López-Morillas, Consuelo, "The Genealogy of the Spanish Qur'ān," *Journal of Islamic Studies* 17:3 (2006), 255–94.

———, "Lost and Found? Yça de Segovia and the Qur'ān among the Mudejars and Moriscos," *Journal of Islamic Studies* 10:3 (1999), 277–92.

Lowe, Dunstan, "Suspending Disbelief: Magnetic and Miraculous Levitation from Antiquity to the Middle Ages," *Classical Antiquity* 35:2 (2016), 247–78.

al-Mahnāwī, Muhammad, "Firearms in Morocco under the Wattāsī Dynasty," in Muhammad Istītū, ed., *Morocco under the Wattāsī Dynasty According to Hasan al-Wazzān's "Description of Africa"* (in Arabic), Rabat, Jamʿiya Hasan al-Wazzān, 2011, 151–60.

Malcolm, Noel, "Comenius, Boyle, Oldenburg, and the Translation of the Bible into Turkish," *Church History and Religious Culture* 87:3 (2007), 327–62.

Mann, Jesse D., "Throwing the Book at Them: Juan de Segovia's Use of the Qur'ān," *Revista Española de Filosofía Medieval* 26:1 (2019), 79–96.

Manstetten, Paula, "Solomon Negri: The Self-Fashioning of an Arab Christian in Early Modern Europe," in Cornel Zwirlein, ed., *The Power of the Dispersed: Early Modern Global Travelers beyond Integration,* Leiden, Brill, 2021, 240–82.

al-Manūnī, Muhammad, *History of Moroccan Bookmaking* (in Arabic), Rabat, Press of Muhammad V University, 1991.

———, "The Phenomenon of Translation into Arabic in Saʿdī Morocco" (in Arabic), *Daʿwat al-Haqq* 10:3, 74–91.

———, "The Production of Firearms in Morocco," *Selected Studies* (in Arabic), Rabat, Ministry of Culture, 2000, 245–56.

Martínez Medina, Francis Javier, "La inmaculada concepción en los libros plúmbeos de Granada: Su influjo en el catolicismo contrarreformista," *Magallánica: Revista de Historia Moderna* 3:5 (2016), 6–47.

Marquez Villanueva, Francisco, "La voluntad de leyenda de Miguel de Luna," *Nueva Revista de Filología Hispánica* 30:2 (1981), 359–95.

Massignon, Louis, *Le Maroc dans les premières années du XVIème siècle, Tableau géographique d'après Léon l'Africain,* Algiers, Adolphe Jourdan, 1906.

Matar, Nabil, *Britain and Barbary, 1589–1689,* Gainesville, University Press of Florida, 2005.

———, "Confronting Decline in Early Modern Arabic Thought," *Journal of Early Modern History* 9, 1–2 (2005), 51–78.

———, *Europe through Arab Eyes, 1578–1727*, New York, Columbia University Press, 2009.

———, *In the Lands of the Christians: Arabic Travel Writing in the Seventeenth Century,* New York, Routledge, 2003.

———, *Mediterranean Captivity through Arab Eyes, 1517–1798*, Leiden, Brill, 2020.

Mejdell, Gunvor, "Changing Norms, Concepts, and Practices of Written Arabic: A 'Long Distance' Perspective," in Jacob Høigilt and Gunvor Mejdell, eds., *The Politics of Written Language in the Arab World: Writing Change,* Leiden, Brill, 2017, 68–89.

Meziane, Leila, *Salé et ses corsaires, 1666–1727: Un port de course marocain au XVIIe siècle,* Caen, Presses Universitaires, 2007.

Michel, Francisque, *Histoire des races maudites de la France et de l'Espagne,* vol. 2, Paris, Franck, 1847.

Miller, Peter N., "Making the Paris Polyglot Bible: Humanism and Orientalism in the Early Seventeenth Century," Herbert Jaumann, ed., *Die europäische Gelehrtenrepublik im Zeitalter des Konfessionalismus,* Wiesbaden, Harrassowitz Verlag, 2001, 59–85.

———, "Peiresc and the Study of Islamic Coins in the Early Seventeenth Century," reprint in *Peiresc's Orient: Antiquarianism as Cultural History in the Seventeenth Century,* Farnham, Ashgate-Variorum, 2012, 103–57.

———, *Peiresc's Mediterranean World,* Cambridge, MA, Harvard University Press, 2015.

Mills, Simon, *A Commerce of Knowledge: Trade, Religion, and Scholarship between England and the Ottoman Empire, c. 1600–1760,* Oxford, Oxford University Press, 2020.

———, "Learning Arabic in the Overseas Factories: The Case of the English," in Jan Loop, Alastair Hamilton and Charles Burnett, eds., *The Teaching and Learning of Arabic in Early Modern Europe,* Leiden, Brill, 2017, 272–93.

Missoum, Sakina, "Andalusi Immigration and Urban Development in Algiers (Sixteenth and Seventeenth Centuries)," in Mercedes García-Arenal and Gerard Wiegers, eds., *The Expulsion of the Moriscos from Spain: A Mediterranean Diaspora,* Consuelo López-Morillas and Martin Beagles, trans., Leiden, Brill, 2014, 329–56.

Molinié, Antoinette, "Les deux corps de la Reine et ses substituts: La souveraineté d'une Vierge andalouse," *Archives de Sciences Sociales de la Religion* 161 (2013), 269–91.

Monneret de Villard, Ugo, *Lo studio dell' Islam in Europa nel XII e nel XIII secolo,* Vatican City, Biblioteca Apostolica Vaticana, 1944.

Mulsow, Martin, "Socianism, Islam, and the Radical Uses of Arabic Scholarship," *Al-Qantara* 31:2 (2010), 549–86.

al-Musawi, Muhsin J., *The Medieval Islamic Republic of Letters: Arabic Knowledge Construction,* Notre Dame, IN, University of Notre Dame Press, 2015.

al-Nāsirī, Ahmad, *Kitāb al-Istiqsā,* vol. 5, Muhammad Hajjī, Ibrāhīm Abū Tālib, and Ahmad al-Tawfīq, eds., Casablanca, Ministry of Culture, 2001.

Noble, Thomas F. X. "Why Pope Joan?" *Catholic Historical Review* 49:2 (2013), 219–38.

Olender, Maurice, *Les Langues du Paradis, Aryens et Sémites, un couple providentiel,* Paris, Gallimard-Le Seuil, 1989.

Oliver Asín, Jaime, "Ahmad al-Hayarī Bejarano: Apuntes biográphicos de un Morisco notable residente en Marruecos," *Conferencias y apuntes inéditos,* Madrid, Agencia Española de Cooperación Internacional, 1996, 151–64.

———, "Noticias de Bejarano en Granada," *Conferencias y apuntes inéditos,* Madrid, Agencia Española de Cooperación Internacional, 1996, 127–50.

———, "Un Morisco de Tùnez, admirador de Lope," *Al-Andalus* 1:2 (1933), 409–50.

———, *Vida de Don Felipe de Africa, Principe de Fez y Marruecos (1566–1621),* Granada, Editorial Universidad de Granada, 1955.

Park, Katherine, and Lorraine Daston, "Introduction: The Age of the New," in Katherine Park and Lorraine Daston, eds., *The Cambridge History of Science,* vol. 3, *Early Modern Science,* Cambridge, Cambridge University Press, 2008, 1–17.

Parr, Adrian ed., *The Deleuze Dictionary,* New York, Columbia University Press, 2005.

Parra Pérez, María José, "Estudio y edición de las traducciones al árabe del Almanach perpetuum de Abraham Zacuto," PhD diss., Department of Semitic Philology, University of Barcelona, 2013.

Penella Roma, Juan, "Introduction au manuscrit D. 565 de la Bibliothèque Universitaire de Bologne," in Mikel de Epalza and Ramon Petit, eds, *Recueil d'études sur les moriscos andalous en Tunisie,* Madrid and Tunis, Dirección General de Relaciones Culturales, Instituto Hispano-Árabe de Cultura; Société Tunisienne de Diffusion, 1973, 258–63.

Pérez-Mallaína, Pablo E., *Spain's Men of the Sea: Daily Life on the Indies Fleets in the Sixteenth Century,* trans. Carla Rahn Phillips, Baltimore, Johns Hopkins University, 1998.

Piechocki, Katharina N., *Cartographic Humanism: The Making of Early Modern Europe,* Chicago, University of Chicago Press, 2019.

Pizzorusso, Giovanni, "Les écoles de langue arabe et le milieu orientaliste," in Bernard Heyberger, ed., *Orientalisme, science et controverse: Abraham Ecchellensis (1605–1664),* Turnhout, Brepols, 2010, 59–80.

———, "Tra cultura e missione: La congregazione de *Propaganda fide* e le scuole di lingua araba nel XVII secolo," in Antonella Romano, ed., *Rome et la science moderne,* Rome, École Française, 2008, 121–52.

Portundo, María M., "Cosmography at the *Casa, Consejo,* and *Corte* during the Century of Discovery," in Daniela Bleichmar et al., eds., *Science in the Spanish and Portuguese Empires, 1500–1800,* Palo Alto, CA, Stanford University Press, 2009, 57–77.

———, *Spanish Cosmography and the New World,* Chicago, University of Chicago Press, 2009.

Pouillon, François, ed., *Léon L'Africain,* Paris, Karthala–IISMM, 2009.

Pratt, Mary Louise, "Arts of the Contact Zone," *Profession* 1991, 33–40.

al-Qaddūrī, ʿAbd al-Majīd, *Moroccan Ambassadors in Europe, 1922–1610* (in Arabic), Rabat, Publications of the Faculty of Letters and Human Sciences, 1995.

Rabbat, Nasser, "Architects and Artists in Mamluk Society: The Perspective from the Sources," *Journal of Architectural Education* 52:1 (1998), 30–37.

Ramachandran, Ayesha, "A War of Worlds: Becoming 'Early Modern' and the Challenge of Comparison," in David Porter, ed., *Comparative Early Modernities, 1100–1800*, New York, Palgrave-Macmillan, 2012, 15–46.

———, *The Worldmakers: Global Imagining in Early Modern Europe,* Chicago, University of Chicago Press, 2015.

Raphael, Pierre, *Le Rôle du collège maronite romain dans l'orientalisme aux XVIIe et XVIIIe siècles,* Beirut, Presses de l'Université Saint Joseph, 1950.

Rauchenberger, Dietriech, *Leo der Afrikaner,* Wiesbaden, Harrassowitz Verlag, 1999.

Razali, W. M. F. A. W., et al., "The Fourth Source: *Isrāʾīliyyāt* and the Use of the Bible in Muslim scholarship," in Daniel J. Crowther et al., eds., *Reading the Bible in Islamic Context. Qurʾanic Conversations,* London, Routledge, 2018, 103–15.

Razzūq, Muhammad, *The Andalusians and Their Emigration to Morocco, 16–17*th *centuries* (in Arabic), Casablanca, Afrique-Orient, 1997.

Reimann, Caren, "Ferdinando de Medici and the *Typographia Medicea*," in Nina Lamal, Jamie Cumby, and Helmer J. Helmers, eds., *Print and Power in Early Modern Europe (1500–1800),* Leiden, Brill, 2021, 220–38.

Reynolds, Dwight F., ed., *Interpreting the Self: Autobiography in the Arabic Literary Tradition,* Berkeley, University of California Press, 2001.

———, "Shaykh ʿAbd al-Wahhāb al-Shaʿrānī's Sixteenth-Century Defense of Autobiography," *Harvard Middle Eastern and Islamic Review* 4:1–2 (1997–98), 122–37.

Rietbergen, Pieter J. A. N., "A Maronite Mediator between Seventeenth-Century Mediterranean Cultures: Ibrāhīm al-Hākilānī, or Abraham Ecchellense (1605–1664) between Christendom and Islam," *LIAS* 16:1 (1989), 13–41.

Rodríguez Mediano, Fernando, "Fragmentos de orientalismo español del s. XVII," *Hispania* (2006), 243–76.

Römer, Claudia, "An Ottoman Copyist Working for Sebastian Tengnagel, Librarian at the Vienna Hoftbibliothek, 1608–1636," *Archiv Orientální* 7 (1998), 331–50.

Rooden, Peter T. van, *Theology, Biblical Scholarship, and Rabbinical Studies in the Seventeenth Century,* Leiden, Brill, 1989.

Root, Deborah, "Speaking Christian: Orthodoxy and Difference in Sixteenth-Century Spain," *Representations* 23 (1988), 118–34.

Rosenberger, Bernard, and Hamid Triki, "Famines et épidémies au Maroc aux XVIe et XVIIe siècles" (part 1), *Hespéris-Tamuda* 14 (1973), 109–75.

Roth, Ulli, "Juan of Segovia's Translation of the Qurʾān," *Al-Qantara* 35:2 (2014), 555–78.

Rothman, E. Natalie, "Dragomans and 'Turkish Literature': The Making of a Field of Inquiry," *Oriente Moderno,* new series 93:2 (2013), 390–421.

————, *The Dragoman Renaissance: Diplomatic Interpreters and the Routes of Orientalism,* Ithaca, NY, Cornell University Press, 2021.

Saavedra, Eduardo, "Índice general de la literature aljamiada," *Memorias de la Real Academia Española* 6 (1889), 237–320, 287–89.

Said, Edward H., *Orientalism,* London, Penguin Books, 2003 (1st ed., 1978).

Sajdi, Dana, *The Barber of Damascus: Nouveau Literacy in the Eighteenth-Century Ottoman Levant,* Stanford, CA, Stanford University Press, 2013.

Saliba, George, "Artisans and Mathematicians in Medieval Islam," *Journal of the American Oriental Society* 119:4 (1999), 637–45.

Salibi, Kamal S., "The Maronites of Lebanon under Frankish and Mamluk Rule," *Arabica* 4 (1957), 288–303.

————, "The Secret of the House of Ma'n," *International Journal of Middle East Studies* 4 (1973), 272–87.

Samsó, Julio, "Abraham Zacut and José Vizinho's *Almanach Perpetuum* in Arabic (16th–19th c.)," *Centaurus* 46 (2004), 82–97.

Santoni, Pierre, "Le passage des Morisques en Provence (1610–1613)," *Provence Historique* 185 (1996), 333–83.

Sarnelli Cerqua, Clelia, "La fuga in Marocco di al-Shihāb Ahmad al-Andalusī," *Studi Magrebini* 1 (1966), 215–229.

————, "Al-Hajarī in Andalusia," *Studi Magrebini* 3 (1970), 161–203.

————, "Lo scrittore ispano-marochino al-Hajarī e il suo *Kitāb Nāsir al-Dīn,*" in *Atti del III Congreso di Studi Arabici e Islamici,* Ravello, Istituto Universitario Orientale, 1966, 597–614.

Sayyid, Fu'ād, *Fihrist al-makhtūtāt,* vol. 2, Cairo, Dār al-kutub, 1963.

Schaefer, Donovan O., *Religious Affects: Animality, Evolution, and Power,* Durham, NC, Duke University Press, 2015.

Schmidt, Jan, "Between Author and Library Shelf: The Intriguing History of Some Middle Eastern Manuscripts Acquired by Public Collections in the Netherlands Prior to 1800," in Alastair Hamilton, Maurits H. van den Boogert, and Bart Westerweel, eds., *The Republic of Letters and the Levant,* Leiden, Brill, 2005, 27–51.

————, *Catalogue of Turkish Manuscripts in the Library of Leiden University and Other Collections on the Netherlands: Minor Collections,* Leiden, Brill, 2012.

————, "An Ostrich Egg for Golius: The John Rylands Library MS Persian 913 and the History of the Early Modern Contacts between the Dutch Republic and the Islamic World," *The Joys of Philology: Studies in Ottoman Literature, History, and Orientalism (1500–1923),* vol. 2, Istanbul, Isis Press, 2002, 9–74.

Secord, James, "Knowledge in Transit," *Isis* 95:4 (2004), 654–72.

Secret, François, *L'Ésotérisme de Guy Le Fèvre de La Boderie,* Geneva, Droz, 1969.

————, "Guillaume Postel et les études arabes à la Renaissance," *Arabica* 9 (1962), 21–36.

————, *Les Kabbalistes chrétiens de la Renaissance,* Paris, Dunod, 1963.

Seed, Pat, "Celestial Navigation: The First Translational Science," in Patrick Manning and Abigail Owen, eds., *Knowledge in Translation: Global Patterns of*

Scientific Exchange, 1000–1800 CE, Pittsburgh, University of Pittsburgh Press, 2018, 275–91.

Seigworth, Gregory J., and Melissa Gregg, "An Inventory of Shimmers," in G. J. Seigworth and M. Gregg, eds., *Affect Theory Reader*, Durham, NC, Duke University Press, 2010, 1–25.

Smith, Pamela H., *The Body of the Artisan: Art and Experience in the Scientific Revolution*, Chicago, University of Chicago Press, 2004.

Soesilo, Daud, "Celebrating 400 years of Ruyl's Malay Translation of Matthew's Gospel," *Bible Translator* 64:2 (2013), 173–84.

Soto, Teresa, and Katarzyna Starcweska, "Authority, Philology, and Conversion under the Aegis of Martín García," in Mercedes García-Arenal, ed., *After Conversion: Iberia and the Emergence of Modernity*, Leiden, Brill, 2016, 199–228.

Stearns, Justin, *Revealed Sciences: The Natural Sciences in Islam in Seventeenth-Century Morocco*, Cambridge, Cambridge University Press, 2021.

———, "Science, Secondary Causation, and Reason in the Early Modern Ottoman Empire and Morocco: Al-Yūsī and his Students," *Proceedings of the International Congress on the Maghreb and the Western Mediterranean in the Ottoman Era*, Istanbul, IRCICA, 2013, 43–52.

Steele, Brett D., and Tamera Dorland, eds., *The Heirs of Archimedes: Science and the Art of War through the Age of Enlightenment*, Cambridge, MA, MIT Press, 2005.

Stivale, Charles J., ed., *Gilles Deleuze: Key Concepts*, Montreal, McGill-Queen's University Press, 2005.

Stolzenberg, Daniel, "Une collaboration dans la *cosmopolis* catholique: Abraham Ecchellensis et Athanasius Kircher," in Bernard Heyberger, ed., *Orientalisme, science et controverse: Abraham Ecchellensis (1605–1664)*, Turnhout, Brepols, 2010, 81–88.

Subrahmanyam, Sanjay, "Connected Histories: Notes toward a Reconfiguration of Early Modern Eurasia," *Modern Asian Studies* 31:3 (1997), 735–62.

———, *Courtly Encounters: Translating Courtliness and Violence in Early Modern Eurasia*, Cambridge, MA, Harvard University Press, 2012.

———, *Empires between Islam and Christianity, 1500–1800*, Albany, State University of New York Press, 2019.

———, "Intertwined Histories: 'Crónica' and 'Tā'rikh' in the Sixteenth-Century Indian Ocean World," *History and Theory* 49:4 (2010), 118–45.

Sumira, Sylvia, *Globes: 400 Years of Exploration, Navigation, and Power*, Chicago, University of Chicago Press, 2014.

Swart, Eric, "'Qualifications, Knowledge, and Courage': Dutch Military Engineers, c. 1550–c. 1660," in Bruce P. Lenman, ed., *Military Engineers and the Development of the Early-Modern State*, Dundee, Dundee University Press, 2013, 47–70.

Szpiech, Ryan, *Conversion and Narrative: Reading and Religious Authority in Medieval Polemic*, Philadelphia, University of Pennsylvania Press, 2013.

————, "A Witness of Their Own Nation: On the Influence of Juan Andrés," in Mercedes García-Arenal ed., *After Conversion: Iberia and the Emergence of Modernity*, Leiden, Brill, 2016, 174–98.

Tageldin, Shaden M., *Disarming Words: Empire and the Seductions of Translation in Egypt*, Berkeley, University of California Press, 2011.

Terzioglu, Derin, "Where *'Ilm-I Hāl* Meets Catechism: Islamic Manuals of Religious Instruction in the Ottoman Empire in the Age of Confessionalization," *Past and Present* 220 (2013): 79–114.

Thuilier, Guy, "Un 'politique' au XVIIᵉ siècle: Savary de Brèves (1560–1628)," *La Revue Administrative* (2009) 62:68, 124–29.

Tinto, Alberto, *La tipografia medicea orientale*, Lucca, Fazzi, 1987.

Toledano, Henry, "Sijilmāsī's Manual of Maghribī *'Amal, al-'Amal al-mutlāq*: A Preliminary Examination," *International Journal of Middle East Studies* 5:4 (1974), 484–96.

Tommasino, Pier Mattia, "Bulghaith al-Darawi and Barthélemy d'Herbelot: Readers of the Qur'ān in Seventeenth Century Tuscany," *Journal of Qur'ānic Studies* 20:3 (2018), 94–120.

————, "Lire et traduire le Coran dans le grand-duché de Toscane," *Dix-Septième Siècle* 268 (2015), 459–80.

————, "*Per l'italiano odeporico europeo:* Il Serai Enderun di Alberto Bobovio (1665)," *Carte di Viaggio* 4 (2011), 109–22.

————, "Textual Agnogenesis and the Polysemy of the Reader: Early Modern European Readings of Qur'ānic Embryology," in Mercedes García-Arenal, ed., *After Conversion: Iberia and the Emergence of Modernity*, Leiden, Brill, 2016, 155–73.

Toomer, Gerald J., *Eastern Wisdom and Learning: The Study of Arabic in Seventeenth-Century England*, Oxford, Clarendon Press, 1996.

————, "Ravius in the East," in Jan Loop and Jill Kraye, eds., *Scholarship between Europe and the Levant: Essays in Honour of Alastair Hamilton*, Leiden, Brill, 2020, 110–27.

al-Turkī, 'Abd al-Majīd, "Documents of the Last Morisco Emigration to Tunisia" (in Arabic), *Hawliyyāt al-jāmi'a al-tūnsiyya* 4 (1967), 23–82, 64–69.

Verdera Franco, Leoncio, "La evolución de la artillería en los siglos XVII y XVIII," in Alicia Cámara, ed., *Los ingenieros militares de la monarquía hispánica en los siglos XVII y XVIII*, Madrid, Ministerio de Defensa; Asociación Española de Amigos de los Castillos; Centro de Estudios Europa Hispánica, 2005, 113–30.

Vérin, Hélène, *La Gloire des ingénieurs: L'intelligence technique du XVIe au XVIIIe siècle*, Paris, Albin-Michel, 1993.

Vers l'Orient . . . (exhibition catalogue), Paris, Bibliothèque Nationale, 1983.

Versteegh, Kees, ed., *Encyclopedia of Arabic Language and Linguistics*, 5 vols., Leiden, Brill, 2006–11.

Villanueva Zubizarreta, Olatz, "The Moriscos in Tunisia," in Mercedes García-Arenal and Gerard Wiegers, eds., *The Expulsion of the Moriscos from Spain: A Mediterranean Diaspora*, trans. Consuelo López-Morillas and Martin Beagles, Leiden, Brill, 2014, 357–88.

Vincent, Bernard, "Les Morisques d'Estrémadure au XVIe siècle," *Annales de Démographie Historique* (1974), 431–48.

Vrolijk, Arnoud, "The Prince of Arabists and His Many Errors: Thomas Erpenius's Image of Joseph Scaliger and the Edition of the 'Proverbia Arabica' (1614)," *Journal of the Warburg and Courtauld Institutes* 73 (2010), 297–325.

———, "Scaliger and the Dutch Expansion in Asia: An Arabic Translation for an Early Voyage to the East Indies (1600)," *Journal of the Warburg and Courtauld Institutes* 78 (2015), 277–309.

Vrolijk, Arnoud, and Richard van Leeuwen, *Arabic Studies in the Netherlands: A Short History in Portraits, 1580–1950*, trans. Alastair Hamilton, Leiden, Brill, 2014.

Wacks, David, *Medieval Iberian Crusade Culture and the Mediterranean World*, Toronto, University of Toronto Press, 2019.

Walton, Steven A., "The Art of Gunnery in Renaissance England," PhD diss., Institute for the History and Philosophy of Science and Technology, University of Toronto, 1999.

———, "Mathematical Instruments and the Creation of the Scientific Military Gentleman," in Steven A. Walton, ed., *Instrumental at War: Science, Research, and Instruments between Knowledge and the World*, Leiden, Brill, 2005, 17–46.

———, "State Building through Building for the State: Foreign and Domestic Expertise in Tudor Fortification," *Osiris* 2:25 (2010), 66–84.

———, "Technologies of Pow(d)er: Military Mathematical Practitioners' Strategies and Self-Presentation," in Lesley B. Cormack, Steven A. Walton, and John A. Schuster, eds., *Mathematical Practitioners and the Transformation of Natural Knowledge in Early Modern Europe*, Cham, Springer, 2017, 87–113.

Weiner, Jerome Bruce, "Fitna, Corsairs, and Diplomacy: Morocco and the Maritime States of Western Europe, 1603–1672," PhD diss., Political Science, Columbia University, 1976.

Werrett, Simon, *Fireworks: Pyrotechnic Arts and Sciences in European History*, Chicago, University of Chicago Press, 2010.

Wiegers, Gerard, "The Andalusī Heritage in the Maghrib: The Polemical Works of Muhammad Alguazir (fl. 1610)," in Otto Zwartjes, Geert Jan van Gelder, and Ed de Moor, eds., *Poetry, Politics, and Polemics: Cultural Transfers between the Iberian Peninsula and North Africa*, Amsterdam, Rodopi, 1996, 107–32.

———, "The Expulsion of 1609–1614 and the Polemical Writings of the Moriscos Living in the Diaspora," in Mercedes García-Arenal and Gerard Wiegers, eds., *The Expulsion of the Moriscos from Spain. A Mediterranean Diaspora*, trans. Consuelo López Morillas and Martin Beagles, Leiden, Brill, 2014, 389–412.

———, *Islamic Literature in Spanish and Aljamiado: Yça of Segovia (fl. 1450), His Antecedents and Successors*, Leiden, Brill, 1994.

———, *A Learned Muslim Acquaintance of Erpenius and Golius: Ahmad b. Kāsim al-Andalusī and Arabic Studies in the Netherlands,* Leiden, Documentatiebureau Islam-Christendom, 1988.

———, "Managing Disaster: Networks of the Moriscos during the Process of the Expulsion from the Iberian Peninsula around 1609," *Journal of Medieval Religious Cultures* 36:2 (2010), 141–68.

———, "Moriscos and Arabic Studies in Europe," *Al-Qantara* 31:2 (2010), 587–610.

———, "Polemical Transfers: Iberian Muslim Polemics and Their Impact in Northern Europe in the Seventeenth Century," in Mercedes García-Arenal, ed., *After Conversion: Iberia and the Emergence of Modernity,* Leiden, Brill, 2016, 229–48.

Wilkinson, Robert J., *The Kabbalist Scholars of the Antwerp Polyglot Bible,* Leiden, Brill, 2007.

———, *Orientalism, Aramaic, and Kabbalah in the Catholic Reformation: The First Printing of the Syriac New Testament,* Leiden, Brill, 2007.

Winter, Michael, *Society and Religion in Early Ottoman Egypt: Studies in the Writings of 'Abd al-Wahhāb al-Sha'rānī,* New Brunswick, NJ, Transaction Publishers, 2007 (1st ed., 1982).

Witkam, Jan Just, "The Leiden Manuscript of the *Kitāb al-Musta'īnī,*" in Charles Burnett, ed., *Ibn Baklarish's Book of Simples: Medical Remedies between Three Faiths in Twelfth-Century Spain,* London and Oxford, Arcadian Library and Oxford University Press, 2008, 75–94.

Wolf, Anne Marie, *Juan de Segovia and the Fight for Peace: Christians and Muslims in the Fifteenth Century,* Notre Dame, IN, University of Notre Dame Press, 2014.

Yerasimos, Stéphane, "Les Ingénieurs ottomans," in Élisabeth Longuenesse, ed., *Bâtisseurs et bureaucrates: Ingénieurs et société au Maghreb et au Moyen-Orient,* Lyon, Maison de l'Orient, 1990, 47–63.

Zhiri, Oumelbanine, *L'Afrique au miroir de l'Europe, fortunes de Jean Léon l'Africain à la Renaissance,* Geneva, Droz, 1991.

———, "A Captive Library between Morocco and Spain," in Marcus Keller and Javier Irigoyen-García, eds., *Dialectics of Orientalism in Early Modern Europe,* London, Palgrave Macmillan, 2018, 17–31.

———, "Les corps, les âmes et le droit: Isaac de Razilly et les captifs français du Maroc au XVIIème siècle," in Nicolas Lombard and Clotilde Jacquelard, eds., *Les Nouveaux mondes juridiques du Moyen Âge au XVIIème siècle,*" Paris, Classiques Garnier, 2015, 227–51.

———, "Lecteur d'Ibn Khaldoun," in François Pouillon, ed., *Léon L'Africain,* Paris, Karthala–IISMM, 2009, 211–36.

———, "'Sauvages et Mahométans,'" *Esculape et Dionysos: Mélanges en l'honneur de Jean Céard,* Geneva, Droz, 2008, 1125–39.

———, *Les Sillages de Léon l'Africain, du XVIème au XXème siècle,* Casablanca, Wallada, 1996.

———, "The Task of the Morisco Translator in the Early Modern Maghreb," *Expressions Maghrébines* 15:1 (2016), 11–27.

———, "Turcs et Mores: Monarques musulmans dans les *Histoires tragiques* de Boaistuau et Belleforest," *L'Esprit Créateur* 53:4 (2013), 33–45.

———, "Voyages d'Orient et d'Occident: Jean Léon l'Africain et Ahmad al-Hajarī dans la littérature de voyage," *Arborescences* 2 (2012), 1–15.

Zouber, Mahmoud A., *Ahmad Bābā de Tombouctou (1556–1627): Sa vie et son œuvre*, Paris, Maisonneuve et Larose, 1977.

INDEX

Page numbers in italics indicate illustrations.

Dutch East Indies Company (Vereenigde Oost-Indische Compagnie/VOC), 152, 153
Dutch Republic. *See* Netherlands
Duval, Jean-Baptiste, 27

Eastern Christians, as Orientalists, 65–69, 71–73. *See also* Maronites
Ecchellensis, Abraham (Ibrāhīm al-Hāqilānī), 67–68, 69, 239n129
Egidio da Viterbo, 51–52, 56, 60
Egypt: al-Azhar, College of, Cairo, 38, 41, 136, 181; Bonaparte's invasion of (1798), 41; Coptic Orientalists, 27, 68; cosmography, Hajarī's interest in, 122; Hajarī in, 38, 83–85, 87, 90–92; Orientalists from, 27, 64, 68, 74; religious debates of Hajarī in, 108, 110
Eighty Years' War, 183
Elements (Euclid), 123
Elias (Maronite), 65
Elisabeth of France, 30
Elizabeth I (queen of England), 127, 167, 194
engineers and engineering: Dutch military engineering, 149; early modern emergence of, 144, 163–64, 168–73, 174–75; Ghānim on gunners versus, 172–73; Golius, as engineer, 5, 146, 160, 163, 164, 168, 169–70; mathematics and, 168–74; *muhandis*, 170–73, 174–75, 258–59n99; in Ottoman army, 173. *See also* Atlantic harbor project
England, 24, 68, 75, 127, 140, 149, 163, 165, 167, 176, 182, 184, 194
Erpenius, Thomas, 1–2, 3, 8; Arabic language, Hajarī's proficiency in, 89, 91, 92; Arabic New Testament published by, 1, 3; atlas sent to Mūlay Zaydān by, 126–27, 129; East Indian text in Arabic, Hajarī's access to, 140; Golius as student of, 1, 2, 34–35; *Grammatica arabica*, 32; Hajarī's first acquaintance with, 27; Hajarī's relationship with, 2, 8, 11, 154; Le Gendre on, 1–3; Leo Africanus, use of, 58; letter from Hajarī to, 35–36, *37*; Netherlands, Hajarī's visit to, 32–33; portrait of, *28*; religious debates of

Hajarī with, 108; as translator of letters from Morocco to Dutch Republic, 36, 151, 154, 228n85; at University of Leiden, 71
Escorial library, Arabic texts at, 53, 54, 57, 148
Esmain/Daime, Catherine and Marie, 119, 121
Espinosa, Fernández de, 176
Les Estats et Empires du monde (Davity), 125
Euclid, 123
Europe: Hajarī on, in *Supporter* and *Kitāb al-ʿizz*, 201; Hajarī's awareness of European expansion, 129; Hajarī's travels in, 24–33
European geography, Hajarī's use of, 134–40
European Republic of Letters: cultural connections between Arabic Republic of Letters and, 2–10, 11–13, 25, 43–44, 217–20 (*See also* Orientalism); *Republica litteraria*, concept of, 11
experts and expertise: Atlantic harbor project and early modern development of, 168–73; rhetoric of technical expertise in *Kitāb al-ʿizz*, 193–98

Fabre, Jacques, 34
don Fadrico of Toledo, 161
Fakhr al-Dīn (Druze emir), 74, 239n129
falsafa, 179, 195, 197
faqīh, 48, 49, 59, 180, 199, 261n26
al-Fārābī, Abū Nasr, 169, 170, 171
Fāris ibn al-ʿIlj, 105
al-Fāsī, ʿAbd al-Rahmān, 212, 267n139
al-Fāsī, al-Hāj ʿAbdallāh b. al-Husayn, 243n184
al-Fāsī, Muhammad, 42
fatwa, 34, 61
Fayard (Bordeaux parliamentarian), 31, 111, 112, 227n62, 248n46
Felipe II (king of Spain), 53
Felipe III (king of Spain), 24
Felipe IV (king of Spain), 30, 164
Ferdinand and Isabella (king and queen of Spain), 48
Ferdinand II of Aragon (king of Spain), 48

harbor project. *See* Atlantic harbor project

al-Ḥarīrī, 35

Harmatta, János, 253n144

Harrison, John, 105

Harvey, L. P., 42, 206, 265n120

al-Ḥasrūnī, Yūhannā (Johannes Hesronita), 67

al-Ḥaytī al-Marūnī, Aḥmad ibn ʿAbd Allāh, 72

Henri III (king of France), 25

Henri IV (king of France), 25, 113, 119, 124

Herrera, Jorge Gil, 226n51

Hesronita, Johannes (Yūhannā al-Ḥasrūnī), 67

Heylan, Francisco, *19, 105*

Hindī, Iḥsān, 259–60n2

Hippocrates, 26, 112

Histoire de Barbarie et de ses corsaires (Dan), 176, 182–83

Historia veradera del Rey Don Rodrigo (The True History of King Don Roderigo; Luna), 53–54, 233n45

Hodgson, Marshall, 254n3

Holland. *See* Netherlands

Hondius, Jodocus, 125

Hornachos, Extremadura, Spain, 17, 24, 140

Hottinger, Johann Heinrich, 58, 64, 233n43, 239n131

Hubert, Étienne: abbey of Saint-Denis visited with Hajarī, 138–39, *139*; collaborations with Eastern scholars, 27, 63, 67, 68, 71, 225n37; at Collège Royal, Paris, 26, 67; employment of converted "Turk" by, 63; *Grammatica Arabica Maronitarum*, 27, 67; *Lāmiyyat al-afʿāl* (Ibn Mālik) copied by Hajarī for, 227n60; Paris, Hajarī in, 25–27, 30–31, 33, 40, 63, 82; as physician at Moroccan court, 25–26; religious debates of Hajarī with, 110, 111; water pump shown to Hajarī by, 198

Hues, Robert, 127

humanities and sciences, early modern intermingling of, 5–6

Ibn ʿAbd al-Rafīʿ, Muhammad, 39, 105

Ibn Abī Dīnār, 172, 173

Ibn Abī Maḥallī, 147, 148

Ibn Ajurrūm, Muhammad al-Sanhājī, 33

Ibn ʿAradūn, 261n26

Ibn ʿAtiyya, 35

Ibn al-ʿAyyāshī (Muhammad b. al-ʿAyyāshī al-Miknāsī), 40–41

Ibn Baklārish, 35, 155, *157*

Ibn al-Bannāʾ, 124

Ibn Hamādūsh, ʿAbd al-Razzāq, 181–82, 187–88, 212

Ibn Khaldūn, ʿAbd al-Rahmān, 35, 58, 179, 258–59n99

Ibn al-Khaṭīb, Lisān al-Dīn, 96.

Ibn Khallikān, 35

Ibn Mālik, Badr al-Dīn, 243n1

Ibn Mālik, Muhammad, 26, 40, 82, 104, 227n60, 227n69

Ibn al-Qāḍī, Ahmad, 62, 236n88

Ibn Sīnā (Avicenna), 26, 63, 112, 236n93

Ibn al-Tawq, 181

Ibn Tūda, ʿAbd al-Karīm, 21, 22, 224–25n19

Ibrāhīm, Darwīsh, 63

Idrīsī (geographer), 63, 67, 75, 106, 135

al-Ifrānī, Muhammad, 41, 42, 93, 95, 123

Iḥṣāʾ al-ʿUlūm (Enumeration of the Sciences; al-Fārābī), 169

Ikhlāṣī, Sheikh Mehmed, 126

Immaculate Conception, doctrine of, 55

India, Mughal empire in, 136, 146, 254n3

Innocent XI (pope), 18

Iran, 68, 70, 74, 146, 243n1

Isabella I of Castile (queen of Spain), 48

ʿĪsā ibn Jābir (Yça Gedelli), 48, 231n12

al-Iskandarī, Ibn ʿAṭāʾ Allāh, 265n120

Islam: captive Easterners in Europe, 56–65; global spread of, and Hajarī's use of European geography, 136–40, 253n139; hadith cited by Hajarī, 35, 206–7, 213; Lead Books or *libros plúmbos/plomos* affair, 18–20, *19*, 40; Orientalism in Spain aimed at conversion of Muslims, 46–50; polemical tradition in Spain and Morocco, 103–4; Quran, Spanish translation of, 48; religious debates of Hajarī with Christians and Jews, 31, 33, 38, 102, 107–17, 131; Spain, ambiguity about Islamic history in, 47, 53; Spanish birth and life of Hajarī as crypto-Muslim, 9, 17–21. *See also* conversion to Islam; Moriscos; polemic; Quran

Morocco *(continued)*
149; Wādī al-Makhāzin, defeat of
Portguese at (1578), 146. *See also* Atlantic harbor project; Zaydān; *specific cities and towns*
Moses of Mardin, 66, 238n116
Mudéjars, 47
Mughal empire, India, 136, 146, 254n3
Muhammad (prophet), 35, 50, 85, 109,
111–13, 206–7, 218, 265n120
Muhammad III (king of Morocco), 187
Muhammad V (king of Morocco), 145
Muhammad al-Burtuqālī (Wattāsī
sultan), 57
Muhammad al-Mutawakkil, 161, 224n19
Muhammad ibn ʿAbd Allāh al-Saʿīdī
al-ʿAdawī (Egyptian imam), 64, 237n106
Muhammad ibn Abī al-ʿĀsī (Muhamed
Vulhac/Pérez Bolhaç), 19, 20, 30
muhandis, 170–73, 174–75, 258–59n99
Mūlay Zaydān (Saʿdī sultan). *See* Zaydān
Muley, Francisco Núñez, 17
Muqaddima (Ibn Khaldūn), 58, 258–59n99
Murād IV (Ottoman sultan), 207
Murat Rais (Jan Janszen), 148
al-Murrākushī, ʿAlī b. Muhammad
al-Andalusī al-Gharnatī, 243n184
Murūj al-dhahab (Masʿūdī), 155
Mūsā, al-Hāj (Jamiro al-Andalusī
al-Gharnātī), 171, 172, 173, 208, 214
Mūsā b. Mikhāʾīl ibn Atiyā (Moses
Michaelis), 70–71
Muslims. *See* Islam
al-Mustaʿīnī (Ibn Baklārish), 35, 155, *157,*
158, 205
Mystico ramillete historico... (Barnuevo), *19*

Nairone, Fausto (Mirhij al-Bānī
Nimrūnī), 68
Nebuchadnezzar's dream, 132
Negri, Solomon, 72–73
Neophytes, College of, Rome, 62–63, 66, 68
Nero (Roman emperor), 105
Netherlands: Brazilian sugar captured in
Spanish ships by, 150; Hajarī in, 32–33,
148–49; Iranian embassy to, 70;
Morocco, Dutch embassy to, 1–2, 3, 5,
11, 34–35, 129, 149–51; Ottoman Porte

and, 30, 32; saltpeter, Morocco's aim to
import, 145; Spain, wars of independence from, 149; States General, 34, 121,
145, 149–51, 153–54, 158–59, 167, 221n1,
256n52; Treaty of Friendship and Free
Commerce with Morocco, 149. *See also*
Atlantic harbor project; *specific cities
and towns*
networks: connecting Spain, France, and
North Africa, 226n51; Hajarī's participation in, 2, 7, 8, 9, 12–13, 21, 30, 32, 40,
45, 77, 100, 217, 218; of Moriscos, 19,
24–25, 29, 31, 226n51, 227n64; network
studies, 6; of Orientalism, 8, 10, 25, 29,
43, 44, 58, 61, 63, 76, 77, 81; *Supporter*
on, 120, 126, 129, 141; technological
culture and, 143, 209. *See also* Arabic
Republic of Letters; European Republic
of Letters
Nimrūnī, Mirhij al-Bānī (Fausto
Nairone), 68
Niqūlāwus ibn Butrus al-Halabī (Nicolaus
Petri), 71–72
nisba, 16
Nova Scientia (Tartaglia), 196
nuevos christianos. See Moriscos
Nūlash, Granada, Spain, 177
Nuyts, Pieter, 33

Old Christians: ability of Hajarī to pass as,
17, 20, 21, 85–86; defined, 17; Ghānim's
ability to pass as, 86; Lead Books affair
and, 55; Spanish artillerymen required
to be, 184
Olearius (Adam Öhlschläger), 70
Olonne, France, 30, 113
One Thousand and One Nights, 73, 88
Orientalism, 45–77; Atlantic harbor
project and, 146, 151–58, 174; Hajarī's
broadening representation of world
through, 121–22; captives, prisoners,
and slaves, contributions of, 56–65, 141;
Christian Kabbalist readers of Spanish
Muslim converts, 50–52; concept of,
2–8; conversion of Muslims in Spain, in
service of, 46–50; cultural connections
between European/Arabic Republics of
Letters, 2–10, 11–13, 25, 43–44, 217–20;

defined, 6–7, 222n13; Eastern Christians and, 65–69, 71–73; Eastern intellectuals' involvement in, 4–5, 6, 7, 45–46, 75–76, 79–80; European enterprise, envisioned solely as, 2–4, 6, 45; globalization, as product of, 100–101; Golius, as Orientalist, 152, 155, 169–70, 174; Hajarī as Orientalist scholar, 2, 5, 152; Hajarī in context of world of, 79–82; humanities and sciences, early modern intermingling of, 5–6; librarians and booksellers, 74–75; Moriscos and, 20, 52–56; networks of, 8, 10, 25, 29, 43, 44, 58, 61, 63, 76, 77, 81; polemic and, 46, 47, 49–52, 55, 56, 61, 62, 65, 69, 72, 76, 121; prestige of, as field of knowledge, 3; Ruyl, as pragmatic Orientalist, 152–55; Said's theory of, 4, 6–7; sites of intellectual exchange outside Europe, 73–75; travellers and diplomats, contributions of, 69–73; world, Hajarī's vision of, 140–41

Orsino, Paul, 236n93
Orthodox Christians, 71
Osman Efendi, 187, 263n51
Ossin (Husayn), 71
Ottomans: embassy to French king on behalf of Moriscos from, 30; engineers in Ottoman army, 173; French embassy to, 26, 30; as "gunpowder empire," 146, 254n3; Hajarī on, 136–37; Lepanto, Battle of (1571), 53; Morocco, struggle for control of, 146; Netherlands and, 30, 32; Tunisia as province of, 207–8; Turkish embroiderers of French queen, 32, 118–21, 249–50n81. *See also* Istanbul
Oualidia, harbor at. *See* Atlantic harbor project
Overijssel (ship), 149, 150

Pallache, Isaac, 71, 240n147
Pallache, Joseph, 121, 149, 151
Pallache, Moses, 149, 150, 153, 154, 155
Pallache, Samuel, 120–21, 249n80
Pallache family, 149–50, 159
Paraclete, Muhammad viewed as, 108
paratext, 199, 205–6, 209

Paris: Collège Royal, 25, 26, 67, 68; Hajarī in, 25–32, 40, 45, 63, 82–83, 92; letter of Hajarī to Morisco friends in Istanbul from, 16, 20, 25, 30, 39, 45, 113; Maronite scholars in, 27, 67–68, 73; religious debates of Hajarī in, 106, 107, 109–10; Saint-Denis, Hubert and Hajarī visiting abbey of, 138–39, *139*
Paris Polyglot Bible, 67
Park, Katherine, 267n144
Parra Pérez, María José, 251n99
el Partal, 22
patrons and patronage, 57, 58, 67, 68, 93, 119, 124, 126, 141, 144, 177, 182, 208, 210, 218, 219
Pauw, Petrus, 33, 248n51
Pedro de Alcalà, 48
Pedro de Navarro, 183
Peiresc, Nicolas Fabri de, 63–64, 74, 75, 119
Peiresc's Mediterranean World (Miller), 63
Pérez-Mallaína, Pablo E., 260n7
El perfecto capitan instruido en la disciplina militar y nueva ciencia de la artilleria (Alava), 264n86
Perron, Jacques Davy du, 26–27, 226n46
Petrarch, 196
Petri, Nicolaus (Niqūlāwus ibn Butrus al-Halabī), 71–72
Piechocki, Katharine N., 137–38
Plática manual de artillería (Practical Manual of Artillery; Collado), 183
Pliny the Elder, 265n122
plomos affair. *See* Lead Books or *libros plúmbos/plomos* affair
Pococke, Edward, 71, 74, 75, 242n167
polemic: abrogation, 116, 131–33; affective connections through, 111–15, 247n38; broadening representation of world through, 116–22; cosmography and, 123, 127; Hajarī as polemicist, 9, 103–7, 217–18; Moriscos addressed by, 117–20; Orientalism and, 46, 47, 49–52, 55, 56, 61, 62, 65, 69, 72, 76, 121; religious debates of Hajarī with Christians and Jews, 31, 33, 38, 102, 107–17, 131; *Supporter* and, 41, 102–3
Polyglot Bibles, 67239n126
polyglot psalter of Giustiniani, 57

Pope Joan, 108
Portugal, 21–22, 122, 124, 135, 146, 161, 164, 224n19
Portundo, Maria M., 250n85
Postel, Guillaume, 50–51, 57, 66
practical/technical knowledge, early modern writing about, 176, 178–82, 260n10, 261n15
Propaganda Fide, 66
Puerto San Maria, Cadiz, Spain, 21
pure blood *(limpieza di sangre)*, 15, 184
Pynacker, Cornelis, 243n182

al-Qabitān, 125, 127
al-Qalbu, Yūsuf, 106
al-Qāliʿ, Ibrāhīm, 155, 255n42
al-Qānūn (Yūsī), 212, 261n15
Qānun al-tibb (Canon of Medicine; Ibn Sīnā), 26, 63, 236n93
al-Qāsim al-Zamakhsharī, Abū, 61
al-Qazwīnī, 71, 74, 242n168
qisas al-anbiyā (Tales of the Prophets), 132
Quran: Arabic copy with Latin translation by Juan Gabriel, 52, 56; on autobiographical writing, 98–99; Bible, Hajarī on agreement with, 118; *Confusión* (Juan Andrés) on, 49, 50; Daniel not mentioned in, 132; Erpenius and, 27, 35; French translation of, 64; on God's possession of Original Book, 131; Hajarī on his lack of exegetical mastery of, 92; Moroccan scholarly education and, 92; Mūlay Zaydān's exegesis of, 129; Orientalists making use of, 47, 49–51, 60, 70, 72; polemic, use in, 49, 131; religious debates of Hajarī and, 110, 113, 116; scientific study and, 129; sodomy, offensive gloss on, 110; Spanish translations of, 48, 231n12; al-Targhī and, 96

Rabat-Salé, 36–38, 83–85, 87, 148, 149
Rachman (Spanish Muslim), 72
Radtmann, Bartholomeus, 63
al-Ragrāguī, Muhammad b. ʿAbd Allāh, 24, 25, 41, 93, 95–96, 110
Raimondi, Giovanni Battista, 63, 71
Ramachandran, Ayesha, 133–34
Ramusio, Gian Battista, 234n60

Ravius, Christian, 71, 74, 233n43
al-Rāzī, Fakhr al-Dīn, 35
Razilly, Isaac de, 63
Razzūq, Muhammad, 42
Redi, Francesco, 64
Reina, Cassiodoro de, 247n19
Relaciones (Teixera), 136
religion. *See* Christianity; Islam; Jews and Judaism; polemic; *Supporter of Religion against the Infidels*
Republics of Letters. *See* Arabic Republic of Letters; European Republic of Letters
Respublica litteraria, concept of, 11
reterritorialization, 89–90, 100, 244n16
Reynolds, Dwight F., 246n52
al-Ribāsh. *See* Ghānim, Ibrāhīm
Richelieu, Cardinal de, 63, 208, 225n28
Rihla al-Shihāb ilā liqāʾ al-ahbāb (The Voyage of Shihāb Toward the Meeting of His Loved Ones; Hajarī), 38, 40–41, 85, 91, 96–97, 103
al-Risāla al-Zakūtiyya (The Epistle of Zakūt; Zacuto), 125, *126*
al-Rizzi, Sarkīs (Sergio Rizzi), 238n120
Rothman, E. Natalie, 12
Rouen, France, 25, 32, 107, 112
Rubio, Muhammad, 15, 39
al-Rūdānī, Muhammad b. Sulaymān, 181, 261n26
Ruscelli, Girolamo, 195–96
Ruyl, Albert Corneliszoon: Atlantic harbor project, opposition to, 151, 159–60, 161, 163, 167, 174; on Dutch embassy to Morocco, 3, 5, 146, 149–51, 158–59; East Indies, travels in, 140, 152, 154, 253n146; Golius and, 160; Hajarī and, 34, 139–40, 153–54; in Le Gendre's memoir, 3; as pragmatic Orientalist, 152–55; Saint-Mandrier and, 167; *Spieghel van de Maleysche tale* (Mirror of the Malay Language), 152; in *Supporter,* 139–40, 154; translations into Malay by, 152–53
Ryer, André du, 64

Saavedra, Eduardo, 42
Sacromonte, Granada, 18, 104, 106, 107
Saʿdī (Persian poet), 70

Saʿdīya ben Levi, 70, 240n143
Safavid empire, Iran, 146, 254n3
Safi (shah of Iran), 70
Safi, Morocco: Atlantic harbor project and, 148–51, 153–55, 159, 161, 174; Hajarī in, 23, 25, 34; Latin books stolen from ship in, 252n116
al-Sahyūnī, Jibrāʾīl (Gabriel Sionita), 66–67, 226n47, 238n123
Said, Edward, 4, 6–7, 222n13
Saʿīd ibn Ahmad of Tārūdānt, 63–64
Saint-Denis, abbey of, Paris, 138–39, *139*
Sainte-Marie, Antoine de, 34, 130, 228n77
Saint-Jean-de-Luz, France, 29–30
Saint-Mandrier, Antoine de Salettes, sieur de, 148, 160–61, 163, 164–72, 174, 182, 208, 214
Sajdi, Dana, 261n22
al-Saktī. *See* Suktānī
saltpeter, Morocco's aim to export, 145, 167
al-Samarrai, Q., 42
Sancy, Achille Harlay de, 30, 250n81
sangre limpia (pure blood), 15, 184
al-Sanūsī, Muhammad, 98
Sarnelli Cerqua, Clelia, 42
Savary de Brèves, François, 26, 64, 71, 119, 121, 226n44
Sayyid, Fuʾād, 42
Scaliger, Joseph, 26, 71
Schwartz, Berthold, 189
Sciadrensis, Isaac (Ishāq al-Shidrāwī), 238n122
sciences. *See* technological culture
Scientific Revolution, Western mythology of, 143–44, 267n144
Sebastian (king of Portugal), 224n19
Séguier, Jean, lord of Autry, 30
Seigworth, Gregory J., 247n38
Selden, John, 239n131
Septem horae canonicae, 57
Seville, 17, 20–21, 29, 86, 122–23, 136, 177
sextants, 262n28
Shāhīn Kandī, 72
al-Shaʿrānī, ʿAbd al-Wahhāb, 98, 99, 127, 180–81, 245–46n47
al-Shaykh (son of Muhammad al-Murawakkil), 224n19

al-Shaykh al-Maʾmūn, Muhammad, 33, 147, 161
Sheykhzāde Muhammad Efendi, 74
al-Shidrāwī, Ishāq (Isaac Sciadrensis), 238n122
Shihab al-Din, 16. *See also* Hajarī
as-Shuwaikh Abū Al-Hasan ʿAlī al-Daqqāq, 236n95
Sīdī Muhammad al-Hāj, 237n105
Sillery, Nicolas Brûlart de, 30
al-Simʿānī (Assemani) family, 238n120
Simon (Maronite bishop of Tripoli), 66
Sionita, Gabriel (Jibrāʾīl al-Sahyūnī), 66–67, 226n47, 238n123
slaves in Europe as Orientalists, 56–65
Smith, Pamela H., 260n10
Social History of Knowledge (Burke), 180
sodomy, offensive gloss of Quran on, 110
Spain: ambiguity about Islamic history in, 47, 53; Arabic language, prohibition of, 17, 52; artillerymen, training for, 177–78, 184–86; Brazilian sugar, Dutch capture of, 150; *chronologias* and *chronographias* from, 131, 134; conquest of Muslim kingdoms by, 47, 48, 146; conversion of Muslims, Orientalism in service of, 46–50; cosmography in, 122–23, 124–25; Dutch wars of independence from, 149; early scientific development in, 250n85; escape of Hajarī to Morocco from, 21–24, *22–23*; expulsion of Jews from (1492), 48, 124; expulsion of Moriscos from (1609), 17, 24–25, 55, 226n51; Hajarī as translator in, 18, 19, 29, 34; Hajarī's birth and early life as crypto-Muslim in, 9, 17–21; inheritance of brother of Mūlay Zaydān, legal case involving, 33–34; Moroccan ports controlled by, 147, 148, 149, 161; networks connecting France, Spain, and North Africa, 24–25, 226n51; polemical tradition in, 103
Spanish Inquisition, 17, 19, 21, 30, 48, 53, 54, 60, 90, 104, 106–7
Spanish language: Arabic/Spanish bilingualism of Hajarī, 82–87, *84*, 90, 219; Quran, Spanish translation of, 48; translation by Hajarī of Islamic religious texts into, 38–39, 87

Founded in 1893,
UNIVERSITY OF CALIFORNIA PRESS
publishes bold, progressive books and journals
on topics in the arts, humanities, social sciences,
and natural sciences—with a focus on social
justice issues—that inspire thought and action
among readers worldwide.

The UC PRESS FOUNDATION
raises funds to uphold the press's vital role
as an independent, nonprofit publisher, and
receives philanthropic support from a wide
range of individuals and institutions—and from
committed readers like you. To learn more, visit
ucpress.edu/supportus.

Milton Keynes UK
Ingram Content Group UK Ltd.
UKHW041046150824
446776UK00002BA/3/J